Accountability of Judicial Power

This book brings together a group of international scholars to discuss theoretical and comparative considerations of judicial accountability. Accountability of the judiciary is an essential element in a democratic state ruled by law. Its design must take into account the need to ensure both the legitimacy of the judiciary and its independence. The work discusses accountability in the light of recent research, including studies on the crisis of the rule of law in the contemporary world. The book adopts a broad approach to accountability, which has various facets, referring both to the courts, that is the organisational element of the judicial branch of government, and to judges, its individual dimension. It is divided into four parts: the first deals with the essence of the concept of accountability of the judiciary; the second discusses the emerging standards relating primarily to the individual accountability of judges; and the third discusses the position of constitutional judges through the lens of accountability. The fourth and final part provides a detailed consideration of the specific accountability mechanisms. The book will be a valuable resource for academics, researchers, and policymakers working in the areas of constitutional law and politics, and accountability studies.

Piotr Mikuli is a full professor of law at the Jagiellonian University in Kraków.

Routledge Frontiers in Accountability Studies

Routledge Frontiers in Accountability Studies series promotes state-of-the-art analyses that reflect and interrogate the shifting accountability landscape from a range of perspectives.

The series welcomes proposals for monographs, edited collections and shorter works by established and early-career academics from a range of disciplines that span the arts, humanities and social sciences. Inter-disciplinary studies are particularly encouraged, as are approaches that seek to challenge dominant frameworks of 'self-evident' truths. The series is designed for a global audience, welcoming contributions that address national, comparative and international issues.

Other titles in this series:

Accountability, Impeachment and the Constitution
The Case for a Modernised Process in the United Kingdom
Chris Monaghan

British Origins and American Practice of Impeachment
Edited by Chris Monaghan and Matthew Flinders

Impeachment in a Global Context
Law, Politics, and Comparative Practice
Edited by Chris Monaghan, Matthew Flinders and Aziz Z. Huq

Accountability of Judicial Power
Theoretical and Comparative Perspectives
Edited by Piotr Mikuli

Accountability of Judicial Power

Theoretical and Comparative Perspectives

Edited by Piotr Mikuli

Routledge
Taylor & Francis Group
LONDON AND NEW YORK

First published 2025
by Routledge
4 Park Square, Milton Park, Abingdon, Oxon OX14 4RN

and by Routledge
605 Third Avenue, New York, NY 10158

Routledge is an imprint of the Taylor & Francis Group, an informa business

British Library Cataloguing-in-Publication Data
A catalogue record for this book is available from the British Library

Library of Congress Cataloging-in-Publication Data
Names: Mikuli, Piotr, 1977- editor.
Title: Accountability of judicial power: theoretical and comparative perspectives/edited by Piotr Mikuli.
Description: Abingdon, Oxon [UK]; New York, NY: Routledge, 2025. | Series: Routledge frontiers in accountability studies | Includes bibliographical references and index.
Identifiers: LCCN 2024058558 (print) | LCCN 2024058559 (ebook) | ISBN 9781032904085 (hardback) | ISBN 9781032904092 (paperback) | ISBN 9781003557852 (ebook)
Subjects: LCSH: Judicial power. | Judicial independence. | Judges. | Liability (Law) | Administrative responsibility.
Classification: LCC K3367 .A33 2025 (print) | LCC K3367 (ebook) | DDC 347/.012–dc23/eng/20241205
LC record available at https://lccn.loc.gov/2024058558
LC ebook record available at https://lccn.loc.gov/2024058559

ISBN: 978-1-032-90408-5 (hbk)
ISBN: 978-1-032-90409-2 (pbk)
ISBN: 978-1-003-55785-2 (ebk)

DOI: 10.4324/9781003557852

Typeset in Galliard
by Apex CoVantage, LLC

Contents

Contributors

Nóra Bán-Forgács is a researcher at the Institute for Legal Studies, Centre for Social Sciences, Hungarian Research Network (Hun-Ren). She earned her LLM degree from Yale University, United States, and her PhD from ELTE School of Law, Hungary. She is also an associate professor at Milton Friedman University, Budapest. She has two decades of experience in the theory and practice of human rights. Her recent focus in research is constitutional theory, separation of powers.

Cristóbal Caviedes is an Assistant Professor at Universidad Andrés Bello Faculty of Law in Santiago, Chile, where he coordinates the Public Law Department. He obtained his PhD at Queen's University at Kingston, Canada, in 2020. He also holds an LLB from Pontificia Universidad Católica de Chile, a Master of Laws from Universidad de Chile, an LLM from University College London, and a visiting scholarship at the Max Planck Centre for Public Law and Public International Law in Heidelberg, Germany. He writes on theory of law and comparative constitutional law. His most recent publication is the book Supermajority Voting in Constitutional Courts: The Problem of Majority Rule for Democracy and Legislation (Routledge 2024). His research has also appeared in the *International Journal of Constitutional Law*, the *Oxford Journal of Legal Studies*, and the *American Journal of Jurisprudence*, among other journals.

Micol Ferrario is a postdoctoral research fellow in comparative public law at Bocconi University, Milan. She holds a PhD in law from the University of Neuchâtel. She previously worked as research and teaching assistant at the Università della Svizzera italiana, Lugano, where she now lectures Swiss constitutional law. Her research fields are the judicial interpretative use of comparative law, emergency powers and courts, and the law of neutrality.

Natalie Fox, an adjunct professor at the Chair of Comparative Constitutional Law at Jagiellonian University in Kraków. Her teaching and research focus on constitutional law, with a particular emphasis on analysing the British constitutional system in the context of the UK's EU membership and Brexit-related issues. She was a principal investigator in the research project *The British Constitutional Law and the Membership in the European Union* financed by the National Science Centre in Poland. The aim of the project was to analyse British constitutional law in the context of membership of the United Kingdom in the EU.

Elżbieta Gudowska-Natanek, PhD, is affiliated with the Chair of Comparative Constitutional Law and a teaching associate at the Institute of Sociology, Jagiellonian University. She is a practicing attorney at law, member of the Cracow Bar Association, and chief specialist at the Cracow City Office with a decade of local government experience. She is an active participant in national conferences and seminars. She is an author and co-author of publications on public law, including constitutional law, and a contributor to legal drafts and opinions. She lectures at Jagiellonian University and conducts training sessions for local government and civil service employees, while also providing pro bono legal education to Cracow high school students. Her research focuses on constitutional law, judicial organisation, administrative law, and public sector management.

Jelena Kostić is a senior research fellow at the Institute of Comparative Law in Belgrade, Serbia. Prior to joining the Institute, she worked as an associate expert in the Financial Secretariat of the Belgrade City Administration and internal auditor of the Belgrade City Administration. She has previously worked as a consultant for the Organization for Security and Co-operation in Europe, in projects funded by the European Union, as well as for the World Bank. Her main area of expertise is criminal law. She has published a number of papers in English and Serbian and a few monographs and holds a doctoral degree in criminal law. Her recent publication is *Whistleblowers' Protection: An Analysis of the Regulatory Frameworks in Selected Western Balkan Countries* (2022), published by the Institute of Comparative Law. Jointly with Marina Matić Bošković in 2022 she wrote 'Financial Accountability and Transparency of Public Sector Institutions in the Republic of Serbia', published in *Accountability and the Law, Rights, Authority and Transparency of Public Power* (Piotr Mikuli and Grzegorz Kuca, eds., Routledge, 2022).

Grzegorz Kuca is an associate professor at the Department of Comparative Constitutional Law at the Faculty of Law and Administration of the Jagiellonian University, Vice-Director of the Center for Interdisciplinary Constitutional Studies at Jagiellonian University, and an attorney at law and a member of the District Bar Association in Krakow. He holds a PhD in law and a habilitation in law, with a specialisation in constitutional law. He is the author or co-author of more than 140 publications, as well as a co-editor of a collective volume published by Routledge and author of papers/chapters published by Oxford University Press. He is a member of the International Society of Public Law, the Polish Society of Constitutional Law, and the Legal Sciences Commission of the Polish Academy of Sciences (Krakow Branch). He has actively contributed to numerous international projects coordinated by foreign partners, including one funded by the Visegrad Fund. His work has been presented at various national and international conferences, notably those organised by the International Association of

Constitutional Law and the International Society of Public Law (ICON-S). His research interests encompass the theory of the separation of powers, constitutional dimensions of public finance, and electoral law

Alexander Lazović is a researcher at the European University Institute in Florence and a judge in Berlin. Currently he is working on his PhD project, 'Structuring Perception. How Structures of Practice Influence Decision-Making at the Court of Justice of the European Union'. He is the author of 'Converging on Structures – The Influence of Court Structure on Convergence and Divergence among Judges' in *Accommodating Diversity in Multilevel Constitutional Orders* (Maja Sahadžić et al., eds., Routledge 2023), among other publications.

Marina Matić Bošković is a senior research fellow at the Institute of Criminological and Sociological research in Belgrade, Serbia. She has extensive experience as a justice reform consultant working predominantly for the World Bank and EU in the Western Balkans and Eastern Partner countries. Her main area of expertise is criminal law, EU law, and justice reform. She is president of the Program Council of Serbian Association of Public Prosecutors and has been an honourable member since 2007. She has published a number of papers in English and Serbian and a few monographs and holds a doctoral degree in criminal law. Her recent publications are *Criminal Procedural Law of EU* (2022), published by the Institute of Criminological and Sociological Research; and *Public Procurement: An Analysis of the Regulatory Frameworks in Selected Western Balkan Countries* (2022) published by the Institute of Comparative Law. Jointly with Jelena Kostić in 2022 she wrote 'Financial Accountability and Transparency of Public Sector Institutions in the Republic of Serbia', published in *Accountability and the Law, Rights, Authority and Transparency of Public Power* (Piotr Mikuli and Grzegorz Kuca, eds., Routledge, 2022).

Piotr Mikuli is a full professor of law at the Jagiellonian University in Kraków. He graduated from the University of Warsaw and completed his LLM at University of Swansea. He was awarded his PhD and habilitation degrees at Jagiellonian. He has a track record in international publications. Inter alia, he is a co-author of the monograph *Ministers of Justice in Comparative Perspective* (2019) and the author of many other international publications dealing with constitutional issues, including book chapters and articles. In 2022 Routledge published (under his co-editorship) a collective volume, *Accountability and the Law: Rights, Authority and Transparency of Public Power*. He has an excellent international profile, having served as a visiting fellow and conducted research at several European universities, including Oxford University, University of Dalarna (Sweden), University of Lucerne, and University of Glasgow. He also held a research position at the University Sheffield. Currently, he is an associate member of the Centre of Public Law and Internationalisation, School of Law, Leicester University.

Teodora Miljojković is a PhD candidate at the Central European University, Department of Legal Studies, Vienna; a member of the Belgrade Legal Theory Group; and an intern at the Democracy Institute in Budapest. She completed her undergraduate studies at the Faculty of Law in Belgrade in 2018 and her master's studies at the Central European University in Budapest in 2019 with the thesis, 'The Importance of the Constitutional Court in the Democratization Process – The Case of Slovenia, Croatia and Serbia'. In her doctoral thesis, she deals with comparative legal analysis of the issue of judicial reform from the perspective of the principles of the rule of law and judicial independence under the mentorship of professor and former judge of the European Court of Human Rights, András Sajó. In 2021 she was engaged in the project of the Judicial Research Center CEPRIS (Serbia), which aimed at monitoring and critically assessing the ongoing judicial reforms in Serbia.

Ryszard Piotrowski, PhD with habitation (law), is an associate professor at the University of Warsaw and a member of the Committee of Legal Sciences of the Polish Academy of Sciences. His research interests include constitutional law, human rights, comparative constitutional law, theory and axiology of the constitution, theory and practice of legislation, parliamentary law, law and new information, and communication technologies.

Radosław Puchta works currently as researcher and lecturer at the Faculty of Law of the University of Bialystok (Poland). Moreover, he conducts professional activity as assistant to judge of the Polish Constitutional Tribunal. In 2009, he graduated in law at the Faculty of Law and Administration of the University of Warsaw (Poland), where he completed doctoral studies in 2015 and defended his PhD thesis in 2017. He publishes and lectures on Polish constitutional law, comparative constitutional law, constitutional review, and human rights. His main area of scientific interests remains French public law. In addition, he is a member of the Polish Constitutional Law Association since 2020 and the Warsaw Bar Association since 2020.

Arnisa Tepelija is a doctoral candidate (SJD) in comparative constitutional law at the Central European University. She is interested in the issues of the rule of law and the fight against corruption in transformative processes such as EU enlargement in the Western Balkans and especially in Albania.

Arianna Vedaschi is Full Professor of comparative public law at Bocconi University. She is a Coordinator of the Research Group on Constitutional Responses to Terrorism within the International Association of Constitutional Law, Member of the Steering Committee of the Associazione Italiana di Diritto Comparato, and Secretary-General of the Italian Association of Comparative and European Public Law. She is also a vice-director of the law review *Diritto Pubblico Comparato ed Europeo* and Member of Académie Internationale de Droit Comparé/International Academy of Comparative Law. She has served as a visiting professor in several prestigious universities and academic institutions in Europe, the United States, and Latin America.

1 Conceptualising accountability of the judiciary

Piotr Mikuli

The principle of judicial independence is a cornerstone of the rule of law.[1] Respect for the rule of law has become one of the most important factors in assessing the development of democracy in the contemporary world. Judicial independence is closely linked to the principle of the separation of powers,[2] which aims to prevent the concentration of authority in a single decision-making centre. This requirement of separation, both in terms of structure and personnel, is particularly crucial in safeguarding the independence of the judiciary. The indispensable independence of the judiciary must not, however, preclude its accountability. Yet, the mechanisms designed to ensure such accountability must be crafted with due diligence, so as not to erode or compromise judicial autonomy. Nevertheless, deficiencies in accountability, or disruptions in the balance of powers within the state's machinery, may entail negative consequences that could further impair the democratic effectiveness of the

1 Tom Bingham, *The Rule of Law* (Penguin Books 2011); Richard H. Fallon, '"*The Rule of Law" as a Concept in Constitutional Discourse*' (1997) 97 Colum L Rev, 1–56; Paul Craig, '*Formal and Substantive Conceptions of the Rule of Law: An Analytical Framework*' (1997) Vol. Autumn(3), pp. 467–487; David Dyzenhaus, *The Constitution of Law: Legality in a Time of Emergency* (Cambridge University Press 2006); Ronald Dworkin, *A Matter of Principle* (Harvard University Press 1985); Trevor R. S. Allan, *Constitutional Justice: A Liberal Theory of the Rule of Law* (Oxford University Press 2001); Martin Krygier, *The Rule of Law: Legality, Teleology, Sociology* (Peeters 2016); Nick Barber, *The Principles of Constitutionalism* (Oxford University Press 2018).

2 William B. Gwyn, *The Meaning of the Separation of Powers: An Analysis of the Doctrine from its Origin to the Adoption of the United States Constitution* (Tulane University Press 1965); M.J.C. Vile, *Constitutionalism and the Separation of Powers* (2nd edn, Liberty Fund 1998); Bruce Ackerman, *We the People: Foundations* (Harvard University Press 1991); Geoffrey Marshall, *Constitutional Conventions: The Rules and Forms of Political Accountability* (Oxford University Press 1984); Eoin Carolan, *The New Separation of Powers: A Theory for the Modern State* (Oxford University Press 2009); Roger Masterman, *The Separation of Powers in the Contemporary Constitution: Judicial Competence and Independence in the United Kingdom* (Cambridge University Press 2010); Keith E. Whittington, *Separation of Powers and the American Constitution* (Oxford University Press 2014); Louis Fisher, *Constitutional Conflicts Between Congress and the President* (University Press of Kansas 2014); Richard A. Posner, *The Federal Courts: Challenge and Reform* (Harvard University Press 1996).

DOI: 10.4324/9781003557852-1

constitutional system. The significant role of the judiciary, including constitutional courts, in modern constitutionalism[3] makes it all the more important to ensure the impeccable reputation of judges and the transparent organisational positioning of courts within the constitutional system of state bodies.

The issue of accountability is broad and complex, with the term being applied in a wide range of contexts.[4] It carries different meanings and connotations depending on the situation and author, often being used somewhat intuitively without a precise definition. Despite its varied usage, the concept remains expansive and encompasses numerous aspects of responsibility in both individual and institutional settings. Whilst considering the issue of judicial accountability, one may primarily refer to the notion of accountability as, according to Bovens, 'a specific social relation or mechanism that involves an obligation to explain and justify conduct'.[5] This relation usually consists of at least three elements or stages. First, in an accountability relationship, the actor must be or feel obliged to inform the forum of their conduct by providing various types of data on their task performance, results or procedures. Second, the forum must be able to question the actor/agent and challenge the adequacy of the procedure. Third, the forum must possess the capability to scrutinise the actor and critically evaluate both the sufficiency of the information presented and the rationality of their actions. The forum can endorse annual reports, provide feedback on policies or publicly denounce the actions of an official or organisation. Additionally, it can be inferred that the term *accountability* in English originates from 'account', largely in the sense of holding someone to account, which primarily involves compelling someone to justify their decisions or inactions. Accountability, therefore, appears intrinsically linked to the duty of reporting. This kind of accountability may be named as accountability in a strict sense. However, once again, it should be borne in mind that the term *accountability* is used in many contexts and seems to comprise various related phenomena. Scholars also use other words, particularly equivalents of the English term *responsibility*, which has various connotations, including casual, moral or legal dimensions, generally referring to some kind of obligation to act and criteria for being blamed or sanctioned[6]

3 Ran Hirlsh, *Towards Juristocracy: The Origins and Consequences of the New Constitutionalism* (Harvard University Press 2004).

4 See P. Mikuli and G. Kuca, 'Introduction' in P. Mikuli and G. Kuca (eds), *Accountability and the Law Rights, Authority and Transparency of Public Power* (Routledge 2022).

5 Mark Bovens, 'Two Concepts of Accountability: Accountability as a Virtue and as a Mechanism' (2010) 33(5) *West Eur Politics* 951. I discuss this in: P. Mikuli, 'Disciplinary (Professional) Responsibility of Judges as a Type of Accountability' in Matthew Flinders, Gergana Dimova and Elizabeth Milner-Roberts (eds) *Understanding Accountability: Power, Politics and Particularities* (Routledge, in press).

6 Conf. Ted Honderich (ed.), *The Oxford Companion to Philosophy* (2nd edn, Oxford University Press 2015) (online), <www.oxfordreference.com/view/10.1093/acref/9780199264797.001.0001/acref-9780199264797-e-2205?rskey=9I7eqA&result=5>.

(accountability in a broader sense). Legal requirements often involve using the term liability to describe legal accountability.[7]

The term accountability, with its various understandings, can be applied to judicial power. Diana Woodhouse, referring to distinctions found in the discourse on political accountability, distinguishes between explanatory, amendatory and sacrificial judicial accountability.[8] Explanatory accountability refers to the obligation to provide adequate reasoning for judicial decisions. Amendatory accountability relates to the losing party's right to appeal an unfavourable decision. Sacrificial accountability involves a willingness to bear the consequences of one's legally wrongful act or omission, which can include tendering one's resignation.

Given the unique nature of the judiciary, which should remain independent from other branches of government, the distinction between strict and broader accountability seems quite helpful. When discussing accountability in the strict sense, the focus is generally less on sanctions for a judge's actions or omissions and more on reporting mechanisms, with an emphasis on fostering transparency within the state apparatus.

In terms of reporting, accountability regulations consist of an obligation to inform a certain entity about the activities of the courts and judges. The entity to which such information is to be provided may be the parliament or the minister of justice, or a report may be released for public information purposes. The information may contain references to substantive judicial cases or issues related to the administrative and organisational activities of judges and courts. The function of such reports is to ensure the transparency of the judiciary's activities and to draw attention to existing problems arising from the functioning of the judiciary.

In turn, a broad understanding of judicial accountability may include supervisory activities related to the dispensation of justice. In this context, a certain organisational subordination of judges in judicial administrative matters to non-judicial bodies may raise concerns about the judiciary's autonomy, above all because some judicial administrative activities may also concern matters related to the issuing of judicial decisions, such as the suspension of proceedings or the frequency or adjournment of hearings. In contemporary constitutional systems, special offices or bodies are often created to deal with court administration.

However, in academic and public discourse, when talking about accountability in relation to the judiciary, attention is also – or perhaps mostly – paid to the concept of responsibility-liability. This is how the concept of judicial

7 Jonathan Law and Elizabeth Martin, *A Dictionary of Law* (Oxford University Press 2014) (online), <www.oxfordreference.com/view/10.1093/acref/9780199551248.001.0001/acref-9780199551248-e-2255?rskey=ACsCvl&result=2381>.

8 Diana Woodhouse, 'The Constitutional and Political Implications of a United Kingdom Supreme Court' (2004) 24(1–2) *Leg Stud* 150.

accountability is understood by Emilio Meyer and Thomas Bustamante, among others: 'Judicial accountability can be defined as the set of mechanisms aimed at making judges and courts personally or institutionally responsible for behaviours and decisions contrary to constitutional or legal standards'.[9]

In a similar vein, Kosař and Spáč emphasise that accountability fundamentally pertains to the notion that individual judges bear responsibility to entities either within or beyond the judiciary.[10] Here, the most important concepts are disciplinary liability and other types of liability (i.e. civil/criminal), especially regarding judges' actions or omissions related to the judicial process.

The notion of accountability may also include the detailed justification of judgements and may thus involve Woodhouse's concept of explanatory accountability, which implicitly involves the evaluation of the performance of judges by higher courts (amendatory liability).

Judicial appointments can also be regarded as a mode of accountability; however, this runs the risk of distorting the precision of our concepts. Appointments are, in this sense, an *ex ante* issue in relation to democratic accountability[11] because the manner and procedure of appointment may influence the application of sanctions in the form of removal from office in the enforcement of accountability. This is because of the possible involvement of similar actors in nomination procedures and the nature of appointments (usually for an indefinite period).[12]

The scope of judicial accountability must take into consideration, under the condition of a democratic state based on the rule of law, the specific nature of judicial power resulting from the complementary principles of the separation of powers and the independence of the judiciary. The legitimacy of the judiciary is derived primarily from its legal legitimacy and not from democratic legitimacy in a simple sense. Legal legitimacy, in turn, is derived from the written constitution (in countries where it operates) or from general rules of law, rather than from a direct mandate resulting from a democratic vote. The judiciary's legitimacy can be derived from the pure principle of constitutionalism, primarily understood as the concept of the limitation of public power, but also from the necessity of existence in the modern state of various institutions,

9 Emilio Meyer and Thomas Bustamante, 'Judicial Accountability' in Rainer Grote, Frauke Lachenmann and Rüdiger Wolfrum (eds), *Max Planck Encyclopaedia of Comparative Constitutional Law* (Oxford University Press 2018) <https://oxcon.ouplaw.com/view/10.1093/law-mpeccol/law-mpeccol-e329?rskey=E9iwpd&result=1&prd=MPECCOL> accessed 15 November 2024.

10 David Kosař and Samuel Spáč, 'Conceptualization(s) of Judicial Independence and Judicial Accountability by the European Network of Councils for the Judiciary: Two Steps Forward, One Step Back' (2018) 18(3) *IJCA* 37–46.

11 Anna Dziedzic, 'Selection of Judges' in Grote and others (n 9).

12 Mark Tushnet, 'Judicial Accountability in Comparative Perspective' in Nicholas Bamforth and Peter Leyland (eds), *Accountability in the Contemporary Constitution* (Oxford University Press 2013) 61.

which, shaped differently thanks to diverse skills and legal instruments, are well suited to modifying a given state policy. Therefore, it cannot be assumed that elected state bodies empowered by the constitution are more legitimate than unelected bodies, such as the courts. Thus, judges have a duty of accountability to the popular sovereign (Bovens's 'forum') only to a symbolic and indirect extent, while having a direct duty to state organ/bodies depending on the type of accountability.

This book consists of four parts: theoretical insights (Part I), the issue of standards regarding accountability (Part II), the issue of accountability of courts and constitutional judges (Part III: *Quis custodiet ipsos custodes?*), and a discussion of selected accountability mechanisms (Part IV). In Part I, the authors delve into foundational concepts and frameworks that shape our understanding of the concept of accountability of the judiciary. Part II systematically examines the standards that govern accountability, providing a comprehensive overview of the expectations placed upon accountability mechanisms. Part III poses a critical question regarding who oversees the overseers, exploring the challenges of ensuring that constitutional judges and constitutional courts remain accountable while preserving their independence. Finally, Part IV presents a selection of mechanisms designed to enhance accountability, analysing their effectiveness and potential drawbacks. Together, these sections aim to provide a nuanced understanding of the complexities surrounding judicial accountability in modern legal systems.

In Chapter 2 Ryszard Piotrowski provides a general overview of judicial accountability, both at the institutional level (the judiciary as a whole) and the individual level (judges' accountability). Judicial independence and its safeguards apply not only to individual judges but also to the judiciary as a body in relation to the legislative and executive branches. Conflicts between these branches are almost inevitable, as each seeks to assert its power, often creating a cycle of negative tension.

In Chapter 3 Nóra Bán-Forgács focuses on constitutional identity and judicial independence. The author argues that judicial accountability in the current sovereignty/constitutional identity debate is impeded. Accountability requires an independent judiciary, emphasising the separation of powers. The chapter highlights three key questions: first, regarding the supremacy of either the EU or Member States over national judiciaries; second, who has true ownership and supreme power over the judiciary; and third, the judicial monopoly on law interpretation under populist constitutionalism.

In Chapter 4 Natalie Fox analyses individual responsibility and the disciplinary accountability of judges within emerging EU standards. The chapter highlights the inadequacies of domestic constitutional law in safeguarding judicial independence, emphasising the importance of the Court of Justice of the EU (CJEU) jurisprudence in resolving disputes between national governments and the EU, especially regarding disciplinary matters in Poland.

In Chapter 5 Marina Matić Bošković and Jelena Kostić investigate the equilibrium between judicial independence and accountability, with particular emphasis on the disciplinary frameworks governing judges and prosecutors. They examine ethical standards, disciplinary offences, sanctions, and the procedures upheld by relevant bodies, ensuring fair trials. The authors highlight the need to safeguard independence while addressing public calls for stronger accountability mechanisms, especially in countries undergoing judicial reforms. Drawing on principles from the European Court of Human Rights, the CJEU, and the Venice Commission, the chapter stresses that disciplinary actions must not be used for political influence. Continuous evaluation of national laws is recommended to strengthen both independence and accountability.

In Chapter 6 I shift the focus to the liability of judges for ordinary criminal and civil wrongs, particularly examining models of judicial immunity. I explore how immunity varies across different legal systems, noting that in some countries, such as the United Kingdom, United States and France, judges enjoy full immunity from civil liability for actions taken in office, often paired with limited criminal immunity. In other systems, like Poland and Hungary, judges are granted formal immunity for criminal acts outside the courtroom, which can be lifted through specific legal procedures. I endeavour to show the various solutions that exist today and to identify the requirements for the regulation of judges' immunity from the point of view of the principle of judicial independence. I point out that reforming judicial immunity can be assessed in the light of the so-called non-regression doctrine, which prohibits the erosion of constitutional rights.

In Chapter 7 Cristóbal Caviedes argues that when judges assess the constitutionality of laws, their accountability to citizens can be evaluated by determining whether they engaged in genuine deliberation. This involves assessing whether they were open to being persuaded by their peers through rational debate. To explore how decision procedures in constitutional courts affect this deliberation, the author proposes three hypotheses. First, early voting, compared to non-opposition, makes judges less likely to change their views. Second, unanimity rules force dissenting judges to conform in unconstitutional rulings. Third, publicising judicial debates discourages agreement. The author suggests empirical studies to test these hypotheses using court comparisons and statistical analysis.

In Chapter 8 Radosław Puchta explores mechanisms to ensure the accountability of constitutional courts both as institutions and through individual judges. The chapter emphasises that independence should not preclude accountability of the constitutional court and its members. The author points out that the existence of a constitutional court is a hallmark of modern constitutionalism. Unlike ordinary judges, constitutional judges are accountable only to the constitution's framers, theoretically exempt from legislative or executive interference. However, being a state authority, the court must operate within the law. The author observes that in illiberal democracies, these courts may be manipulated to undermine rather than uphold the constitution.

In Chapter 9 Alexander Lazović notes that the rule of law crisis highlights the tension between judicial independence and accountability. While autonomy is crucial, judges must remain bound to the law to avoid unchecked power. However, excessive external accountability could compromise their independence, leading to undue influence. Instead, the focus should be on internalising both values, allowing judges to feel independent yet responsible. The author examines the European Court of Justice, wherein judges from politically diverse governments converge around shared legal values. This internal judicial discourse ensures accountability through peer review, discouraging political motivations and promoting genuine legal reasoning.

In Chapter 10 Arnisa Tepelija and Teodora Miljojković explore the evolving justification for judiciary vetting in EU candidate countries, where radical vetting contrasts with the traditional liberal democratic requirement for judicial independence. Recently employed in Albania and Moldova due to EU accession conditions, vetting aims to address corruption and bolster judicial integrity. Countries like North Macedonia, Georgia and Kosovo are also considering vetting as they pursue EU candidacy.

In Chapter 11 Arianna Vedaschi and Micol Ferrario elaborate on the issue of the accountability and independence of military courts. Through the lens of comparative constitutional law, this chapter explores whether and to what extent these issues define military justice systems in major developed Western democracies. By examining the Italian case study, the chapter proposes certain reforms to existing models, aimed at ensuring that military courts – tasked with ruling on highly complex and sensitive matters – adhere to the fundamental principles of justice that must underlie any legal system grounded in the rule of law. While transitional justice standards were effective for early institutional reforms, they are insufficient for current judicial vetting. Pre-accession reforms often prioritised structural independence but lacked robust accountability, leading to corporatism, nepotism, and politicisation. Vetting procedures have been introduced to tackle these issues, shifting the focus from addressing past wrongs to reinforcing the rule of law and improving judicial efficiency.

In Chapter 12 Grzegorz Kuca and Elżbieta Gudowska-Natanek examine how performance-based budgeting can influence judges' remuneration and how this relates to the issue of judicial accountability. The level of pay should reflect the importance and significance of the tasks they perform, while also safeguarding them from external interference. However, due to the need to address crisis impacts, judges' salaries may be frozen or even reduced. The chapter aims to reconstruct the constitutional standard for judicial remuneration and justify such freezes or reductions, referring to the case of Poland and its Constitutional Court's rulings.

The themes explored within the chapters underscore the intricate and multifaceted nature of judicial accountability. These chapters illustrate the diverse interpretative frameworks and methodological approaches encountered in the constitutional law scholarship. Through these lenses, the authors endeavour to illuminate the various dimensions of accountability, highlighting its critical role in ensuring the effective functioning of the judiciary within contemporary democratic systems based on the rule of law.

Part I

Theoretical insights

2 Accountability of the judiciary as a constitutional value

Ryszard Piotrowski

Judicial accountability in the spectrum of judicial independence

Judicial independence based on accountability is a fundamental value defining the constitutional identity of the rule of law. Constitutional identity can be understood as 'the features of a constitution so that we can identify that document as a constitution when we see certain attributes incorporated in a particular legal document'.[1] However, if there is no constitution per se – as written down in a single document – the existence of an actual unwritten constitution may be authoritatively attested to by the attributes of constitutional culture that make up its identity, and which have been confirmed by judicial decisions.[2] In keeping with contemporary constitutional theories, these attributes include the separation of powers, the rule of law and judicial independence.[3] They are the universal constitutional values that define the meaning of democratic constitutionalism 'irrespective of any controversy regarding their interpretation',[4] even if their 'jurisprudential status is a subject of considerable contestation, and their meaning and significance for courts vary markedly across national boundaries'.[5]

1 Gary Jeffrey Jacobsohn, *Constitutional Identity* (Harvard University Press 2010) 5.

2 Albert Venn Dicey, *Introduction to the Study of the Law of the Constitution* (first published 1915; ed. Roger E. Michener, Indianapolis, Liberty Fund 1982) <http://oll.libertyfund.org/title/1714> accessed 22 April 2024.

3 Roderick A. Macdonald and Hoi Kong, 'Judicial Independence as a Constitutional Virtue' in Michel Rosenfeld and András Sajó (eds), *The Oxford Handbook of Comparative Constitutional Law* (Oxford University Press 2013) 831.

4 Dennis Davis, Alan Richter and Cheryl Saunders (eds), *An Inquiry into the Existence of Global Values Through the Lens of Comparative Constitutional Law* (Hart Publishing 2015) 11ff.

5 Gary Jeffrey Jacobsohn, 'Constitutional Values and Principles' in Rosenfeld and Sajó (n 3) 777.

DOI: 10.4324/9781003557852-3

The keystone among them is judicial independence based on accountability of judges and the judiciary, a prerequisite for the right to a fair trial before an independent and impartial court.[6] This right is considered to be

> of paramount importance; in a way, it is a defining element of the rule of law. Indeed, it can be thought of as a fundamental right with the status of a 'meta-right', whose respect is necessary to ensure the respect of all other rights.[7]

According to Marek Safjan and Łukasz Gwóźdź, within the rule of law, the judicial power can only play its protective role 'if members of the judiciary exercise their function independently and impartially. There is no doubt that there is a correlation between the lack of judicial independence and defectiveness, weak character, and inefficiency of the rule of law'.[8]

From the perspective of a scholarly analysis, the historical experiences and the systemic practice of the last few decades seem to confirm that

> the quality of the rule of law is increasingly determined by the respect of fundamental rights and effective judicial protection. This observation finds support in the examples offered by many legal systems: judicial protection allows the operationalisation of goals related to the rule of law; indeed, it is the only real remedy to protect the rights of individuals and guarantee legal security against dangers that can easily appear in well-functioning democracies.[9]

Safjan and Gwóźdź further note:

> [A] purely formal normative declaration of adherence to the rule of law is meaningless if it is not backed by the possibility of relying on adequate control mechanisms, and legal consequences in cases of violation of this principle. It is no coincidence that the biggest threats to the rule of law go hand in hand with attempts to undermine judicial independence by exercising political control of courts' decision-making process.[10]

6 On the notion of accountability see Piotr Mikuli and Grzegorz Kuca, 'Introduction' in Mikuli and Kuca (eds), *Accountability and the Law: Rights, Authority and Transparency of Public Power* (Routledge 2022) 1ff. See also Carol Harlow, 'Accountability and Constitutional Law' in Mark Bovens, Robert E. Goodin and Thomas Schillemans (eds), *The Oxford Handbook of Public Accountability* (Oxford University Press 2014) 195ff.

7 Marek Safjan and Łukasz Gwóźdź, *Revival of the Rule of Law* (Report for the General Congress of International Academy of Comparative Law, Asuncion 2022) 19.

8 Safjan and Gwóźdź (n 7).

9 Safjan and Gwóźdź (n 7) 41.

10 Safjan and Gwóźdź (n 7).

However, according to H. P. Lee,

> [in countries] with a constitutionally entrenched bill of rights, the role of the judiciary becomes more pronounced. The courts are entrusted with the role of 'constitutional watch-dog'. They then stand between citizens and the state. The might of the apparatus of a government is kept in check by the courts, and occasions will arise when an impatient government becomes irate with the tempering effect of judicial decisions.[11]

Therefore, as posited by Shimon Shetreet, judicial independence should be based on certain constitutional principles, creating infrastructure of such independence, namely the following: (1) a rule against ad hoc tribunals, (2) a prohibition against intentionally depriving courts of their jurisdiction and diverting cases to other tribunals with a view to having those cases disposed of by tribunals that do not enjoy the same conditions of independence as the original courts, (3) the standard-judge principle, or the ordinary-judge principle, which requires that judges be selected to hear cases by a predetermined internal plan or assignment schedule prior to the commencement of the case, (4) the post-decisional independence of the judgement and its respect by the other branches of the government, (5) the requirement that judges must not be part of the administrative arm of the executive branch, rather they should be viewed as independent constitutional or statutory officers of the state, and completely separate from the civil service; and (6) changes in the terms of judicial office should not be applied to present judges unless such changes serve to improve the terms of judicial service.[12]

Absent judicial independence – with the courts subordinated to the legislature or the executive – checks and balances are no longer working, and one branch of government (or two of them) gets the upper hand.

A non-authoritarian state cannot exist without independent courts and independent judges, who play a special role in the process of legitimisation of the authorities.

Judicial independence and impartiality underpins the rule of law and is the keystone of modern constitutional democracies. These democracies have embraced the principle of the separation of powers, and also the principle of representation, which is coessential with the former. The separation of powers is one of the fundamental constitutional values, reflecting this principle's linkage with human rights protection – that is, with the very essence of the Constitution, which lays down rules restricting the powers of the majority

11 H. P. Lee, 'The Judiciary: A Comparative Conspectus' in Lee (ed.), *Judiciaries in Comparative Perspective* (Cambridge University Press 2011) 534.

12 Shimon Shetreet, 'Judicial Independence and Accountability: Core Values in Liberal Democracies' in Lee (n 11) 20ff.

in accordance with the rights and freedoms of the individual. At the same time, this principle – that is, the separation of powers – is crucially linked with the essence of the democratic system, understood as a system where majority rule is constrained by human rights.[13] An extraordinary cultural and political project developed in Western Europe and North America which we call 'liberal democracy' constrains the power of the majority in accordance with human rights.[14] It is founded on the rule of law, a concept that invokes the belief, expressed by Plato, that a 'state in which the law is subject and has no authority' is 'on the road to ruin', whereas 'the state in which the law is above the rulers, and the rulers are the inferiors of the law, has salvation, and every blessing which the Gods can confer'.[15]

As Shetreet observes, the doctrine of the separation of powers – which provides the theoretical basis for judicial independence – in its modern form does not mean total separation of the branches of government but, rather, a system of 'checks and balances'. The judicial branch has to be independent in order to carry out its function of controlling and balancing vis-à-vis the other two principal branches of government: the executive and the legislature.[16]

The separation of powers[17] has been present in human reflection – as an aspect of good governance – ever since questions were asked about a just and fair government, worthy of man, thus emerging as an underlying theme in constitutionalism since its very inception.[18] The experiences accumulated since time immemorial, including the tragedies of the twentieth century, have confirmed the sense of the age-old anxieties about too much power being vested in too few hands. These experiences also confirm the accuracy of the eighteenth-century belief that a society in which 'the separation of powers is not defined has no Constitution at all'.[19]

The experience of the past century made it clear that the rule of law in a democratic state relies on values consistent with human dignity, which delineate

13 Ryszard Piotrowski, 'Independence of the Courts and Constitutional Democracy: Rethinking the Contemporary Experience of Poland' in Monika Bator-Bryła, Stanisław Adam Paruch and Kamil Spryszak (eds), *Main Challenges for Democracy, the Rule of Law, and the Protection of Human Rights in the Modern World: Studies in Honour of Professor Jerzy Jaskiernia* (Adam Marszałek 2022) 228ff.

14 Piotrowski (n 13).

15 Plato, *Laws* Book IV, 255ff. See also Ryszard Piotrowski, 'Judges and European Democracies' (2019) 12 *Państwo i Prawo* 39ff.

16 Shetreet (n 12) 9ff.

17 Ryszard Piotrowski, 'Separation of Powers, Checks and Balances, and the Limits of Popular Sovereignty: Rethinking the Polish Experience' (2019) 79 *Stud Iurid* 78ff. See also Piotrowski, 'Zasada podziału władz w Konstytucji RP' (2007) 4 *Przegl Sejmowy* 3ff, with the literature cited therein and referred to in the present article.

18 On the history of this principle, see Ryszard Małajny, *Trzy teorie podzielonej władzy* (Wydawnictwo Sejmowe 2001).

19 The Declaration of the Rights of Man and of the Citizen (Paris 1798) art. XVI.

the power of the majority and the powers of the sovereign.[20] The guardians of those values and the guarantors of freedom are independent courts which can review the constitutionality of acts of the legislature and the executive. This is of fundamental importance to the role of the judiciary in a democratic state.[21]

The independence and accountability of the judiciary is a pillar of the democratic state and the rule of law, and a linchpin of contemporary constitutional democracies. Such judiciary relies on the principle of the separation of powers, which significantly changes the traditional concept of national sovereignty and the corresponding principle of representation.

The separation of powers is one possible answer to the question of what system of governance would align with ideas about human dignity. It is also intended to counter the pursuit of concentration of power in conditions of partisan competition, where success in fulfilling electoral promises tends to boost a party's chances for re-election. The question of the limits to majority power and of minority protection defines the basic dilemma of the vast intellectual tradition usually referred to as constitutionalism.[22] In the light of this tradition, a system worthy of the human being should be so designed as to safeguard individuals from mutual aggression, unite people for the sake of the common good rather than divide them and, most importantly, shield citizens from the perils that may arise from a power pursuing its own interests, often at the expense of the life, liberty and property of the governed. From this perspective, tyranny is both highly effective and mightily corrupt, as it prioritises its own benefits over those of society.[23]

The principle of the separation of powers has been the subject of many critical assessments and commentaries focused on analysing the practice of constitutional systems that respect this principle, even if those systems are not necessarily immune to mistakes and failures. The principle itself can make it easier for rulers to justify their ineffectiveness, and it discourages the governed from participating in public life.[24]

However, it can be argued, particularly in the face of contemporary threats to democracy, that this principle – which is of a piece with the principles of a democratic state ruled by law – remains a crucial aspect of constitutionalism, given its significance for affirming and guaranteeing human rights, and also its role in shaping the structure and rules of a democratic state.[25] From this per-

20 Piotrowski (n 15) 41ff.

21 Piotrowski (n 15).

22 William B. Gwyn, 'The Separation of Powers and Modern Forms of Democratic Government' in Robert A. Goldwin and Art Kaufman (eds), *Separation of Powers – Does it Still Work?* (American Enterprise Institute for Policy Research 1986) 65.

23 Gwyn (n 22) 66. See also David Held, *Models of Democracy* (Polity Press 2006).

24 See, e.g., Charles Hardin, 'The Separation of Powers Needs Major Revision' (n 22) 99.

25 On linkage between the principles of the rule of law and separation of powers, see in particular Mirosław Wyrzykowski, 'Zasada demokratycznego państwa prawnego' in Wojciech Sokolewicz (ed.), *Zasady podstawowe polskiej Konstytucji* (Wydawnictwo Sejmowe 1998) 69ff. See

spective, the principle of the separation of powers comes as part of normative universalism, a notion which encompasses the values underpinning the mechanisms of governance. The presence of these values in constitutions and their evolution over time has been the subject of both constitutional law and human rights analyses.[26] Due to these values, the government should simultaneously be capable of effective action and also constrained by laws, which the majority in power could not change and whose interpretation should be the province of independent judges. These principles – and thus, in essence, the principle of the separation of powers – can be categorised as rules of constitutional natural law.[27]

The principle of the separation of powers – in that aspect of it which rules out a concentration of power, threatening human rights – is recognised as the universal basis of constitutional democracy.[28] A state where unlimited power is exercised, i.e., power not divided among the state's constituent entities, cannot be considered democratic. However, this does not imply that the principle of the separation of powers, as understood in this way, determines specific solutions and systemic relations in the state.[29]

According to Safjan and Gwóźdź, if judicial control of the legal system is to be the most effective way of securing the rule of law, 'such control must be external to the sovereign recognised by that system, i.e., must have a different normative grounding than the content of law subject to such control' and, besides, 'the essence of the rule of law cannot be reduced to the presence of a democratically elected majority that makes and applies laws'.[30]

Judicial independence, accountability and constitutionalism

Without judicial independence, it is impossible to exercise the principle of the rule of law, understood as preventing the law from 'turning itself into a sheer tool of domination, a manageable servant to political monopoly and instrumentalism'.[31]

---

also Lech Garlicki, *Polskie prawo konstytucyjne* (Wolters Kluwer 2023, pp. 76ff); Mirosław Wyrzykowski, 'Legislacja – demokratyczne państwo prawne – radykalne reformy polityczne i gospodarcze' in Hanna Suchocka (ed.), *Tworzenie prawa w demokratycznym państwie prawnym* [Law-Making in a Democratic State Ruled by Law] (Wydawnictwo Sejmowe 1992).

26 See in particular Sujit Choudhry (ed.), *The Migration of Constitutional Ideas* (Cambridge University Press 2006) 68ff.

27 Hardin (n 24) 91.

28 Hubert Izdebski notes that departures from the formula linking constitutionalism with separation of powers should be regarded as exceptional, and that 'the only argument in its favour could possibly be that in a given case the principle of unity of power must not pose a threat to democracy'. See Izdebski, *Fundamenty państw współczesnych* (LexisNexis 2007) 170.

29 See also Piotr Mikuli, *Zasada podziału władz a ustrój brytyjski* (Wydawnictwo Sejmowe 2006).

30 Safjan and Gwóźdź (n 7) 43.

31 Gianluigi Palombella, 'The Rule of Law as an Institutional Ideal' in Leonardo Morlino and Gianluigi Palombella (eds), *Rule of Law and Democracy: Internal and External Issues* (Brill 2010) 3ff.

The independence of the judiciary is crucial to the realisation of the principle of constitutionalism, understood as 'not identical to the legalisation of public power'.[32] According to this principle, 'no extraconstitutional bearers of public power and no extraconstitutional ways and means to exercise this power are recognised'.[33] Independent courts serve as guardians of this principle only if they maintain their independence. This very independence and impartiality is crucial for the success of particular economic projects and, indeed, for overall economic prospects, whether nationally or globally.[34]

The concept of judicial independence and its guarantees refers not only to individual judges, but also to the judiciary as a whole, in relation to the other branches of government, i.e., the legislative and the executive. Conflicts among them are all but inevitable, as each seeks to strengthen its own position at the expense of the others, thus initiating and reinforcing negative feedback.[35]

The literature on the subject contains a proposition positing that the judiciary, of which judges are a part, operates on the principles of 'procedural fairness, efficiency, accessibility, public confidence in the courts, judicial independence, [and] constitutional protection of the judiciary'.[36] However, according to Neil Andrews, the core values of the justice system may be formulated in 24 principles: judicial independence; judicial impartiality; public or open justice; the principle of due notice; judicial duty to give reasons; avoidance of undue delay; litigants not prejudiced by the court's culpable shortcomings; access to justice; right to choose a lawyer; confidential legal consultation; procedural equality; protection against bad or spurious claims and defences; simplicity of procedure; judicial control of the civil process; proportionality; disclosure; oral proceedings; procedural equity; promoting settlement; accuracy; fair play between litigants; protection of non-parties; effectiveness; and finality.[37] These interconnected values are reflected differently in various countries that are considered democratic. However, the basic condition for respecting judicial independence, as resting on the previously mentioned values, is compliance with the provisions of the constitution relating to the judiciary. Failure to respect the constitution, for whatever reason, by any authority, renders judicial

32 Dieter Grimm, *Constitutionalism: Past, Present, and Future* (Oxford University Press 2016) 363.
33 Grimm (n 32) 363.
34 Shetreet (n 12) 43.
35 For insightful remarks on the subject by judges, see Sandra Day O'Connor, 'Judicial Accountability Must Safeguard not Threaten, Judicial Independence: An Introduction' (2008) 86 *Denv U L Rev* 1; Ewa Łętowska, 'Władza sądownicza a pozostałe władze – stan równowagi czy jej zachwiania?' in Ryszard Piotrowski (ed.), *Pozycja ustrojowa sędziego* (Wolters Kluwer 2015) 124ff.
36 Shetreet (n 12) 4.
37 Neil Andrews, *The Modern Civil Process: Judicial and Alternative Forms of Dispute Resolution in England* (Mohr Siebeck 2008).

independence meaningless, resulting in constitutional vacuity. This erodes the rights of citizens and undermines the legitimacy of the judiciary.[38]

The tragic legacy of the twentieth century – reflecting the weaknesses of a representative democracy that proved unable to contain totalitarianism – highlights the fundamental importance of the guarantees of individual rights and freedoms.

The experiences of the past century helped us understand that the rule of law in a democracy must be founded on values coessential with the dignity of the human person – the values which set the limits to majority rule and, simultaneously, the limits to sovereign rule.[39] These values are guarded, and the freedoms protected, by independent and impartial courts, competent to judge the constitutionality of executive and legislative actions. This fundamentally determines the judiciary's role in a democracy. Judicial independence and impartiality is the foundation of the democratic state ruled by law, and the linchpin of modern liberal democracies.

The question of the role played by law in a democracy – in other words, the relationship between the state ruled by law, whose tenets are made flesh thanks to an independent judiciary, and a democracy understood as the right of the parliamentary majority to determine the rules – is closely linked to the question of delineating limits to the authority of the sovereign. In modern specialist literature, this question takes the form of an antinomy between legal constitutionalism and political constitutionalism. In terms of legal constitutionalism, the judiciary plays a special role in the state, as the ultimate guardian of the legal system which governs the operation of the other branches of government, and also as the defender of human rights.[40] But in the perspective of political constitutionalism, the legal system is a time-limited arrangement of rights, duties and competences that changes in accordance with the majority will, representing the sovereign.[41] In this view, the separation of powers, interpreted in a strict orthodox manner, may result in an 'impossibilism', restricting the majority's capacity to act.[42] It is not clear, the argument goes, why disputes in which law and politics are closely interwoven should be adjudicated by judges, not by elected politicians. In modern US constitutional doctrine, these doubts are reflected in the following passage, which for the time being at least remains a minority opinion:

> The Supreme Court is our servant and not our master: a servant whose seriousness and knowledge deserves much deference but who is

38 Ryszard Piotrowski, 'The Issue of Legitimation of the Judicial Power in a Democratic State Ruled by Law' in Anna Machnikowska (ed.), *The Legitimation of Judicial Power* (Gdańsk University Press 2017) 9ff.

39 Piotrowski (n 13) 230.

40 T.R.S. Allan, *The Sovereignty of Law: Freedom, Constitution and Common Law* (Oxford University Press 2015) 1ff.

41 Adam Tomkins, *Our Republican Constitution* (Hart Publishing 2005) 37ff.

42 Allan (n 40) 3ff.

> ultimately supposed to yield to our judgements about what the Constitution means and not the reverse. The Supreme Court is not the highest authority in the land on constitutional law. We are.[43]

In the light of the US Constitution, though, the notion of 'we' represents a legislature operating within a system – known as the economy of influence – that is seen as restricting citizens' power in favour of corporations.[44]

In British constitutional doctrine, the relationship between judges and the sovereign takes a slightly different, noteworthy form. Given the Parliament's special status as the 'immediate sovereign', the Constitution is consequently seen as the 'ultimate or normative sovereign'.[45] In the literature on the subject we can find the opinion that the sovereignty of the British Parliament reflects the sovereignty of the unwritten Constitution, from which the Parliament derives its extensive powers that make up a legislative supremacy within the rule of law.[46] The judges derive their authority not only from the will of the Parliament but also from the principles of the common law, which require judges to adjudicate in accordance with their own perception of how the rule of law ideal should be applied in a given case. The British common law constitution is seen by some as representing a compromise between parliamentary sovereignty and constraints thereon arising from the rule of law. The British concept of parliamentarianism denotes an unbreakable linkage between the sovereignty of the people, the sovereignty of the Parliament and the sovereignty of the Constitution – that is, the linkage between the sovereignty of the people and the sovereignty of law, as reflected in judicial independence and impartiality.[47] The independence of the judiciary and its separation from other branches of government is of paramount importance for the system of integral democracy. Judicial autonomy provides the guarantee of individual rights and liberties, and a promise of respect for the common good, exposed as it is to threats from multiple vested interests.[48]

In a democratic state ruled by law – where the power of the majority is limited by the rights of the minorities, as reflected in the formula of constitutional democracy – the judicial power derives its legitimacy not from election results but from its ability to adjudicate independently of the will and interests of political parties. The political parties control the legislative power but sometimes also the constitutional courts dependent on the parliamentary majority.[49]

43 Larry D. Kramer, *The People Themselves: Popular Constitutionalism and Judicial Review* (Oxford University Press 2004) 248.
44 *Lawrence* Lessig, *Republic, Lost: How Money Corrupts Congress – and a Plan to Stop it* (Twelve 2011).
45 Sir Ernest Barker, *Political Thought in England* (Oxford University Press 1963) 212ff.
46 Allan (n 40) 133.
47 Piotrowski (n 13) 242.
48 Piotrowski (n 13).
49 Piotrowski (n 13).

They also control the executive power. Therefore, citizens are essentially subordinate to politicians, even if not providing them with electoral support. Only the judicial power can put up defences against that subordination, provided that judges and courts are independent.[50] Thus, this ability resulting from the systemic position of the judicial power, intrinsically related to balancing the role of politicians and judges in the process of judges' appointment, is the factor determining the legitimation of the judicial power in the State, whose Basic Law reflects the rules referred to as liberal constitutionalism.[51]

The identity of liberal democracy is informed not so much by uniform systemic solutions but rather by consistency with the values rooted in the legal tradition which gives legitimacy to the judiciary in a democratic system.[52] The cornerstone of the system and the foundation for the judges' role in democracies is provided by the principle of the separation of powers, combined with safeguards of human rights, which reaffirm inviolable and inalienable human dignity.[53] That principle is materialised in the independence of courts and judges. The independence of judges precludes their appointment according to political criteria, even if judges are, as a rule, appointed by the highest powers: presidents, kings, or parliaments. However, judicial candidates have to meet professional criteria, and judges cannot be removed from office for political reasons. In particular, changes of the retirement age of judges cannot be retroactive in effect. Another fundamental principle of a democratic system is that judges are answerable for their actions before the judiciary, not before the other branches. However, the judiciary reports on its activities to the highest authorities of the other branches. In democratic European states, judges are subject to laws, i.e., the constitution and the statutes, rather than political directives. Judges, not politicians, pass judgements. Judges have the exclusive power to resolve legal disputes, which may include all types of controversies.

It is a distinctive feature of liberal democracies that the judiciary can restrain the other branches by reviewing the constitutionality of laws and the legality of acts of the executive. Checks and balances in European states allow for only very limited dependence of the judiciary on the other branches. The more dependent the judiciary is on the other branches, the higher the risk of its excessive irresponsibility.[54]

The growing importance of the judiciary is part of a process initiated in democratic states in the mid-twentieth century, which reversed the eighteenth-century trend of minimising the importance of the judiciary in the system of power, as expressed in the opinions typical of legal illuminism:

50 Piotrowski (n 38) 11ff.

51 Mark Tushnet, *Advanced Introduction to Comparative Constitutional Law* (Edward Elgar 2014) 114ff.

52 Piotrowski (n 15) 40.

53 Piotrowski (n 17) 78ff.

54 Daniel Smilov, 'The Judiciary: The Least Dangerous Branch?' in Rosenfeld and Sajó (n 3) 859ff.

judges are but the mouthpiece of the law; they should speak when the law speaks and keep silent when the law is silent or imprecise; there should be no interpretation of the law and no place for legal authorities in the courtroom. The objective was to avoid divergences in case law, criticised by Voltaire. It seemed that the law could be rational, clear and concise, and that its only acceptable interpretation was a literal one. To limit the importance of judges, nineteenth-century Europe barred other-than-literal interpretations of laws and forbade the publication of commentaries to the criminal code. A different approach eventually prevailed, tough, as expressed in the Napoleonic Code which provides that '[t]he judge who shall refuse to determine under pretext of the silence, obscurity, or insufficiency of the law, shall be liable to be proceeded against as guilty of a refusal of justice' (Article 4). This prevailing conviction is that for the constitution to perform its functions in the system, judges must have power over statutes by way of constitutional review. Such approach is consistent with the legal culture of judge-made laws.

The importance of the judiciary has been on the rise in contemporary democratic states, a trend often called the 'government of judges'. The reasons include the growing role of judges: they resolve conflicts between rival politicians, disputes concerning competences between different segments of public authorities, and disputes between proponents of secular and religious propositions; judges also address the universal demand for condemnation of the corruption and inefficiency of the legislature and the executive. However, the importance of the judiciary has also been increasing due to a crisis of the system of law.

Contemporary democracy is, at its heart, a system of growing litigiousness of everyday life[55] and litigiousness of politics.[56] Founded on the aspiration to exercise effective review of the legality of the political branch and of the constitutionality of laws, this is a system where political decisions have been transferred to courts. The role of courts has been growing since sovereignty is based on human rights and the rule of law, i.e., respect for the rights of minorities and the rights of the opposition.

The dilemma of the legitimacy of the judiciary in a democratic state may be resolved by an interpretation of the constitution which takes into consideration the mutual axiological relations among the underlying systemic principles: inalienable human dignity, sovereignty of the people, and the separation of powers. The paradigm of the democratic system is the right to have rights,[57] but that right is ineffective without judges. The independence of judges in a democratic state implies independence from the one and only legitimate opinion of the majority and the one and only point of view. The culture of 'one truth' may pose a serious risk to that independence. The autonomy and

55 Antoine Garapon, 'La question du juge' (1995) 74 *Pouvoirs* 16ff.

56 C. Neal Tate and Torbjorn Vallinder (eds), *The Global Expansion of Judicial Power* (NYU Press 1995) 5ff. See also Ran Hirschl, *Towards Juristocracy* (Harvard University Press 2004) 221ff.

57 Stefano Rodotà, *Il diritto di avere diritti* (Editori Laterza 2012) 41ff.

independence of courts represents a challenge to those who believe that the majority that wins the parliamentary election has an unfettered right to implement the projects of its leaders.[58]

The principle of the sovereignty of the people is often evoked in support of the claim that the parliament and the government, as an emanation of the will of the sovereign, are powers superior to courts and tribunals. However, that concept has no standing in the light of the values of constitutional democracy, which rule out any opposition of democracy versus the rule of law, or national sovereignty versus the constitution. In this system, the constitution as the supreme law of the state is intrinsically linked with the people and their sovereignty, but also with the independence of courts and judges because 'in questions of power, let no more be heard of confidence in man, but bind him down from mischief by the chains of the constitution'.[59]

An independent judiciary strengthens the state and its position among other states. When courts are controlled by the government, their credibility is compromised and they can no longer maintain the legality of the existing order through their own ability to perform constitutional functions independently of politicians.[60] That would restrict the capacity of the sovereign to rule regardless of whichever political party wins the elections. It would eventually erode the boundary between political parties exercising public power and the state; instead of the common good, the objective of politics would be for political factions to come to power. The judiciary's independence of politicians is crucial in stopping a constitutional democracy from turning into the supremacy of the majority, which would also mean turning the sovereignty of the people into precisely such supremacy.

According to Shimon Shetreet, the importance of the principle of an independent judiciary has grown and received increased attention, particularly as a result of the expanding role of the judiciary in society.[61] This increasing judicialisation is in part a result of social developments, such as massive industrialisation or the expansion of the welfare state. Wide-ranging primary and secondary legislation has been enacted and, consequently, there has been a corresponding expansion in litigation against government services, as well as the development of 'social rights', a typical by-product of the welfare state. Shetreet notes that the increasing role of the judiciary in society may be seen as natural and objective, but some processes behind growing judicialisation may actually be viewed as convenience based. This refers to the judicialisation of issues largely for the political convenience of the other branches of government.[62]

58 Piotrowski (n 15) 40.

59 Thomas Jefferson, *The Writings of Thomas Jefferson* (ed. A. A. Lipscomb) (Washington; Memorial Association 1903) Vol. II, 163.

60 Piotrowski (n 15).

61 Shetreet (n 12) 10.

62 Shetreet (n 12).

As the independence of the judiciary is a crucial constitutional value in a liberal democracy, its constitutional counterpart, judicial accountability, comes as equally important. The constitutional significance of the independence of judges, who uphold the law, highlights the relevance of the question of who guards the guards, echoing the long-familiar doubt, *Quis custodiet ipsos custodes*?[63]

Judicial accountability as a core guarantee of judicial independence

Judicial independence and judicial accountability, which are both constitutional values of a democratic state, tend to remain in potential, and sometimes real, conflict.

It is clear that if government is to be conducted in accordance with the law, the law must be administered by as independent a judiciary as possible, otherwise there is a danger that the law will serve the ends of government rather than the interests of justice: the two may not always be synonymous.[64] The clear trend which has emerged is a more pronounced and vigorous evaluation of the functioning of the courts, particularly in the arena of human rights protection. The emergence of that trend has led to expressions of concern over the state of independence of the judicial institution. In evaluating the importance of judicial independence, there is a need to reconcile the requirement for judicial 'accountability' and the notion of 'judicial independence'.[65] According to H. P. Lee, since it is a fundamental feature of the judicial system that a judge is not only impartial but must be seen to be impartial, when claims of judicial bias are raised the issue of recusal arises.[66] At the same time, it has been pointed out that decisions by judges to disqualify themselves should not be made lightly; otherwise it would lead to a situation where litigants may exploit this avenue in order to choose their own judges.

The courts can perform their function as an institution to resolve disputes in society 'only if they enjoy public confidence'.[67] The courts have recognised the indispensability of this value to the functioning of the legal system. The courts can enjoy such confidence only if they are seen as independent and unbiased, and if the process of resolving the dispute is fair, efficient, expedient and accessible.[68] Nevertheless, there is a continuous tension between judicial independence and the public accountability of judges in a democracy. As Shimon Shetreet argues, this tension 'should be reconciled by the exercise of

63 Juvenal, *Satires*, 6, 347–348.
64 A. W. Bradley and K. D. Ewing, *Constitutional and Administrative Law* (Pearson 2007) 381.
65 Lee (n 11) 535.
66 Lee (n 11) 538.
67 Shetreet (n 12) 6.
68 Shetreet (n 12).

wisdom and good judgement, so that the proper balance between these very important principles is maintained'.[69]

For the judiciary to be considered politically accountable, its performance must be evaluated by a body – either outside or within the judiciary – that is external to the judges being evaluated. It would seem that the more this evaluation is detached from judges themselves, the less illusory and the more objective the accountability of judges will be. However, this may lead to the subordination of judges to the entity to which they are held accountable.

According to scholarly literature:

> [Individual judges] must enjoy both personal and substantive independence, both of which are necessary to protect judges from threats to their personal or professional security that may influence their official duties. Characteristics of personal independence include security of office, life tenure and adequate remuneration and pensions. Substantive independence refers to the freedom of judges to perform their judicial functions independently.[70]

From the scholarly perspective, the development of the judiciary as a significant social institution with an important constitutional role requires that the concept of judicial independence should not be confined to the independence of the individual judge. It must also extend to the independence of the judiciary as a whole under the rubric of collective independence. It is widely recognised that interference with the independence of individual judges is considered a serious infringement of the rule of law. Interference with the collective independence of the judiciary also has an adverse impact on individual judges as they discharge their official duties.

This is due to the fact that the traditional sense of social responsibility that the judiciary imparts on individual judges is a strong instrument for ensuring its independence. Interference with the judiciary as a whole is, therefore, likely to have a negative impact on the sense of independence of individual judges. The collective independence is protected by the rules outlined, which deals with the constitutional position of the judiciary.[71]

In this context, it is worth noting the distinction made in the extensive and diverse literature on the subject – a discussion of which is beyond the scope of this chapter – between political accountability and accountability to the law.[72] Understood in this way, political accountability is a responsibility to the people that judges bear in the same way as others who exercise public authority

69 Shetreet (n 12) 9.

70 Shetreet (n 12) 15.

71 Shetreet (n 12).

72 Mark Tushnet, 'Judicial Accountability in Comparative Perspective' in Nicholas Bamforth and Peter Leyland (eds), *Accountability in the Contemporary Constitution* (Oxford University Press 2013) 57ff.

to the extent conferred on them by law. Accountability to the law, which is interpreted and applied by judges, means accountability for whether or not the manner in which they do so conforms to the rigours of the law. Mark Tushnet argues that accountability to the law is a derivative accountability, given that the law itself is accountable to the people.[73] An excessive independence of judges leads them to exercise power for their own ends, which are narrower than the good of the community. The good of the community is a constitutional value, the realisation of which requires accountability on the part of the judiciary to ensure that the various particular interests are not served by ignoring the common good.

Accountability as a value requires that a balance be struck between political accountability and accountability to the law. Excessive political accountability may lead judges to favour the political expectations of those to whom they are accountable. Conversely, exaggerated accountability to the law may encourage judges to invoke the rigours of the law in order to justify their own intentions which only ostensibly comply with the law.[74]

According to Safjan and Gwóźdź, a good and important standard allowing one to discern the loss of independence by the judiciary is provided by the 'impartial bystander' test.[75] It aims to measure the degree to which the general public perceive their judiciary as independent and impartial. The general public thus become the ultimate point of reference.[76] Judicial accountability may be transformed into judicial subordination to political control. Safjan and Gwóźdź note that the loss of independence by courts invariably comes as a symptom of a

> deep structural crisis in the legal system, with defective mechanisms leading to a systematic reproduction of patterns of political dependence of judges. Individual instances of judges who let themselves be politically influenced, if very dangerous in themselves, are not yet evidence of such a structural crisis.

It is necessary to take into consideration the system as a whole, including mechanisms of judicial appointments, career progression instruments, and the disciplinary regime. In a broken system, the judicial power loses its credibility in the eyes of 'impartial bystanders', who begin to perceive it 'as a simple executor of the political will'. Political interference with judicial independence varies in intensity and does not necessarily lead to a complete loss of this independence. Most commonly, 'it comes in stages, and is manifested through an incremental weakening, and then elimination of mechanisms that guarantee

73 Tushnet (n 72).
74 Tushnet (n 72).
75 Safjan and Gwóźdź (n 7) 21.
76 Safjan and Gwóźdź (n 7) 20.

judicial independence'. The politicisation of judicial appointments is 'highly dangerous, as it lowers popular trust in judges and courts, at the same time leading to the erosion of the criteria and substantive requirements applied to candidates for judicial posts'. This politicisation sometimes results from the legal solutions adopted in a given system, letting political bodies have the final say on judicial appointments.[77]

One manifestation of a judge's direct political accountability is the possibility that he or she may be removed from office because of the judgements they have made. This type of accountability must be regarded as limiting judicial independence to an extent that is constitutionally impermissible, except in cases of physical or mental disability, corruption and administrative malfeasance.[78]

According to Safjan and Gwóźdź, one method politicians employ in eliciting such submission is to create instruments, often of disciplinary nature, allowing them to threaten judges who refuse to comply with their directives, thus producing a 'chilling effect' to prevent courts from deciding cases in a politically inconvenient way.[79] Unfortunately, quite often

> [politicians are also able] to shape public opinion about the constitutional role of courts, with a view to undermining the credibility and prestige of the judicial branch. The judiciary do not dispose of any instruments other than their own case-law to defend their position before the public opinion; the judicial branch has no formalised established presence in the media and does not partake in the political game.[80]

As a result, 'this vulnerability is often exploited by hostile political actors'.[81] H. P. Lee notes that judges are today faced with a diminution of the traditional deference accorded to judicial officers and the judiciary as a whole. On many occasions the media has taken an aggressive approach in its reporting of court matters. It is now commonplace for the media, politicians and commentators to attack judges when they disagree with the results of judicial decisions, such as sentences handed down by the courts, particularly in highly publicised trials, or with decisions which lead to the invalidation of significant legislation. It is quite clear that a traditionally complacent and deferential approach towards the judiciary is giving way to more critical and vocal demands for greater judicial accountability. On the other hand, thoughtful concerns have been raised about the fundamental importance of protecting the independence of the judicial institution and judicial officers.[82]

77 Safjan and Gwóźdź (n 7) 39ff.
78 Tushnet (n 72) 60ff.
79 Safjan and Gwóźdź (n 7) 40.
80 Safjan and Gwóźdź (n 7) 40.
81 Safjan and Gwóźdź (n 7) 40.
82 Lee (n 11) 533ff.

Indirect manifestations of political accountability of judges may include the influence exerted by politicians on the budget of the judiciary and the remuneration of judges. This is particularly relevant when the government has organisational oversight over a judiciary which does not have budgetary autonomy. The literature on the subject argues that any reduction in the salaries of judges, other than under austerity programmes affecting other branches as well, does threaten the independence of the judiciary to an extent that is difficult to reconcile with judicial accountability under the rule of law.[83]

The judiciary's political accountability is executed through a process of appointment and promotion of judges, whereby their independence is susceptible to limitation – in the name of accountability – by means of manipulation of a number of variables, including the appointment of judges for either a fixed or indefinite period of time (while restricting the vacation of office to statutorily defined non-political cases). The idea is that political considerations should not provide a cause for removal from office of the judges whose rulings do not meet the expectations of the legislative or executive branches. From this point of view, guarantees of independence are available to the Justices of the Supreme Court of the United States, who serve 'during good behaviour' and are not subject to mandatory retirement age.[84] In the case of constitutional courts, the non-renewable term of office is fixed for a period of up to a dozen years or more, which fosters the independence of the judges.

Also indicative of the judiciary's political accountability is an arrangement whereby judges are appointed by election, as is the case at the state level in the United States. The literature on the subject is ambivalent about that system, arguing that – while meeting the requirement of accountability – it leads to the politicisation of state courts and thus threatens the independence of the judiciary.[85] After all, in accordance with the rules governing state elections for judges, the results depend on factors such as campaign effectiveness and media persuasiveness. Another, inherent risk is that judicial decisions may be subordinated to the anticipated expectations of the electorate, and there is also the role that political leaders play in the candidate selection process.[86]

A similar pattern can be observed when it comes to the appointment of Supreme Court Justices in the United States, made by the President 'with the advice and consent of the Senate'. Tushnet believes that predictions about future decisions are rarely the sole consideration that presidents have in mind when selecting nominees.[87] This opinion notwithstanding, we can see in this instance a kind of indirect accountability to the political environment to which the President (making the nomination) and the Senators (providing advice

83 Tushnet (n 72) 61ff.
84 Tushnet (n 72).
85 Melinda Gann Hall, *Attacking Judges* (Stanford University Press 2015) 25ff.
86 Tushnet (n 72) 61ff.
87 Tushnet (n 72) 63ff.

and consent) are linked. The substantive qualification requirements, though, largely neutralise the political nature of the appointment and, in any case, strengthen the role of accountability for respecting the primacy of law over politics. This assessment also applies to the arrangements whereby judges, especially constitutional court judges, are selected by parliament. The higher the professional requirements for candidates, who may be also vetted by non-governmental organisations, the lower the risk that the accountability associated with the process will pose a threat to the independence of the judge.

According to the scholarly literature, nomination commissions established for the purpose of appointing judges – comprising judges, representatives of other legal professions, Members of Parliament, officials, and members of the public – may sometimes allow judges to take control of the nomination law.[88] Limiting the role of politicians in a nomination process so structured may not necessarily strengthen the independence of judges, if it so happens that accountability to constitutional values takes a back seat to the judicial corporation's standards and vested interest. In any event, though, the inclusion of a committee set up specifically for the nomination process can strengthen the credibility of the process and dispel doubts about judicial independence. Judges can then be perceived as independent guardians of the law. The correct model for balancing accountability and independence of judges has to be commensurate with the varied systemic arrangements that different liberal democracies may apply.

Safjan and Gwóźdź observe that political pressure and attempts to limit judicial independence vary in intensity. Some tensions between political and judicial powers are inevitable even in old, secure democracies:

> When we speak of the lack of judicial independence, we also mean the presence of structural mechanisms oriented towards producing this lack. Moreover, given that separation of powers cannot be taken to require absolute independence of branches of state from one another, but rather a proper balance founded on mutual control, one cannot infer a rule of law crisis from the mere fact that actors of the political power, such as Parliament or the Minister of Justice, exercise some control over the judiciary.[89]

It seems that the influence that the legislative majority or the executive power may have over the process of judicial appointments does not per se suggest an absence of judicial independence. Such prospect, however, emerges 'when there is a politicisation of the process of appointments, often combined with a politicisation of related mechanisms of control that impact the career progression of judges, including the removal of politically inconvenient judges

88 Tushnet (n 72) 65.
89 Safjan and Gwóźdź (n 7) 20.

through disciplinary procedures'.[90] This can have a chilling effect on judges, 'with visible consequences for their decision making'.[91] Judicial appointment procedures, Safjan and Gwóźdź note, vary significantly between different legal systems, and, in any event,

> [a] full separation between the political and the judicial does not seem ideal from the point of view of separation of powers based on a system of checks and balances. However, there is room for real concern when solutions adopted by the given legal system create an impression, in the eyes of the general public, that the courts submit to political influence in a way that impacts their decision making.[92]

To balance the constitutional values of independence and accountability, it is crucial to have suitable mechanisms for removing judges from office, if such need arises. Standing out in the literature on the subject is a system of removing judges who fail the 'good behaviour' test, having committed a serious criminal offence. The exclusion of these judges is served by an impeachment procedure, which, however, must not invoke the judgements they have passed.[93] As legal scholarship has it, disciplinary liability of judges in a liberal democracy can be enforced either in accordance with narrowly defined criteria – within or outside the judiciary – or by more broadly defined criteria.[94] The process of removing a judge from office, regardless of the path followed, poses a greater risk to judicial independence than the risk associated with the nomination process.

Safjan and Gwóźdź argue that even 'sound institutional guarantees are not sufficient to counter expansionist tendencies of political power backed by parliamentary majority'.[95] The erosion of judicial independence, and further, of the rule of law, tends to be incremental, and takes the form of step-by-step eradication of guarantees on which this independence rests. Only a general, high-level 'survey of the legal system allows one to diagnose this structural problem'.[96] This process of eradication can be significantly hindered by the judges themselves, provided that

> they withstand political pressure and use available instruments to secure the quality of their decisions; such instruments can include the primacy of constitutional norms over ordinary laws, creative interpretation of laws to achieve constitutionality and conformity with international law,

90 Safjan and Gwóźdź (n 7).
91 Safjan and Gwóźdź (n 7).
92 Safjan and Gwóźdź (n 7) 40.
93 Tushnet (n 72) 67.
94 Tushnet (n 72) 66.
95 Safjan and Gwóźdź (n 7) 22.
96 Safjan and Gwóźdź (n 7).

and finally, appealing to international institutions suited to the role of rule of law watchdogs.[97]

The literature also distinguishes accountability to the law.[98] It results from judges' subordination to the control exercised by their superiors in the judicial hierarchy, if such superiors are in place. Unlike political accountability, which carries the risks of politics trumping the law, accountability to the law involves responsibility to uphold the law in isolation from current politics. This type of accountability 'refers to people and their representatives in the more distant past'.[99]

A judge's subordination to statutory laws does not relieve them of the obligation to obey the Constitution. Accountability to the Constitution and to the values it encompasses, therefore, itself comes as a constitutional value. Ultimately, then, fidelity to Radbruch's formula, *lex iniustissima non est lex*, could also be counted among constitutional values. In a liberal democracy, for judicial accountability to be considered a constitutional value, it must affirm the axiological foundations of that democracy, which include limiting the power of the majority in the name of human rights.

Judicial accountability and the independence of universities

Judicial accountability also involves judges' accountability to legal scholarship, which examines the judicial decisions of individual judges and the current case law trend. Such impartial, non-political examination is possible where universities, especially their law faculties, remain independent of political authority.

The concept of constitutionalism is meaningless unless understood as restrictions imposed on majority power through human rights; it is meaningless without the principle of the separation of powers (which requires respect for the separation and independence of courts as opposed to other branches), without political pluralism, without a democratic state ruled by law, and without universities in their classical European form, ruling out subordination to the power of political parties and corporations.[100] Universities as a social phenomenon thrive on independence and autonomy in the sense that their 'research and teaching must be morally and intellectually independent of all political authority and economic power'.[101] Independent universities become a source of interpretations and evaluations alternative to those used by governments. The independence of universities limits the predominance of political

97 Safjan and Gwóźdź (n 7).
98 Tushnet (n 72) 68ff.
99 Tushnet (n 72) 69.
100 Ryszard Piotrowski, 'Konstytucja i uniwersytety' in Stanisław Bożyk (ed.), *Prawo. Parlament i egzekutywa we współczesnych systemach rządów. Księga poświęcona pamięci Profesora Jerzego Stembrowicza* (TEMIDA2 2009) 151.
101 Magna Charta of the European Universities 1988 <www.magna-charta.org/magna-charta-universitatum/mcu-1988> accessed 23 April 2024.

parties in public life. Consequently, the judiciary and universities perform the same social function in the democratic system: it is to restrict power on the grounds of values which are independent of such power.[102] This is the role of universities in a democratic state and that of judges in a constitutional democracy.[103]

A salient feature of liberal democracy is the potential identity of the public functions of constitutions and universities, where an authority is limited by values that are independent of it. Such limitation, in fact, defines both the role of universities and the role of judges in a constitutional democracy.[104]

Universities, being centres of free thinking, independent of current political authority, are of particular significance for the separation of powers, that is, for such a manner of state organisation where the law-making process – while respecting society's current needs, economic and political interests, and recommendations from experts – enables, above all, a respect for values. The separation of powers provides an answer to the question about such a form of government that would uphold the idea of human dignity. The separation would not be possible without citizens' capacity to think freely, which is also a necessary condition for the sovereign people to exercise their constitutional rights. And it is universities – if only they stay independent of banks, multinational corporations, owners of electronic media, political parties and governments – that enable citizens to maintain this capacity of free thinking. Therefore, universities undermine the domination of official propaganda which uses all possible channels to tell people how they should think and how they should vote. Universities provide a forum for debate about values – a debate which helps to balance values in the course of both the legislative process and judicial review.[105] This is of particular importance when public debate is brutalised, trivialised and turns formulaic. As matters stand, however, the autonomy of universities is being effectively constrained. University organisation and research are micromanaged by government and, in addition, university autonomy is in fact constrained by banks, to whom students have to turn for credit to finance the high costs of university education. Meanwhile, the independence of universities provides a foundation of liberal democracy, in the same way as judicial autonomy does.[106]

One of the most important problems facing modern democracy – the ease with which voters can be controlled, turning in effect the voice of *the* people into the voice of *some* people – can be resolved primarily through the diffusion of education, on which civil society is predicated. This highlights the

102 Piotrowski (n 100) 151.
103 Walter F. Murphy, *Constitutional Democracy: Creating and Maintaining a Just Political Order* (The Johns Hopkins University Press 2007) 147.
104 Piotrowski (n 13) 238ff.
105 Piotrowski (n 100) 152ff.
106 Piotrowski (n 13) 238.

fundamental importance of universities and higher education for the future of democracy and its survival in a world of multiple crises.

Scholars, especially in the humanities, act as guardians of memory – and this memory often differs from what those in power, seeking legitimisation, would like to disseminate. Universities, where time is not measured by the rhythm of successive electoral campaigns, 'produce, examine, appraise and hand down culture' – a hard-to-overestimate quality vis-à-vis political competition for public support.[107] Bent on winning a battle for memory,[108] those who seek power, and also those already in power, tend to construct their own politics of history and their own sets of values, yearning for such universities that they could call their own.

However, the essence of the university as a social phenomenon lies in its independence, inherent to an autonomous institution, which means precisely that its 'research and teachings must be morally and intellectually independent of any political authority and economic power'.[109] By virtue of this independence, universities offer interpretations and opinions alternative to those propounded by people in power. They also serve as guardians of rationality, without which the law could no longer perform the art of judging what is good or just – an art so much needed when attempting to convince the majority that there are limits to its power.

The independence of academic centres is also important as a factor limiting the actual capture of public life by political parties, which impedes civil society.

Consequently, one cannot fail but notice the fundamental identity of the social function performed in a democratic system by the Constitution and by universities, namely to limit power in the name of values that are outside the control of that power, for this is essentially the role assigned to universities in a democratic state, and to the Constitution in a constitutional democracy.[110]

The importance of universities as centres of thought independent of the current political power is particularly pronounced in the context of the separation of powers, i.e., such form of governance where law-making abides by both current and longer-term social, economic and political interests, the guidance of experts and, above all, where it respects values. The university provides space for debate on values, making their balancing possible, whether in the legislative process, in constitutionality review proceedings, or in judicial decisions.

Conclusion

Judicial accountability, as lying with the judges, is coextensive with the judiciary's answerability to the public. It represents a moral duty to uphold the

107 Magna Charta (n 101).
108 Luciano Canfora, *Libro e liberta* (Editori Laterza 1994) 64ff.
109 Magna Charta (n 101).
110 Murphy (n 103) 147ff.

public's confidence in the credibility not only of the judicial branch but also of the entire State, which then, based on this confidence, can demand obedience to the law. While individual judges are held accountable for professional misconduct and (in accordance with the relevant regulations) for infringement of universal laws binding on all, their independence must never be compromised. As a constitutional value of an importance comparable with the independence of the judiciary, judicial accountability is held both to disciplinary panels and to the public at large. At its core, it represents each and every judge's accountability to their own conscience for enforcement of the constitutional values of the judicial branch of government.

A judge, following the dictates of conscience, may find himself or herself in conflict with the opinions of those in power or the sentiments of the public. In a democracy, judges must not be held responsible for the content of their judgements just because these judgements – even if not violating the law – do not conform to what those in power perceive as the proper understanding of the law. And the independence of the judiciary may collide with the belief that a parliamentary victory empowers the elected majority to do whatever they think is right in pursuit of their leaders' projects.

Judicial accountability remains a constitutional value unless it undermines other constitutional values, including the separation of powers and the rule of law. With modern democracies' social and political life increasingly subjected to the process of juridification, the heft of the judges has grown, but it also became easier to blame them for failures on the part of the legislative and judicial branches of government. This erodes the importance of judges' accountability, which consists in truly streamlining the operation of the judiciary and effecting such a change in the conduct of judges that would indeed benefit the public.

The attainment of judicial accountability, as a constitutional value, is contingent on the characteristics of a society's legal and political culture, notably the delineation of the boundary between law and politics and adherence to the rule of law as the foundation of governance.

3 Constitutional identity as an 'actor' of judicial accountability

Nóra Bán-Forgács

Introduction

This chapter focuses on constitutional identity and judicial independence and accountability.[1] First, we anchor the discourse on constitutional identity in the context of judicial independence. By doing so, we seek to link constitutional identity and national sovereignty in the context of judicial independence. Then, we link the current debate on sovereignty and judicial independence with the scholarly literature on autocratic populism.[2] I argue that judicial

1 The author owes special thanks for comments and ideas to Associate Prof. Judit Tóth and Assistant Prof. Endre Orban and Senior Researcher Boldizsár Szentgáli-Toth.

2 Tjitske Akkerman, 'Populism and Democracy: Challenge or Pathology?' (2003) 38 *Acta Pol* 147–159; Daniele Albertazzi and Duncan McDonnell, *Populists in Power* (Routledge 2015); Manuel Anselmi, *Populism: An Introduction* (Routledge 2018); Rogers Brubaker, 'Why Populism?' (2017) 46 *Theory Soc* 357–385; Jack Balkin, 'Constitutional Crisis and Constitutional Rot' in Mark A. Graber, Sanford Levinson and Mark Tushnet (eds), *Constitutional Democracy in Crisis?* (Oxford University Press 2018) 16–17; Paul Blokker, 'Populist Counter-Constitutionalism, Conservatism, and Legal Fundamentalism' (2013) 15 *EuConst* 519, 520, 542; Paul Blokker, 'Constitutional Reform in Europe and Recourse to the People' in Xenophon Contiades and Alkmene Fotiadou (eds), *Participatory Constitutional Change: The People as Amenders of the Constitution* (Routledge 2016) 31–51; Paul Blokker, 'EU Democratic Oversight and Domestic Deviation from the Rule of Law: Sociological Reflections' in Carlos Closa and Dimitry Kochenov (eds), *Reinforcing Rule of Law Oversight in the European Union* (CUP 2016) 249–269; Paul Blokker, 'Populism as a Constitutional Project' (2019) 17 *ICON* 536–553; Alessandro Ferrari, Kaul Volker and David Rasumussen, 'The Populist Upsurge and the Decline of Diversity Capital' (2018) 44 *Philos Soc Crit* 345–504; Martin Krygier, 'The Challenge of Institutionalisation: Post-Communist "Transitions", Populism, and the Rule of Law' (2019) 15 *EuConst* 544–573.; Silvia Suteu, 'The Populist Turn in Central and Eastern Europe: Is Deliberative Democracy Part of the Solution?' (2019) 15 *EuConst* 488–518; Nicola Lacey, 'Populism and the Rule of Law' (2019) 15 *Annu Rev L Soc Sci* 79–96; Steven Levitsky and Daneil Ziblatt, *How Democracies Die* (Crown 2018); Cas Mudde and Cristobal Rovira Kaltwasser, *Populism: A Very Short Introduction* (OUP 2017); Jan-Werner Müller, *What Is Populism?* (University of Pennsylvania Press 2016); Laurent Pech and Kim Lane Scheppele, 'Rule of Law Backsliding in the EU' (2017) 19 *CYELS* 3–47; Kim Lane Scheppele, 'The Opportunism of Populists and the Defense of Constitutional Liberalism' (2019) 20 *GLJ* 314; Boldizsár Szentgáli-Tóth and Marco Antonio Simonelli, 'Populism and Liberal Constitutionalism: A Proposal to Define the Impact of Populism on the Constitutional Framework' (2023) 7 *Pub Gov*

DOI: 10.4324/9781003557852-4

independence can only be understood in relation to illiberal populist constitutionalism through a hyper-concentration of power in the hands of the Executive, and this serves as an antithesis to the doctrine of the separation of powers in the Hegelian sense and thus contributes to a vision of the unity of the state.[3]

We claim that judicial accountability in the current sovereignty/constitutional identity debate is hampered. The concept of accountability can only be conceptualized within judicial independence and the separation of powers. Accountability of judges presupposes a judicial body with integrity as a point of reference to whom or by which administration of justice is carried out. So, I argue in this chapter that the idea of judicial accountability operates in a medium, in a forum in which judicial supremacy is underlined. There are certain preconditions to judicial accountability, and judicial independence plays a paramount role in it.

We reason in this chapter that the current debate about judicial independence and sovereignty is a game-changing struggle over a threefold problem, or more precisely, a three-dimensional question:

1 According to the sovereignty argument, the judiciary comes under the domain of national legislation since states are not restricted in designing their own constitutional structure, including their judicial system. The claim is that an independent sovereign state must have an independent judiciary. Accordingly, the question is, who has supremacy over the national judiciary, the Union or Member States?
2 The second question is, who has (real) ownership of the judiciary under the doctrine of the separation of powers in a sovereign Member State, or more precisely, who has supreme power over the judiciary?
3 And third, who has a monopoly over the interpretation of the law? We further argue that challenging the judicial monopoly on interpreting the law is indeed a very strong forward move in populist constitutionalism.

Admin Fin L Rev 139–155; Nadia Urbinati, 'Populism and the Principle of Majority' in Rovira Kaltwasser, Paul A. Taggart, Paulina Ochoa Espejo and Pierre Ostiguy (eds), *The Oxford Handbook of Populism* (Oxford University Press 2017) 571–587; Sean Leo Hanley and Milada Anna Vachudová, 'Understanding the Illiberal Turn: Democratic Backsliding in the Czech Republic' (2018) 34 *E Eur Pol* 276; Neil Walker, 'Populism and Constitutional Tensions' (2018) 17 *IJCL* 515–535; Fareed Zakaria, 'The Rise of Illiberal Democracy' (1997) 76 *Foreign Aff* 22–43.

3 Kosař argues that Central European countries have always gravitated towards a centralisation of power (often culminating in a cult of personality) and that basic imperatives of the principle of the separation of powers have been sidelined even during the occasional democratic periods in these countries' histories. Moreover, the interwar regimes left little room for an active and pluralistic civil society and the communists openly suppressed this. These historical legacies of Central European countries, a strong push toward centralization, and a lack of a robust civic political and legal culture, have left a deep imprint on the Central European mindset. See David Kosař, Jiri Baroš and Pavel Dufek, 'The Twin Challenges to Separation of Powers in Central Europe: Technocratic Governance and Populism' (2019) *EuConst* 459.

Our hypothesis is that those actors who have a monopoly on the interpretation of statutes (and the interpretation of the text of the Constitution), together with those who have real ownership of the judiciary in illiberal constitutionalism, are totalitarian-like states, in contrast to constitutional democracies where the concept of judicial supremacy and the separation of powers prevails. We further argue that Europe represents a laboratory in which these arguments about the consequences of undercutting judicial independence can be empirically examined.[4]

In our analyses, we mainly use examples from Hungary and aim to conceptualize our findings on a higher abstract level. The ultimate goal of this chapter is to provide a synthesized overview and a systematic analysis of the theory and practice of judicial independence in the context of constitutional sovereignty.

The concept of constitutional identity in a judicial context

We do not know what constitutional identity is. We do, however, know that Member States call for constitutional identity when they want to deviate from the law of the European Union. Neither scholarship nor the jurisprudence of constitutional courts nor the Court of Justice of the European Union (CJEU) has provided a reliable standard concerning what constitutes an ultra vires argument from constitutional courts. One might conclude that there are "risks associated with its use, including the fact that opponents of constitutional democracy can use it as a great weapon, as there is no objective standard in terms of its content."[5]

The first academic works of this kind on constitutional identity only appeared at the turn of the millennium and are associated with the inconsistency and uncertainty that has accompanied the whole identity discourse to this day. Constitutional identity is a popular topic in modern public law,[6] although

4 Pedro C. Magalhães and Nuno Garoupa, 'Populist Governments, Judicial Independence, and Public Trust in the Courts' (2023) 15 *JEPP* 427.

5 Endre Orbán, 'Constitutional Identity in the Jurisprudence of the Court of Justice of the European Union' (2022) 2 *Hun J Leg Stud* 142.

6 Leonard F. M. Besselink, 'National and Constitutional Identity Before and After Lisbon' (2010) 6 *Utrecht LR* 36–49; Laurence Burgorgue-Larsen, 'The Constitutional Dialogue in Europe: A "Political Dialogue"' (2015) 21 *Eur J Curr L Stud*; Armin von Bogdandy and Stephan Schill, 'Overcoming Absolute Primacy: Respect for National Identity Under the Lisbon Treaty' (2011) 48 *CMLR* 1417–1454; Laurence Bourgorgue-Larsen (ed.), *L'identité constitutionnelle saisie par les juges en Europe* (Pedone 2011); Christian Callies and Gerhard van der Schyff (eds), *Constitutional Identity in a Europe of Multilevel Constitutionalism* (CUP 2019); Marta Cartabia, *'"Taking Dialogue Seriously" The Renewed Need for a Judicial Dialogue at the Time of Constitutional Activism in the European Union'* (New York USL 2007); Monica Claes and Jan-Herman Reestman, 'The Protection of National Constitutional Identity and the Limits of European Integration at the Occasion of the Gauweiler Case' (2015) *GLJ* 917–970; Monica Claes, 'National Identity: Trump Card or Up for Negotiation?' in Alejandro Saiz Arnaiz and Carina Alcoberro Llivina (eds), *National Constitutional Identity and European Integration* (Intersentia 2013) 109–140; Tímea Drinóczi, 'Constitutional Identity in Europe:

it is not always clear exactly what scholars mean by this concept.[7] Furthermore, the question of constitutional identity is closely related to the question of state identity. Indeed, the identity of constitutions can be understood within a broad framework. One may argue that the concept of constitutional identity can be defined as a set of key characteristics of a given constitution. On the other hand, the notion of constitutional identity can also mean a linkage between the constitution and the culture it represents, as well as the national, religious, and ideological identity of a country.[8]

The main reason for uncertainty stems from the vagueness of the basic assumptions. What is constitutional identity really about? Is it the identity of the people or the nation? Is it the identity of a state as a public entity? Is it the identity of the Constitution as such? It also remains an open question of how to derive constitutional identity or identities. Should this be done from the community which drafted the constitution? Or rather, in relation to those historical and political moments when constitutional documents were drafted or adopted? (Some refer to the latter as 'constitutional moments'[9].) Or should one focus only on the most essential elements of the current constitution in force when formulating constitutional identity? What does identity have to do with the idea of constitutional values?[10] These questions, which stem from the inherent ambiguity of the concept being discussed, remain to be answered.

When formulating the concept of constitutional identity, American legal scholars tackled the characteristics of individual identity and endeavored to apply them appropriately within the legal framework. This approach was pioneered by Gary J. Jacobsohn. According to Jacobsohn, the identity of a constitution derives from its text, the practice based on it, and the traditions

The Identity of the Constitution. A Regional Approach' (2020) 21 *GLJ* 105–130; Pietro Faraguna, 'Constitutional Identity in the EU – a Shield or a Sword?' (2017) *GLJ* 1617–1640; Mattias Kumm and Victor Ferreres Comella, 'The Primacy Clause of the Constitutional Treaty and the Future of Constitutional Conflict in the European Union' (2005) 3 *ICON* 491, 492; Mattias Kumm, 'Rethinking Constitutional Authority: On the Structure and Limits of Constitutional Pluralism' in Matej Avbelj and Jan Komárek (eds), *Constitutional Pluralism in the European Union and Beyond* (Hart 2012) 39–65, at 51; Mattias Wendel, 'Lisbon Before the Courts: Comparative Perspectives' (2011) 1 *EuConst* 96–137; Anna Śledzińska-Simon, 'Constitutional Identity in 3D: A Model of Individual, Relational, and Collective Self and its Application in Poland' (2015) 1 *ICON* 124–155; Julien Sterck, 'Sameness and Selfhood: The Efficiency of Constitutional Identities in EU Law' (2018) 24 *ELJ* 281–296; Monika Polzin, 'Constitutional Identity as a Constructed Reality and a Restless Soul' (2017) 7 *GLJ* 1595–1616; Orbán (n 5) 142–173; Ernő Várnay, 'The Hungarian Sword of Constitutional Identity' (2022) 2 *Hun J Leg Stud* 80.

7 Michel Rosenfeld, 'The Identity of the Constitutional Subject: Selfhood, Citizenship, Culture, and Community' in András Sajó and Renáta Uitz (eds), *Constitutional Topography: Values and Constitutions: The Hague* (Eleven International Publishing; additionally, Jacobsohn 2010).

8 Michel Rosenfeld, *The Identity of the Constitutional Subject* (Routledge 2010) 30–41.

9 Bruce Ackerman, *We the People, Vol 1: Foundations* (Harvard University Press 1991).

10 Ivan Halasz, 'Az alkotmányos identitás fogalmaés funkciója' in Fruzsina Gárdos-Orosz-Ivan Halász (ed.), *Bevezetés az Alkotmányjogba* (Dialog Campus 2019) 125–127.

of the past. This is ventured through a process of political, judicial, and academic dialogue. Thus, constitutional identity is a dynamic concept that develops and is shaped through discourse.[11] Moreover, it is often based on a collective memory, which – by nature – is part of the cultural identity of a nation.[12]

The concept was further developed by Michel Rosenfeld. Rosenfeld puts constitutional identity into a broader historical context. He argues that constitutional identity is, in fact, an integral interface between the Constitution and those for whom it was constituted.[13] In his study, Rosenfeld also draws on historical processes, models of constitutional identity, and, in this context, types of constitutionalism.[14]

Constitutional identity is currently one of the most frequently discussed concepts in European constitutional discourse. The debate was initially boosted by the adoption of the Lisbon Treaty in Article 4(2) of the Treaty on European Union (TEU). Accordingly, the Union must respect Member States' national identities inherent in their fundamental political and constitutional structures, inclusive of regional and local self-government. It must respect their essential State functions.[15]

It is clear from this wording that the whole provision is intended to protect the essential elements of the Member States with particular reference to their constitutional arrangements. The adoption of this provision of the TEU has thus further specified and politicized the academic debate on constitutional identity. Constitutional identity is no longer a dogmatic-theoretical question. Instead, it has become a technical point of reference, a toolbox in the hands of national constitutional courts and supreme courts, and is used to object to EU provisions. As a result, the whole issue has shifted further away from the initial academic dimension to take on a political dimension.

11 Gary Jeffrey Jacobsohn, *Constitutional Identity* (Harvard University Press 2010) 133–135.

12 Gary Jeffrey Jacobsohn, 'Constitutional Identity' (2006) 68(3) *Rev Politics* 370, 373.

13 Michel Rosenfeld, 'Constitutional Identity' in Michel Rosenfeld and András Sajó (eds), *The Oxford Handbook of Comparative Constitutional Law* (Oxford Handbooks Online 2012).

14 Some theories that support nationality (national identity) within the framework of liberal democratic offsets, including individual autonomy and social equality, are: Kymlicka, Miller and Canovan. See: Will Kymlicka, *Multicultural Citizenship* (Oxford University Press 1995); David Miller, *On Nationalism* (Oxford University Press 1995); Margaret Canovan, *Nationhood and Political Theory* (Edward Elgar 1996).

15 Article J. 4 of the Treaty on the European Union (1992) OJ C191/108. Article 4 (2) TEU does not use the term 'constitutional identity'. It operates simply with the requirement to respect 'national identity'. However, the latter concept is considered to be equivalent to the obligation to respect constitutional identity in the vast majority of the literature. See Denys Simon, 'L'identité constitutionnelle dans la jurisprudence de l'Union européenne' in Laurence Bourgorgue-Larsen (ed.), *L'identité constitutionnelle saisie par les juges en Europe* (Pedonne 2011) 27; Orbán (n 5) 145; Gerhard van der Schyff, 'The Constitutional Relationship Between the European Union and its Member States: The Role of National Identity in Article 4(2) TEU' (2012) 37 *ELJ* 563.

The Treaty of Lisbon opened the doors to a new framework of interpretation of the margin of maneuver for Member States and their institutions. In relation to the collective characteristic of constitutional identity, Member States provide little latitude to their national institutions within the European legal space. At this point, the inherent tension should be highlighted: Member States can preserve their unique character but should also conclude agreements in specific fields to help establish unitary regulation within the European Union.[16] Some argue that this leads to cooperation and coordination – or, to use another term, 'dialogue' between Member States and the Union.[17] 'European constitutional dialogue' is very fashionable[18] and a permanent reference in contemporary academic literature; it means something like informal and formal communication between the EU court and national courts, as well as between national courts, "in the application of comparative law methodology, also in the way courts are inspired by one another."[19]

As noted, the Lisbon Treaty of 2009 fertilized the discourse over constitutional identity. The current chapter addresses constitutional identity and judicial independence. In the context of colliding competencies among EU courts and national (mostly constitutional) courts, I argue that constitutional identity is an idea national courts rely on to prevail over EU jurisdiction.

We further argue that the identity argument in the judicial context is a single-edged sword applied to EU courts by nation-states. According to Faraguna, constitutional identity protects nation-states (serving as a shield). If national courts use constitutional identity as a weapon against the values of the European Union, the identity argument is a sword deployed against European constitutionalism.[20]

Scholarship distinguishes two or three periods in the practice and institutional development of constitutional identity.[21] All contributors to the debate agree, however, that the starting point is the 1970s, the fundamental period

16 Armin von Bogdandy, 'The European Constitution and European Identity: Text and Subtext of the Treaty Establishing a Constitution for Europe' (2005) 2–3 *ICON* 295–315.

17 See, for example, Constitutional Dialogues Alec Stone Sweet and Jud Mathews, *Proportionality Balancing and Constitutional Governance: A Comparative and Global Approach* (Oxford University Press 2019) 127–161.

18 The notion has become à la mode. See Ernő Várnay, 'The Hungarian Sword of Constitutional Identity' (2022) 2 *Hun J Leg Stud* 80; Christian Callies and Gerhard van der Schyff (eds), *Constitutional Identity in a Europe of Multilevel Constitutionalism* (CUP 2019); Luke Dimitrios Spieker, *Framing and Managing Constitutional Identity Conflicts: How to Stabilise the Modus Vivendi Between the Court of Justice and National Constitutional Courts'* (2020) 2 *CMLR* 361–389; Orbán (n 5) 143; Glenn Alexander Magee, *The Hegel Dictionary* (A & C Black 2010) 262.

19 Tímea Drinóczi, 'Hungarian Constitutional Court: The Limits of EU Law in the Hungarian Legal System' (2017) 1 *ICLJ* 146.

20 Faraguna (n 6) 1617–1640; Luigi Corrias, 'Populism in a Constitutional Key: Constituent Power, Popular Sovereignty and Constitutional Identity' (2016) 12 *EuConst* 6–26.

21 Orbán (n 5) 144.

of rights reservation, featuring the *Solange I*[22] or (from an EU perspective) the *Handelsgesellschaft* decisions.[23] The focal point is the ultra vires reservation, which was invented in relation to the Maastricht Treaty.[24]

We do not share the notion that the CJEU is of much concern to national courts in terms of widening the interpretation at the expense of the EU's self-restraint. Hungarian scholar László Blutman goes as far as referring to the ultra vires period of national courts as a "rebellion (or revolution) of constitutional courts." He argues that, as of 2012, a new chapter opened, which began an era of active protection of sovereignty, followed by a number of case laws, that has continued to the present day[25] (the Czech *Landtová* decision C-399/09 was the first in this line).

Identity, patriotism and populism

It is paramount for states to ensure that citizens identify to some degree with their own state: without a minimum measure of self-identification, it is implausible for elites to be governed and public policies enacted. Given the functional imperatives of the modern state, it is therefore inevitable that a sense of cultural commonalities will be developed to rule the elites and mobilize support for ambitious regulatory programs.[26]

In the long term, a monopoly on violence alone (as exercised by the state) is not enough to bring together a disunited nation. According to Habermas, historically, the notion of 'the nation' has transformed and framed the community's collective identity, vested with a homogeneous national language and national culture, helping to convert populations into disciplined armies and efficient labor forces.[27] Not surprisingly, modern nation-states have usually attempted to transform themselves into political and moral communities. In doing so, they have enforced legal ties (formulated in citizenship) and developed cultural ties and educational links.[28]

> This resulted in a double coding of citizenship – as a legal status defined by possession of equal rights, on the one hand, and as membership in an

22 BVerfGE 37, 271, Solange I.

23 *Internationale Handelsgesellschaft mbH v. Einfuhr- und Vorratsstelle für Getreide und Futtermittel* (1970) ECR 1125 (Case 11/70).

24 Maastricht, BVerfG (Urteil vom 12. 10. 1993) 2 BvR 2134/92 und 2159/92; BVerfGE 89, 155.

25 László Blutman, 'Az uniós jog elsőbbsége: alkotmánybíróságok lázadása [Primacy of EU Law: The Rebellion of Constitutional Courts]' (2022) 1 *Közjogi Szemle* 1.

26 Ciaran Cronin, 'Democracy and Collective Identity: In Defence of Constitutional Patriotism' (April 2003) 11(1) *Eur J Philos* 19.

27 Jürgen Habermas, *The New Conservatism: Cultural Criticism and the Historians' Debate* (ed. and trans. S. Weber Nicholsen) (Cambridge; MIT Press 1989) 253–254.

28 Ivan Halasz, 'Az alkotmányos identitás fogalma és funkciója' in Fruzsina Gárdos-Orosz and Ivan Halász (eds), *Bevezetés az Alkotmányjogba* (Dialog Campus 2019) 107.

> ethnoculturally defined community, on the other – and a corresponding split in the concept of sovereignty between internal sovereignty, defined in terms of citizen self-rule, and external sovereignty understood in terms of national self-assertion.[29]

In the case of nation-states, it would be pointless to deny that national feeling has certainly played an important integrating role. It has often been this notion which led to the emergence of patriotism. Ethnicity as a source of national feelings contributed to the idea of national identity throughout the long nineteenth century until the Second World War. This theory laid the foundations for the later-developed idea of constitutional patriotism that emerged from German scholarship after World War II. Political philosopher Dolf Sternberger, a student and follower of Hannah Arendt, coined the theory of constitutional patriotism in the German context;[30] it was subsequently taken up by Jürgen Habermas,[31] and through his work, became better known in contemporary academic literature.[32]

Habermas was concerned about whether particularistic identities are compatible with a commitment to universal values such as freedom and equality.[33] Among prominent representatives of this view, Habermas proposed probably the most comprehensive theory: he argued for a model based on loyalty to the principles and institutions of the constitution, or more precisely, loyalty to constitutional democracy. Accordingly, in his theory, *Verfassungspatriotismus* (constitutional patriotism) is a credible – and democratic – alternative to nationalism.

Habermas argues that collective identity can be framed by procedures. "Constitutional patriotism designates the idea that political attachment ought to center on the norms, the values, and, more indirectly, the procedures of a liberal democratic constitution."[34] To this end, democratic deliberation creates the interface through which citizens can constitute a normative collective identity through participation in a democratic 'constitutional project'.

Correspondingly, Habermas advocates for a cosmopolitan approach to citizenship; a collective membership in relation to all cultural and human

29 Cronin (n 26) 3.

30 Dolf Sternberger, 'Verfassungspatriotismus [Constitutional Patriotism]' *Frankfurter Allgemeine Zeitung* (23 May 23 1979).

31 Jürgen Habermas, 'On Social Identity' (1974) 19 *Telos* 91–103; Jürgen Habermas, 'Moral Development and Ego Identity' in Habermas (ed.), *Communication and the Evolution of Society* (trans. T. McCarthy; MIT Press 1979) 69–94; Habermas, 'Citizenship and National Identity' in Ronald Beiner (ed.), *Theorizing Citizenship* (State University of New York Press 1995) 491–516; Habermas, 'Popular Sovereignty as Procedure' in Deliberative Democracy: Essays on Reason and Politics. Edited by James Bohman, William Rehg, The MIT Press. 1997. DOI: https://doi.org/10.7551/mitpress/2324.001.0001 ISBN electronic: 9780262268936.

32 Jan-Werner Müller and Kim Lane Scheppele, 'Constitutional Patriotism: An Introduction' (2008) 6(1) *ICON* 68.

33 Cronin (n 26) 1.

34 Jan-Werner Müller and Kim Lane Scheppele, 'Constitutional Patriotism: An Introduction' (2008) 6(1) *ICON* 67.

rights, and collective identification with a post-national European Union.[35] The vision is based on a post-national and integrative European constitutional identity – European citizenship. It is a vision that promises a framework for the community of citizenry that can identify with European political values.

According to Habermas, we need to define "what forms of patriotic attachment are still possible in pluralistic liberal democracies,"[36] especially in the light of the most obvious dilemma concerning the idea of national identity: that identity as such (individual or collective) is usually formed in opposition to something. Thus the political conception of 'the nation' is ethnoculturally predetermined and can be easily appropriated to stigmatize non-nationals as inferiors, aliens, or enemies.[37] "The ethnocultural component of nationalist conceptions of citizenship and sovereignty inspired or facilitated internal repression of 'aliens' and external aggression against 'enemies' in the name of national self-assertion."[38] According to Habermas, the history of German nationalism represents an extreme example of the "discriminatory potential of an ethnocultural definition of the nation."[39] As Hungarian scholar András Sajó summarized in 1999: "the constitution offers identity, while identification is perhaps impossible. We are the people, but whom can we exclude from among us? And to voice the more dangerous possibility, when can *we* be excluded?"[40]

The emergence of populism as a counterargument to constitutional patriotism

Habermas's thesis is that pluralistic democracies should foster a 'post-national' form of identification because "nationalism is beset by an inherent ambivalence that fosters discrimination in the domestic sphere and chauvinistic self-assertion in international relations."[41]

In contrast to the post-national universal notion proposed by Habermas and his followers,[42] in the early twenty-first century modern autocratic populism

35 Jürgen Habermas, *Between Facts and Norms: Contribution to a Discourse Theory of Law and Democracy* (MIT Press 1996) 491–515, 566–567; Jürgen Habermas, *The Inclusion of the Other* (MIT Press 1998) 105–154.

36 Cronin (n 26) 1.

37 Cronin (n 26) 1.

38 Cronin (n 26) 3.

39 Cronin (n 26) 1. Footnote 7. See: Jürgen Habermas, *The New Conservatism: Cultural Criticism and the Historians' Debate* (ed. and trans. S. Weber Nicholsen; Cambridge: MIT Press 1989) 254–255.

40 András Sajó, *Limiting Government: An Introduction to Constitutionalism* (CEU Press 1999) 6.

41 Cronin (n 26) 2.

42 See, for example: Attracta Ingram, 'Constitutional Patriotism' (1996) 22(6) *Philos Soc Crit* 1–18; B. R. Barber, 'Constitutional Faith' in J. Cohen (ed.), *For Love of Country: Debating the Limits of Patriotism* (Beacon Press 1996) 30–37; Andrew Mason, 'Political Community, Liberal-Nationalism, and the Ethics of Assimilation' (January 1999) 109(2) *Ethics* 261–286.

emerged, basically as an antithesis to universality and the 'European constitutional project' and as a backlash against European integration.

Paul Blokker denotes that populist constitutionalism rejects the existing legal-constitutional order to restore (an ideal of) a preceding, historical order.[43] The hierarchy of the legal, constitutional order is not to be replaced by an inclusive, more universalistic order but rather by a realization of the past, that is, of a traditional order based on 'natural' hierarchies related to ethnicity, family, and tradition.[44] According to populists, constitutional patriotism and universality led to the erosion of the historical nation. Consequently – I argue – populists are Euroskeptics.

Populism has different aspects. Hungarian scholar Gárdos-Orosz emphasizes that the reinterpretation of popular sovereignty, constitution-making, and the creation of a constitutional identity are three elements that may be appraised in populist constitutional change.[45] Similarly, Luigi Corrias underlines that populism can be seen as a constitutional theory that combines specific readings of the theories of constituent power, popular sovereignty, and constitutional identity.[46] Paul Blokker claims that the four aspects of popular sovereignty are, at present, popular will, majoritarianism, legal resentment, and constitutional instrumentalism.[47]

Hungarian scholar András Pap argues that constitutional identity, under the current challenges of autocratic populism, means nothing more than that the community takes priority over individuals, and state protection no (longer) defends individual autonomy; instead, it safeguards the autonomy of the community.[48] The best example of this may be found in the Hungarian Prime Minister's speech on the national holiday in 2024. Namely:

> It does not make us free if everyone does what they like. That is not enough for us. Freedom for us is to be able to build a homeland without a landlord over our heads. That is why it is important for none but us Hungarians to survive. We know [that] the Hungarian quality of existence is a special, unparalleled, high form of human life. The greatest thing that can happen to us is to be born Hungarian. In the Western world, it is also imagined that man just exists, in himself. It is entirely up to his free choice

43 Blokker, 'Populism as a Constitutional Project' (n 2) 5.

44 Blokker, 'Populism as a Constitutional Project' (n 2) 5.

45 Fruzsina Gárdos-Orosz, 'The Reference to Constitutional Traditions in Populist Constitutionalism – the Case of Hungary' (2020) 61 *Hun J Leg Stud* 23, 25–31.

46 Corrias (n 20) 6–26.

47 Blokker, 'Populism as a Constitutional Project' (n 2) 2–9.

48 András László Pap, 'Who Are "We, the People?" Biases and Preferences in the Hungarian Fundamental Law' in Zoltán Csehi, Balázs Schanda and Pál Sonnevend (eds), *Viva Vox Iuris Civilis: Studies in Honor of László Sólyom on the Occasion of His 70th Birthday* (Szent István Society 2015); Zsuzsanna Fejes, Fanni Mandák and Zoltán Szente (eds), *Challenges and Pitfalls in the Recent Hungarian Constitutional Development, Discussing the New Fundamental Law of Hungary* (L'Harmattan 2015) 59–67.

> which state he becomes a citizen of[;] he decides whether he will be a boy or a girl, the family is what he invents for himself, and the homeland is just a field of action. We Hungarians do not believe in that. We know that if you stand alone in the world, you are not free, you are lonely.[49]

The position of citizens who do not necessarily believe in the meaning of the 'Hungarian' community as the basis of membership in the political community is fragile.[50] The Prime Minister continues:

> there are great opportunities ahead. We are facing a sovereign revolution in America and Europe. Accordingly, all can find their own identity, and we can open a new great era for . . . nations. For everyone, except those who have broken their oath to serve the nation. Those who have betrayed their country, treasonously stabbed it in the back. No, they will not find consideration.[51]

Political philosopher János Kis argues that the populist Hungarian Fundamental Law (FL; Constitution) of 2012 identifies the sovereign people as the totality of ethnic Hungarians, excluding Hungarian citizens of a non-Hungarian ethnicity but including individuals of Hungarian ethnicity not living under Hungarian law. It contributes to the legacy of the Hungarian Holy Crown, a symbol of the Greater Hungary that was ruled for a millennium by the ethnic Hungarian nobility.[52] The national Avowal of the FL provides, for example:

> We honor the achievements of our historic constitution, and we honor the Holy Crown, which embodies the constitutional continuity of Hungary's statehood and the unity of the nation. We hold that the protection of our identity rooted in our historic constitution is a fundamental obligation of the State.

Populists are not blind to equality. They link equality and national identity.[53] However, the populist understanding of identity is restrictive in the sense that it aims to narrow down identity to sameness and radicalize this notion.[54]

49 Prime Minister Viktor Orbán's speech on the 176th anniversary of the 1848–1849 revolution and fight for liberty (15 March 2024).

50 András László Pap, 'Személyiségkép és alkotmányos identitás a Nemzeti Együttműködés Rendszerében (I. rész) [Images of Personality and Constitutional Identity in the System of National Cooperation (Part I)]' (2014) 4 *Közjogi Szemle* 1.

51 Prime Minister Viktor Orbán's speech on the 176th anniversary of the 1848–1849 revolution and the fight for liberty (15 March 2024).

52 János Kis, 'Introduction: From the 1989 Constitution to the 2011 Fundamental Law' in Gábor Attila Tóth (ed.), *Constitution for a Disunited Nation, on Hungary's 2011 Fundamental Law* (CEU Press) 2.

53 Corrias (n 20) 6–26.

54 Corrias (n 20) 15.

Corrias further argues that the blueprint of political legitimacy in modernity is when the same people are both ruling and being ruled.[55] Here, we should realize, however, that by no means is the absolutization of Rousseau's *volonté général* – the legacy of the supreme political will – alien to the European tradition. What is new here is that under populist constitutionalism, it is not counterbalanced by an equally important tradition derived primarily from the Anglo-Saxon concept of limited government, in which the representative of the majority exercises self-restraint and ties its own hands. Regarding the notion of limited government, we sometimes use the metaphor of Ulysses. As Norwegian social scientist Jon Elster points out, in this famous metaphor, Ulysses ties himself to the mast to avoid listening and giving into the seductive voice of the sirens, knowing that he will not be able to resist their temptation.[56] The current temptation in the metaphor is the unrestrained power of the state. Perhaps the most picturesque elaboration of the limited government doctrine is provided by Hungarian scholar András Sajó in his classic book, *Limiting Government*.[57] He argues that the denial of absolute power and the desire for plurality are motivated by historical fears of tyranny.[58] Sajó notes that "'Power corrupts and absolute power corrupts absolutely,' so says Lord Acton. This is also true about our own power. 'People have one serious enemy, their own government,' as Saint-Just noted."[59] Sajó argues that constitutionalism means the restriction of state power for the preservation of public peace.[60] Hence, we can conclude that state power is limited in constitutional democracy, whereas it is unrestrained in illiberal democracy.

Sovereignty and judicial independence

As we noted earlier, recent developments in Central Europe in the area of constitutional identity are associated with the idea of national sovereignty, in which the margin of movement for Member States to shape their judiciary is very much tolerated, if not triggered; in political philosophy, this approach is related to Euroskepticism, with some analysts using the distinction between nation-states and post-Westphalian states.[61] We also argued earlier that the sovereignty argument is often used by populist scholarship against the idea of a

55 Corrias (n 20) 15.

56 Jon Elster, *Ulysses and the Sirens: Studies in Rationality and Irrationality: Revised Edition* (CUP 2013). Also cited by András Sajó, see Sajó (n 40) 7–8.

57 Sajó (n 40) 9.

58 Sajó argues that constitutionalism is the restriction of state power in the preservation of public peace. Although this definition is obviously inadequate, the imperfection is comforting, says Sajó. See Sajó (n 40) 9.

59 Sajó (n 40) 7.

60 Sajó (n 40) 7.

61 Orbán (n 5) 144.

'collective European identity', we linked populist scholarship to the notion of sovereignty. (We elaborate on this notion in details later in this section).

The national visions of constitutional identity rely on the arguments of Emmanuel Sieyès,[62] Carl Schmidt,[63] and Carl Bilfinger,[64] especially on the distinction between constitution-making and constitution-amending power, which envisage a greater margin of movement for Member States to shape their constitutional structure, including their judiciary. This line of argumentation is based on different assumptions, with one notably authoritative argument suggesting that each national constitution includes some core principles that should not be amended unless a new constitution is enacted by the sovereign power. This model might serve as a coherent interpretative framework in the German constitutional context,[65] where the eternity clause has been identified as the core provision of the German Basic Law as the source of constitutional identity;[66] however, in Hungary, for instance, the Constitutional Court failed to identify these core principles.[67] Moreover, due to a supermajority of populists representatives, the Hungarian Parliament serves both as a constitution-making and constitution-amending power.

I argue in this chapter that in illiberal populist states 'the people' are present as one, with one (common) interest and one will. This is the true meaning of sovereignty.[68] As a matter of principle, the counterclaim for separation of powers is the supremacy of the state, 'a unitary power' that is 'the sole representative' of popular will. Therefore, every illiberal, autocratic, hybrid, or anti-constitutional populist state, as a matter of principle,[69] refuses judicial independence. As Corrias emphasizes, accordingly, populist leaders are the sole representatives of state unity.

What we find makes this constitutional debate very special is that judicial independence is connected with the idea of popular sovereignty. In contrast,

62 Emmanuel Joseph Sieyès, *The Third State* (1789).

63 Carl Schmitt, *Verfassungslehre* (Duncker & Humblot 2017) 55.

64 Panu Minkkinen, 'Political Constitutionalism Versus Political Constitutional Theory: Law, Power, and Politics' (2013) 3 *ICON* 560–610.

65 Monika Polzin, 'Constitutional Identity, Unconstitutional Amendments and the Idea of Constituent Power: The Development of the Doctrine of Constitutional Identity in German Constitutional Law' (2016) 14 *ICON* 411–438.

66 Armin von Bogdandy and Stephan Schill, 'Die Achtung der nationalen Identität unter dem reformierten Unionsvertrag' (2010) 4 *Zeitschrift für ausländisches öffentliches Recht und Völkerrecht* 712.

67 Petra Bárd, Nóra Chronowski and Zoltán Fleck, 'Use, Misuse and Abuse of Constitutional Identity in Europe' in Mark Tushnet and Dimitry Kochenov (eds), *Research Handbook on the Politics of Constitutional Law* (Edward Elgar 2023) 619–620.

68 Corrias (n 20) 10.

69 Some authors use the expression 'authoritarianism': Ozan O. Varol, 'Stealth Authoritarianism' (2015) 100 *Iowa L Rev* 1673–1742. For an overview and roadmap of different concepts of autocratic populism, see: Fabio de Sa e Silva, 'Law and Illiberalism: A Sociolegal Review and Research Road Map' (2022) 18 *Ann Rev L Soc Sci* 193–209.

the separation of powers is 'part of Europe's DNA',[70] associated with the idea of judicial supremacy and the rule of law.

On the other hand, in illiberal states,[71] the idea of 'judicial independence' is affiliated with national sovereignty. We may argue that most contemporary constitutional scholars somehow bridge constitutional identity, sovereignty, and illiberal constitutionalism.[72]

We conclude in this section that an important aspect of constitutional identity is its proud manifestation of the sovereignty of the Member States against the enlarging power of the Union and its jurisdiction. An obvious example from Hungary is Article R (4) of the FL, which provides that the protection of the constitutional identity and Christian culture of Hungary shall be an obligation of every organ of the State. To protect constitutional identity, an independent organ established by a cardinal Act shall operate.

The jurisprudence of the Court of Justice of the European Union regarding judicial independence, sovereignty, and constitutional identity

National identity in the judicial context first emerged in the European context in the *O'Brien* case, where the request for a preliminary ruling on behalf of a British court aimed to clarify the applicability of EU law to judges employed part-time.[73] The Latvian Government, in its intervention, held that the application of EU law to the judicial system of a Member State infringes the national identities of the latter. The CJEU held that the competence of the Member States to construct their own judiciary should not lead to a disregard for fundamental values derived from EU law. Therefore, Member States could decide whether judges could be categorized as employed persons. However, the potential exclusion of certain judges from this group should not be arbitrary.[74]

70 The conceptual development of judicial independence is part of the European Union, its organs and its agencies' DNA. See, for example, Gisbert R. Bustos, 'Judicial Independence in European Constitutional Law' (2022) 18 *EuConst* 591.

71 In the academic literature, some argue that we are experiencing so-called illiberal constitutionalism. See, for example, Gábor Halmai, 'Illiberal Constitutionalism in East-Central Europe' in Antonina Bakardjieva Engelbrekt, Andreas Moberg and Joakim Nergelius (eds) *Rule of Law in the EU: 30 Years After the Fall of the Berlin Wall* (Hart 2021) 51–74; Martin Belov (ed.), *Populist Constitutionalism and Illiberal Democracies: Between Constitutional Imagination, Normative Entrenchment and Political Reality* (Intersentia 2021).

72 See also: Andreas Kalyvas, 'Popular Sovereignty, Democracy, and the Constituent Power' (2005) 12 *Constellations* 223; Martin Loughlin, 'The Concept of Constituent Power' (2013) 12 *Eur J Pol Theory*; András Sajó, *Ruling by Cheating, Governance in Illiberal Democracy* (Cambridge University Press 2021).

73 Orbán (n 5) 142–173.

74 CJEU, Case C-393/10 *Dermod Patrick O'Brien v. Ministry of Justice*, ECLI:EU:C:2012:110.

In the *Torresi* case, the CJEU once again rejected the argumentation of a Member State based on national identity.[75] An Italian citizen who had obtained his law degree in Spain intended to establish a law practice in Italy, his country of original citizenship. However, the Italian Bar Association turned to the CJEU and argued that the freedom to practice law does not mean an individual is free to obtain a legal qualification in another Member State and then immediately return to his country of origin to open a law firm. The CJEU did not agree with this approach and ruled that the freedom to establish such a legal practice should not be restricted by a Member State's constitutional structure.[76]

As elaborated in detail below, the Hungarian constitutional framework was changed in 2011, including the system of the administration of justice. The new Hungarian legislation radically lowered the age of retirement for judges from 70 to 62 years in a sudden procedure without an admission period. The CJEU held that the altering of the retirement age was discriminatory according to 2000/78/EC concerning equal treatment in employment and occupation. Consequently, the fundamental values of the EU legal order should prevail. However, in this case, the judiciary was scrutinized, but Hungary did not rely on the constitutional identity argument when reacting to the directive,[77] and, as we shall see in more detail in this chapter, it was only years later, after the Polish case of 2019, that Hungary started to call on sovereignty arguments against changes in the Hungarian judicial system.

In 2019, Hungary supported Poland in a case involving the compulsory retirement of judges (case C-619/18). In this case, similarly to Hungary in 2012 as referred in the paragraph above, Polish legislation lowered the retirement age limit from 71 to 65 with a very short deadline, and judges who had already reached this new limit could not continue their activity unless requested to do so by the president of the Polish Republic. Unfortunately, the decision of the President of the Republic was not made subject to any objective criteria.[78] Poland, with the support of Hungary, argued in case C-619/18 that national rules on the judicial system cannot be the object of a review of the CJEU (in light of the second subparagraph of Article 19(1) TEU and Article 47 of the Charter). Because the organization of the national justice system constitutes a competence exclusively reserved for Member States, the EU cannot arrogate competences in that domain. Poland claimed that, regarding the judiciary, there is no link whatsoever between EU law and national legislations

75 Orbán (n 5) 142–173.

76 CJEU, Case C-58/13 *Angelo Alberto Torresi and Pierfrancesco Torresi v. Consiglio dell'Ordine degli Avvocati di Macerat*, ECLI:EU:C:2014:2088.

77 CJEU, Case C-286/12 *European Commission v. Hungary*, ECLI:EU:C:2012:687.

78 Jakub Jaraczewski, 'Age Is the Limit? Background of the CJEU Case C-619/18 Commission v Poland' *VerfBlog* (28 May 2019) <https://verfassungsblog.de/age-is-the-limit-background-of-the-cjeu-case-c-619-18-commission-v-poland> accessed 10 May 2022.

to call for or rely upon. Moreover, under TEU and the Charter of the EU,[79] general principles of EU law, such as the principle of judicial independence, are applicable only in situations governed by EU law.

The CJEU in its judgment in case C-619/18 declared its supremacy and the infringement of Article 19 of TEU and stated that the principle of the rule of law and effective judicial protection provides for the removability of judges. The Court clearly declared that judicial independence is a value protected by Union law. The court emphasized that even if the organization of justice in the Member States falls under the competence of those Member States (as Hungary and Poland argue), the fact remains that when exercising that competence, Member States are required to comply with their obligations deriving from EU law.[80] Moreover, the Court stated that, in requiring the Member States to comply with those obligations, the European Union is not claiming to exercise that competence itself or arrogating that competence to itself.

The CJEU, in its judgment, interpreted the requirement of independence for the judiciary in details. The Court ruled that according to the TEU, this involves two aspects.[81] The first aspect requires that the court concerned exercise its functions wholly autonomously, without being subject to any hierarchical constraint or subordinated to any other body and without taking orders or instructions from any source whatsoever; thus, it is protected against external interventions, pressure, or influence.

The second aspect is linked to impartiality and seeks to ensure that an equal distance is maintained from the parties. This requires objectivity and the absence of any interest in the outcome of the proceedings apart from the strict application of the rule of law. Those guarantees of independence and impartiality require rules, particularly as regards the composition of the judicial body and the appointment, length of service, and grounds for abstention, rejection, and dismissal of its members, that are such as to dispel any reasonable doubt in the minds of individuals as to the imperviousness of that judicial body to external factors and its neutrality, in particular, the freedom of the judges from all external intervention or pressure, which is essential for a fair justice system.

The European Court held that the principle of the irremovability of judges requires, in particular, that judges may remain in post until they have reached the obligatory retirement age or until the expiry of their mandate. The Court noted that in the present case, it must be outlined that the Polish judicial reform raised reasonable concerns as regards compliance with the principle of the irremovability of judges. Moreover, by granting the President of Poland

79 TEU, Article 19(1), second subparagraph; Charter, Article 47.

80 See, by analogy, Case C-247/17 *Oikeusministeriö v. Denis Raugevicius*, EU:C:2018:898 [45]; Case C-202/18 *Rimšēvičs and ECB v. Latvia*, C 202/18 and Case C-238/18, EU:C:2019:139 [57] and, in particular, from the second subparagraph of Article 19(1) TEU (see, to that effect, Case C-64/16 Associação Sindical dos Juízes Portugueses, EU:C:2018:117 [40]).

81 Case C-64/16 Associação Sindical dos Juízes Portugueses, EU:C:2018:117 [44] and the case-law cited.

discretion to extend the period of judicial activity of judges beyond their fixed retirement age, Poland had failed to fulfill its obligations under the second subparagraph of Article 19(1) TEU.[82]

In a recent case from 2023 (*Commission v Poland*, C-204/21), the Commission (supported by Belgium, Denmark, the Netherlands, Finland, and Sweden) initiated an infringement procedure against Poland for failure to fulfill obligations under Article 258 TFEU. The Court declared Poland's failure to fulfill obligations under Article 19(1) TEU and Article 47 of the Charter of Fundamental Rights of the EU. We should note that the previous decisions on the judicial system in a Member State did not rely on direct provisions of the Charter.[83]

The Court held, inter alia, that the reorganization of court jurisdiction in a Member State is covered, in principle, under the freedom of the Member States guaranteed by Article 4(2) TEU and that any reorganization must not, in particular, undermine respect for the rule of law set out in Article 2 TEU and the requirements arising from the second subparagraph of Article 19(1) TEU, especially those relating to independence, impartiality, and the previous establishing by law of the courts and tribunals called upon to interpret and apply EU law.[84]

According to the CJEU, the European Union respects the national identities of Member States, which are inherent in their fundamental political and constitutional structures. Therefore, states enjoy a certain degree of discretion in implementing the principles of the rule of law. While separate national identities are inherent to their fundamental constitutional and political structures, which the European Union respects, the Member States adhere to a concept of 'the rule of law', which they share as a value common to their own constitutional traditions and which they have undertaken to respect at all times as members of the European Union.[85]

Member States cannot be exempt from the obligation to comply with the requirements arising from the principle of rule of law, judicial independence, and the right to effective judicial protection. Therefore, Article 4(2) TEU must be read considering the provisions of the same rank, as enshrined in Article 2 and the second subparagraph of Article 19(1) TEU.[86]

The Court held that there is no ground for maintaining that the requirements arising in the European Union from respect for values and principles such as the rule of law, effective judicial protection, and judicial independence, enshrined in Article 2 and the second subparagraph of Article 19(1) TEU, are

82 Case C-64/16 Associação Sindical dos Juízes Portugueses, EU:C:2018:117 [49] and the case law cited.

83 Case C-204/21 *European Commission v. Poland*, ECLI:EU:C:2023:442.

84 CJEU, Case C-204/21 *European Commission v. Poland*, ECLI:EU:C:2023:442 [263].

85 CJEU, Case C-204/21 *European Commission v. Poland*, ECLI:EU:C:2023:442 [73].

86 CJEU, Case C-204/21 *European Commission v. Poland*, ECLI:EU:C:2023:442 [72].

capable of affecting the national identity of a Member State, in line with the meaning of Article 4(2) TEU.[87]

The obligations of Member States to respect judicial independence and the competence of the EU to review national judicial reforms in this respect were also confirmed in 2018 in a case concerning the salary of Portuguese judges. Although the temporary deduction of payments in the judiciary did not in itself breach EU law, the CJEU underlined its demand that national judicial reforms be reviewed to avoid the serious undermining of common European values.[88]

Populist legal scholarship against European Courts' arguments on judicial independence

Since the Hungarian judicial reform is inextricably linked to the jurisprudence of the Chief Justice of the Hungarian Curia (Supreme Court), Professor András Zs. Varga, it is worth elaborating on an article he wrote on the jurisprudence of the CJEU, in particular[89] on Polish judgment C-619/18,[90] and subsequently, on the order of the CJEU in Case C-791/19 R *Commission v Poland*, in which in April 2020, the CJEU, inter alia, suspended the right of the Polish Disciplinary Chamber of the Supreme Court to hold cases.[91] The Court of Justice's order in Case C-791/19 R is unprecedented to the extent that the Court demanded the immediate suspension, until delivery of the final judgment, of the processing of all disciplinary cases.[92]

Professor Varga points out that the CJEU's decision seems fine on first reading, but it is substantially wrong. There is no mandate for any EU institution – not even the EU Court – to determine the judicial system of its Member States. More worryingly, the ruling is a clear challenge to judicial independence, quite ironically made in the name of judicial independence. According to Professor Varga, the independence of the judiciary in Hungary is an achievement of our historical constitution, which has become an element of identity and which would, therefore, be difficult to

87 CJEU, Case C-204/21 *European Commission v. Poland*, ECLI:EU:C:2023:442 [72].

88 Case C64/16 *Associação Sindical dos Juízes Portugueses v. Tribunal de Contas*, ECLI:EU:C:2018:117.

89 András Varga Zs., 'Védi vagy kiüresíti a bírói függetlenséget az EU Bírósága? [Will the Court of Justice of the EU Protect or Undermine Judicial Independence?]' Mandiner (2020) <https://mandiner.hu/kulfold/2020/04/vedi-vagy-kiuresiti-a-biroi-fuggetlenseget-az-eu-birosaga> accessed 10 May 2022; See also: Dobrotka Mayer Annamária, 'Interjú Varga Zs. Andrással, a Kúria elnökével [Interview with Andras Zs. Varga, Chief Justice of the Curia]' (2021) 7 *Fontes Iuris* 5.

90 CJEU, Joint Cases C-585/18, C-624/18 and C625/18 *A. K. and Others v. Sąd Najwyższy, CP v. Sąd Najwyższy and Do v. Sąd Najwyższy* ECLI:EU:C:2019:982.

91 https://curia.europa.eu/jcms/upload/docs/application/pdf/2020-04/cp200047en.pdf, accessed 10 May 2023.

92 Laurent Pech, 'Protecting Polish Judges from Poland's Disciplinary "Star Chamber": *Commission v. Poland* (Interim Proceedings)' (2021) 58 *CMLR* 137–162.

give up, even if one wished to do so. However, the order of the Court of Justice of the European Union in the case of Poland not only allows but also expects Member States, even traditional constitutional democracies such as Poland or Hungary, to surrender the independence of their courts. Chief Justice Varga is of the opinion that the Polish judgment served as a pretext for the urgent Opinion of the Venice Commission[93] that reinforced the supremacy of EU law. It shows only that the European Council and the Commission are unduly intertwined.[94] According to the sovereignty argument, when the legislature passes a law that judges do not agree with, it is not a violation of judicial independence but a manifestation of independence. As a hard limit, a judge cannot depart from the text of the legislation when interpreting it. Unlimited freedom of interpretation would unilaterally elevate the judiciary above the legislature. And therefore, the Chief Justice concludes that the CJEU's position is a challenge against which it is urgent to rediscover and reassert the natural limits on judicial independence.[95]

Sovereignty and judicial independence in Hungary: theory and practice

The theory of sovereignty in populist Hungary

The post-2010 system is based on a particular concept of sovereignty in Hungary – the notion that the government (through Parliament, but often bypassing it) is the only sovereign entity based on its legitimacy. We maintain that this concept of sovereignty challenges the courts' monopoly of the interpretation of the law, so I argue that the 'real' game-changing struggle is for the monopoly on (or authority over) the interpretation of the law.

In this subsection, we focus exclusively on the doctrinal-theoretical aspects of the separation of powers to provide an academic concept regarding the nature of judicial independence in an illiberal state. We take our analysis of Hungary only as an example, since Hungary is a laboratory case for populist illiberalism and it serves as a litmus test.

The independence of the judiciary in Hungary turned into a sovereignty argument after the political changes of 2010, which resulted in a super-majoritarian victory for right-wing forces in the Hungarian Parliament.

93 CDL-PI(2020)002-e Poland – Urgent Joint Opinion on the amendments to the Law on organisation on the Common Courts, the Law on the Supreme Court and other Laws, issued pursuant to Article 14a of the Venice Commission's Rules of Procedure.
94 Varga Zs. (n 89).
95 Varga Zs. (n 89).

This majority soon turned its political will into a *pouvoir constituant* (a constituent power)[96] for the framing and adoption of the new Hungarian FL.

As we noted earlier, an inevitable consequence of this reading of the doctrine of popular sovereignty is the open denial of the separation of powers and – to a large extent – the denial of an independent judiciary, a doctrine that prevailed for 150 years in the history of European law.

I argue that under illiberal anti-constitutionalism,[97] the judiciary is outweighed by the sovereign will of the state.[98] According to political philosopher János Kis, the new Hungarian FL of 2012 violates the principle of separation of powers by limiting the powers of the Constitutional Court, by increasing the number of constitutional justices, and by allowing the present majority to appoint new justices without the agreement of the opposition, by mandating early retirement for judges and placing the power to appoint their replacements in the hands of a politically appointed chief of the judiciary, and by allowing the chief prosecutor (elected by the populist majority Parliament) to designate the proceeding court.[99]

96 Christoph Möllers argues that the idea of a *pouvoir constituant* designates the subject of the founding act, the people, and it guarantees its application. Regimes under strong popular sovereignty usually have a revolutionary approach to the constitution-making process vis-à-vis the evolutionary approach favoured by some German traditions. Accordingly, the sovereignty approach is based on revolutionary tradition, and its claim is that their constituant and legislative decisions have greater normativity. See C. Christoph Möllers, 'Pouvoir Constituant-Constitution-Constitutionalisation' in Armin von Bogdandy and Jürgen Bast (eds), *Principles of European Constitutional Law* (Hart 2009) 169–170 and further. See also: Corrias (n 20) 14 and further.

97 The Hungarian prime minister, Viktor Orbán in 2014 stated that "the new state we are building is an illiberal state, a non-liberal state', similar to Singapore, China, India, Turkey, and Russia as countries of reference for Hungary. See Hungarian Spectrum, 'Viktor Orbán's Speech at the XXV Bálványos Free Summer University and Youth Camp, July 26, 2014, Băile Tuşnad (Tusnádfürdő)' *hungarianspectrum.wordpress.com* (2014) <http://hungarianspectrum.wordpress.com/2014/07/31/viktor-orbans-speech-at-the-xxv-balvanyos-free-summer-university-and-youth-camp-july-26-2014-baile-tusnad-tusnadfurdo/> accessed 10 May 2022. The expression of anti-constitutionalism was coined by W. Sadurski. See Martin Krygier, Adam Czarnota and Wojciech Sadurski (eds), *Anti-Constitutional Populism: Cambridge Studies in Law and Society Series* (CUP 2022) 401–433.

98 For an account of populist/authoritarian or illiberal constitutionalism, see Gárdos-Orosz (n 45) 1. See also: Anselmi (n 2); Walker (n 2) 515; Théo Fournier, 'From Rhetoric to Action, a Constitutional Analysis of Populism' (2019) 20 *GLJ* 362–381; Zoltán Szente, 'Populism and Populist Constitutionalism' in Fruzsina Gárdos-Orosz and Zoltán Szente (eds), *Populist Challenges to Constitutional Interpretation in Europe and Beyond* (Routledge 2021); Kurt Weyland, 'Clarifying a Contested Concept: Populism in the Study of Latin American Politics' (2001) 34(1) *Comp Pol* 1–22.

99 Kis (n 52) 1–2.

The practice of judicial independence and sovereignty in populist Hungary

As early as 2011, the Venice Commission signaled that adopting a new Constitution (FL) represents a backsliding, a significant step, which "appears to be only the beginning of a longer process of establishing a comprehensive and coherent new constitutional order. This implies adoption or amendment of numerous pieces of legislation, new institutional arrangements, and other related measures."[100] The Venice Commission was concerned about whether the processes were based on the greatest consensus possible within Hungarian society.[101] Similarly, Hungarian civil society representatives claimed in 2011[102] that the new Hungarian constitutional order regarding the judiciary can be identified as the centralization and "concentration of powers."[103] Hungarian scholar Mátyás Bencze also noted that the "Hungarian judiciary is highly centralised, and judges are under administrative control."[104] The new populist FL was enacted in April 2011. Not much later, the same populist supermajority in the Parliament ratified the new legislation on the organization and administration of the Hungarian court system and the status and remuneration of judges,[105] which generated salient international criticism for putting unprecedented superpowers in the hands of the very few.[106]

As we have already underlined in this chapter, our main claim is that the concept of judicial independence can only be understood in populist (illiberal) constitutionalism through the concentration of powers and the unity of the state. We claim that this defines the discourse within which judicial independence is (re) interpreted. We further argue that under these circumstances, the real questions

100 AD(2011)016-e, Opinion on the new constitution of Hungary Adopted by the Venice Commission at its 87th Plenary Session (Venice, 17–18 June 2011).

101 AD(2011)019-e, European Commission for Democracy through Law, the advisory body of the Council of Europe, Venice Commission's Opinion on the new constitution of Hungary adopted by the Venice Commission at its 87th plenary session (Venice, 17–18 June 2011).

102 Such as the Hungarian Helsinki Committee, the Hungarian Civil Liberties Union and the Eötvös Károly Public Policy Institute.

103 Joint opinion of the Eötvös Károly Policy Institute, the Hungarian Helsinki Committee and the Hungarian Civil Liberties Union on the Hungarian legislative package on justice reform. Similarly, The Venice Commission was concerned about the judicial administration being under unified control, without proper balancing of powers. See CDL-REF(2012)034-e Act CXI of 2012 and CDL-AD(2012)020-e Opinion on the Cardinal Arts.

104 Mátyás Bencze, 'Judicial Populism and the Weberian Judge – the Strength of Judicial Resistance Against Governmental Influence in Hungary' (2021) *GLJ* 1297.

105 Hungary, Act CLXI of 2011 on the Organisation and Administration of the Courts (hereinafter: Act CLXI); Act CLXII of 2011 on the Legal Status and Remuneration of Judges.

106 Magyar Helsinki Bizottság, 'A módosított bírósági törvények kritikája' *Helsinki.hu* (2012) <https://helsinki.hu/wp-content/uploads/MHB-TASZ-EKINT_Modos%C3%ADtott_birosagi_torvenyek_kritikaja_201209.pdf> accessed 10 May 2022; Magyar Helsinki Bizottság, 'Assessment of the Amended Hungarian Laws on the Judiciary' *Helsinki.hu* (2012) <https://helsinki.hu/wp-content/uploads/HHC-HCLU-EKINT_Assessment_of_the_Amended_Hungarian_Laws_on_the_Judiciary_092012.pdf> accessed 10 May 2022.

at stake are (1) who has (real) ownership of the judiciary, or more precisely, who has the supreme power over the judiciary? and (2) who has a monopoly on the interpretation of the law? We further argue that questioning the judicial monopoly of interpreting the law is indeed adopting a very strong position vis-à-vis the law. This is a direct challenge to liberal constitutionalism.[107]

As for the latter argument (who has a monopoly on the interpretation of the law), I argue that it is clearly indicated in Article 28 of the new Hungarian Constitution (FL) that courts should interpret the law according to the guidance laid down in the Constitution. And the Constitution is designed and drafted in accordance with the will of the parliamentary supermajority. So, the FL stipulates binding rules on the judiciary concerning how to interpret the law. This is a fairly new and restrictive approach, given that the Hungarian Constitution of 1989–2011 did not have provisions on judicial interpretation, leaving it to the judicial branch to decide how and when to exercise their right to interpret legislation. Accordingly, Article 28 of the FL further provides that the "the courts shall in principle interpret the laws in light of their purpose and in accordance with the Fundamental Law." Additionally, the Seventh Amendment to the Fundamental Law in 2018 further circumvented the freedom of interpretation of the Judiciary by stating that in the course of legal interpretation, preambles of legal norms and their explanatory memorandums shall be primarily taken into consideration.[108]

These deliberate restrictions on the freedom of interpretation of the judiciary can only be understood as a limitation of the scope of scrutiny of the courts to avoid the empowerment of the judicial branch, which prevents them from fully exercising control over the sovereign power of the legislature and the government. In this context, the idea of an absolute sovereign representing the highest will of the people is against the idea of judicial counterbalance.

In the same account, one might emphasize the underdetermined language of the FL in relation to describing the functioning and role of the judiciary: the lack of description of the latter's structure and the composition of the courts. Meanwhile, the same restraint in the text cannot be traced in relation to the retirement age of judges, which, it might easily be argued, is unduly overarticulated in the Constitution, rather than these provisions being regulated at the sub-constitutional level.

I argue that this overregulation is deliberate political interference with the integrity of the judiciary.[109] (Because as a result, from now on, the FL

107 So, for example, Barber in his influential book argues that the main aspect of the separation of powers is the requirement that the judiciary be independent of the executive branch. See Nicholas William Barber, *The Principles of Constitutionalism* (Oxford University Press 2018) 12.

108 László Detre and Endre Orbán, 'The Main Dimensions of Constitutional Interpretation of Judicial Independence in Hungary' (2022) 19 *Revista de derecho constitucional europeo* 1.

109 This provision of the Fundamental Law was adopted by Article 26.2 of the FL in 2011. Later, this provision was reinforced by the Cardinal Law on the Judiciary. The Cardinal Law, however, was subsequently subject to constitutional scrutiny. In decision 33/2012 the Hungarian Constitutional Court declared the provisions of the retirement age unconstitutional.

dictates the conditions under which judges retire and new judges become eligible for the position, instead of conceding these decisions to judicial self-determination).[110]

I argue that in the struggle over the monopoly of the interpretation of the law between courts and lawmakers (often with the notion of *pouvoir constituant*), different peak points can be traced, such as the curtailing of the power of the courts, including the constitutional court, narrowing courts' scope of scrutiny and the implementation of new procedures and new legal institutions to expand the scope of the executive power at the expense of limiting judicial power. Further, by removing judicial control mechanisms (on the one hand) and restricting the freedom of constitutional and legal interpretation on the other.

What remains constant in this conflict is that the courts are gradually tied up, and their room for maneuver gradually shrinks until they are degraded to a de facto technical player (some would argue that courts become non-playing characters) in the art of interpretation.

Distinguished Czech legal scholar Zdeněk Kühn argues that non-liberal regimes are very skeptical of the nature of the interpretation of the law, which – in their opinion – is nothing other than pure politics concealed behind a veil of legalistic jargon. Kühn argues that unfortunately, some court decisions prove non-liberal politicians right. Too often, the courts raise doubts about the integrity of their decisions.[111]

Regarding the interpretation of the law, the Hungarian Constitutional Court was reshaped by the new FL (New Constitution of Hungary) in 2012. Accordingly, the Constitutional Court lost some of its important – some would argue its main – jurisdiction over the legislation of Parliament, and its mandate was adjusted towards the control of the judicial branch, a type of jurisdiction over the courts that the Constitutional Court in Hungary has never had before. And therefore, the competing competencies of the regular courts and the Constitutional Court have resulted in the erosion of the domains of both branches (courts and the Constitutional Court) as a mutually adverse solution.[112]

The Court argued that it can be deduced from the text of the Constitution that an age limit is constitutional only if it means a rise in and not an arbitrary reduction of the age limit unless it is introduced gradually, over a sufficient transitional period, without prejudice to the principle of the immovability of the judge. Subsequently, Decision C-286/12 of the ECJ declared that Hungary had failed to fulfil its obligations under EU Law for establishing a general framework for equal treatment in terms of the employment of judges.

110 As noted earlier, the original language of the Constitution was basically repeated and reinforced by the Cardinal Law on the Judiciary. Decision C-286/12 of the ECJ declared that Hungary had failed to fulfil its obligations under EU Law for establishing a general framework for equal treatment in employment for judges.

111 Zdeněk Kühn, 'The Judiciary in Illiberal States' 22 (2021) *GLJ* 1245–1246.

112 Zoltán Szente and Fruzsina Gárdos-Orosz, 'Juridical Deference or Political Loyalty?' in Zoltán Szente and Fruzsina Gárdos-Orosz (eds), *New Challenges to Constitutional Adjudication in Europe* (Routledge 2018) 89–110.

In 2019, the Constitutional Court was granted oversight over complaints from government bodies.[113] Due to international criticism, these provisions were revoked in 2023.[114] These provisions are imbued with the risk that government bodies may 'complain' against regular court decisions at a politically appointed Constitutional Court as a way of circumventing rather than complying with those unfavorable court decisions. (As noted earlier, the Hungarian Constitutional Court has the power to overrule regular court decisions.) Thus these provisions interfere with the original intent of constitutional complaint to provide a remedy against state actions in cases of fundamental rights violations.

Regarding the interpretation of the law, another controversial provision granted the Prosecutor General the right to challenge the legality of references for preliminary rulings from proceeding judges to the CJEU. Accordingly, a preliminary ruling from a proceeding judge was overturned by the Hungarian Curia, which found it illegal 'in the interests of legality' to refer a case to the European Court. The CJEU ruled that such a decision by the Curia is contrary to EU law. EU law prevents national supreme courts from interfering with the legality of the lower courts when referring cases directly to the CJEU.[115] Although this case has never been referred to as a constitutional identity case, in fact, the merit of the case is based on a sovereignty argument,[116] which claims that the Hungarian Curia has the final say in referring a case to the CJEU against a national judge. In the present case, the referring court, sitting as a single-judge formation at the Central District Court in Budapest on a criminal proceeding, referred a case to the CJEU. Among other things, the referring judge asked:

1 "Must Article 267 [TFEU] be interpreted as precluding a national practice whereby the court of last instance, in proceedings to harmonise the case law of the Member State, declares as unlawful a decision by which a lower court makes a request for a preliminary ruling, without altering the legal effects of the decision in question?"

"If [Question 1] is answered in the affirmative, must Article 267 [TFEU] be interpreted as meaning that the referring court must disregard contrary decisions of the higher court and positions of principle adopted in the interest of harmonizing the law?"

"If [Question 1] is answered in the negative, can the suspended criminal proceedings be continued, given that the preliminary ruling proceedings are pending?"

113 See: Hungary, Act CXXVII of 2019, Article 55, in force since 20 December 2019.

114 2023 Rule of Law Report, European Rule of Law Mechanism.

115 CJEU, Case C-564/19 *IS (Illégalité de l'ordonnance de renvoi)*, ECLI:EU:C:2021:949. The Court also held that within the scope of preliminary ruling, no national judge shall be sanctioned for referring a case to the European Court by any disciplinary measure.

116 See Ernő Várnay and Mónika Papp, *Magyarázat az Európai Unió jogáról* (Wolters Kluwer 2023) 371.

2 Must the principle of judicial independence, established in the second subparagraph of Article 19(1) TEU, in Article 47 of the Charter and the case law of the Court of Justice, read in the light of Article 267 TFEU, be interpreted as meaning that that principle precludes disciplinary proceedings being brought against a judge for having made a request for a preliminary ruling?'

According to Advocate General Pikamäe's opinion, the Curia reviewed the lawfulness of the initial order for reference in the light of Hungarian national law. Thus the Curia's judgment seems to undermine the referring judge's right to refer questions to the European Court for a preliminary ruling and, therefore, infringes Article 267 TFEU.[117] The CJEU judgment further declared that Article 267 TFEU must be interpreted as preventing the supreme court of a Member State from declaring a preliminary ruling by a lower court unlawful on the grounds that the questions referred to are not relevant and necessary for the resolution of the dispute. According to the principle of the primacy of EU law, the lower court must disregard such a decision of the national supreme court.[118]

In another account, a case was brought to the ECHR in 2022 by a judge from the metropolitan tribunal who claimed that, in an undue decision, she was classified as incompetent in her position as a judge and had lost her job.[119] The applicant complained that there was no remedy against the classifications (of judges); therefore, she could not appeal.[120] Accordingly, it could seriously undermine public confidence in the judiciary if neither the selection nor the dismissal of judges is based on foreseeable rules and cannot be challenged afterward in a fair procedure.[121]

The freedom of interpretation for preceding judges was further restricted in Hungary in 2020 by the introduction of the so-called limited precedent system. (This also resulted in a greater concentration of power in the hands of the Chief Justice). Accordingly, each leading decision of the Curia is legally binding on all

117 Case C-564/19, ECLI:EU:C:2021:292.

118 Case C-564/19. Section 85. Since this time, in the rule of law negotiations between the EU and Hungary, Hungary has adopted amendments to the law to withdraw the challenged provisions.

119 Eszter Zalán, 'Hungarian Judge Claims She Was Pushed Out for Political Reasons' *Euobserver* (2021)<https://helsinki.hu/en/another-scandal-at-the-judiciary-no-effective-remedy-for-judges-dismissed-from-the-bench/> accessed 10 May 2022.

120 Zalán (n 119).

121 The applicant is represented by the Hungarian Helsinki Committee. Magyar Helsinki Bizottság, 'Újabb bírósági botrány: nincs hatékony jogorvoslati lehetőség kirúgott bíróknak' Helsinkifigyelő, 'Egy bírónő meghurcolása, avagy fenyegetés minden magyar bírónak' *Helsinki figyelő* (2021) <https://helsinkifigyelo.444.hu/2021/07/06/egy-birono-meghurcolasa-avagy-fenyegetes-minden-magyar-bironak> accessed 10 May 2022.

lower courts.[122] Any deviation from the precedent must be justified by the lower courts, and this justification can be overruled by the higher courts.[123]

The centralization of powers in the judicial branch without counterbalance

Considering the fact that the Chief Justice of the Curia has key powers within the judiciary in most countries – including Hungary – in the final adjudication of cases, in ensuring the uniformity of the jurisprudence of Hungarian courts, and in the management of the apex courts, it goes without further explanation that when a further concentration of power is granted by law to the Chief Justice – such as the right to appoint lower court judges, to directly impact the career path of judges, to delegate cases and judges between different jurisdictions, and to interfere directly with the composition of court panels – this will result in a 'hyper power' in the hands of the (a politically appointed) head of the Branch.[124]

The undue and premature termination of the mandate of András Baka, former President of the Supreme Court in 2011 in the midst of populist constitutional changes, resulted in the first step in a series of systemic attacks against the integrity of the Hungarian judiciary. The President of the Court lost his mandate in the midterm due to the provisions of the new Constitution and its reinforcing cardinal laws. This resulted in ECHR decision 20261/12 against Hungary, declaring the termination of the applicants' mandates as President (Mr. Baka) and Vice-President (Mr. Erményi)[125] unlawful. (The expressions "undue" and "premature" are contained in the language of the ECHR decision.)

Next, the political appointment of the new Chief Justice (Mr. András Zs. Varga) of the Curia was a further step[126] in a "far-reaching reform of the judicial system" starting in 2010–2011.[127] The main effect – if not the main goal – of these measures

> has been to hamper the constitutionally protected principle of judicial independence in Hungary. As a result, the independence of the

122 See Article 185 of Act CXXVII of 2019 that modifies Act CLXI of 2011 on the Organization and Administration of Courts: leading decisions published in the official gazette of the Curia are binding. Analyses: Hungarian Helsinki Committee, *New Law Threatens Judicial Independence in Hungary – Again* (Hungarian Helsinki Committee 2020).

123 See Zoltán Szente, 'Hungary' in André Alen and David Haljan (eds), *International Encyclopaedia of Laws: Constitutional Law* (Kluwer 2022) 209–210.

124 Amnesty International, 'Nem vész el, csak átalakul – a kormány tovább korlátozza a bíróságok függetlenségét' *amnesty.hu* (2020) <www.amnesty.hu/wp-content/uploads/2020/10/ELEMZE%CC%81S.pdf> accessed 10 May 2022.

125 *Baka v. Hungary* App no 20261/12 (ECHR, 20, 23 June 2016).

126 Szente (n 123) 209.

127 AL HUN 2/2021. Report by the UN Special Rapporteur on the independence of judges and lawyers.

justice system and institutional checks and balances under the separation of powers, are now under threat, as noted by several international and regional bodies, such as the Human Rights Committee, the Venice Commission, the CoE Commissioner for Human Rights and the European Commission.[128]

The Chief Justice of the Curia was appointed in spite of the manifest objection of the competent judicial body (NJO) to evaluating the application. The Chief Justice was elected in 2021 after a series of legislative enactments that paved the way to making his appointment legally possible.

In undermining judicial independence, as noted earlier in this chapter, criticism also arose concerning the underdetermined language of the FL of 2012 in respect of its description of the functioning and role of the judiciary, including its structure and composition, basically providing carte blanche for the Legislator. We have already noted that the functioning of courts was arbitrarily underdetermined in the FL, while the constitutionally redesigned retirement age of judges was arbitrarily overrepresented in the text, resulting in a counterexample of legal certainty.

The concentration of power as a counterpoint to the separation of powers is particularly noticeable in the academic scholarship of the Chief Justice. Professor Varga, head of the department of administrative law at the Catholic University, Budapest,[129] has elaborated on his concept of the rule of law quite articulately.

Varga notes that the separation of powers cannot mean that, in the name of the rule of law, judicial bodies acquire for themselves the final, unconstrained right to decide. It is the task of constitutional courts to defend so-called normative justice and nothing more.[130] The Chief Justice refers to the work of Canadian Professor Ivan Martin, who in a book refers to courts as "The Most Dangerous Branch."[131] The Chief Justice relies on Martin when he adds: "we once thought that the judiciary is the least dangerous branch of power;[132] we have now had to admit that they are the most dangerous. And why? Because it has no limits."[133] Professor Varga highlights that modern constitutional

128 AL HUN 2/2021. Report by the UN Special Rapporteur on the independence of judges and lawyers.

129 Pázmány Péter Catholic University, Budapest.

130 András Zs. Varga, *From Ideal to Idol?* (Dialóg Campus 2019) 22–24.

131 Ivan Martin, *The Most Dangerous Branch* (McGill-Queen's UP 2003).

132 Ivan Martin borrows his title from American scholar Alexander M. Bickel's *The Least Dangerous Branch*. Bickel's book was written in defence of judicial review and in the wake of what he called the School Desegregation Decisions. See Alexander M. Bickel, *The Least Dangerous Branch: The Supreme Court at the Bar of Politics* (Yale University Press 1986).

133 Martin specifically implies that the Canadian Supreme Court is the most dangerous branch. See Ivan Martin, *The Most Dangerous Branch* (McGill-Queen's UP 2003) 7. See also: Aranka Szávuly, 'Az életben a legtöbb döntést nem én hoztam meg' (2016) <https://jogaszvilag.hu/szakma/az-eletben-a-legtobb-dontest-nem-en-hoztam-meg/> accessed 10 May 2022.

democracies are heading towards an arbitrary system of rule of law and judicial supremacy under the unlimited power of (constitutional) courts.[134]

According to the theory of the Chief Justice, constitutional courts and their highly powerful international counterparts are essentially institutions with unlimited power; whatever they decide is the only rule of law, and there is nowhere else to go from there. In contemporary legal scholarship, the concept of the rule of law serves as a magic wand for constitutional courts to justify their arbitrary decisions.[135]

Varga notes: "EU-interpretation of the rule of law, despite the endeavour to provide legal security, yields ground for arbitrary interpretation enforceable by judicial means. Albeit, in order to recognise that arbitrariness has become tyrannical, moreover, totalitarian."[136]

Varga complemented that the situation is less damaging in Hungary because if an ordinary court decides in one way, it can be corrected by amending the law and even the Constitution.[137] "In international terms, this is more dangerous, since is it possible to amend the European Convention on Human Rights because someone does not like the Strasbourg ruling? And many people do not like that they cannot [do this]"[138] – the European Union is a Union ruled by courts.[139] The Chief Justice notes that today's rule-of-law state has no natural constraints; today's rule of law is a judicial rule of law and nothing but a state of totalitarianism. There is reason to ask whether the rule of law by the judiciary has an anti-serum or counter-agent.[140]

So, the Chief Justice goes on: there is "a serious question in other countries as to what is the counterweight, what is the constraint or the limitation on the courts?" He concludes that giving too much power to courts is like providing 'carte blanche,' a blank mandate to act arbitrarily. It is like living under the tyranny of a monarch because the judiciary's decision is just as arbitrary as the decision of the absolute monarch; it is not made by the crown prince but by the crown body.[141]

With regard to the scholarship of Chief Justice Varga, at the center of his argument is how to circumscribe the unlimited power of courts. His central claim is that the absolute power of courts should be limited. (I argue, this is a kind of reverse idea of limited government and separation of powers, in which the judiciary and not the executive is restricted in order to maintain the constitutional order.)[142] According to Varga, against the courts, the "counter-

134 Varga (n 130) 8–10, 101–102.
135 Varga (n 130) 14.
136 Varga (n 130) 19.
137 Szávuly (n 133).
138 Szávuly (n 133).
139 Varga (n 130) 25–29.
140 Varga (n 130) 27.
141 Szávuly (n 133).
142 It is common sense that the purpose of the separation of powers is to protect the liberty of the individual by making tyrannical and arbitrary state action more difficult. See Barber (n 107) 4.

weight cannot be solely the executive power"; however, it is a good starting point.[143] Eventually, only the legislative power, as the bearer of legitimacy, and the executive power, as the acting branch of the state, can serve together as a counterbalance against the courts.[144] He further argues that "against the tyranny of the rule of law," another counter-agent is the FL of Hungary itself and its interpretation by the restructured Hungarian Constitutional Court.[145] In this regard, the Chief Justice argues, Hungary took significant steps in provision R (3) of the FL providing Article R (1), which stipulates that "Laws shall be interpreted in accordance with their purposes, the National Avowal contained therein and the achievements of our historic constitution." With the same weight, the above-mentioned provisions of Article 28 of the FL provide that "courts shall interpret laws in accordance with their purposes". When ascertaining the purpose of a law, consideration "shall be given primarily to the preamble of that law and the justification of its proposal". When interpreting the Constitution (FL) or laws, it shall be presumed that they serve moral and economic purposes in accordance with common sense and the public good.[146]

The public good, according to the Chief Justice, is a theory behind which we find cooperation and collaboration between branches of government, a dialogue between the legislature and the courts as administrators of justice. Then public good is the substantive serum against the tyranny of the rule of law, based on the "mutual respect and loyal co-operation between state organs" formulated in the opinion of the Venice Commission.[147] In this approach, the legislator or, in fact, the constitution-maker themselves, does not commit heresy if they change the laws or the constitution itself in response to a previous judicial decision.[148] (Meaning, the 'uninvited' court or constitutional court decisions in principle can be modified by amending the Constitution itself).

To reflect the practice associated with the aforementioned theory, the best example in Hungary is the annihilation of specific court decisions by a legislative act. First, in 2011, the Fidesz-majority Parliament, by an Annulment Act, declared null and void a range of judgments of the judicial branch related to a violent political protest that occurred in 2006. Parliament annulled criminal court judgments concerning convictions for vandalism and violence

143 András Varga Zs., *Eszményből bálvány?* (Századvég 2019) 29.
144 Varga (n 130) 24–25; Varga (n 143) 29.
145 Varga (n 130) 130–132.
146 Varga (n 130) 29–30, 130–132.
147 CDL-AD(2012)026 Opinion no. 685/2012 on the compatibility with constitutional principles and the rule of law of actions taken by the government and the parliament of Romania in respect of other state institutions and on the government emergency ordinance on amendment to the law no. 47/1992 regarding the organisation and functioning of the constitutional court and on the government emergency ordinance on amending and completing the law no. 3/2000 regarding the organisation of a referendum in Romania. <www.venice.coe.int/webforms/documents/CDL-AD(2012)026-e.aspx>
148 Varga (n 130) 25.

committed during a right-wing riot against the former democratic left-wing government.[149] (The riots targeted the left-wing Hungarian Government, demanding its resignation after the speech of the Prime Minister from his party reunion was leaked in which the Prime Minister denounced his party as dishonest and blamed the 'left' environment fraudulent and dishonest).

Later, after the right-wing takeover in Hungary in 2010, the Annulment Act was referred to the Constitutional Court for constitutional scrutiny. The politically packed Hungarian Constitutional Court found the provisions of this Act constitutional and upheld them.[150] Presidential pardons or amnesties were not initiated by the Fidesz-led new supermajority to support politically motivated mischief (and vandalism) committed previously, because, under presidential amnesty, convicts continue to be criminalized and, therefore, stigmatized, thus a presidential pardon would have provided only an exemption from further criminal sanction.

Therefore, I argue, the Hungarian legislator chose to deny the court's competent power to base its judgment on its jurisdiction. This is an open denial of judicial supremacy and the principles of the rule of law. In this constitutional drama, the Hungarian Constitutional Court was assigned the role of a non-playing character. The majority of the literature on this case has indicated that the Hungarian Constitutional Court did not simply err by upholding the Annulment Law on criminal convictions but that it also surrendered to politics over 'law', which meant a clear denial of judicial supremacy.[151] I argue in this chapter that this was a symbolic capitulation of the rule of law. The active metaphor here is of a journey from the rule of law to autocratic populism. The legislator's open agenda was to provide a symbolic remedy for political purposes.[152]

To a lesser extent, the aforementioned 'loyal co-operation and mutual respect' between court and executive can be tackled symbolically, as the Hungarian Government construed it, in a number of court cases when the Government exercised pressure on the judiciary by commenting, counter-arguing, or complaining against the courts' decisions in individual judgments. I argue, however, that under the doctrine of separation of powers, the government is not by any means in a position to be the interpreter of or commentator on the independent judicial branch.[153]

149 See Hungary, Act XVI of 2011 on remedies for the convictions in connection with the riots of autumn 2006. Remedy was granted against public officials, criminal damage, and criminal trespass, if the judgement was based exclusively on a police report or police testimony.

150 See 24/2013(X.4) AB Decision.

151 Mátyás Bencze and Ágnes Kovács, '"Mission: Impossible": alkotmánybíráskodás az alkotmányos értékek védelme nélkül' (2014) 6 *Jogtudományi Közlöny* 273.

152 The preamble of Act XVI of 2011 declares the purpose of the Act "to remedy the violations of the democratic rule of law and the fundamental constitutional rights of citizens in the autumn of 2006".

153 Mátyás Bencze, 'A magyar bírósági rendszer rezilienciája 2012 és 2021 között' in Fruzsina Gárdos-Orosz (ed.), *A Magyar Jogrendszer rezilienciája 2010–2020* (TTK – ORAC 2022) 376–394. Moreover, According to EU Rule of Law Report, pro-government media launched

So, we can conclude that the pattern of the sovereignty argument in constitutional populism is to shift emphasis from the rule of law and separation of powers to the 'shared responsibility' of the administration of justice between branches of government (which many argue in practice means nothing more than the denial of judicial supremacy). Then, a politically mutilated judicial body is granted a new Chief Justice with unprecedented superpowers to demonstrate how cherished judicial independence under a sovereign state is with a fully empowered chief of the branch. The newly appointed chief has wide competencies, including competencies over the arbitrary system of the allocation of court cases and, more generally, exercises a unilateral concentration of power over court administration to designate cases among jurisdictions and to appoint judges to the branch without adequate checks and balances.[154]

Arbitrary decisions about the careers of judges have been a concern expressed by the EU. The Chief Justice did not respect the applicable rules when appointing a number of judges to the branch.[155] Moreover, the evaluation system in the application process prioritized candidates from the public administration over judiciary candidates.[156] Accordingly, it can seriously undermine public confidence in the judiciary if neither the selection nor the dismissal of judges is based on foreseeable rules and cannot be challenged afterward in a fair procedure.[157]

In 2018, the Hungarian Parliament passed legislation establishing a separate branch for administrative courts. The de facto establishment of administrative courts was postponed multiple times, and eventually, the idea was withdrawn by the Hungarian Government due to substantial international criticism. Therefore, as I have noted in general terms, now, in the case of administrative courts, the new law (again) intended to put a great deal of power in the hands of the very few without any substantial counterbalance. The Minister of Justice had too much authority over the (new) design, structure, budget, and size of the administrative courts, including the right to appoint new politically suitable judges to the administrative branch.[158]

A further concentration of powers was enhanced in 2020 by the introduction of the above-mentioned 'limited precedent system'.

---

smear campaigns against members of the Judicial Branch to silence judges. See 2022 Rule of Law Report, Country Chapter on the rule of law situation in Hungary.

154 See CD-AD(2012)001-e Opinion on Act CLXXI of 2011.

155 See CD-AD(2012)001-e Opinion on Act CLXXI of 2011.

156 2022 Rule of Law Report, Country Chapter on the rule of law situation in Hungary.

157 The applicant is represented by the Hungarian Helsinki Committee. See Helsinkifigyelő (n 121).

158 Kosař argues: to make it sure, neither Orbán nor Kaczyński (nor Babiš nor Fico) is an anti-institutionalists in an unequivocal sense. They like institutions as long as those institutions pursue their agendas, or at least behave in a neutral way and do not put up unwelcome obstacles. As Müller notes, populists 'only oppose those institutions that, in their view, fail to produce correct political outcomes'. See Kosař, Baroš and Dufek (n 3).

Czech scholar Zdeněk Kühn highlights:

> It is well known that interpretation of the law is a contextual exercise. Nonetheless, if we give up on the idea that the law is capable of being at least partially an autonomous phenomenon . . . that is capable of limiting the government and parliament relatively independently of the value preferences of the individual judges, a gate will soon be wide open for government of the current political majority which is limited by nothing and no one. From this perspective, non-liberal democracy is, in fact, merely a transient phenomenon because, sooner or later, it will no longer be a democracy at all. If the ruling power is not limited in its activities in any way, it becomes completely unclear why it should let its own political support be repeatedly tested in democratic elections. Such unlimited political power will naturally acquire an appetite for adapting election rules to suit it or modifying the media environment for its own benefit. If we admit this, we will have to relive our recent history, even if with a different ideology, different political arrangements, and different actors.[159]

Conclusion

Judicial supremacy as part of the rule of law, which is an inherent part of the DNA of European constitutionalism, has suffered almost irreparable damage due to recent developments associated with the new concept of constitutional identity (mainly but not exclusively in Hungary, to some extent in Poland and Czechia, and increasingly in Slovakia),[160] which openly denies the supremacy of the separation of powers as a core value of Europe, its people, and its ideas. This has a devastating effect on judicial independence and accountability. I argue that the prerequisite for judicial independence is the integrity of the judiciary protected by the separation of powers doctrine. And the precondition for judicial accountability is the independence of the judiciary. Therefore, judicial accountability is indivisible and inalienable from judicial independence and the supremacy of law.

Constitutional identity (and its theory) have offered a conceptual framework for judicial independence to be interpreted in a 'national way', removed from European constitutional traditions.

Accordingly, the pattern is that nation-states first declare a withdrawal from the mainstream understanding of the supremacy of law, using as a disclaimer that the courts are ruling instead of the 'people' governing. Thus, they argue, the

159 Kühn (n 111) 1246.
160 See Kosař, Baroš and Dufek (n 3) 429–430.

courts have taken over and are dominating the public discourse through the interpretation of the law.

Therefore, Member States in the 'stage of constitutional identity' (whatever constitutional identity means) first rely on ultra vires arguments to withdraw from the principle of rule of law, then call for a new concept of public good, which means 'loyal co-operation between branches of government' by scaling back the powers and competences of the courts in favor of the executive and legislative branch. Finally, a new head of the judiciary is appointed to the mutilated courts, creating an unprecedented concentration of powers (in terms of the appointment of new judges, the final adjudication of cases, transferring cases between court jurisdictions, designating different courts of jurisdictions, deciding on the retirement of judges, exercising final administrative decisions in the justice system, and so forth) in the hands of a political appointee.

I claim in this book chapter that under the umbrella of European civilization complemented by the US traditions of limited government from the Magna Carta to the US Constitution, from John Locke to the Federalists, there is no viable alternative to the idea of judicial supremacy and the rule of law. As Armin von Bogdandy put it, Europe is at high risk today. Much is at stake. Kosař adds that we usually only realize what the separation of powers is and what value it is to us once we have lost it.[161] However, the constitutional European project is not yet lost.[162] Let us conclude: breath is held and eyes are on Hungary.

161 See Kosař, Baroš and Dufek (n 3) 431.

162 Armin von Bogdandy, 'A Potential Constitutional Moment for the European Rule of Law: The Importance of Red Lines Defending Checks and Balances in EU Member States' in Armin Bogdandy, Piotr Bogdanowicz, Iris Canor, Christoph Grabenwarter, Maciej Taborowski and Matthias Schmidt (eds), *Defending Checks and Balances in EU Member States* (Springer 2021) 399.

Part II

Standards

4 EU standards regarding individual accountability of judges[*]

Natalie Fox

Introduction

The judges' and the judiciary's independence in the context of European Union (EU) standards of the rule of law is an issue that has generated considerable interest in international law in recent years, particularly in light of the case law of the Court of Justice of the European Union (CJEU). The solutions introduced in Poland after 2016 following the so-called reform of the judiciary have undermined the importance of judges' independence, impartiality and accountability, which are crucial issues for the very idea of democracy, as well as the principles of the rule of law and separation of powers. These principles constitute the cornerstone for the protection of individual rights, which are deemed undeniable values in a contemporary democratic state ruled by law. In this context, it should be emphasised that the possibility for individuals to pursue their rights before a body independent of the executive and legislative powers should be treated as a fundamental human right, on one hand, and as a guarantee of the protection of all human rights, on the other hand.[1] This principle is expressed in Art. 6 of the European Convention on Human Rights (ECHR), as well as in Art. 45(1) of the Constitution of the Republic of Poland of 1997.[2] The proper implementation of the right to a fair trial is possible only within the framework of an existing organised justice system in a state. The changes that are currently observing are the subjects of extensive political and legal disputes in Poland and in other EU member states. To provide effective mechanisms for defending values such as the independence and accountability of judges, there is an emerging need to reach out to the EU.

* The publication has also been supported by the funds from the Law and Administration Faculty of the Jagiellonian University granted within the Priority Research Area 'FutureSoc' under the programme 'Excellence Initiative – Research University'.

1 Ensuring the independence of the judiciary is a necessary element for the observance of human rights. *See* Kathleen Pitchard, 'Comparative Human Rights: An Integrative Explanation' (1986) 1 *PSJ* 110.

2 The Constitution of Poland, which is in force, was ratified on 2 April 1997 (hereinafter, the Polish Constitution of 1997).

DOI: 10.4324/9781003557852-6

Increasingly, in this context, the CJEU's jurisprudence is becoming crucial in terms of resolving legal disputes between national governments and EU institutions, enforcing the law through infringement proceedings in cases against national governments for their non-compliance with EU law. Recently, some standards have emerged in the CJEU's jurisprudence related to the independence of national judicial bodies operating in EU member states authorised to assess disciplinary torts (e.g. the cases in Poland, Hungary and Romania). For example, national laws may not provide for sanctions disciplining judges for applying the principle of primacy of EU law. The need to ensure the effectiveness of EU law requires member states to recognise and comply with the standards developed in the CJEU case law and in force, which constitute guarantees of the independence of the judges and the judiciary. The complexity of this issue requires defining the main aim of this chapter, that is, to present the emerging EU standards for the protection of the rule of law in the EU member states against the background of the CJEU case law developed in the context of the responsibility of judges and the independence of the judiciary. The standards understood in this way include, in particular, unhindered cooperation between the CJEU and national courts within the preliminary ruling mechanism of Art. 267 of the Treaty on the Functioning of the European Union (TFEU), the principle of effective judicial protection expressed in Art. 19(1), Para. 2 of the Treaty on the European Union (TEU) or the principle of Art. 47 of the EU Charter of Fundamental Rights (hereinafter, the Charter), which regulates the right to an effective remedy and to a fair trial.

Effective judicial protection in the realms enshrined in EU law in light of Art. 19 of the TEU

The CJEU's role in building a European standard of effective judicial protection, in accordance with Art. 19(1), Para. 1 of the TEU, consists of ensuring that the law is respected in the application and interpretation of the treaties. This provision serves as a guarantee of the member states' fulfilment of their obligation to provide the measures necessary for this protection by means of national legal protection mechanisms. The equivalent of this obligation of the member states is the right of individuals to have full access to an effective remedy and to an impartial court under Art. 47 of the Charter.[3] It should be emphasised that in the modern world, supranational processes have an increasingly intensive impact on the functioning of nation-states. The role of supranational judicial bodies is gaining in importance. As a supranational organisation,

3 Under Art. 6 of the TEU, the EU Charter of Fundamental Rights has a binding force equal to that of the Treaties, which formally confirms that the right of individuals in Art. 47 of the EU Charter of Fundamental Rights is part of the catalogue of EU fundamental rights and therefore has the status of a general principle of law. In this spirit, see the CJEU judgement of 4 June 2013, *C-300/11 ZZ v. Secretary of State for the Home Department*, ECLI:EU:C:2013:363.

the EU serves as a tool for influencing these processes through traditional structures and mechanisms of democratically legitimised power. Not only do the EU judicial bodies exercise influence with their decisions on the functioning of integration structures, but they do so more intensively on national legal orders, which makes them occupy a special position.[4] On one hand, EU rulings influence globalisation processes by controlling these in some way; on the other hand, they are accused of unjustified interference in a state's legal order and of going beyond the scope of their areas of competence. Currently, when national constitutional law fails and, in particular, when a state's constitution does not provide effective mechanisms as safeguards to defend such values as judicial accountability provided by principles of democracy and the separation of powers, as well as the rule of law, EU member states and their citizens are compelled to invoke EU law.

The organisation of the national judicial system, previously deemed to be essentially the domain of national sovereignty, is enshrined in the guarantees of the EU principle of effective judicial protection before national courts, resulting from Art. 19(1), Para. 2 of the TEU, and the scope of protection of the right to an independent court, resulting from Art. 47 of the Charter. In the important CJEU judgement of 27 July 2018 in case C-64/16 *Associação Sindical dos Juízes Portugueses*,[5] the case law emphasised the EU law's potential to defend the rule of law in the member states through the possibility of applying the rule of law clause in Art. 19 of the TEU, establishing the principle of effective judicial protection before national courts. This provision facilitates the enforcement of rule of law standards against EU member states compared to the enforcement of Art. 47 of the Charter.[6] In the future, Art. 19, para. 1 of the TEU could be enforced by means of infringement proceedings under Art. 268 of the TFEU to counteract the undermining of judicial independence at the national level. According to Art. 2 of the TEU, the EU is founded on values, such as the rule of law, that are common to the member states in a society in which, inter alia, justice prevails. In this regard, it should be noted that mutual trust between the member states and, in particular, their courts and tribunals is based on the fundamental premise that the member states share a set of common values on which the EU is founded, as stated in Art. 2 of the TEU.[7] Art. 19 of the TEU, which gives concrete expression to the value of the rule of law stated in Art. 2, entrusts the responsibility for ensuring judicial review in the EU legal order not only to the Court of Justice but also to national courts and tribunals.[8] The member states are therefore obliged, by

4 *See* Anna Kalisz, *Wykładnia i stosowanie prawa wspólnotowego* (Wolters Kluwer Polska 2007).
5 ECLI:EU:C:2018:117.
6 Michał Krajewski, 'Associação Sindical Dos Juízes Portugueses: The Court of Justice and Athena's Dilemma' (2018) 3(1) *Eur Papers* 395–407.
7 Para. 30 of the C-64/16 judgement of the CJEU.
8 Para. 32 of the C-64/16 judgement of the CJEU.

reason, inter alia, of the principle of sincere cooperation set out in Art. 4(3), Subpara. 1 of the TEU to ensure the application of and respect for EU law in their respective territories. In the same vein, as provided for in Art. 19(1), Subpara. 2 of the TEU, member states have to provide sufficient remedies to guarantee effective judicial protection for individual parties in the fields covered by EU law. Therefore, it is for the member states' obligation to establish a system of legal remedies and procedures, ensuring effective judicial review in those fields.[9] In this regard, the CJEU notes that in assessing whether a body is a 'court or [a] tribunal', the following factors, inter alia, should be considered: whether the body is established by law, whether it is permanent, whether its jurisdiction is compulsory, whether its procedure is *inter partes*, whether it applies rules of law and whether it is independent.[10] The guarantee of independence, inherent in the task of adjudication, is required not only at the EU level as regards the Judges of the Union and the Advocates-General of the CJEU, as provided for in Art. 19(2), Subpara. 3 of the TEU, but also at the member-state level as regards national courts.[11] The concept of independence presupposes, in particular, that the body concerned wholly exercises its judicial functions autonomously, without being subject to any hierarchical constraint or subordinated to any other body and without taking orders or instructions from any source whatsoever, and that it is thus protected against external interventions or pressure liable to impair its members' independent judgement and influence their decisions.[12]

Disciplinary responsibility of judges in the context of the violation of the ban on holding judges accountable for the content of their judgements

On numerous occasions, the CJEU has had the opportunity to comment on the relation between EU law and national regulations on disciplinary proceedings, setting fairly clear standards that apply to national legislators in this respect. Disciplinary responsibility prevents the abuse of official supervision over a judge. Court administration bodies may not, in any form, apply penalties to judges that may only be imposed as a result of initiated disciplinary proceedings. In the event that a disciplinary offence also meets the criteria for a crime, disciplinary responsibility is fully independent, meaning that a judge

9 Para. 34 of the C-64/16 judgement of the CJEU.

10 Para. 38 of the C-64/16 judgement of the CJEU.

11 Para. 42 of the C-64/16 judgement of the CJEU.

12 Para. 44 of the C-64/16 judgement of the CJEU. See also Jacek Barcik, 'Niezawisłość sędziowska jako wartość konstytucyjna Unii Europejskiej. Glosa do wyroku TS z 27.02.2018 r., C-64/16, Associação Sindical dos Juízes Portugueses' (2018) 5 *EPS* 23–29; Matteo Bonelli and Monica Claes, 'Judicial Serendipity: How Portuguese Judges Came to the Rescue of the Polish Judiciary: ECJ 27 February 2018, Case C-64/16, Associação Sindical dos Juízes Portugueses' (2018) 14(3) *EU Const* 622–643.

who is held criminally responsible is not released from professional accountability. A judge is therefore independently liable to both criminal and disciplinary responsibility. The disciplinary court makes an independent assessment of an act recognised in a final judgement as a crime in terms of determining whether it also constitutes a disciplinary offence.[13] Currently, dealing with a constitutional crisis, whose source is perceived as a violation of the constitutional principles that form the basis of judicial power. The limitation of the independence of courts is manifested in the lack of compliance with the provisions of the national constitution, the change in the role of the law, which becomes the exclusive instrument for achieving political goals because unconstitutional statutory revisions lead to the replacements of presidents of common courts and changes in the substantive, procedural and structural bases of disciplinary proceedings.

In the Polish legal system, the issue of responsibility of court judges[14] is regulated by the Act of 27 July 2001 – Law on Common Courts Organisation (Journal of Laws of 2020, item 365), as amended (hereinafter, LCCO), containing provisions enforcing criminal responsibility (by regulating the procedure for waiving immunity) and disciplinary responsibility for misconduct in office. The previous wording of the LCCO provided for disciplinary responsibility of a judge for misconduct in office, including obvious and gross violations of legal provisions and detriment to the dignity of the office (the so-called disciplinary misconduct).[15] Under the so-called Muzzle Act (also

13 See Supreme Court judgement of 27 February 2008, file reference SNO 7/08, OSNSD 2008, item 31, LEX 1288974, and Jarem Sawiński, 'Komentarz do Art. 107' in Antoni Górski (ed.), *Prawo o ustroju sądów powszechnych. Komentarz* (LEX 2013) and the literature cited therein. A disciplinary offence may in principle only concern procedural provisions that are not directly related to adjudication itself. In turn, recognition of a disciplinary offence with respect to the interpretation and application of substantive law in the decision-making process would conflict with the constitutional principle of independence under Art. 178(1) of the Polish Constitution of 1997. *See* Maciej Szuleka and Małgorzata Kalisz, 'Disciplinary Proceedings Against Judges and Prosecutors' *Helsinki Foundation of Human Rights* (2019) <https://archiwum.hfhr.pl/wp-content/uploads/2019/02/HFHR_Disciplinary-proceedings-against-judges-and-prosecutors.pdf> accessed 18 August 2024.

14 In Poland, judges do not form a single and uniform corps of judges operating based on the same legal regulations but function according to separate legal acts, although connected by numerous references to acts. For example, Art. 43 of the Act of 25 June 2015 on the Constitutional Tribunal (Journal of Law of 2015, item 1064) referred, in matters not regulated, to the rights and obligations and disciplinary responsibility of judges of the Constitutional Tribunal to the appropriate application of the provisions concerning the rights and obligations and disciplinary responsibility of judges of the Supreme Court (currently the Act of 30 November 2016 on the Status of the Judges of the Constitutional Tribunal (Journal of Law of 2018, item 1422), and the Act of 23 November 2002 on the Supreme Court (Journal of Law of 2013, item 499, as amended) referred, in matters not regulated, to the appropriate application of the provisions of the Act of 27 July 2001 – Law on Common Courts Organisation (Journal of Laws of 2020, item 365), currently the Act of 8 December 2017 on the Supreme Court (Journal of Law of 2024, item 622).

15 The indicated normative content of Art. 107 of the LCCO was in force from 1 October 2001 to 14 February 2020 (Act of 27 July 2001, LCCO (Journal of Law of 2019, item 52).

known as the Act Disciplining Judges) of 20 December 2019 amending the Act – Law on Common Courts Organisation, the Act on the Supreme Court and certain other acts (Journal of Laws of 2020, item 190), Art. 107 of the LCCO was amended. Currently, disciplinary responsibility covers – apart from obvious and gross violations of legal provisions (point 1 of Art. 107, §1 of the LCCO) – actions or abandonments that can disable or relevantly obstruct the functioning of a judiciary organ/body (point 2 of Art. 107, §1 of the LCCO); actions that question the office status of a judge, the effectiveness of the appointment of a judge or the legitimacy of the constitutional body of the state (point 3 of Art. 107, §1 of the LCCO); public activities incompatible with the principles of independence of the judiciary and judges (point 4 of Art. 107, §1 of the LCCO – corresponding to Art. 178(3) of the Polish Constitution of 1997); and impairment of the authority of the office (point 5 of Art. 107, §1 of the LCCO). Pursuant to point 4a of Art. 4 of the Act of 9 June 2022 amending the Act on the Supreme Court and certain other acts (Journal of Laws of 2022, item 1259), another ground for disciplinary responsibility for official (disciplinary) misconduct was introduced in point 1a of Art. 107, §1 of the LCCO, that is, for refusing to administer justice. In the above-mentioned manner, derogations from the prohibition of holding judges liable for issued judgements have acquired a statutory basis, being of a systemic and universal nature.[16]

The legal responsibility of judges has always been a significant issue. Judges are subject to disciplinary responsibility for acts related to the performance of their office. The sources of disciplinary responsibility are disciplinary torts that violate the dignity of the judges' office unrelated to the performance of their office and offences related to the performance of their office. Transferring the responsibility of a judge to the level of disciplinary proceedings does not eliminate the conflict between the independence and the responsibility of a judge for violating the law. There is no precise definition of a disciplinary offence in the Poland's legal doctrine and case law. Nevertheless, the Polish Supreme Court judgement of 18 June 2015, SNO 31/15, emphasised that a disciplinary offence consists of a judge's breach of specific duties, which is an obvious and flagrant offence against the provisions. However, there is uncertainty regarding the possibility of recognising an incorrect interpretation or a wrong application of the provisions as a basis for the content of the issued judgement as a disciplinary tort. Until recently, such events were considered disciplinary

16 Piotr Tuleja, 'Odpowiedzialność dyscyplinarna sędziego za wydane orzeczenie jako instrument naruszenia sędziowskiej niezależności' in Adam Bodnar and Adam Ploszka (eds), ***Wokół kryzysu praworządności, demokracji i praw człowieka: księga jubileuszowa Profesora Mirosława Wyrzykowskiego*** (Wolters Kluwer 2020) 344–345; Mirosław Wróblewski, 'Polski system odpowiedzialności dyscyplinarnej sędziów w świetle standardów prawa Unii Europejskiej' (2020) 4(56) *PPK* 183–200; Michał Laskowski, 'Granice wolności wypowiedzi sędziów w warunkach kryzysu praworządności' (2023) 3 *PS* 7–17.

torts only in exceptional cases.[17] It should be pointed out that disciplinary responsibility for a judgement issued under Art. 107, §1 of the LCCO was admissible if it met two requirements. First, the error in the interpretation of the law had to be an obvious violation of the provisions that could be clearly established without a deeper analysis. Second, the error in the application of the law had to cause gross consequences, consisting of a significant violation of a person's rights. In turn, regarding criminal responsibility (the so-called formal immunity), judges were responsible for their actions related to the exercise of their office, their conduct that had the characteristics of a crime and their actions beyond sentencing. Against this background, legal scholars raised the question of whether the basis for a judge's criminal responsibility could also be Art. 231 of the Polish Penal Code[18] when the charge of exceeding powers or breaching duties concerned the content of the issued judgement. In Poland, until recently, holding a judge criminally liable for the content of an issued judgement was rare.[19] Both criminal responsibility and disciplinary responsibility result in similar limitations on judicial independence. Since the enactment of the Polish Constitution of 1997, its provisions have been consistently interpreted and excluded criminal or disciplinary responsibility of judges for the content of an issued judgement.[20] Judges certainly cannot constitute a group exempt from legal responsibility, but such responsibility may violate their independence. In this context, the legal responsibility of judges may violate the right to an independent and impartial court. Determining the scope of substantive and formal liability of judges is a challenge, as is establishing appropriate procedural standards of responsibility.[21]

In this context, attention should be paid first to the CJEU judgement of 5 June 2023 in case C-204/21,[22] concerning, inter alia, the Muzzle Act. The judgement states that the CJEU has full control of a member state's compliance with values and principles, such as the rule of law, effective judicial protection and judicial independence. In these circumstances, there is no ground for maintaining that the requirements for both accession to and participation in the EU, arising from the respect for values and principles such as the rule of law, effective judicial protection and judicial independence, enshrined in Art. 2

17 *See* judgement of the Supreme Court of 16 June 2016, SNO 21/16, LEX 2064239 and judgement of the Supreme Court of 27 June 2002, SNO 18/02, LEX 470242.

18 Act of 6 June 1997, the Penal Code (Journal of Law 2024, item 17 with amendments).

19 *See* the resolution of the Supreme Court of 30 August 2013, file reference SNO 19/13, LEX 1375241 – the Supreme Court recognises the responsibility of a judge for the content of a judgement under Art. 231 of the Penal Code as *ultima ratio*, that is, as the final remedy.

20 *See* judgement of the Constitutional Tribunal of 24 June 1998, K 3/98 OTK 1998/4, item 52 and judgement of the Supreme Court of 22 February 2007, SNO 6/07, OSNSD 2007, item 6.

21 *See especially* Maciej Jakub Zieliński, *Niezależność władzy sądowniczej a model stosunku służbowego sędziego* (Wolters Kluwer 2024).

22 ECLI:EU:C:2023:442.

and Art. 19(1), Subpara. 2 of the TEU, are capable of affecting the national identity of a member state, within the meaning of Art. 4(2) of the TEU. Therefore, the latter provision, which must be read by taking into account the provisions, of the same rank, enshrined in Art. 2 and Art. 19(1), Subpara. 2 of the TEU, cannot exempt member states from the obligation to comply with the requirements arising from those provisions.[23] Thus, the CJEU has held that as apparent from Art. 4(2) of the TEU, although the EU respects the separate national identities of the member states – inherent in their fundamental political and constitutional structures, such that they enjoy a certain degree of discretion in implementing the principles of the rule of law – it in no way follows that such an obligation as to the result to be achieved may vary from one member state to another. The member states adhere to their shared concept of the rule of law as a value common to their own constitutional traditions, which they have undertaken to respect at all times.[24]

The mere prospect of exposing judges, who are supposed to apply EU law, to the risk that a body such as the Disciplinary Chamber of the Supreme Court in Poland could rule on issues concerning the status of judges and the exercise of their office – particularly by authorising the holding of criminal proceedings or the detention of a judge or by issuing rulings on important aspects of labour law, social security or retirement applicable to judges – may undermine their independence. Poland has failed to comply with its obligations to guarantee the independence and impartiality of the Disciplinary Chamber, even though that chamber, as a 'court or tribunal', forms part of the Polish judicial system in the 'fields covered by EU law', within the meaning of that provision, and has been accorded exclusive jurisdiction to rule in certain cases concerning the status and performance of judges' duties, which is liable to affect their independence.[25] In this respect, the interim order of 14 July 2021, which required Poland to immediately suspend the application of national provisions relating specifically to the powers of the Disciplinary Chamber of the Supreme Court, was pivotal. Pending the final judgement of 5 June 2023 in case C-204/21 (the Final Judgement), all of the European Commission's (hereinafter, Commission) requests have been upheld. The Commission filed a motion with the Supreme Court, in the proceedings concerning interim measures against Poland, issuing the following requirements: (1) Suspend, first, the application of the provisions under which the Disciplinary Chamber is competent to rule on cases concerning authorisation to hold judges and assessors criminally liable or to temporarily arrest, detain or forcibly bring them into custody, and, second, to suspend the effects of the resolutions already issued by the Disciplinary

23 Para. 72 of the C-204/21 judgement of the CJEU.

24 Para. 73 of the C-204/21 judgement of the CJEU; see *also* CJEU judgement of 16 February 2022, *Hungary v. Parliament and Council*, C-156/21, EU:C:2022:97, Para. 233–234.

25 Para. 84 of C-204/21 judgement of the CJEU.

Chamber authorising the holding of a judge criminally liable or his/her temporary arrest, as well as to refrain from referring the above-mentioned cases for examination by a judicial body that does not meet the requirements of independence indicated in particular in the aforementioned judgement in the A.K. case.[26] (2) Suspend the application of the provisions under which the Disciplinary Chamber is competent to adjudicate in cases concerning the status of judges of the Supreme Court and their performance of their duties, particularly in cases about labour law and social security concerning judges of the Supreme Court and in cases involving the retirement of judges of the Supreme Court, and to refrain from referring these cases for examination by a judicial body that does not meet the requirements of independence indicated, particularly in the above-mentioned judgement in the A.K. case. (3) Suspend the application of the provisions permitting disciplinary proceedings against judges for examining whether the requirements of independence and impartiality of a court previously established under the Muzzle Act have been met. (4) Suspend the application of national provisions to the extent that they prohibit national courts from examining compliance with the EU requirements concerning an independent and impartial tribunal previously established by law. (5) Suspend the application of provisions transferring the examination of allegations of a judge's or a tribunal's lack of independence to the exclusive competence of the Extraordinary Control and Public Affairs Chamber. (6) Inform the Commission, no later than one month from the notification of the order (of the Vice President) of the Polish Constitutional Tribunal of all the measures it has adopted to fully comply with that order. Due to the broad and imprecise nature of the provisions of the Muzzle Act and the specific context in which they were enacted, they may be subject to an interpretation that allows the application of the system of disciplinary liability of judges and the penalties provided for in that system. The purpose is to prevent national courts from assessing whether a court or a judge meets the requirements of EU law related to effective judicial protection (if necessary, also by referring the so-called preliminary questions to the CJEU). Consequently, these provisions are contrary to EU law.

Concerning the rules governing the disciplinary regime applicable to judges, it thus follows from the settled case law of the Court that the requirement of independence derived from EU law, and, in particular, from Art. 19(1), Subpara. 2 of the TEU, means that such regime must provide the necessary guarantees to prevent any risk of its being used as a system of political control over the content of judicial decisions. In this regard, rules that define both the conduct amounting to disciplinary offences and the penalties actually applicable, rules that provide for the involvement of an independent body in accordance

26 Judgment of the Court (Grand Chamber) of 19 November 2019 in the joined cases C-585/18, C-624/18 and C-625/18 *A. K. and Others v. Sąd Najwyższy, CP v. Sąd Najwyższy and DO v. Sąd Najwyższy*, ECLI:EU:C:2019:982 (hereinafter, A. K. case).

with a procedure that fully safeguards the rights enshrined in Arts 47 and 48 of the Charter, especially the rights of the defence, and rules that lay down the possibility of bringing legal proceedings challenging the disciplinary bodies' decisions constitute a set of guarantees that are essential for safeguarding the judiciary's independence.[27] It should also be emphasised that national provisions requiring judges to submit a written declaration indicating their membership in an association, involvement in a foundation that does not conduct economic activity or membership in a political party, as well as to provide the same information in electronic form,[28] violate the judges' fundamental rights to the protection of their personal data and respect for their private lives. Their provision of such information in electronic form could enable free access to the said data by persons who, for reasons unrelated to the declared objective of general interest, seek to obtain information about the personal situation of a judge. According to the Commission, in so far as those national provisions require the judges of the various courts concerned to submit a written declaration concerning their membership in an association, a non-profit foundation or a political party, as well as the positions held therein, and require the publication of such information in the *Biuletyn Informacji Publicznej*, these involve the processing of personal data, since such information concerns clearly identified natural persons acting in the private sphere. Furthermore, the Commission submits that the collection and publication of those personal data fall outside the scope of the organisation of justice and, in any event, any functional link between those data and the performance of judicial office does not allow such measures to be excluded from the scope of the General Data Protection Regulation (GDPR). Those measures are intended to influence the careers of judges and the performance of their duties and are liable to affect their independence, whereas the protection of that office should be guaranteed under Art. 19(1), Subpara. 2 of the TEU when those judges are called upon to apply and interpret EU law. The personal data at issue also fall under the category of sensitive data subject to the regime of prohibition and enhanced protection established in Art. 9(1) of the GDPR, as data capable of revealing the political opinions or philosophical beliefs of the judges concerned.[29]

27 Para. 95 of the C-204/21 judgement of the CJEU; *see also* the CJEU judgement of 15 July 2021, *Commission v. Poland (Disciplinary regime for judges)*, C791/19, EU:C:2021:596, Para. 61 and the cited case law.

28 Art. 88a of the amended Law relating to the ordinary courts (LCCO), Art. 45(3) of the amended Law on the Supreme Court and Art. 8(2) of the amended Law relating to the administrative courts infringe Art. 7 and Art. 8(1) of the EU Charter of the Fundamental Rights and points (c) and (e) of Art. 6(1), Subpara. 1, Art. 6(3) and Art. 9(1) of the General Data Protection Regulation (GDPR) 2016/679 of the European Parliament and of the Council of 27 April 2016 on the protection of natural persons regarding the processing of personal data and on the free movement of such data and repealing Directive 95/46/EC.

29 Paras. 294–296 of the C-204/21 judgement of the CJEU.

The CJEU's role in building EU standards of individual judicial accountability

The dialogue between national constitutional courts and the CJEU occasionally turns into a serious conflict on the international stage. EU judges are taking an increasingly active part in the development of European integration. Since the beginning of the functioning of the CJEU (formerly known as the European Court of Justice (ECJ)) judicial body, and certainly at least since the judgement of 5 February 1963 in case C-26/62 *Van Gend en Loos*, they have perceived themselves as guardians and promoters of EU values. While EU institutions such as the Council or the Parliament make decisions through political channels, the CJEU is the only body authorised to legally interpret and rule on the validity of EU law.[30] CJEU judges often make decisions that are not just readings of treaties but, in fact, also law-making activities. Judicial decisions constitute the legitimacy of the entire European integration project. The effectiveness of the EU judicial body seems extremely desirable in the context of protecting democracy in the member states.[31]

The CJEU case law contains direct indications regarding EU standards of disciplinary proceedings regarding the prohibition of holding judges liable for the content of their judgements. The analysis of the CJEU case law should begin with a reference to the CJEU judgement of 25 July 2018, *Minister for Justice and Equality (Deficiencies in the system of justice)*, C-216/18 *LM PP*,[32] which emphasised that due to the principle of judicial independence, national disciplinary regulations concerning judges guarantee the impossibility of using these proceedings to politically influence the content of judicial decisions. In turn, the CJEU judgement of 24 June 2019, in case C-619/18 *Commission v Poland (Independence of the Supreme Court)*,[33] emphasised that preventing or hindering the use of the preliminary ruling procedure, similar to preventing the execution of a preliminary ruling issued by the CJEU, may be the subject of proceedings under Art. 258 of the TFEU.[34]

In the scope of the issue of initiating disciplinary explanatory proceedings in connection with the national court's referral of a preliminary ruling to the

30 *See* Agnieszka Sołtys, *Obowiązek wykładni prawa krajowego zgodnie z prawem unijnym jako instrument zapewnienia efektywności prawa UE* (Wolters Kluwer 2015).

31 *See* Roberto Adam, Marek Safjan and Antonio Tizzano, *Zarys prawa Unii Europejskiej* (Wolters Kluwer 2014); Anna Zawidzka-Łojek, 'Trybunał Sprawiedliwości Unii Europejskiej na straży przestrzegania prawa unijnego' in Jan Barcz and Anna Zawidzka-Łojek (eds), *Sądowe mechanizmy ochrony praworządności w Polsce w świetle najnowszego orzecznictwa Trybunału Sprawiedliwości UE* (Dom Wydawniczy ELIPSA 2018).

32 ECLI:EU:C:2018:586.

33 ECLI:EU:C:2019:531, Para. 77.

34 *See also* Paweł Filipek, 'Nieusuwalność sędziów i granice kompetencji państwa członkowskiego do regulowania krajowego wymiaru sprawiedliwości – uwagi w świetle wyroku Trybunału Sprawiedliwości z 24.06.2019 r., C-619/18 Komisja Europejska przeciwko Rzeczypospolitej Polskiej' (2019) 12 *EPS* 4–14.

CJEU regarding the judges sitting on the bench of the court that referred the question, it is crucial to mention the preliminary ruling submitted to the CJEU by the Regional Court in Łódź and the Regional Court in Warsaw regarding the new system of disciplinary measures against judges in Poland. Of significance in this respect was the CJEU judgement of 26 March 2020 in the joined cases C-558/16 and C-563/18, which emphasised that the mere prospect (as the case may be) of being the subject of disciplinary proceedings as a result of making such a reference or deciding to maintain it after it was made would likely undermine the effective exercise of the discretion and the functions of the national judges concerned.[35] In this context, it is important to note (as is clear from the CJEU settled case law) that the keystone of the judicial system established by the TFEU is the preliminary ruling procedure provided for in Art. 267 of the TFEU, which, by setting up a dialogue between one court and another, between the CJEU and the courts and tribunals of the member states, has the object of securing uniformity in the interpretation of EU law, thereby serving to ensure its consistency, full effect and autonomy, as well as, ultimately, the particular nature of the law established by the EU Treaties.[36]

In turn, regarding the issue of judicial enforcement of the CJEU's preliminary ruling, it is necessary to point out the disciplinary proceedings initiated against Judge Paweł Juszczyszyn and the judges from Kraków and Katowice, in connection with the actions they took to assess the correctness of the appointment of the National Council of the Judiciary (NCJ) according to the criteria formulated by the CJEU.[37] The culmination of the CJEU's interpretation of the principle of effective judicial protection and the right to an independent court, arising from Art. 19(1), Subpara. 2 of the TEU and Art. 47 of the Charter, is the CJEU judgement of 19 November 2019 in the joined cases C-585/18, C-624/18 and C-625/18 *A.K. v National Council of the Judiciary*.[38] Its first national implementation, that is, execution by the referring court, using the criteria for resolving the case presented by the CJEU, was the judgement of the Supreme Court of 5 December 2019, file reference III PO 7/18, in the scope concerning disciplinary proceedings, the most important of which are the theses of the CJEU judgement regarding the status of the Disciplinary Chamber of the Supreme Court as a 'court' within the meaning of EU law and consequently within the meaning of national law.[39] Along with the reform of the judiciary, a change was made to the system of electing members of the NCJ in Poland.[40] The NCJ has some additional powers regarding the judiciary, namely to safeguard the independence of courts and

35 Para. 58 of the C-558/16 judgement of the CJEU.

36 Para. 55 of the C-558/16 judgement of the CJEU.

37 ECLI:EU:C:2019:982.

38 ECLI:EU:C:2019:982.

39 *See also* Anna Rakowska-Trela, 'Sądy i sędziowie wobec niedemokratycznych przemian', (2018) 47 *Studia Politologiczne* 299–315.

40 Act of 8 December 2017 amending the Act on the National Council of the Judiciary (NCJ) and certain other acts (Journal of Laws of 2018, item 3) abolished the model established

judges (Art. 186(1) of the Polish Constitution of 1997), select a disciplinary prosecutor for judges and express an opinion in the case of the dismissal of the president of a court.[41] Currently, the NCJ's members are elected by the Sejm (first chamber of the parliament). This kind of solution must be assessed as incompatible with Art. 187(1) of the Polish Constitution of 1997, which in this provision, limits the Sejm's appointment function to the election of four deputies of the NCJ and is inconsistent with Art. 186(1), which states that the NCJ 'shall safeguard the independence of courts and judges'.[42] By the NCJ resolution of 27 July 2019, a negative opinion was issued in the case of the judge with the initials A.K. regarding the latter's further holding of the position of judge of the Supreme Administrative Court. Judge A.K. filed an appeal against the above resolution, indicating a violation of Art. 19(1), Para. 2 of the TEU and Art. 47, Para. 2 of the Charter, whose provisions establish the principle of effective judicial protection and thus oppose the arbitrary retirement of a judge solely because he has reached the age (i.e. 65 years) required by law, in a situation where, when he took up the function of a judge of the Supreme Administrative Court, the retirement occurred only after reaching the age of 70. Art. 47 of the Code of Criminal Procedure and Art. 9, para. 1 of Council Directive 2000/78/EC of 27 November 2000, establishing a general framework for equal treatment in employment and occupation must be interpreted as precluding disputes concerning the application of EU law from falling within the exclusive jurisdiction of a body that is not an independent and impartial tribunal within the meaning of the first of those provisions.

The latter situation occurs when the objective circumstances in which the body in question was created and its characteristics, as well as the manner in which its members were appointed, are such that they raise justified doubts regarding the independence of that body from external factors, particularly from the direct or indirect influence of the legislative and executive powers, and its neutrality concerning the interests before it, and thus the lack of any appearance of independence or impartiality on the part of that body, which could undermine the confidence that the judiciary must inspire in individuals in a democratic society. It is for the referring court to determine, taking into account all the relevant information available to it, whether that is the case with regard to a body such as the Disciplinary Chamber of the Supreme Court. If that were the case, the principle of primacy of EU law should be interpreted as requiring the referring court to disapply the provision of national law

in 1990, according to which the judicial self-government elected 15 judge-members of the NCJ.

41 Art. 3 of the statute of 12 May 2011 on the NCJ.

42 Piotr Mikuli, 'An Explicit Constitutional Change by Means of an Ordinary Statute? On a Bill Concerning the Reform of the National Council of the Judiciary in Poland' *Int J Const L Blog* (23 February 2017) <https://verfassungsblog.de/an-explicit-constitutional-change-by-means-of-an-ordinary-statute-on-a-bill-concerning-the-reform-of-the-national-council-of-the-judiciary-in-poland/> accessed 17 August 2024.

that reserves the jurisdiction to hear the disputes in the main proceedings to such a body, so that those disputes may be heard by a court that satisfies the above-mentioned requirements of independence and impartiality and would have jurisdiction in the relevant field, were that provision not prevent it. The CJEU emphasised that the assessment of the independence of the Disciplinary Chamber of the Supreme Court should take into account all legal and factual circumstances – even if individual elements did not determine the lack of independence of that chamber, their cumulative confluence and joint assessment might justify the finding that the chamber did not meet the required standard. Using the criteria formulated by the CJEU for the assessment of a body such as the Disciplinary Chamber of the Supreme Court, the Supreme Court, in the above judgement, ruled that the chamber was not a court within the meaning of Art. 47 of the Charter, Art. 6 of the European Convention on Human Rights and Art. 45(1) of the Polish Constitution of 1997. As a result of this ruling, the Supreme Court refused to apply the provisions of the Supreme Court Act, assuming the exclusive jurisdiction of the Disciplinary Chamber of the Supreme Court to decide the case of Judge A.K.[43] As Piotr Mikuli and Maciej Pach rightly point out in Poland's case, the creation of the Disciplinary Chamber of the Supreme Court, staffed in violation of the constitution by lawyers connected with the ruling party, was nothing else than establishing an external political machine of harassment and intimidation.[44]

In another judgement concerning the compatibility of the Polish system of disciplinary responsibility of judges with EU law, in the CJEU judgement of 15 July 2021 in case C-791/19 *European Commission v Republic of Poland*,[45] the Commission found it inadmissible that Polish national law allowed the possibility that the right of courts to refer preliminary references to the CJEU was limited by the possibility of initiating disciplinary proceedings. The Commission initiated infringement proceedings against Poland, alleging the latter's failure to fulfil the obligations arising from Art. 19(1), Subpara. 2 of the TEU and Arts 267(2) and (3) of the TFEU. The CJEU stated that the requirement of independence and impartiality derived from, inter alia, Art. 19(1), Subpara. 2 of the TEU – which must be met by national courts or tribunals that (similar to the Polish ordinary courts) may be called upon to interpret and apply EU

43 The Resolution of the Supreme Court in a joint composition of the Civil Chamber, the Criminal Chamber and the Labour Law and Social Security Chamber of 23 January 2020, file reference BSA I-4110-1/20, which constitutes a binding decision of all compositions of the Supreme Court on the manner of national implementation of the CJEU judgement of 19 November 2019 in joined cases C-585/18, C-624/18 and C-625/18 *A. K. v. National Council of the Judiciary*, ECLI:EU:C:2019:982. *See* Agnieszka Grzelak and Andrzej Sakowicz, 'Wymóg niezależności sądu krajowego jako element skutecznej ochrony sądowej (uwagi na tle wyroku TS z 19.11.2019 r. dla polskiego wymiaru sprawiedliwości)' (2020) 5 *PiP* 59–77.

44 Piotr Mikuli and Maciej Pach, 'Disciplinary Liability of Judges: The Polish Case' in Piotr Mikuli and Grzegorz Kuca (eds), *Accountability and the Law: Rights, Authority and Transparency of Public Power* (Routledge 2022).

45 ECLI:EU:C:2021:596.

law – requires such a regime to include rules defining the forms of conduct constituting a disciplinary offence. The reason is to avoid any risk that the disciplinary regime applicable to those whose task is to adjudicate would be used as a system of political control over the content of judicial decisions.[46] The CJEU responded in this way to four allegations. In its first allegation, the Commission found an inadmissible failure to guarantee the independence and impartiality of the Disciplinary Chamber of the Supreme Court, which is responsible for reviewing decisions issued in disciplinary proceedings against judges (Art. 3(5), Art. 27 and Art. 73, § 1 of the new Law on the Supreme Court in conjunction with Art. 9a of the Law on the NCJ). In its second allegation, the Commission submitted that it was incompatible with EU law that the content of judicial decisions might be classified as a disciplinary offence involving judges of common courts by allowing the content of judicial decisions to be classified as a disciplinary offence involving judges of the ordinary courts (Art. 107, § 1 of the Law on the ordinary courts and Art. 97, §§ 1 and 3 of the new Law on the Supreme Court).

In this judgement (C-791/19), it was stated that in defining the forms of conduct constituting a disciplinary offence on the part of judges of the ordinary courts as covering, respectively, any 'obvious and gross violations of the law' and any 'error' entailing an 'obvious violation of the law', Art. 107, § 1 of the Law on the ordinary courts and Art. 97, §§ 1 and 3 of the new Law on the Supreme Court permit such political control, as evidenced by the various specific cases where those provisions have been applied that have been referred to by that institution.[47] In this regard, as should be noted at the outset, it is true that the disciplinary regime applicable to judges falls within the organisation of justice and therefore within the member states' competence, and, in particular, the possibility that a member state's authorities may raise the issue that the disciplinary responsibility of judges can, inter alia, depending on the member states' choice, be a factor that contributes to the accountability and effectiveness of the judicial system. However, in exercising that competence, the member states must comply with EU law by safeguarding, inter alia, the independence of the courts called upon to rule on questions concerning the application or interpretation of EU law in order to ensure the effective judicial protection of individuals as required by Art. 19(1), Subpara. 2 of the TEU.[48] In its third allegation, the Commission considered that EU law had been infringed by conferring on the President of the Disciplinary Chamber the discretionary power to designate the disciplinary tribunal with jurisdiction at first instance in cases concerning judges of the ordinary courts (Art. 110, § 3 and

46 Para. 134 of the C-791/19 judgement of the CJEU. *See also* Marek Skwarcow, 'Odpowiedzialność dyscyplinarna sędziów oraz postępowanie przed rzecznikiem dyscyplinarnym na podstawie Prawo o ustroju sądów powszechnych (po ostatnich zmianach ustawowych i wyroku Trybunału Sprawiedliwości Unii Europejskiej z 15.07.2021 r., C-791/19)' (2021) 11–12 *PS* 65–84.

47 Para. 135 of the C-791/19 judgement of the CJEU.

48 Para. 136 of the C-791/19 judgement of the CJEU.

Art. 114, § 7 of the Law on the ordinary courts) and therefore by failing to guarantee that disciplinary cases would be examined by a tribunal 'established by law'. In the fourth allegation, the Commission stated that Poland violated Art. 112b, § 5 of the Law on the ordinary courts by granting the Minister of Justice the power to appoint the Disciplinary Commissioner of the Minister of Justice and thus failing to guarantee that disciplinary cases against judges of the ordinary courts would be examined within a reasonable time. Art. 112b, § 5 of the Law on the ordinary courts was also violated by providing that actions relating to the appointment of the defence counsel and the taking up of the defence by that counsel did not have a suspensory effect on the course of the disciplinary proceedings. Additionally, the CJEU found that the disciplinary tribunal violated Art. 115a, § 3 of the Law on the ordinary courts by conducting the proceedings despite the justified absence of the notified accused judge or his or her defence counsel and therefore by failing to guarantee the respect for the right of defence of accused judges of the ordinary courts.[49]

As for the provisions regulating the system of disciplinary responsibility of judges, reference should also be made to the CJEU judgement of 18 May 2021 in joined cases C-83/19, C-127/19, C-195/19, C-291/19, C-355/19 and C-397/19 *Asociația 'Forumul Judecătorilor din România' and Others*.[50] This judgement stated that the requirement of independence of judges resulting from EU law, particularly from Art. 19(1), Subpara. 2 of the TEU, means that in accordance with settled case law, that regime must provide the necessary guarantees to prevent any risk of its being used as a system of political control over the content of judicial decisions. Rules that define both the forms of conduct amounting to disciplinary offences and the penalties actually applicable provide for the involvement of an independent body in accordance with a procedure that fully safeguards the rights enshrined in Arts. 47 and 48 of the Charter, particularly the rights of the defence, and lay down the possibility of bringing legal proceedings challenging the disciplinary bodies' decisions constitute a set of guarantees that are essential for safeguarding the judiciary's independence.[51]

Conclusions

Strengthening the independence of judges and the judiciary is currently a crucial domain. The CJEU case law provides direct indications regarding the EU standards of disciplinary proceedings, the prohibition of holding judges responsible for the content of their judgements and preventing or hindering the use of the preliminary ruling procedure by national courts. The case law presented in this

49 *See* Anna Siewierska, 'Odpowiedzialność dyscyplinarna sędziego w Polsce w świetle wyroku TS UE z 15 lipca 2021 r., C-791/19. Aspekty materialne i procesowe' (2021) 4 *RPZN* 11–28.

50 ECLI:EU:C:2021:393.

51 Para. 198 of the joined cases C-83/19, C-127/19, C-195/19, C-291/19, C-355/19 and C-397/19 judgement of the CJEU and the cited case law.

chapter has become an important element of the identity of the EU legal order as a supranational constitutional system of the rule of law in the EU.

In light of the foregoing considerations, the following findings are presented:

1 It is worth emphasising that the existing legal remedies, such as the disciplinary responsibility of judges and its legal bases, cannot pose a threat to the fundamental EU principle of the obligation to establish and apply the measures necessary to ensure effective judicial protection in areas covered by EU law.
2 Disciplinary responsibility is not the basic form of response to errors made in the adjudication process. Errors are inherently connected with the process of interpretation and application of legal provisions, and erroneous or unjustified judgements should, above all, be annulled or amended by a higher court, including the Supreme Court. The provisions amending the laws on the judiciary in Poland, particularly those concerning the meaning and scope of disciplinary responsibility of judges, were aimed at politicising judges. The idea of democracy and the principle of the separation of powers were undermined by taking political control over independent institutions and state bodies.
3 It is significant that the legal status of a judge is shaped by the principle of judicial independence, which includes a number of historically formed elements called guarantees, which have the features of the existing tradition and are confirmed in many acts of international law. In the context of the significance and scope of the disciplinary responsibility of judges, it indicates that the use of formal disciplinary proceedings against judges as a reprisal for judicial decisions has accelerated over time, creating a strong chilling effect on judicial functions and de facto establishing the political control of judges.[52]
4 The lack of systemic guarantees results in transferring constitutional disputes to the supranational level, that is, the EU. The changes regarding the disciplinary regime for judges introduced in Poland, as well as in other countries (i.e. Hungary or Romania) were inconsistent with the national constitutions and EU standards. Currently, there is a strong desire to strengthen control over the disciplinary responsibility of judges. The separation of the judiciary from the legislative and the executive powers is necessary to implement the rule of law as a safeguard for a contemporary democratic state ruled by law (by the provisions of the constitution and of judicial procedures, by the political elite and society's legal and political culture as a whole and by the jurisprudence of international courts, especially the CJEU).

52 Wojciech Sadurski, *Poland's Constitutional Breakdown* (Oxford University Press 2019) 119.

5 Challenges of disciplinary liability of judges and public prosecutors

Marina Matić Bošković and Jelena Kostić

Introduction

Each branch of government bears the responsibility of upholding the legality of its actions and safeguarding the rule of law, with the judiciary playing a pivotal role in this endeavour.[1] Judicial office holders are tasked with preserving the independence of the judiciary, ensuring that their impartiality and objectivity are maintained to protect human rights and fundamental freedoms. Their impartiality and objectivity is important for the protection of human rights and fundamental freedoms. Prosecutors, acknowledged as the gatekeepers of the courtroom, are expected to act with unwavering integrity and impartiality, exercising autonomy to uphold professional confidentiality while respecting human rights throughout the criminal proceedings.[2]

Judicial independence and prosecutorial autonomy and discretion need to be counterbalanced by a certain level of accountability.[3] The Consultative Council of European Prosecutors highlights that "accountability does not contradict the concept of independence; on the contrary, the more independence there is, the more accountability is required."[4] The concept of accountability is inherent in the rule of law. Specifically, the rule of law, inter alia, implies the

1 Jelena Kostić and Marina Matić Bošković, 'Financial Accountability and Transparency of Public Sector Institutions in the Republic of Serbia' in Piotr Mikuli and Grzegorz Kuca (eds), *Accountability and the Law, Rights, Authority and Transparency of Public Power* (Routledge 2022) 46–59; International Commission of Jurists, *International Principles of the Independence and Accountability of Judges, Lawyers and Prosecutors – a Practitioners Guide* (International Commission of Jurists 2007). <www.refworld.org/reference/manuals/icjurists/2007/en/92043> accessed 26 June 2023.

2 Marina Matić Bošković and Goran Ilić, *Javno tužilaštvo u Srbiji – Istorijski razvoj, međunarodni standardi, uporedni modeli i izazovi modernog društva* (Institute of Criminological and Sociological Research 2019).

3 *OECD, The Independence of Prosecutors in Eastern Europe, Central Asia and Asia Pacific* (OECD 2020) *<https://web-archive.oecd.org/2020-12-08/573087-The-Independence-of-Prosecutors-in-Eastern-Europe-Central-Asia-and-Asia-Pacific.pdf> accessed 26 June 2023.*

4 Consultative Council of European Prosecutors, *Report of the 22nd Meeting of the Working Group of 8–9 February 2018* (Council of Europe 2018) <https://rm.coe.int/report-of-the-22nd-meeting-of-the-ccpe-gt-8-9-february-2018-strasbourg/168089ff4f> accessed 26 June 2023.

DOI: 10.4324/9781003557852-7

mechanisms and procedures prescribed by law regulating the establishment of accountability, enhancing the transparency, fairness, integrity and predictability of conduct of the state and the state institutions.[5] Judicial independence is a precondition for achieving the political criterion of upholding public confidence.[6] When judges and public prosecutors are alleged to have failed to meet their duties, the accountability mechanism is triggered. While forms of accountability may vary from one jurisdiction to another, judicial accountability includes some or all of the following elements: evaluation of judges and public prosecutors against objective indicators, the complaints procedure, disciplinary responsibility/liability[7] and removal, recusal, work transparency including publishing periodic reports and decisions, inspections, and the audit committee.[8]

This chapter focuses on the disciplinary responsibility/liability of judges and public prosecutors. The disciplinary responsibility of the judiciary is a necessary consequence of the need for the judiciary to be accountable for their actions, and thereby ensure public trust.[9] However, it is crucial to ensure impartiality and objectivity in setting limits and determining disciplinary liability to prevent discretionary decision-making from jeopardising the independence of judges and public prosecutors.[10]

While a disciplinary regime is seen as an important component in regulating judicial and prosecutorial conduct, it should also not be used to sanction prosecutors for arbitrary or unfounded reasons.[11] In line with the European standards, disciplinary action needs to be regulated by law and governed by transparent and objective criteria, in accordance with impartial procedures,

5 Albuquerque e Silva, Gabriela Knau de, *Report of the Special Rapporteur on the Independence of Judges and Lawyers*, UN Doc. A/HRC/6/32 (28 April 2014), 5, para. 19.

6 Richard Devlin and Sheila Wildeman, *Disciplining Judges – Contemporary Challenges and Controversies* (Edward Elgar Publishing 2021) 42.

7 As noted by the editor in the introduction to this volume, the term *liability* may have some drawbacks, however in this chapter we use both terms *liability* and *responsibility* in reference to disciplinary regime of accountability of judges.

8 European Network of Councils for the Judiciary, *Independence and Accountability of Judiciary – ENCJ Report 2013–2014* (European Network of Councils for the Judiciary 2014) <www.encj.eu/images/stories/pdf/workinggroups/independence/encj_report_independence_accountability_adopted_version_sept_2014.pdf> accessed 26 June 2023.

9 The human rights standards and principles establish that "prosecutors are responsible in the performance of their duties and may be subject to disciplinary procedures," paragraph 85 of the Explanatory Note to the Rome Charter; See also the Interim report of the Special Rapporteur on the independence of judges and lawyers, A/65/274, 10 August 2010.

10 Piotr Mikuli and Maciej Pach, 'Disciplinary Liability of Judges: The Polish Case' in Piotr Mikuli and Grzegorz Kuca (eds), *Accountability and the Law, Rights, Authority and Transparency of Public Power* (Routledge 2022) 64 and 65.

11 The United Nations Office on Drugs and Crime (UNODC), *The Status and Role of Prosecutors, a United Nations Office on Drugs and Crime and International Association of Prosecutors Guide* (United Nations 2014) 32.

excluding any discrimination and allowing for impartial review.[12] Furthermore, the disciplinary system should be clear and transparent, with well-defined rules.[13] Each European country should ensure that the standards set out in the main international and human rights documents relating to judges and public prosecutors are respected. The main European standards relating to judges are specified in the Basic Principles on the Independence of the Judiciary;[14] the Bangalore Principles of Judicial Conduct;[15] Independence and Impartiality of the Judiciary, Jurors and Assessors and the Independence of Lawyers;[16] Integrity of the Judicial System;[17] the Universal Charter of the Judge;[18] the European Charter on the Statute for Judges (1998); the Magna Carta of Judges adopted by the Consultative Council of European Judges in 2020; the Recommendation on Judges: Independence, Efficiency and Responsibilities;[19] and the Report on the Independence of the Judicial System Part I: The Independence of Judges adopted by the Venice Commission at its 82nd Plenary Session (Venice, 12–13 March 2010).

The key European standards for public prosecutors are found in the UN Guidelines on the Role of Prosecutors from 1990;[20] the European Convention on Human Rights, the Recommendation of the Committee of Ministers of the Council of Europe to Member States on the role of public prosecution in the criminal justice system;[21] various opinions and a study of the Venice

12 Paragraph XII of the Rome Charter, reaffirmed in paragraph 20 of Bureau of the Consultative Council of European Prosecutors (CCPE-BU), Report on the independence and impartiality of the prosecution services in the Council of Europe Member States in 2017, CCPE-BU(2017)6; See: Marina Matic Boskovic, 'EU Court of Justice Role in Establishment of EU Judicial Standards', *EU and Comparative Law Issues and Challenges Series (ECLIC), EU 2020 – Lessons from the Past and Solutions for the Future* 4 (2020) *Faculty of Law Osijek* 329–351.

13 UNODC, *The Status and Role of Prosecutors, a United Nations Office on Drugs and Crime and International Association of Prosecutors Guide* 32.

14 Adopted by the Seventh United Nations Congress on the Prevention of Crime and the Treatment of Offenders held at Milan from 26 August to 6 September 1985 and endorsed by General Assembly resolutions 40/32 of 29 November 1985 and 40/146 of 13 December 1985.

15 Endorsed by the UN Economic and Social Council Resolution (ECOSOC Resolution) 2006/23, *Strengthening Basic Principles of Judicial Council* <www.refworld.org/legal/resolution/ecosoc/2006/en/47016> accessed 26 June 2023.

16 United Nation, Human Rights Council Resolution A/HRC/RES/44/9 on Independence and impartiality of the judiciary, jurors and assessors and the independency of lawyers (2020).

17 United Nation Human Rights Council Resolution A/HRC/RES/25/4 on the Integrity of Judicial System (2014).

18 Adopted by the International Association of Judges on 17 November 1999, and updated on 14 November 2017.

19 Recommendation CM/Rec(2010) of the Committee of Ministers of the Council of Europe on 17 November 2010.

20 Adopted by the Eighth United Nations Congress on the Prevention of Crime and the Treatment of Offenders, Havana, Cuba, 27 August to 7 September 1990 (the United Nations Guidelines).

21 Adopted by the Committee of Ministers on 6 October 2000 at the 724th meeting of the Ministers' Deputies (Recommendation Rec(2000)19).

Commission;[22] two opinions of the Consultative Council of European Prosecutors (CCPE)[23] and the recommendations by the Group of States against Corruption (GRECO);[24] the Standards of Professional Responsibility and Statement of the Essential Duties and Rights of Prosecutors adopted by the International Association of Prosecutors (IAP) in 1999;[25] a guide produced in 2014 by the IAP; and the UN Office on Drugs and Crime on the Status and Role of Prosecutors.[26] The lack of a uniform European public prosecutor model, and different structures and principles across the European jurisdiction, have influenced prosecutorial accountability. In the mandatory prosecution systems, prosecutors may be less vulnerable to pressures to terminate proceedings than in the systems where prosecutors have broader discretionary powers to drop charges. The practice shows that in both these systems, prosecutors may be subject to interferences, and it is crucial that the prosecutorial discretionary powers (e.g. entering into plea agreements or dismissing charges based on the principle of opportunity) are regulated by law and subject to a form of judicial review. Furthermore, external oversight mechanisms can also ensure that public prosecution actions are subject to public scrutiny, thus limiting the likelihood of unlawful decisions such as unduly terminating a case against a specific suspect. Such mechanisms include private prosecution (such as in Hungary or Spain) or the judicial review of decisions to terminate cases (as is the case in Lithuania or Italy).[27]

22 European Commission for Democracy Through Law (Venice Commission) *Compilation of Venice Commission Opinions and Reports Concerning Prosecutors* (CDL- PI(2018)001) (European Commission for Democracy Through Law (Venice Commission, November 2017) <www.venice.coe.int/webforms/documents/?pdf=CDL-PI(2018)001-e> accessed 26 June 2023; European Commission for Democracy Through Law (Venice Commission) *the Report on European Standards as regards the Independence of the Judicial System: Part II – The Prosecution System* (Study No. 494/2008, CDL-AD(2010)040) ((European Commission for Democracy Through Law (Venice Commission), January 2011) <https://rm.coe.int/1680700a60> accessed 26 June 2023.

23 Council of Europe, Consultative Council of European Prosecutors, *Opinion No. 4 on Judges and Prosecutors in a Democratic Society, (the Bordeaux Declaration)* (Council of Europe, Consultative Council of European Prosecutors December 2009); Council of Europe, Consultative Council of European Prosecutors, *Opinion No. 9 (2014) on European Norms and Principles Concerning Prosecutors (the Rome Charter)* (Council of Europe, Consultative Council of European Prosecutors December 2014).

24 In its Fourth Evaluation Round, concerned with issues relating to the prevention of corruption in respect of members of parliament, judges and prosecutors (Fourth Evaluation Round).

25 International Association of Prosecutors (IAP), *The Standards of Professional Responsibility and Statement of the Essential Duties and Rights of Prosecutors'* (International Association of Prosecutors April 1999). These were endorsed by the United Nations Commission on Crime Prevention and Criminal Justice (Resolution 17/2, 14–18 April 2008).

26 A United Nations Office on Drugs and Crime, *The Status and Role of Prosecutors* (The UNODC and IAP Guide 2014) <www.unodc.org/documents/justice-and-prison-reform/14-07304_ebook.pdf> accessed 26 June 2023.

27 OECD, *The Independence of Prosecutors in Eastern Europe, Central Asia and Asia Pacific* (OECD 2020) 101.

This chapter puts special attention on the EU member states, focusing on the EU-11[28] to ensure a combination of different practices and factors. The selected countries are grouped in two categories: the old EU member states and the EU-11. The old EU member states (i.e. Italy, Spain, Austria) are selected as they present good practices developed over the course of centuries with the aim to ensure the separation of powers and introduce accountability. Furthermore, different models have been taken into account: Italy and Spain are the representatives of the Southern model of Judicial Councils, while Austria is included as the country that does not have a Judicial Council. Furthermore, the position of public prosecutor in Italy and Spain is different from that in Austria. In Italy and Spain, public prosecutors are part of the magistracy and judges and public prosecutors are subject to mirroring rules. Contrary to that, public prosecutors in Austria are part of the executive branch and are subject to the rules that apply to civil servants. Irrespective of the position of public prosecutors, the selected countries respect the values of the rule of law. The EU-11 countries, Slovenia and Croatia, are thus a good example of former communist countries that have reformed their prosecution in line with the EU requirements.[29]

Independence versus accountability

Judicial independence and accountability are two fundamental values of equal importance for the rule of law.[30] While it provides an important guarantee, independence also has the potential to serve as a shield behind which judges and public prosecutors can cover up unethical behaviour. Thus, judicial independence does not mean that judges and public prosecutors are free to behave as they please. In the judicial reform debate, judicial independence and accountability are considered the values that are in tension with one another.[31] However, judicial independence is not a value in itself, and it is rather a necessary means for achieving an impartial tribunal.[32] The key dilemma is how to protect the independence of the judiciary while ensuring its accountability.[33] Europe has been witnessing abuse of disciplinary proceedings against judges and their removal because political actors disagree with their rulings. The key

28 Poland, Czech Republic, Slovakia, Slovenia, Estonia, Lithuania, Latvia, Hungary, Romania, Bulgaria and Croatia.

29 Some EU-11 countries, like Poland and Hungary, were not taken into consideration as they are facing the rule of law backsliding.

30 Shivaraj S. Huchhanavar, 'Conceptualising Judicial Independence and Accountability from a Regulatory Perspective' (2023) 9(2) *Oslo L Rev* 111.

31 Amy B. Atchison Laurence Tobe Liebert and Denise K. Russell, 'Judicial Independence and Judicial Accountability: A Selected Bibliography' (1999) 3 *South Calif L Rev* 723.

32 Francesco Contini and Richard Mohr, 'Reconciling Independence and Accountability in Judicial Systems' (2007) 3(2) *Utrecht L Rev* 28.

33 Jerold Waltman and Kenneth M. Holland (eds), *The Political Role of Law Courts in Modern Democracies* (Palgrave Macmillan 1988) 1.

challenge is to regulate adequately the disciplinary mechanism and removal based on precise grounds for disciplining and place the decision with the judiciary and public prosecution control.[34] In their paper, Mikuli and Pach refer to different modalities of competent bodies deciding on disciplinary liability. Thus, in the Federal Republic of Germany, these bodies are often established as part of regular courts, while in other countries, including the Republic of Serbia, disciplinary liability is decided by the Judicial Councils or their internal bodies; in England and Wales, there are special offices connected to judicial authorities; and in Sweden and Finland it is decided by the Ombudsman.[35] However, it is reasonable to ask whether there would be less influence on judges and prosecutors if their disciplinary liability is decided exclusively by the judges and prosecutors who are part of the disciplinary bodies. In the countries where disciplinary liability is decided by the special bodies of the Judicial Council, there is a need to consider independence and professional integrity of the Council members. If the members are appointed in a procedure that allows for political influence, it is certain that the disciplinary proceedings will be used to deal with the "disobedient" judicial office holders.

The position and role of the disciplinary body

To ensure independence, in addition to strengthening the judicial office holders' accountability, the disciplinary responsibility/liability of judges and prosecutors needs to be decided by independent bodies. Consequently, the method of appointing members of such bodies and the procedure applied when deciding on the judicial office holders' disciplinary liability are of particular importance.

The appointment of national judicial councils is important for the functioning of the judiciary as a whole, including the disciplinary proceedings against judicial office holders. Thus, in their paper, Mikuli, Kuca and Gudowska-Natanek write about the problems in the Polish judiciary relating to the appointment of the National Council of the Judiciary in violation of the constitutional provisions. Such a procedure has had implications for the status of the Supreme Court Disciplinary Chamber, whose members were appointed

34 Mark Tushnet, 'Judicial Accountability in Comparative Perspective' in Nicholas Bamforth and Peter Leyland (eds), *Accountability in the Contemporary Constitution* (Oxford University Press 2013) 63.

35 Piotr Mikuli and Maciej Pach, 'Disciplinary Liability of Judges: The Polish Case' in Piotr Mikuli and Grzegorz Kuca (eds), *Accountability and the Law, Rights, Authority and Transparency of Public Power* (Routledge 2022) 65 and 66; Marina Matic Boskovic and Jelena Kostic, 'How to Build Common Features of the Justice Systems in Candidate Countries and EU Member States' in Ondrej Blažo, Lucia Mokra and Andrej Mačaj (eds), *Legal Challenges for the New European Commission* (Comenius University in Bratislava, Faculty of Law 2018) 101–114; Marina Matic Boskovic and Jelena Kostic 'New EU Enlargement Strategy Towards the Western Balkans and its Impact on Rule of Law' (2021) 1 *SYEUL* 37–58.

in a way that is contrary to the constitution. Members of the Chamber used their position for political confrontation with the judges who were against the national judicial reform.[36]

The Consultative Council of European Judges and the Venice Commission have expressed their opinions on the criteria that Judicial Councils need to meet in order to protect the judicial independence, as an important factor in preserving the rule of law, while strengthening the judicial office holders' accountability. According to the Consultative Council of European Judges Opinion No. 24 (2021) on the development of Judicial Councils and their role in independent and impartial judicial systems, due to the judicial independence strengthening, the composition and function of the Councils should be taken into account to guarantee their independence from the legislative and executive authorities.[37] The above Opinion indicates also the need for transparent and responsible work of Judicial Councils in order for the judiciary to ensure public trust and support.[38]

With respect to the composition of the above bodies, according to the Consultative Council Opinion, they should be composed mainly, but not predominantly, of judicial office holders. They should also include non-judicial members.[39] The same position is stated by the Venice Commission (European Commission for Democracy through Law (Venice Commission) in the Compilation of Venice Commission opinions and reports concerning courts and judges.[40] It seems that the prevailing opinion in the international documents is that Judicial Councils should consist of a majority of members elected by their peers, and should therefore have a decisive influence both on the appointment and promotion of judges and on the disciplinary measures against them.[41] Bearing in mind the need to reconcile judicial independence and accountability of judges and public prosecutors, the question arises as to how to ensure their independence and at the same time strengthen their accountability. Therefore, there is a need to ensure that the bodies deciding on the disciplinary liability of judicial office holders are independent, objective and competent to act in such

36 Piotr Mikuli, Grzegorz Kuca and Elżbieta Gudowska-Natanek, 'Poland' in Richard Albert, David Landau, Pietro Faraguna and Simon Drugda (eds), *Global Review of Constitutional Law, I·CONnect-Clough Center* (Routledge 2021) 239.

37 Item 10 of the Opinion No 24 (2021) on the development of Judicial Councils and their role in independent and impartial judicial systems of the Consultative Council of European Judges.

38 Item 12 of the Opinion No 24 (2021) on the development of Judicial Councils and their role in independent and impartial judicial systems.

39 Item 30 of the Opinion No 24 (2021).

40 Items 5.2.1. and 5.2.2. of the Compilation of Venice Commission Opinions and Reports Concerning Courts and Judges CDL-PI(2019)008 (Council of Europe, European Commission for Democracy through Law (Venice Commission) December 2019).

41 Miloš Stanić, *Sudski saveti – sastav i nadležnosti širom Evrope* (Institute of Comparative Law 2022) 33.

situations. This should be considered both during the appointment of these bodies and their members, and during their work.

Judicial office holders are obliged to adhere to ethical standards in their work, and ethical standards must be clearly and precisely defined, including sanctions for non-compliance. Disciplinary proceedings against judicial office holders should not be a tool for exerting political influence. The possibility of political influence may be present, particularly regarding the financial crime and corruption cases.[42]

In their Paris Declaration on Resilient Justice, the European Network of Councils for the Judiciary states the need to ensure at the national level that judicial councils, which are often responsible for the disciplinary procedure against judges, should take measures to improve and strengthen the rule of law, particularly by supporting the judicial office holders' independence and accountability.[43]

According to the Consultative Council of European Judges Opinion, decisions on disciplinary liability of the judicial office holders must have the legally binding force, which however must be conditional on the possibility of appealing to the competent court. The independence of the judiciary must not be above the law or exempt from the judicial review.[44] In situations when the Judicial Council has disciplinary powers, judges who are the subject of the proceedings need to be fully informed of the grounds of the decision. To ensure transparency and responsible action of Judicial Councils, there is a need to publish legally binding decisions establishing the judicial office holders' liability to inform the public of the outcome of the proceedings, and ensure that the judiciary does not seek to facilitate any improper actions by its members.[45] In case C-791/19, the Court of Justice of the European Union, referring to Articles 6 and 13 of the European Convention on Human Rights, found that each member state must ensure that the bodies acting in the disciplinary proceedings against judicial office holders satisfy the conditions of effective judicial protection.[46] Therefore, judges need to be protected from any external interventions or pressures that may threaten their independence. The

42 Marina Matić Bošković and Jelena Kostić, 'Specijalizacija državnih organa u suzbijanju finansijskog kriminaliteta i korupcije' (2019) 3 *Srpska politička misao* 255–279, DOI: 10.22182/spm.6532019.11.

43 Item 5 of the Paris Declaration on Resilient Justice (European Network of Councils for the Judiciary 2017) <www.encj.eu/images/stories/pdf/GA/Paris/encj_paris_declaration_adopted_ga.pdf> accessed 26 June 2023.

44 Item 39 of the Consultative Council of European Judges Opinion No. 10 on the role of the Council for the Judiciary at the service of society.

45 Item 95 of the Consultative Council of European Judges Opinion No. 10 on the role of the Council for the Judiciary at the service of society.

46 Items 60, 61 and 62, *European Commission v. Poland* C-791/19. According to Article 6 of the European Convention on Human Rights, "everyone is entitled to a fair and public hearing within a reasonable time, and no one shall be tried except by an independent and impartial tribunal established by law." <https://curia.europa.eu/juris/document/document.

rules applied to the performance of the judge's duties must not threaten their independence, as it could negatively affect the public confidence in the performance of the judiciary. Lack of public confidence undermines the principle of the rule of law, as a key principle of any democratic society.[47]

Disciplinary wrongs

The general principles of criminal law apply to all administrative sanctions, and consequently, the principle of legality (*nullum crimen sine lege certa*) has to be respected in the field of the administrative sanctioning system. In this context, it has to be recalled that the disciplinary sanctions fall into the category of punitive administrative measures, i.e., into the category of criminal charge for the purposes of the ECHR Article 6.1. The Engel criteria[48] and the safeguards linked to punitive administrative sanctioning systems apply here as well.

The formulation of disciplinary offences should reconcile the requirement for precise language and the use of general terms to cover the issues at hand comprehensively. It is essential that the formulation of any grounds for disciplinary action is not imprecise or vague. The Venice Commission highlights in respect of disciplinary violations that vague provisions are potentially dangerous and could be used to undermine a prosecutor or to control him or her.[49] A similar request has been highlighted by GRECO in their Fourth Evaluation Round.[50] However, the European Court of Human Rights has recognised that in formulation of disciplinary offences it is difficult to prevent the use of general language because otherwise it may not be possible to deal with an

---

jsf?text=&docid=244185&pageIndex=0&doclang=en&mode=lst&dir=&occ=first&part=1&cid=5367570> accessed 26 June 2023.

47 The opinions expressed in the jurisprudence of the European Courts are of great importance for the development of national legislation and practice. More about that in: Marina Matić Bošković and Jelena Kostić, 'The Application of the *Ne bis in idem* Related to Financial Offences in the Jurisprudence of the European Courts' (2020) 25(2) *NBP* 67–77, DOI: 10.5937/nabepo25-27224.

48 In case *Engel and Others v. the Netherlands*, Application No. 5100/71, 5101/71, 5102/71, 5374/71, 5370/72, judgement dated 8 June 1976, in paras. 82 and 83 European Court of Human Rights outlined the criteria for applicability of the criminal aspect of Article 6 of the European Convention of Human Rights: (1) classification in domestic law, (2) nature of the offence, and (3) severity of the penalty that the person concerned risks incurring.

49 European Commission for Democracy through Law (Venice Commission), *Opinion on the Draft Law on the Public Prosecutor Service of Moldova*, CDL-AD(2008)019 (European Commission for Democracy through Law (Venice Commission) 2008) para. 52 <www.venice.coe.int/webforms/documents/?pdf=CDL-AD(2008)019-e> accessed 26 June 2023.

50 In its Fourth Evaluation Round, GRECO recommended that disciplinary offences should be specified clearly or more precisely in Georgia (para. 204.xv), Monaco (para. 198.xiv), Portugal (para. 189.xv), "the former Yugoslav Republic of Macedonia" (para. 251.xvi) and Ukraine (para. 273.xxix).

issue comprehensively and continuous updating may be required to regulate new circumstances.[51]

In most legal systems, disciplinary wrongs (offences) are graded according to their severity. In Spain, the legal provisions classify the misconduct of improper fulfilling of duties and responsibilities as very serious, serious, and minor offences.[52] In Slovenia, there is a distinction between serious and more serious disciplinary violations.[53] To ensure the fulfilment of the requirement for precise language and clear definition of disciplinary violations, some countries have introduced very detailed lists of violations. In Italy, Decree No. 109 includes a general clause on disciplinary liability and goes on to list two subsets of disciplinary violations: violations committed in the performance of duties and violations committed out of office. In total, the number of disciplinary offences listed in Decree No. 109 is 42.[54] However, the Italian legislation includes one violation specified in general language that depends on interpretation (any other behaviour that may undermine the independence, neutrality and impartiality of the magistrate including the appearance thereof).

One of the tools for prevention of a broad interpretation of conduct that could serve as grounds for disciplinary liability is a closed list of very specific disciplinary violations. This approach is used in Slovenia and in Spain. In Slovenia, Article 80 of the Law on State Prosecutor's Office provides a closed list with no general language that could be used to undermine a prosecutor. In Spain, the disciplinary offences are established in Articles 62 and 63 of the Law on Public Prosecutors as *numerus clausus*, which prevents considering any other kind of behaviour as grounds for disciplinary liability.

Croatia has taken a specific approach, and in addition to the list of disciplinary violations, the Law provides definitions for each violation. The list of eight disciplinary violations is provided in the Law on State Prosecutorial Council.[55] Some of the disciplinary violations are clear, such as the violation of official secrecy in relation to the performance of duty or a failure to submit asset declaration, while others are more general, such as the abuse of duty. However, the Law provides definitions of the violations specified in a more general manner, using the same principles as those used to define the crimes in the Criminal Code. According to Article 85(3) of the Law on State Prosecutorial Council, the disciplinary offense of the abuse of duty exists if the deputy state attorney has intentionally caused damage or put the person concerned in

51 *Oleksandr Volkov v. Ukraine*, Application No. 21722/11, 9 January 2013, at para. 178.

52 Article 61 of the Law on Public Prosecutors *Official Journal*, No. 243, 10 October 2007.

53 The Law on State Prosecutor Office *Official Journal*, No. 58/11, 21/12, 47/12, 15/13, 47/13, 48/13, 19/15, 23/17, 36/19, 139/20, 54/21 and 105/22 in Article 80 lists all violations of the prosecutors' duties and provides the distinctions based on their severity.

54 See: <https://rm.coe.int/comparative-study-disciplinary-proceedings/1680a2914a> accessed 26 June 2023.

55 The Law on State Prosecutorial Council *Official Journal*, No. 67/18, 126/19, 80/22.

a more favourable or a less favourable position than the one that would have belonged to him or her given the circumstances, and the features of the criminal offense have not been met.

The comparative legal framework analysis provides an insight into good practices; however, it is important to note that the legal provisions need to be interpreted in line with the legal culture of the country. All comparative jurisdictions use some general language in the description of disciplinary violations, but the active role of the disciplinary body, the uniform decision-making practice, and predictable interpretation of the provisions could serve as proper mitigation measures.

To prevent that one failure in the fulfilment of duty would result in the initiation of the disciplinary proceedings, some jurisdictions envisage that the violations must be serious and repeated. In Italy, undue delays are considered a disciplinary offence only in case of repeated serious and unjustified delays that exceed three times the length of the statutory time limit for the performance of the respective act.[56] In Spain, the Law in Article 63 also includes the term "repeated delays" in the exercise of entrusted prosecutors' functions.

In Italy, the disciplinary liability of judges is prescribed by the Legislative Decree 109/2006. The Law in Article 1 prescribes the main duties that judges must observe when performing their duties. These are the main principles and ethical values that are of crucial importance for the performance of the judicial function. They refer to impartiality, correctness, diligence, dedication, confidentiality and respect for the dignity of individuals. Article 2 of the Decree specifies the cases of violation of discipline in the performance of judicial functions, and Article 3 prescribes the procedures to be carried out in case of a violation of discipline by judicial office holders.[57] In some jurisdictions, specific disciplinary liabilities are connected to the commission of crimes or violations of the ethical code. In Italy, the disciplinary procedure is to be initiated against a prosecutor when he or she has been convicted (final decision) for a crime sanctioned by deprivation of liberty.[58] Furthermore, the Italian Decree No. 109 envisages that the disciplinary procedure can be initiated against a public prosecutor when he or she has committed any crime that may damage the reputation of the prosecution service.[59]

According to the authors, in the German legislation, the law on the disciplinary measures against judges and prosecutors should also be seen in the context of the application of the law on the disciplinary measures against civil servants. The most important duties whose violation triggers disciplinary liability include the obligation to act impartially and fairly, to take into account the welfare of citizens, and to perform duties with enthusiasm, while refraining

56 Legislative Decree 109 on the disciplinary offenses of magistrates, General Series, No. 67.

57 Consiglio Superior della Magistratura, *The Italian Judicial System* (Consiglio Superior della Magistratura 2015) 41 and 42.

58 Article 4 of the Legislative Decree 109 on the disciplinary offenses of magistrates.

59 Article 4d of the Legislative Decree 109.

from political activities. In addition, other very important obligations include protecting information confidentiality in the performance of official duties, refraining from undertaking other jobs and activities without special permission or accepting gifts or bribes, and acting in accordance with the law. The comparative jurisdictions provide examples how "gross violations of legislation" and "inappropriate fulfilment of service duties" could be specified in detail to avoid the use of vague language. The decision makers in the countries in transition could use these examples and prepare comprehensive lists of disciplinary violations, particularly violations of prosecutor's duties. In addition, the authorities may wish to use the Italian example and consider further specifying the violations as repeated and serious, including the indicators for seriousness.[60] Another option is the Croatian approach of defining the disciplinary violations in a similar way as the crimes in the Criminal Code. The Croatian approach provides flexibility while ensuring legal security.

The consequences of the decision on disciplinary wrongs

The consequences of disciplinary violations are rather similar across Europe. The imposed sanctions range from a reprimand or a written warning to financial sanctions (salary reduction over a certain period of time or payment of a fine), transfer of the public prosecutor to a different office, temporary ban on promotion or a dismissal from office.

Disciplinary sanctions must be proportionate to the severity or gravity of the offence committed.[61] Most countries incorporate a legal provision on determination of sanctions in proportion with the disciplinary violations. The countries that classify the violations based on their gravity envisage in their legislation types of sanctions that can be imposed for specific groups of violations. In Spain, minor offences are punishable only by a warning or a fine.[62]

The disciplinary sanctions in Italy as prescribed by the Legislative Decree 109 include admonition, censure, loss of seniority up to a maximum of two years, expulsion or dismissal. The loss of seniority and more severe sanctions are applicable to violations that caused a serious unfair damage or advantage to one of the parties; the habitual use of title to obtain an undue advantage if serious; frequentation or commercial relationships with notorious criminals, convicted criminals and individuals under investigation.[63]

60 Article Article 2(1)n of the Legislative Decree 109.

61 European Commission for Democracy through Law (Venice Commission), Directorate of Human Rights of the Directorate General of Human Rights and Rule of Law (DGI), OSCE Office for Democratic Institutions and Human Rights (OSCE/ODHR) CDL-AD(2015)005, *Joint Opinion on the Draft Law on the Prosecution Service of the Republic of Moldova* (Venice Commission, DGI, OSCE/ODHR 2015), para. 120 <www.venice.coe.int/webforms/documents/?pdf=CDL-AD(2015)005-e> accessed 26 June 2023.

62 Article 66 of the Law on Public Prosecutors of Spain, *Official Journal*, No 243, 10 October 2007.

63 Article 5 of the Legislative Decree 109.

Slovenia has five different sanctions in place: a written warning, salary reduction, ban on promotion, transfer to another state prosecutor office, and a dismissal from service.[64] Promotion may be suspended for a period of maximum of three years in particular for violations related to the performance of state prosecutorial service.[65]

The sanctions that can be imposed on prosecutors for the offences committed in the exercise of their duties in Spain[66] are similar to those in Italy and Slovenia, and include: a warning, a fine in the amount of up to EUR 3,000, forced transfer to another public prosecutor office (at least 100 km away from the office where he or she was serving), suspension of up to three years, and a dismissal. As additional consequences of these sanctions, Article 66 of the Law on Public Prosecution states that the prosecutor sanctioned with forced transfer will not be able to be promoted within a period of one to three years.

The Croatian Law on State Prosecutorial Council stipulates a ban on promotion not as a disciplinary sanction but as a consequence of the imposed sanction.[67] In Croatia, the following disciplinary sanctions may be imposed for committed disciplinary violations: a reprimand, a fine up to one-third of the salary earned in the previous month for the period of up to three months, a fine up to one-third of the salary earned in the previous month for the period of up to six months, up to one-third of the salary earned in the previous month for the period of up to 12 months or a dismissal from duty. The duration of the ban on promotion depends on the severity of the disciplinary sanction. A prosecutor who has been reprimanded by the Council cannot be appointed or permanently transferred to another office within one year of the decision. A prosecutor who has been fined by the Council cannot be transferred or appointed for two years, while a dismissal means that the person concerned cannot be reappointed as a prosecutor for a period of eight years.[68]

Contrary to Italy, Slovenia, Spain and Croatia, the Austrian disciplinary system does not envisage a ban on promotion. In Austria, the disciplinary system for public prosecutors is regulated under the Beamtendienstrechtsgesetz (BDG) 1979.[69] The only possible sanctions are a reprimand, a fine (up to a half of the monthly salary), financial punishment (up to five monthly payments)

64 Article 81 of the Law on State Prosecutor Office of Slovenia, *Official Journal*, No 58/11, 21/12, 47/12, 15/13, 47/13, 48/13, 19/15, 23/17, 36/19, 139/20, 54/21 and 105/22.

65 Article 82(3) of the Law of the Law on State Prosecutor Office of Slovenia.

66 Article 66 of the Law on Public Prosecution of Spain.

67 Articles 86 and 87 of the Law on State Prosecutorial Council of Croatia, *Official Journal*, No 67/18, 126/19, 80/22.

68 Article 87 of the Law on State Prosecutorial Council of Croatia.

69 Beamtendienstrechtsgesetz (BDG) 1979, *Federal Law Gazette I* No. 205/2022.

and a dismissal.[70] Warnings may be given before the disciplinary proceedings is initiated.[71]

The second part of the Legislative Decree 109/2006 prescribes the sanctions for a breach of discipline. These include a warning, a censure, a loss of seniority, which cannot be shorter than two months and longer than two years, a temporary disqualification from performing the function, which cannot be shorter than six months and longer than two years, a suspension from the position including salary suspension or a dismissal from office with the termination of employment.[72]

In Germany, the disciplinary sanctions that can be imposed to judges include a warning, a fine, a salary reduction, a transfer to another judicial position (with lower salary) and a dismissal. In more serious cases, the disciplinary measures can also be applied against retired judges. Court presidents have the right to decide only on warnings and reprimands, while in other situations, the decision is made by the Judicial Service Court.[73] Any disciplinary measure can be contested on the grounds that it violates the principle of judiciary independence.

Conclusion

The independence and accountability of judges and public prosecutors are the key elements of the rule of law. The standards on independence and accountability of judges and public prosecutors have been established at the European Union level to improve the quality of the judiciary and strengthen the public trust in the judiciary. However, it can be difficult to establish the adequate balance between the independence and accountability of judicial office holders. With respect to judicial independence, judges and prosecutors should be independent in their work from any internal or external influences, particularly political. In addition, they are accountable to the public and should act and decide in their interest. When acting in their work, judicial office holders must respect the principles that are precisely defined by the national legislation. To strengthen the judicial office holders' accountability for the violation of the principles specified at the national level by the countries included in the comparative analysis in this chapter, adequate sanctions have been prescribed in the legislation. However, to ensure the protection of judicial independence

70 Article 92 of the Beamtendienstrechtsgesetz (BDG).

71 Giusepe di Frederico (ed.), *Recruitment, Professional Evaluation and Career of Judges and Prosecutors in Europe: Austria, France, Germany, Italy, the Netherlands and Spain* (Istituto di Informatica Giuridica e Sistemi Giudiziari del Consiglio Nazionale delle Ricerche 2005) 21.

72 della Magistratura (n 57); di Frederico (n 71).

73 Cf. s. 48 of the Richter- und Staatsanwälte Gesetz für das Land Nordrhein-Westfalen (Landesrichter- und Staatsanwälte Gesetz – LRiStaG) (Landesrichtergesetz NRW) 8 December2015,<https://recht.nrw.de/lmi/owa/br_text_anzeigen?v_id=13520210318105639395> accessed 26 June 2023.

in parallel with strengthening the judicial office holders' accountability, the disciplinary responsibility of the judiciary needs to be decided by independent bodies to prevent any possibility for undue influence, particularly political. In most countries, the disciplinary decisions are made by the Judicial Councils. An additional guarantee of the Council's independence in deciding on sensitive issues concerning judiciary independence is the Council's composition. Consequently, a general attitude expressed in the relevant standards at the EU level is that the majority of Judicial Council members should be professional judges, and that non-judicial members should be appointed in a way that does not jeopardise their work independence and objectivity. All decisions made in the disciplinary procedure must be reasoned and subject to review by a higher authority. Therefore, such an obligation must be prescribed by the relevant national legislation. The absence of judicial review of the decisions made in the disciplinary proceedings against the judicial office holders could increase the likelihood of arbitrary treatment. In addition, judicial independence must not be above the law or exempt from judicial review. Bearing in mind that one of the roles of Judicial Councils is to condemn any political or other influence on the freedom of decision-making by judges, they should react accordingly to any attempt to influence the decisions on the disciplinary liability of judicial office holders.

Considering that the judiciary is at the service of the public, the decisions made against the judicial office holders in the disciplinary procedure should be published after they become final. Publishing the decisions would ensure transparency and disclosing information on the outcome of the disciplinary proceedings. As a result, the public would gain insight into the judiciary's attitude towards the improper actions by their members. This approach would ensure strengthening both the independence and accountability of the judicial office holders, increasing the public trust in the judicial system.

6 In search of standards for judicial immunity*

Piotr Mikuli

Introductory remarks

In the previous chapter, we considered the matter of disciplinary liability of judges: accountability for actions strictly connected with professional judicial activities. This chapter shifts the focus to liability for ordinary criminal and civil wrongs. A judge performing his or her function may either intentionally (in bad faith) or unwittingly commit civil or criminal wrongs. The principle of judicial independence requires the judge to have enough comfort to adjudicate freely and not be exposed to liability, especially if it were to relate to his or her diligent and bona fide performance of judicial duties. In this context, the appropriate scope of judicial immunity is the central theme of this chapter.

In this chapter, I discuss the scope of judicial immunity and try to show how the limits on liability thus created may interfere with the independence of judges. First, I refer to the notion of civil and criminal liability connected with the sphere of adjudication. Subsequently, after defining judicial immunity, I present a typology of possible legal frameworks and describe the normative measures that exist in the selected countries. I then argue that a certain minimum scope of immunity should be treated as part of the universal concept of judicial independence and that the most important aim of immunity is protecting the judicial decision's content. Then, although I agree with the argument that absolute judicial immunity is not essential and its limitation in certain aspects may be reasonable, I argue that possible changes in existing legal measures in this respect may also evoke some doubts. I also argue that immunity concerning criminal liability for acts not connected with judicial function is not a necessary requirement from the perspective of the rudimental aim of judicial immunity. In the context of possible limitations and reforms of judicial immunity, I support the position adopted in the ECHR case law, namely, a prohibition on lowering the national standard for judicial independence and relate this to the question of immunities.

* The chapter is based on research conducted at Swansea University in 2021 and on research funded by the Polish National Agency for Academic Exchange (NAWA) conducted at the University of Glasgow in 2022. The publication has also been supported by the funds from the Law and Administration Faculty of the Jagiellonian University granted within the Priority Research Area 'FutureSoc' under the programme 'Excellence Initiative – Research University'.

DOI: 10.4324/9781003557852-8

My discussion is based on an analysis of judicial immunity arrangements in the United Kingdom, the United States, France, Poland and Hungary. The intention is to juxtapose the approaches found in stable democracies and in new democracies, which have been (Poland) or are still (Hungary) in the midst of a deep crisis related to violations of the rule of law.

Types of liability

As I indicated in the introduction to this volume, one can individuate a notion of liability within the concept of accountability.

To identify the actions covered by immunity, it is important to distinguish between the various other liability regimes and consider the notion and types of guilt (fault) that can be attributed to the judge.

Since Roman law, several conditions have had to be fulfilled for the implementation of liability. With criminal liability, the basis of this liability is the perpetrator's guilt/fault (*nullum crimen sine culpa*). Guilt or fault is an ambiguous term. Fault can be understood in two ways: as the perpetrator's mental state regarding the act (psychological theory of fault) or as the ability to hold the perpetrator accountable for committing an act that is prohibited by law (normative theory of fault).[1] The degree of fault is also relevant, as the perpetrator may act intentionally or unintentionally (negligence). In civil liability, it is sometimes a matter of the occurrence of damage (understood as a depletion of the victim's assets) and the occurrence of an event with which the law binds an obligation to award damages to compensate for that damage. It may involve a breach of contract[2] or committing an illegal act under civil law (civil tort).[3] The damage may also be non-pecuniary and connected to the infringement of the victim's personal goods or harm done to the victim physically or mentally. Yet, an essential premise here is the causal link between the damage and the given event. Civil liability may also be exercised without the prerequisite of fault, e.g., in the case of strict liability, in which the liable person is responsible for causing the damage from a specific event that must be indicated precisely in a specific provision. In such circumstances, it is irrelevant whether that person is at fault for causing the event that caused the damage. Thus, this kind of tortious liability is independent of intent or negligence. Strict liability may also apply in some jurisdictions

1 See Mikołaj Małecki and Marek Sławiński, 'Guilt in Criminal Law: Guilt in Us or in the Stars?' in Bartosz Brożek and Nicole A. Vincent (eds), *Law and Mind: A Survey of Law and the Cognitive Sciences* (Cambridge University Press 2021) 289–316.

2 The contract creates a relationship in which the debtor is bound directly to fulfil obligations (*dare facere praestare*). See Reinhard Zimmermann, *The Law Of Obligations* (Oxford University Press 1996) 4ff.

3 The idea of tort law is built on the premise that a person is responsible for harm caused to another person through wrongful action. See the discussion in John C. P. Goldberg and Benjamin C. Zipursky, 'Tort Law and Responsibility' in John Oberdiek (ed.), *Philosophical Foundations of the Law of Torts* (Oxford University Press 2014) 17–37.

under criminal law (e.g. the United Kingdom),[4] while in others (e.g. Poland) the perpetrator's mental state is always taken into account. A broader consideration of the scope and conditions of civil and criminal liability lies beyond the focus of this volume, but these fundamental principles are crucial when it comes to the issue of a judge's liability, particularly for acts committed in the exercise of their jurisdictional duties. In the case of a judge's civil liability, tortious liability holds predominant significance, as it involves inflicting pecuniary damage on a third party or infringing on their personal rights. Therefore, contractual liability is irrelevant where it relates to acts within the scope of one's office. Simultaneously, the concept of fault is crucial and must be defined and understood, following the well-established meaning under national law. In particular, it is essential to distinguish between the degree of fault and the type of fault, as these may have a decisive influence on the existence of liability; these understandings may not overlap, i.e., they may be slightly diverse depending on the legal system. For example, it is particularly relevant to distinguish between intentional and unintentional acts that may be unlawful in terms of a judge's responsibility.[5] As far as unintentional acts are concerned, this is a situation in which no intention exists on the perpetrator's part to commit a tort or a criminal offence (e.g. carelessness, negligence). Also in this context, as we shall see below, the law may link the operation of immunity to whether the judge, in the performance of his or her duties, acted in good or bad faith. Theoretically, immunity may refer to all types of liability (except disciplinary liability, for which a judge is, by definition, liable, as it is an internal type of liability).

Typology of judicial immunity

In discussing judicial immunity, I will employ a typology used in constitutional law scholarship primarily in relation to members of the legislature.[6] The basis here is the distinction between substantive/material and formal immunity. Substantive/material immunity refers to substantive (material) law, which excludes criminality of a certain act and therefore also imposes penalties.[7] This kind of immunity may also be described as an absolute one, as this means in practice excluding the unlawfulness of the actions of the person covered by this immunity. It then may be assumed that the act in question cannot be qualified as unlawful (from the perspective of both civil and criminal law) since one

4 See Jonathan Herring, *Criminal Law: Text, Cases and Materials* (9th edn, Oxford University Press 2018) 1–25.

5 I bear in mind here the classic Roman law distinction between the notions of *dolus*, *culpa lata* and *culpa levis*.

6 See for instance Maria Fernanda Palma, *Observations sur l'etendue et la levee des immunites parlementaires, material prepared within the Venice Commission* (n° 714/2013, 6 March 2014) 2.

7 Andrzej Jackiewicz and Artur Olechno, 'Immunity' in Rainer Grote, Frauke Lachenmann and Rüdiger Wolfrum (eds), *Max Planck Encyclopaedia of Comparative Constitutional Law* (Oxford University Press 2018) <https://oxcon.ouplaw.com/display/10.1093/law-mpeccol/law-mpeccol-e310?rskey=jnL3H1&result=2&prd=MPECCOL> accessed 15 November 2024.

cannot be held responsible for acts that are not unlawful. Generally, this scope of substantive immunity applies to parliamentarians' actions falling within the scope of their mandate. Such an immunity exists in several democratic states. Historically, this immunity aimed to protect MPs from being intimidated by a gradually waning, but still important, royal power. Certain analogies to substantive parliamentary immunity can be found wherever the broadest immunity protection for judges exists regarding liability for actions performed in the exercise of judicial office, e.g., the United Kingdom, the United States and France. In Hungary, the law regulating the immunity of judges refers to the provisions relating to parliamentary immunity.[8]

Immunity may also be formal/procedural,[9] where it excludes or limits the applicability of procedural law provisions. In the case of judges (as in case if parliamentarians and holders of other public offices), such immunity in contemporary constitutional systems refers to the procedural norms of criminal law. Its characteristic feature is the relative exclusion of the possibility of prosecution for a committed offence: a given act committed by a person protected under immunity constitutes an offence, but prosecution during the operation of immunity is prevented. This can thus be understood as an exemption from the procedure established by law. This type of immunity usually protects judges from criminal prosecution for acts that fulfil the attributes of an offence committed outside their official capacity but may also extend to possible offences committed in the course of judicial service. Amongst the countries examined, formal immunity for judges currently exists only in Poland and Hungary. It is not very common in the so-called old democracies and has no equivalent in the United Kingdom, the United States or, presently, France (see Table 6.1).

A separate category related to criminal liability is judicial personal inviolability, which is built on the premise that a judge cannot be arrested or detained (in the sense of using this preventive measure) without the consent of the relevant authority (state organ).[10] This institution of personal inviolability amongst the researched jurisdictions occurs only in Poland and Hungary.

The establishment of universally recognised standards for judicial immunity is important for understanding the principle of judicial independence. Due to European integration processes and broader globalisation mechanisms, international courts frequently encounter the problem of assessing these rule of law violations, primarily from the perspective of international provisions that express the right to a fair trial. The vague requirements regarding judicial

8 Art. 2(1) of Act CLXII 2011, on the status and remuneration of judges.

9 Art. 2(1) of Act CLXII 2011, on the status and remuneration of judges.

10 I refer here to the terminology proposed inter alia by Lech Garlicki. In the scholarship, however, the term 'inviolability' may sometimes also signify a broad definition of formal/procedural immunity, which protects a deputy or a judge against any actions within the criminal procedure. cf Leszek Garlicki and Maria Michalik, 'Pologne' (2001) 17 *Annuaire international de justice constitutionnelle*; Olivier Duhamel and Yves Mény, *Dictionnaire constitutionnel* (Presses universitaires de France 1992) 487.

Table 6.1 Types of Judicial Immunity in Five Jurisdictions

Country	*Acts/omissions within and connected with judicial function*		*Acts/omissions done outside the courtroom (in private life)*		*Additional protection within criminal procedures*
	Protection from civil liability	*Protection from criminal liability*	*Protection from civil liability*	*Protection from criminal liability*	*Personal inviolability*
United Kingdom	Substantial immunity	Substantial immunity	None	None	None
United States	Substantial immunity	Partial substantial immunity	None	None	None
France	Substantial immunity	Partial substantial immunity	None	None	None
Hungary	Substantial immunity	Substantial immunity	None	Formal immunity	Personal inviolability
Poland	None	Formal immunity	None	Formal immunity Substantial immunity in case of misdemeanours	Personal inviolability

immunity expressed in various international soft law documents,[11] which prescribe that a certain degree of immunity must be observed to maintain an independent judiciary position, may not be particularly helpful when several different solutions regarding the breadth of immunity protection exist in democratic countries. Therefore, these requirements should be defined more clearly.

In the examined jurisdictions, both the scope of this immunity and how it may be rescinded vary (see Table 6.1). In considering the analysis of legal regulations in the countries studied here, it may be concluded that several models of immunity protection exist. First, complete immunity protection concerns civil liability

11 The requirements included in such acts are often imprecise. Art. 2.24 of the Montreal Universal Declaration on the Independence of Justice States (1983) declares that 'judges shall enjoy immunity from suit, or harassment, for acts and omissions in their official capacity'. One can argue that the declaration does not call for absolute judicial immunity, but rather a limited one, mainly regarding judicial acts within the exercise of judicial actions. The desired international standard regarding immunity was worded in a clearer way in sec. 8.1 of the Mount Scopus International Standards of Judicial Independence (2008), which contend that '[a] judge shall enjoy immunity from legal actions in the exercise of official functions'.

for acts committed in the exercise of office (the United Kingdom, the United States and France). Usually, such a regulation is also accompanied by immunity from criminal prosecution in respect of the judicial acts undertaken, although this may be limited (the United Kingdom, the United States and France). Two other competing solutions may occur regarding judges' criminal liability for acts committed outside the courtroom. Here, one can speak of a model in which the prosecution of judges is entirely permissible (the United Kingdom, the United States and France) or a model of relative protection through the application of formal immunity, which can be lifted under an appropriate procedure (Poland, Hungary). The Polish case is distinguished by the fact that there is no regulation concerning the establishment of material immunity in respect of acts performed in the exercise of the function of the judge, for these are covered by formal immunity, as are any acts or omissions that fulfil the characteristics of a criminal offence. The procedure to lift immunity, as I will explain below, may take the form of a judicial or quasi-political decision. In Poland, the power to lift immunity belongs to disciplinary courts, while in Hungary, the decision, in principle, is rendered by the President of the Republic upon the motion of the President of the Curia (Supreme Court). Table 6.1 shows the types of immunity in the jurisdictions covered by this chapter.

Discerning a particular type of liability and the extent of the fault that may be assigned to a judge is crucial to identifying the actual scope of this immunity in a specific jurisdiction. Determining the scope of a judge's immunity also involves defining actions that fall within a judge's competences as defined by binding legal norms. It is an essential requirement from the perspective of judicial independence that a judge is not responsible for the content of a judicial decision/judgement when it comes to the material scope of disciplinary responsibility. Immunity protection also entails the need for a distinction between a judge's professional and extrajudicial activities. The latter includes all acts or omissions of a judge in his or her private life when he or she is not acting as a judge. However, within his or her professional activities, a judge may undertake certain acts without a legal basis, ultra vires. Therefore, a judge may take specific actions that have no legal basis and through these actions either cause damage (civil liability) or fulfil the attributes of an offence (criminal liability). Thus, one may contend that if in a given legal system immunity excludes civil or criminal liability for actions taken within the scope of the judicial service, then when a judge exceeds their powers (acting ultra vires, beyond their jurisdiction), they cannot be covered under this immunity. However, in practice, it may be quite challenging to prove that a particular procedural decision lies entirely beyond a judge's powers, and the practical approaches to such an abuse of power may vary. In this context, immunity, as I will show below, may depend on whether a judge uses their judicial capacity bona fide.

Immunity for the content of judicial decisions

Traditionally, as mentioned above, the broadest immunity in the scope of acts taken within jurisdiction occurs in Anglo-Saxon countries. It should be noted that although in many situations determining whether the condition of a judge performing judicial duties is met may not be difficult, as I pointed out above, defining the activities that should be regarded as performing judicial functions can sometimes pose problems. The situation is simple when a judge takes action outside the courtroom, in complete isolation from his or her function, i.e., in private life; then it is clear that immunity does not apply.

United Kingdom

In the United Kingdom, generally speaking, common law immunity precludes civil or criminal liability for action taken in a judicial capacity. At common law the broadest immunity traditionally was enjoyed by superior court judges.[12] In principle, a judge shall not be held liable for any act of a judicial nature, even if it was performed outside of his or her jurisdiction, although immunity does not exist if he or she acted in bad faith.[13] This immunity was later extended to judges and magistrates in inferior courts (for example, circuit and district judges in England and Wales as well as justices of the peace) through case law[14] and legislation.[15] Despite the fact that a uniform perspective is not always presented in the case law,[16] it can be concluded that judges in inferior courts are protected by immunity, at least within their jurisdictions.[17] As Shimon Shetreet

12 This included judges sitting in the House of Lords (presently in the Supreme Court of the United Kingdom), in the High Court, in the Court of Appeal in England and Wales and in the Northern Irish counterparts of these courts, as well as judges of the Court of Session and the High Court in Scotland.

13 See Anthony W. Bradley and Keith D. Ewing, *Constitutional and Administrative Law* (Edinburgh 2003) 376. The immunity was conformed inter alia in *Sirros v. Moore* (1975) QB 118, in which it was held that despite erroneous judicial decisions regarding detentions, no action could be taken against the judge, as he had acted in good faith; see also Shimon Shetreet and Sophie Turenne, *Judges on Trial: The Independence and Accountability of the English Judiciary* (2nd edn, Cambridge University Press 2013) 275.

14 This concerns all jurisdictions within the United Kingdom. See, e.g., *McC v. Mullan* (1985) AC 528 or *McCreadie v. Thomson* (1907) SC 1176 at 1182.

15 In England and Wales, justices of the peace enjoy immunity on the grounds of ss 31 and 32 of the Courts Act 2003, which includes acts or omissions (1) in the execution of their duties as a justice of the peace and (2) in relation to matters within their jurisdiction. The immunity extends beyond the jurisdiction of a justice of the peace as long as the judge did not act in bad faith. In Scotland, magistrates in lower civil courts (e.g. justices of the peace) are immune from liability under s 170(1) of the Criminal Procedure (Scotland) Act 1995, which provides that magistrates generally are not liable for damages in connection with proceedings unless the person prosecuted has been deprived of his or her liberty as a result of the magistrate's action, the proceedings have been discontinued or the person prosecuted can demonstrate that the magistrate's action was malicious and without probable cause. See Questionnaire From the Special Rapporteur on the Independence of Judges and Lawyers Regarding the Disciplinary, Civil and Criminal Liability of Judges' Response of the United Kingdom of Great Britain and Northern Ireland <www.ohchr.org/Documents/Issues/IJudiciary/disciplinary-judges/Submissions/States/United-Kingdom.pdf>.

16 See Lord Denning's views in *Sirros v. Moore* (1975) QB 118.

17 They may be liable if they act outside their jurisdiction, even if they do not act in bad faith, e.g., if no jurisdiction exists *ab initio* or they act within their jurisdiction but cause damage

and Sophie Turenne stated, according to the majority in the landmark case *Sirros v Moore*, immunity always should be viewed as coming into play when (1) the judge, in the performance of their duties, acts in good faith, and (2) they act on the belief (however mistaken) that they have relevant jurisdiction over the dispute in question.[18]

However, British judges may be criminally liable for acts related to their profession if they fulfil the elements of a general offence, such as corruption or perversion of justice.[19]

UK judges are sometimes called upon to clarify some public matters out of court (public inquiries); therefore, in practice, the issue arises of whether substantive immunity applies to judges' actions in these various special investigations. In the case of public inquiries conducted under the Inquiries Act 2005, immunity is guaranteed by virtue of s 37 of this Act. However, as Abimbola A. Olowofoyeku contends, if the investigative procedure was initiated on the basis of powers derived from the prerogative, the situation is not clear-cut and will be assessed on the basis of different interpretations of common law.[20]

The Crown Proceedings Act 1947 precludes proceedings against the Crown for any action identified in the exercise of a judicial function (see s 2(5)). The exception to this general principle lies within the purview of the Human Rights Act 1998 (HRA). State liability for judicial decisions is possible in forms prescribed in this Act (see s 8). However, this exception is accompanied by complete immunity for judges, as the Act allows proceedings only against public authorities so that action will be brought against a court, not against an individual judge.[21]

United States

In the United States, regulations concerning judicial immunity resemble the British approach. Immunity refers first of all to civil liability and is wide in its

through malicious or unjustified acts. See Witold Borysiak, *Odpowiedzialność cywilnoprawna sędziego (perspektywa prawnoporównawcza)* (Instytut Wymiaru Sprawiedliwości 2016) 35; Abimbola A. Olowofoyeku, 'Judges and Non-Judicial Functions in the United Kingdom' in Hoong Phun Lee (ed.), *Judiciaries in Comparative Perspective* (Cambridge 2011) 70ff.

18 Shetreet and Turenne (n 13) 278.

19 *Sirros v. Moore* (1975) QB 118.

20 Abimbola A. Olowofoyeku, *Suing Judges* (Clarendon Press 2003) 504.

21 This state liability is connected to infringements of the European Convention on Human Rights. Pursuant to s 6 (1) of HRA, 'It is unlawful for a public authority to act in a way which is incompatible with a Convention right'. In turn, in s 9, a caveat was included, according to which damage may not be awarded under the Act if an action was done in good faith unless the arrest or detention of the victim runs contrary to the ECHR (art 5) or 'to compensate a person for a judicial act that is incompatible with art. 6 of the Convention in circumstances where the person is detained and, but for the incompatibility, the person would not have been detained or would not have been detained for so long'.

scope,[22] precluding suits in situations in which judges act within their judicial capacity.[23] Civil liability is possible when judges commit a tort or breach a contract outside of their judicial functions or act in the complete absence of all jurisdiction.[24] Therefore, a judge will not be deprived of immunity because the action he or she took was in error, was done maliciously or was in excess of his or her authority.[25] Immunity protects a judge even if their behaviour within their judicial capacity has subsequently been found to be obviously wrong from a legal perspective. This rule was confirmed strongly in the famous *Stump v Sparkman* case, amongst others.[26] The judge was immune from being sued over his decision to allow a tubal ligation of a minor under her mother's petition in such a way that the operation's real purpose was not disclosed to the patient, because the order was issued as a judicial function. It seems that immunity from civil actions applies even in cases of corrupt or abusive judicial acts.[27] Currently, judges are also immune from non-monetary relief (such as injunctive or declaratory relief), which, in practice, might have previously resulted in judges being liable for the winning party's court costs and attorney's fees.[28]

In the United States, following the British example, judicial immunity coexists with the exclusion of the State Treasury's liability for judicial decisions. This results from provisions under federal legislation,[29] interpreted in case law[30] precisely in the direction of excluding the possibility of asserting claims against the state in the case of court decisions. Similar regulations, in practice, are in force in state law.[31]

Substantive immunity pertaining to acts or omissions within judicial capacity may extend to the criminal domain, but only in a limited way. Judges may

22 See *Randall v. Brigham* (1868) 74 U.S. (7 Wall.) 523; *Bradley v. Fisher* (1871) 80 U.S. 335.

23 *Pierson v. Ray* (1967) 386 U.S. 547.

24 See *Stump v. Sparkman* (1978) 435 U.S. 349, 356–357 and also *Bradley v. Fisher* (n 22) 352. The court gave a hypothetical example of this distinction. A probate court judge who presided over a criminal trial would be acting in the apparent absence of any jurisdiction over the case, whereas a criminal court judge who presided over a criminal trial for a crime that was not illegal would merely be acting in excess of his jurisdiction.

25 In *Bradley v. Fisher*, the court illustrated the distinction between lack of jurisdiction and excess of jurisdiction with the following examples: if a probate judge, having jurisdiction only over wills and estates, tried a criminal case, he would be acting in clear lack of jurisdiction. In contrast, if a criminal court judge convicted a defendant of a non-existent crime, he would be acting only in excess of his jurisdiction and would be immune from liability.

26 (1978) 435 U.S. 349.

27 See Jeffrey M. Shaman, 'Judicial Immunity from Civil and Criminal Liability' (1990) 27(1) *San Diego L Rev* 182.

28 The rule constituting this kind of exception in judicial immunity was established in *Pulliam v. Allen* (1984) 466 U.S. 522 but was overturned by the Federal Courts Improvement Act 1996 (amending 42 U.S. 1988). The immunity does not operate if a judge was clearly in excess of their jurisdiction.

29 See 28 USC s 2680a.

30 *Cromelin v. United States* (1949) 177 F.2d 275. See Olowofoyeku (n 20) 161–162.

31 *Cromelin v. United States* (1949) 177 F.2d 275. See Olowofoyeku (n 20) 161–162.

not enjoy immunity when they do not exercise their office in good faith;[32] i.e., similarly to the United Kingdom, a judge who acts fraudulently or corruptly remains criminally liable.[33] For example, one may point to the 'kids for cash scandal', in which two judges sentenced minors to severe punishment in return for money from a juvenile facility in Luzerne County, Pennsylvania.[34] While civil action was not possible, the judges were eventually found guilty of criminal offences and sentenced to imprisonment. Despite this constitutional practice, it is worth noting that, in academia, one also encounters the view that Article III of the Constitution, concerning impeachment, precludes judges from being held criminally liable, at least temporarily. In this regard, the only way to remove Supreme Court justices and judges in lower courts established by Congress from the bench would be via impeachment.[35] Thus, one may argue that criminal proceedings may be launched only together with the impeachment procedure.

France

A similar preclusion of civil liability for judicial decisions occurs in France, where judges may only be found personally liable in cases of acts committed outside of judicial service. The state is obliged to repair the damage that the defective functioning of the justice system causes, but the plaintiff must establish the existence of gross fault (*une faute lourde*) or a denial of justice (*un déni de justice*).[36] This kind of liability concerns professional judges in general jurisdiction; however, according to the case law of the *Conseil d'État*, in the case of administrative courts, the principles of compensation are similar, taking into account the grave fault of the judge.[37]

An action for civil liability against a professional judge who has committed a personally culpable act (*faute personnelle*) within the scope relating to the

32 As Shaman argues, 'Immunity Works in (the) Case of Malfeasance or Misfeasance in (the) Absence of Judicial Tasks Undertaken in Good Faith'. See Shaman (n 27) 18 and the case law quoted there. For instance, in *Ex Parte Virginia*, the court decided that immunity cannot protect a judge who, on racial grounds, excluded African Americans from the jury, but qualified this act as a non-judicial act (*Ex Parte Virginia*, *Braatelien v. United States* [1945] 147 F.2d. 888).

33 See Shaman (n 27) 18 and *Ex Parte Virginia*, *Braatelien v. United States* (1945) 147 F.2d. 888.

34 '"Kids for Cash" Judge Gets 28 Years in Pennsylvania Bribery Case' *The Guardian* (11 August2011)<www.theguardian.com/world/2011/aug/11/kids-for-cash-judge-pennsylvania> accessed 15 January 2024.

35 Steven W. Gold, 'Temporary Criminal Immunity for Federal Judges: A Constitutional Requirement' (1987) 53 *Brook L Rev* 699.

36 See art. L. 141-1 of the Code of the Organisation of the Judiciary of 1976. Initially, the concept of grave fault was interpreted more subjectively, but later interpretation moved towards objectification. Thus, the notion of grave fault now also includes any negligence reflecting a failure of justice (e.g. loss of documents).

37 Roger Perrot, *Institutions Judiciaires* (LGDJ Paris 2012) 91; Borysiak (n 17) 25.

exercise of public service of justice (*service public de la justice*) may be brought against such a judge only on the basis of an indemnity claim by the state.[38] The term *faute personnelle* in the French scholarship comes close to that of 'intentional action'.[39]

Non-professional judges in France are not protected on the same basis against civil claims as professional judges. They can be sued for specific acts such as intentional conduct (*dol*), fraud (*fraude*), bribery/corruption (*concussion*) and grave fault (*faute lourde*) committed both during the hearing of a case and in the delivery of a judgement.[40] An action against a non-professional judge is only possible through a special procedure called *la prise à partie*. This involves, amongst other things, having to obtain the special permission of the President of the Court of Appeal in the district concerned. His or her decision in this matter may be appealed to the *Cour de Cassation*.

As far as criminal liability connected with performing the judicial service, in France, as in the United Kingdom, certain types of offences may apply to judges to the extent that they act as public officials, including abuse of authority,[41] an offence of active or passive corruption[42] or denial of justice.[43]

Hungary

In Hungary, on the grounds of art 2(1) of Act CLXII 2011 on the status and remuneration of judges, judges in principle have the same immunity protection as Members of Parliament. With respect to the latter, the Fundamental Law states that 'Members of Parliament shall be entitled to immunity and to adequate remuneration ensuring their independence' (art 4(2)). In turn, art 73(1) of Act XXXVI 2012 on the National Assembly states that 'during and after the term of his or her mandate, the Member shall not be held liable before courts or other authorities for the vote cast or the fact or opinion communicated by him or her in the course of exercising and in connection with his or her mandate'. Thus, in applying this respectively to judges, it must be interpreted in such a way so that liability is generally precluded as far as the adjudicative process is concerned, meaning that a judge's legal opinion expressed in relation to the adjudication of a case cannot lead to criminal or civil liability. This thesis may be based on the general concepts of the separation of powers and judicial independence entrenched in art C (1) and in art XXVIII (1) of the Fundamental Law. Nevertheless, the 2011 Act introduces a certain exception to the principle of absolute immunity. It confers limited liability for judges

38 Art. 11-1[1] of Ordonnance No 58-1270 on the status of judges, with amendments.

39 Perrot (n 37) 91.

40 Art. 141-3 (1)(1) of the Code of the Organisation of the Judiciary of 1976.

41 Criminal Code, art. 432-150.

42 Criminal Code, art. 434-9.

43 Criminal Code, art. 434-7-1. See Guy Canivet and Julie Joly-Hurard, 'La responsabilité de juges, ici at ailleurs' (2006) 4 *Rev Int Droit Comp* 1055.

for damage or infringement of personal rights. The judge is liable up to three months' salary or may be ordered to pay damages if the damage or personal injury was caused by grossly negligent conduct. In the case of intentional damage or personal injury, the judge shall be liable for the full amount of the damage or injury suffered, regardless of his or her salary amount.[44] Liability for damages and claims arising in connection with infringement of personal rights resulting from a judge's professional misconduct is adjudicated in disciplinary proceedings, the provisions of which also apply to proceedings for liability for damages or payment of compensation.

The Hungarian law provides for limiting judges' civil liability relating to the relationship between a judge and their employer, i.e., the state. Pursuant to 131–134/A of the 2011 Act, judges may be held financially liable for any damages caused to the employer from their intentional or grossly negligent conduct within their jurisdiction. The judge's liability for damages, or for payment of any restitution for reasons other than professional misconduct, shall be determined – by a reasoned decision – by the person exercising the employer's rights within 60 days from the day they became aware of the damage.[45] The judge may challenge the employer's decision by filing an appeal with the court within 15 days.

The 2011 Act also confers limited judicial immunity to lay judges. Lay judges shall not be liable for their participation in the dispensation of justice or any fact or opinion which they may have stated in the exercise of their functions (art 2(4)). However, in this respect, immunity, under the Act, 'shall not apply to the misuse of top secret and privileged information, to defamation, slander or to civil liability'.[46] Simultaneously, the immunity covers 'defamation committed against a person in public office or a politician acting in a public capacity and where the lay judge was not aware that the information was substantially false'.[47] In practice, so far, liability issues for non-professional judges have not arisen.[48]

Poland

In Poland, unlike Hungary, no general analogy exists between judicial and parliamentary immunity, which is why no provision exists at the constitutional level that establishes substantive immunity for judges to protect them from

44 Art. 132 of Act CLXII 2011, on the status and remuneration of judges.

45 *Disciplinary, Civil and Criminal Liability of Judges in Hungary – Report Prepared for the Special Rapporteur on the Independence of Judges and Lawyers within the Operation of the Office of the High Commissioner for Human Rights* (OHCHR 17 June 2020), <www.ohchr.org/EN/Issues/Judiciary/Pages/ReportDisciplinaryMeasures.aspx> accessed 12 September 2021.

46 Art. 2 (4) of Act CLXII 2011, on the status and remuneration of judges.

47 Art. 2 (4) of Act CLXII 2011, on the status and remuneration of judges.

48 Tóth Áron László, 'A bírák mentelmi jogával kapcsolatos büntetőjogi és jogállási kérdések' (2017) 3 *Iustum Aequum Salutare* 237.

civil or criminal liability for acts connected with their profession. The Constitution only provides for formal immunity with respect to criminal liability (see below); in this regard, the statuses of judges and MPs are similar. The scholarship maintains, on the basis of the Constitution and the Act on the Common Courts Organisation 2011, that such formal immunity covers all acts (and omissions) of a judge, regardless of when they were committed and whether they were committed in connection with jurisdictional activities or administrative acts or in the judge's private life.[49] Therefore, it would appear that Polish law provides, to some extent, less protection than Hungarian law for actions undertaken by a judge in the exercise of his or her judicial function, as it does not provide for substantive immunity in this regard. On the other hand, as I mentioned above, there is an explicit legal provision in Hungary relating to liability for damages caused by the negligence or intentional act of a judge.

In Poland, there are no clear regulations concerning the civil liability of judges. The opinion of the scholarship is ambiguous.[50] Ewa Łętowska maintains that a judge may be liable for damages if unlawful action and fault can be attributed to him or her.[51] The Supreme Court has held that performing the function of a public official does not automatically eliminate liability for infringement of the personal rights of another person.[52] This infringement, performed within the scope of one's public function, may constitute grounds for liability regardless of the liability of the State Treasury. This means that the possible liability of the State Treasury does not exonerate the judge from liability but rather can exist in parallel with the liability of the judge.

Immunity from criminal liability for acts outside the courtroom

In the old democratic countries, it is quite rare to grant immunity to judges in criminal matters for acts which are committed outside the judge's function and which qualify as crimes in criminal law. In contrast, in Poland, judges enjoy

49 Jerzy Gudowski, Tadeusz Ereciński and Józef Iwulski (eds), *Prawo o ustroju sądów powszechnych. Ustawa o Krajowej Radzie Sądownictwa. Komentarz* (C.H. Beck 2009), note concerning art. 80.

50 Grzegorz Matusik, 'Odpowiedzialność cywilna sędziego za naruszenie czci w postępowaniu cywilnym' (2015) 1(19) *Iustitia* [online].

51 Ewa Łętowska, 'Grube nieporozumienie' *Dziennik Gazeta Prawna* (7 August 2013). This also results from the case law that states the prerequisite for the judge's liability is the unlawfulness of the act or omission infringing on personal goods in the exercise of judicial power (see Judgement of the Court of Appeal in Łódź of 28 April 2015, I ACa 1012/1).

52 See, inter alia, judgements of the Supreme Court of 19 December 2002, II CKN 176/01, unpublished, of 12 February 2010, I CSK 340/09, OSNC-ZD 2010, No C, item 97 and of 8 November 2012, I CSK 177/12, unpublished. The Supreme Court, in a 2013 resolution, obiter dicta also held that judges do not enjoy immunity in civil matters and that no provision excludes their civil tort liability towards the injured party for any damages caused by their unlawful acts and omissions in the exercise of their judicial powers or by their unlawful decisions.

formal immunity from criminal liability, which refers to all acts (and omissions) of a judge, including in the judge's private life. In Hungary, on the other hand, formal immunity applies only to those acts of a judge which are not related to the exercise of his or her judicial function. A characteristic of formal immunity is that it is qualified, in that it can be lifted through a special procedure. Once immunity is lifted, the judge is liable like anyone else, but each system in these countries has its individual aspects. In Poland in particular, from 2015 – until the electoral change in October 2023 – political actors tried to turn the institution of immunity lifting into a machine for disciplining judges.

United Kingdom

UK judges are not protected with procedural or substantive immunity from prosecution for acts outside the courtroom.[53] Furthermore, no personal inviolability exists for judges; therefore, a judge may be arrested and detained in precisely the same way as any other person.

United States

In the United States, like in the United Kingdom, no formal or substantive immunity exists concerning criminal liability for acts committed outside the judicial function.[54] Thus, judges may be charged with committing any ordinary criminal offence.

France

Since law no. 93–2 of 4 January 1993, judges in France also no longer benefit from any jurisdictional immunity for acts committed outside the exercise of their duties and can be prosecuted just like any other citizen, i.e., currently no procedural immunity in criminal matters exists in France.[55] The reform was motivated by the restoration of equality of all citizens and was linked to the abolition of various procedural privileges belonging to other public officials.[56] Before the reform, according to art 679–688 of the Code of Criminal Procedure of 1957 and 1958, the case had to be preliminarily examined by the *Cour de Cassation* after the prosecution. Where the crime or misdemeanour was committed in the course of legal proceedings and involved the violation of a provision of criminal procedure, the indictment might have been issued only if the unlawful nature of the proceedings or of the act carried out on that occasion had been established by a final decision of the criminal court hearing

53 Shetreet and Turenne (n 13) 272–284.

54 Shaman (n 27) 182.

55 Éric Sales, *Le Droit constitutionnel de la Ve République* (Editions Ellipses 2015) 343.

56 Vincent Lecoq, *Contribution à l'étude juridique de la norme locale d'urbanisme* (Presses Universitaires de Limoges 2004) 500.

the case. After reviewing the case, the court could determine that there were no grounds to charge the judge or to refer the case to a court with jurisdiction other than in which jurisdiction the accused exercised his or her functions. The procedure described therefore amounted in practice to an abandonment of formal immunity, which in this case protected actions taken in the exercise of the judicial function. The *Cour de Cassation* also had the power to authorise the arrest of a judge in ongoing criminal proceedings.[57]

Hungary

As I mentioned above, the immunity regulations for judges are analogous to those for Members of Parliament. This means that judges are also protected by formal immunity for acts committed outside the courtroom.

The Hungarian Status of the Members of the National Assembly Act of 2012 introduces two exceptions to deputies' immunity, which must be understood as extending to judges. The immunity shall not apply to the following criminal offences:

1 Agitation against a community, violation of national symbols, public denial of crimes of the national socialist and communist regimes, misuse of top secret and secret data, misuse of confidential data and misuse of restricted data as laid down in Act IV 1978 of the Criminal Code (in force until 30 June 2013) and
2 Incitement against a community, violation of national symbols, public denial of crimes of the national socialist or communist regimes or misuse of classified data as laid down in Act C 2012 of the Criminal Code (entered into force on 1 July 2013).

The procedure to lift immunity, however, may raise deep concerns, particularly in the context of the breakdown of the rule of law. In Hungary, it seems not to be a pure judicial procedure and in many ways is more discretionary, involving a political factor. The President of the Republic decides on the suspension of judicial immunity upon a proposal by the President of the National Office for the Judiciary, and Parliament shall decide on the suspension of immunity of the President of the Curia.[58] The National Office for the Judiciary (*Országos Bírósági Hivatal*, OBH) is a body with certain regulatory competences concerning courts and judges, which was created in 2011 to reduce the powers of the National Judicial Council. The president of the OBH is chosen by Parliament. In the original wording of Act CLXII 2011, the President of the Republic decided on the renunciation of immunity on the proposal of

57 See art. 682 of the Code of Criminal Procedure of 1957 and 1958.
58 Art. 2 paras. 2 and 3 and art. 2 (1) of Act CLXII 2011 on the status and remuneration of judges.

the President of the Supreme Court. In 2014, the power to suspend judicial immunity was transferred from the President of the Supreme Court to the President of the OBH, which appears to be part of a further politicisation of the procedures for holding judges to account in Hungary.

Immunity also protects Hungarian judges against prosecution for misdemeanours. In such cases, judges may also renounce their immunity themselves.[59]

Judges, like members of Parliament, may not be detained unless caught in the act of committing an offence (this constitutes the above-mentioned institution of personal inviolability), and no coercive measures provided for in the criminal procedure may be taken against them without lifting immunity.[60]

Poland

In Poland, as I noted above, the Constitution of 1997 entrenched procedural immunity regarding judges' criminal liability. This kind of judicial immunity has a long tradition. It was introduced by the March Constitution of 1921 and maintained, at least formally, during the Polish People's Republic (1944–1989). The current constitution states in art 181 that '[a] judge shall not, without prior consent granted by a court specified by statute, be held criminally responsible'. Apart from this kind of procedural judicial immunity, the same provision establishes personal inviolability, which precludes judges from being arrested or detained without the prior decision of 'a court specified by statute, except for cases when he has been apprehended in the commission of an offence and in which his detention is necessary for securing the proper course of proceedings'.[61] The Constitution adds in the aforementioned art 181 in fine print that 'the president of the competent local court shall be forthwith notified of any such detention and may order an immediate release of the person detained'.

Furthermore, under the Act on Common Court Organisation 2011 (as amended), judges enjoy absolute substantive immunity for misdemeanours, except for some traffic-related ones. Consequently, they cannot be held liable for misdemeanours before the ordinary courts (the procedure for lifting immunity is simply irrelevant here) and to that extent are liable in the same way as for disciplinary offences.

Returning to constitutional provisions, the Constitution in both cases uses the wording 'court specified by statute'. Until 2020, according to the Act on Common Court Organisation, this role was played by disciplinary courts, which have, first and foremost, jurisdiction in disciplinary matters as far as judges of general jurisdiction are concerned. In 2017, the disciplinary regime for judges changed, but in matters concerned with lifting immunity, in the

59 Art. 74. § (1) of Act XXXVI 2012 on the National Assembly.
60 Art. 74. § (1) of Act XXXVI 2012 on the National Assembly.
61 Art. 181 of the Constitution of Poland of 1997.

first instance, disciplinary courts within courts of appeal were competent. The so-called muzzle law amended the existing model for lifting immunity and made the Disciplinary Chamber of the Supreme Court (presently the Chamber of Professional Liability) the only organ responsible for all matters concerned with judicial immunities with reference to judges of the Supreme Court, common courts and military courts. The aim of this change was evident: the ruling party wanted to seize full control in this respect, as in the case of disciplinary procedures.

Turning back to the legal solutions applied in Poland, according to the procedures to lift judicial immunity, currently, the Chamber of Professional Liability's panel is supposed to issue a resolution 'which permits calling the judge to criminal responsibility if a sufficiently justified suspicion exists that he has committed a criminal offence'.[62] The Chamber's resolution includes the decision granting permission to hold a judge liable for criminal responsibility as well as the statement of grounds.[63] The identical procedure is applied when consenting to a judge's detention. If a resolution permits the prosecution of a judge for criminal liability for an intentional offence prosecuted through public indictment, it *eo ipso* should include suspension of the judge from their duties, as well as a reduction in their remuneration of between 25% and 50% for the duration of the suspension.[64]

As in disciplinary proceedings, in the case of administrative judges, respective benches of the Supreme Administrative Court are competent to lift the immunity. The same applies to the judges of the Constitutional Court, i.e., the decision to lift immunity constitutes a competence of the respective benches (compositions) of the judges of the Court. From a legal perspective, in this case, the independence of the administrative and constitutional judiciary seems to be better protected. Nevertheless, entrusting the competence to lift immunity only to the Constitutional Court judges may raise the question of maintaining impartiality, as in the case of the implementation of disciplinary liability.

The core of judicial immunity and the principle of judicial independence

From the point of view of the principle of judicial independence, it is vital to establish the fundamental nucleus of judicial immunity, which, regardless of

62 Art. 80 para. 2c of the Act on Common Court Organisation. The standard 'reasonable suspicion that an offence has been committed' is not a strict one; therefore, the assessment of whether this condition is met should always depend on the specific circumstances of the case. Cf *Resolution of the Supreme Court of 18 October 2004*, ref. SNO 40/04, OSNSD 2004, No 2, Item 33; *Resolution of the Supreme Court of 16 November 2016*, ref. SNO 38/16, Lex No 2157283.

63 Art. 80 para. 2c in fine.

64 Art. 129 paras. 2 and 3 of the Act on Common Court Organisation.

a given political system, should be permanent. The starting point here, in my view, must be to link immunity with the objective that it serves in the context of ensuring the principle of an independent judiciary, including – above all – judges' internal, individual independence, comprising a correlate of these virtues as judicial impartiality.

Olowofoyeku cites several justifications for absolute immunity is said to be needed before arguing against each of them.[65] The arguments in favour of absolute judicial immunity to civil liability include:

1. It is not right to make judges liable for erroneous decisions, as it is natural that there may be various approaches to a particular case and that a decision could be reviewed by a higher court.
2. For damages arising from judicial misconduct, there are several alternatives to an action for damages, such as criminal proceedings and disciplinary measures.
3. A lack of judicial immunity precludes decision finality, as the parties and judge may sue one another unceasingly.
4. Judges are accountable not to the litigants, but to the state, so liability towards parties should not occur here.
5. Possible actions taken against judicial decisions would deter people from serving in judicial posts.
6. Immunity protects judges in the exercise of their office from being influenced by the threat of litigation.
7. Immunity preserves the independence of the judiciary from both the executive and the public.
8. Immunity protects the integrity of judges and the judicial process, e.g., from degradation if the judiciary faced many actions against it.
9. Immunity is in the interest of the public, as judges should be at liberty to adjudicate without fear of consequences, thereby protecting the stability of the whole system of the administration of justice.
10. Shielding judges from intimidation is more important than redressing harm in an individual case.

Olowofoyeku balances all these arguments and, while agreeing with some points, simultaneously contends that they do not justify absolute immunity. He is of the opinion that limited civil liability allows for redressing a wrong without undermining the values included in the aforementioned points. He also contends that substitutes for civil liability, such as disciplinary or criminal liability, do not work because they often fail in practice: for a person who suffered financial damages, these liabilities are not much consolation. Thus,

65 Olowofoyeku (n 20) 178–201.

Olowofoyeku[66] and other common law authors[67] are in favour of a limited version of judicial immunity from suit – a qualified one that would allow for holding judges liable when they infringe on others' legal rights unlawfully and deliberately through malicious motivation, or when fraud, corruption or conspiracy is involved.

The fundamental issue seems to be ensuring judges' freedom to exercise their powers and guarantee their impartiality. These are essential conditions for the functioning of an independent judiciary. Therefore, immunity is intended to protect against potentially unfair treatment of a judge by litigants in such a way that it could influence judicial decisions and lead to bias on the judge's part. In this context, some arguments favour limiting the possibility of bringing a civil action against a judge for actions that can be qualified as falling within the scope of his or her functions. However, a complete lack of civil liability on a judge's part may result in him or her failing to exercise due care and help cause specific harm due to his or her actions or judgements. Therefore, in the search for a standard, certain exceptions to the principle of full immunity in the adjudication sphere should be allowed. Judicial errors should be remedied on appeal, whether in relation to jurisdiction, procedure, determination, application of the law or assessment of the evidence.[68] Where this is not possible and the question of damage under civil law arises, it is conceivable that civil liability could only be asserted if the judge acted culpably (in bad faith) and only once the appeal route is exhausted and a higher court has validly overturned the judge's erroneous decision that caused damage or infringed on personal rights. This makes it possible to combine the principle of instance control with the principle of personal liability of the judge for the damage. On the other hand, where the judicial wrong arises in connection with a final judgement, the possibility of claims would have to involve some form of resumption of legal proceedings, which obviously complicates the principle of the finality of judicial decisions.

Nevertheless, the need to protect a judge's freedom to make judicial decisions, even erroneous ones, to an extent supports the French approach, which comprises only the possibility of the state's recourse claim against a judge in a situation in which a court ruling is linked to the state's responsibility for causing damage. Of course, this measure can only be implemented in a system in which the state is empowered to pay compensation for unlawful judicial action,

66 Olowofoyeku (n 20) 178–201.

67 See for instance Andrew Nicol, 'Judicial Immunity and Human Rights' (2006) *European Human* 136 (5) *Rights L Rev* 558ff and John Murphy, 'Rethinking Tortious Immunity for Judicial Acts' (2013) 33 (3) *Leg Stud* 455–477.

68 This approach is emphasised by the Consultative Council of European Judges (CCJE), see 'Opinion no. 3 of the Consultative Council of European Judges (CCJE) to the Attention of the Committee of Ministers of the Council of Europe on the Principles and Rules Governing Judges' Professional Conduct, in Particular Ethics, Incompatible Behaviour and Impartiality' <https://rm.coe.int/16807475bb> accessed 6 January 2022.

and only if there is a proper judicial remedy in this respect or the consent of an impartial institution. However, such a solution also carries the potential risk of increasing the judges' fear that they will be powerless when confronted with the machinery of the state.[69] In turn, the exclusion of State Treasury liability for an incorrect, damage-causing ruling, combined with absolute judicial immunity from civil liability, is the most controversial solution, as it makes it *ex lege* impossible to seek any compensation for damages. It is not without reason that calls for limiting judicial immunity appear in British and American[70] academia when dealing with such a situation.[71]

As far as formal immunity from criminal liability is concerned, the argument to justify it would be that it protects judges from harassment using organs of the state, which is reminiscent of the early days of constitutional democracy when deputies' immunity was created so that the monarch would not be able to intimidate parliamentarians by making criminal accusations. As indicated in the analysis above, immunity in criminal matters does not exist in the 'old democracies' discussed here. Therefore, the question arises as to whether this particular kind of immunity falls within the international/European standard of immunity protection. In this respect, the answer may depend on the extent to which a potential reform in a given state comprising a significant reduction in immunity may be perceived as a violation of the principle of judicial independence and, thus, a violation of the right to an independent court in the sense of international and European law. It seems that this issue must be examined on a case-by-case basis, taking into account the political landscape of the country concerned as well as the specificity of the particular criminal justice system. In this respect, the approach that the CJEU presented on the appointment of Maltese judges may be helpful,[72] in which the CJEU recognised the possibility of political appointees making judicial appointments if these decisions are not arbitrary and an independent body is involved in appointing judges. In this ruling, the judges also formulated the important principle of the prohibition of regression, i.e., the legislative deterioration of the protection of rule of law values. Regarding the issue we are interested in here, the ruling may be used as an argument in favour of viewing the deterioration of existing immunity solutions as impermissible. Thus, the lack of immunity protection in criminal proceedings would not in itself violate the principle of judicial independence, but when it already exists under the state's constitutional traditions,

69 Olowofoyeku (n 20) 219.

70 Cf John Bennett Sinclair, 'Casenotes: Torts – Judicial Immunity: A Sword for the Malicious or a Shield for the Conscientious? *Stump v. Sparkman*, 98 S Ct 1099 (1978)' (1978) 8(1) *U Balt L Rev* 141–161.

71 There is also a legitimate criticism concerning the lack of state responsibility for unlawful judicial action in common law countries. See Abimbola A. Olowofoyeku, 'When Courts Get it Wrong: Judicial Errors and Common Law Under Enforcement' (2018) 134 *L Q Rev* 450–477.

72 Judgement in Case C-896 of 19 April 2021.

its limitation or abolition would raise serious doubts. Invoking the principle of non-regression means that any reform that weakens immunity protection is to some extent suspect and must be assessed, for example, through the prism of the requirements of art 6 of the European Convention on Human Rights in the context of the specific situation of judges in a given country and the motives behind the proposal. The opinions expressed by the judges themselves and other participants in the public debate are also relevant here.

Conclusion

This chapter has presented an overview of judicial immunity in selected constitutional systems and has answered questions regarding whether some level of immunity is essential for protecting judicial independence.

It may be concluded that judicial immunity in some form is an essential guarantee of judicial independence, but the scope of immunity appears to be the focus of continued debate. In considering the most important components of the principle of independence of the judiciary, it seems crucial to ensure that a judge is free to make his or her own decisions within judicial remit. I contend that, as a general rule, civil and criminal liability for delivering a specific judgment should be excluded. Exceptions to this principle should only apply in situations where a higher court determines that a lower court's ruling was erroneous, resulted in specific damage, and that such damage was caused by a judge's actions that were unequivocally unauthorised or carried out in bad faith. In turn, criminal liability may relate to a situation in which a judge has committed a type of official criminal offence that is strictly connected with his judicial function, e.g., a corrupt action. Allowing such liability, however, may leave room for autocratic politicians to attack the independent judiciary by defining such 'official crimes' very broadly.

The absence of immunity in many jurisdictions regarding criminal matters does not inherently threaten the principle of independence. However, if immunity is present within a constitutional system, its limitation or abolition could, in specific instances, be viewed as a degradation of the established standard, thereby raising certain concerns. Generally, it also may be said that while a judge lacking absolute immunity in civil cases does not necessarily threaten the independence of the judiciary, proposals for such limitations must be assessed in the specific socio-political context of the country concerned. In practice, limiting substantive immunity from actions carried out within a judicial capacity may also raise doubts in regard to the previously mentioned non-regression principle.

As far as civil liability for an unlawful judicial decision is concerned, the principle of judicial independence might seem less threatened if the state were to bear the costs of compensation and, in extreme cases, seek indemnity from the judge. The condition of such an approach would be an independent judicial assessment of such liability. In the case of direct civil action by a party of the proceedings, the danger here lies in the possible distortion of impartiality by giving judges an excessive fear of future entanglement in a personalised civil action. However, as I mentioned above, the pressure of the state machinery, especially when undermining the rule of law, could also have a disproportionate impact on judicial independence, so this solution is not without its drawbacks.

In summary, immunity is designed to protect a judge from potential harassment by both litigants and other factors, including other state authorities, in particular law enforcement organs. It is therefore intended to safeguard the independence of the judiciary by providing adequate protection for judicial decisions. This rationale for immunity protection makes some form of immunity necessary to maintain the independence of the judges and to enable judges to apply the law without fear of the consequences of reaching any decision made in good faith. Given the purpose of immunity, the minimum requirement is to protect the judicial decision itself. The protection of acting in good faith when exceeding one's powers therefore appears to be an essential condition for a judge's freedom of action.

Part III

Quis custodiet ipsos custodes?

7 Making constitutional judges accountable for deliberating*

Three hypotheses and possible research

Cristóbal Caviedes

Introduction

When checking the constitutionality of legislation, an area in which judges may be made accountable to citizens is whether – before issuing their decisions – they really deliberated among themselves. Put differently, whether they tried to reach widespread reason-based agreements on how the respective case should be solved, and on the justifications behind such a solution. After all, salient theories justifying constitutional adjudication assume that citizens' acceptance of this practice rests upon constitutional courts' decisions[1] being highly thought through, which in turn is seen as being dependent on judicial deliberation.[2]

Still, to make judges accountable for deliberating, there's a data gap that needs to be bridged on how constitutional courts' decision procedures affect, impinge on, or influence their deliberation. Mainly due to the general secrecy of judicial debates, there seems to be relatively little empirical research focused on judicial deliberation. There is detailed quantitative research – particularly on the US Supreme Court – describing judges' decisions.[3] Yet, this research mainly explains those decisions by concentrating on variables other than

* This book chapter belongs to a research project called Procedimientos Decisorios y Consenso Judicial en los tribunales constitucionales y las cortes supremas de las democracias consolidadas [Decision Procedures and Judicial Consensus in the Constitutional and Supreme Courts of Consolidated Democracies]. This project is financed by the FONDECYT programme of Chile's Agencia Nacional de Investigación y Desarrollo [National Research and Development Agency], grant n° 11220386.

1 I use the word 'constitutional courts' broadly. So, I'm including 'Kelsenian' and 'supreme' courts. On these courts, see Alec Stone Sweet, 'Constitutional Courts' in Michael Rosenfeld and András Sajó (eds), *The Oxford Handbook of Comparative Constitutional Law* (Oxford University Press 2012) 817–820.

2 Ronald Dworkin, *A Matter of Principle* (HUP 1985) ch 2; John Rawls, *Political Liberalism* (Expanded edn, Columbia UP 2005); John Ferejohn and Pasquale Pasquino, 'Constitutional Adjudication: Lessons from Europe' (2004) 82 *Texas L Rev* 1671, 1692–1700.

3 David Robertson, 'Appellate Courts' in Peter Cane and Herbert M. Kritzer (eds), *The Oxford Handbook of Empirical Legal Research* (Oxford University Press 2010) 576–577; Brian M. Barry, *How Judges Judge* (Routledge 2021) 3–5.

DOI: 10.4324/9781003557852-10

decision procedures, such as the ideology that judges supposedly espouse,[4] or their incentives to maximise certain goods.[5] And there are studies analysing how decision procedures affect decision making in groups such as juries,[6] legislatures,[7] and mini publics,[8] but considering the differences between these groups and constitutional courts, it is not clear that the results of these studies carry over to such courts.

As in most research, to start bridging this gap, one may consider existing studies on how decision procedures affect deliberation in different kinds of groups, and then build hypotheses tailored to constitutional courts. Once these hypotheses are built, one may suggest empirical studies to probe them. This is the aim of this chapter, in which I review some of the main empirical literature on how certain decision procedures – namely, non-opposition, voting, and publicising judicial debates – affect deliberation in constitutional courts and other groups, and then build three hypotheses on these procedures' effects on judicial deliberation. Afterwards, I briefly suggest some possible empirical studies to probe these hypotheses.

This chapter is divided into three sections. In the first section, I address why, in constitutional adjudication, it matters that judges deliberate with each other. In the second section, I introduce this chapter's hypotheses. I start by hypothesising that, compared with non-opposition, early voting produces a certain resistance to change one's mind that affects judges. Later, I hypothesise that, in constitutional adjudication, unanimity rule coerces dissenting judges into accepting their peers' view. Finally, I hypothesise that publicising judicial debates de-incentivises judges to agree with each other. Before presenting each hypothesis, I analyse relevant empirical literature. In the final section, I propose some studies for assessing these hypotheses. I suggest some comparisons between constitutional courts, along with controlled trials and statistical analyses. Also, I suggest that, since no constitutional court seems to

4 E.g., see Lee Epstein and Jack Knight, *The Choices Justices Make* (CQ Press 1998); Jeffrey A. Segal and Harold J. Spaeth, *The Supreme Court and the Attitudinal Model Revisited* (CUP 2002); Cass R. Sunstein, David Schkade, Lisa M. Ellman and Andres Sawicki, *Are Judges Political? An Empirical Analysis of the Federal Judiciary* (Brookings Institution 2006).

5 E.g., see Richard Posner, 'What Do Judges and Justices Maximize? (The Same Thing Everybody Else Does)' (1993) 3 *Sup Ct Econ Rev* 1; Lee Epstein, William M. Landes and Richard A. Posner, *The Behavior of Federal Judges: A Theoretical and Empirical Study of Rational Choice* (Harvard University Press 2013).

6 For overviews of this research, see Michael J. Saks, 'What Do Jury Experiments Tell Us About How Juries (Should) Make Decisions?' (1997) 6(1) *S Cal Interdisc LJ* 1; Neil Vidmar and Valerie P. Hans, *American Juries: The Verdict* (Prometheus Books 2007); Dennis J. Devine, *Jury Decision Making: The State of the Science* (New York University Press 2012).

7 E.g., see Jürg Steiner, André Bächtiger, Markus Spörndli and Marco R. Steenbergen, *Deliberative Politics in Action: Analysing Parliamentary Discourse* (Cambridge University Press 2004).

8 For overviews of this research, see Jürg Steiner, *The Foundations of Deliberative Democracy: Empirical Research and Normative Implications* (Cambridge University Press 2012); Michael A. Neblo, *Deliberative Democracy Between Theory and Practice* (Cambridge University Press 2015).

use unanimity rule to declare statutes unconstitutional, in principle, the main way of testing unanimity rule's potential coercive effects is through controlled trials.

Now, I must clarify that most of the studies suggested here can only assess judicial deliberation indirectly, by measuring levels of judicial agreement when deciding. Thus, these studies must assume that, *ceteris paribus*, there's a positive or direct association, correlation, or link between judicial agreement and judicial deliberation. Meaning, all else equal, the more judicial agreement there is on a decision or set of decisions, the likelier it is that the respective judges deliberated on them. This link would have to be assumed since, along with the usual secrecy of judicial debates, there are inherent difficulties in empirically analysing people's motives for agreeing on decisions. And these studies may only be considered by courts in which judges can publish separate opinions, since only then one can measure judicial agreement.

Naturally, this approach may be subject to criticism since judicial agreements may not stem from deliberation, but rather from peer pressure or from what psychological research refers to as 'social influences'[9] – that is, our bent, tendency, or inclination to (even unconsciously) agree to what we perceive as the group's dominant opinion. Yet, in constitutional courts, there are at least four reasons to assume that peer pressure and social influences are partially controlled for.

First, if a constitutional court has effective rules protecting judicial independence (both regarding other institutions and other judges), peer pressure and social influences are mitigated since such mitigation is one of these rules' main aims. Second, in many constitutional courts, judges are jurists, that is, they are legal experts.[10] So, they are likely confident at rendering individual judgements[11] without being unduly pressured by their peers. Third, if judges can publish separate opinions, there's little reason to assume that they were coerced into agreeing on some decisions since they can openly oppose them, and since those decisions may be issued without their support.[12] Finally,

9 Cass R. Sunstein, *Infotopia: How Many Minds Produce Knowledge* (Oxford University Press 2006) 67–69, 86–88; Devine (n 6) 152–153, 158–167, 185–186.

10 The big outlier here is the French Constitutional Council. On the Council, see Louis Favoreu, 'The Constitutional Council and Parliament in France' in Christine Landfried (ed.), *Constitutional Review and Legislation* (Nomos Verlagsgesellschaft 1988) 81–88; John Bell, *Judiciaries within Europe* (Cambridge University Press 2006) 94–100.

11 I'm using the word *judgement* in a philosophical sense, not a legal sense. So, when referring to judicial decisions, I use the word *decisions* rather than *judgements*. On judgements in a philosophical sense, and how they differ from preferences, see Lewis Kornhauser and Lawrence Sager, 'Unpacking the Court' (1986) 96(1) *Yale LJ* 82, 101.

12 It isn't fully accurate that, in civil law countries, judges can't publish separate opinions. In most European and Latin American constitutional courts, judges may do so. On European courts, see European Parliament, 'Dissenting Opinions in the Supreme Courts of the Member States' (PE 462.470, Directorate-General for Internal Policies. Policy Department C, Citizens' Rights and Constitutional Affairs, November 2012) 17–19; Katalin Kelemen, *Judicial Dissent in European Constitutional Courts: A Comparative and Legal Perspective* (Routledge

peer pressure and social influences tend to occur in groups whose members have high status differences,[13] but this does not fully apply to constitutional courts since – at least formally – judges have roughly the same status between them. So, in principle, the assumption that, all else equal, there are direct links between judicial agreement and judicial deliberation seems reasonable.

It is also worth pointing out that, in this chapter, I use a flexible concept of accountability.[14] I understand accountability as requiring judges to explain their actions to others – not as requiring judges to follow the preferences or judgements of people they are accountable to.[15] Particularly, in this chapter, accountability is interpreted as requiring judges to explain to others whether they really deliberated with their brethren, colleagues, or peers. This matters since some conceptions of accountability may be somehow at odds with deliberation. As we see further, a key aspect of deliberation is the willingness to change one's judgements when presented with sound reasons to do so. Thus, if accountability implies that one must exactly follow the judgements of people one's accountable to, accountability goes against deliberation since it doesn't allow for judgement change. Conversely, if accountability is understood more broadly, simply as requiring one to explain one's actions to others, accountability is compatible with deliberation. I use the term *accountability* in this latter sense.

After these provisos, let's proceed with the rest of this chapter.

Why must judges deliberate?

Despite the differences between legal theorists, an assumption that most of them share is that, when checking the constitutionality of legislation, judicial deliberation is a cognitively or epistemically sound decision procedure. This means that, to correctly interpret the constitution, judges must deliberate among themselves:[16] they must exchange arguments based on impartial reasons[17] on how constitutional provisions should be understood. And they must

2019). On Latin American courts, see Eduardo Ferrer Mac-Gregor (coord), *Crónica de Tribunal Constitucionales en Iberoamérica* (UNAM Marcial Pons 2009).

13 Garold Stasser and William Titus, 'Pooling of Unshared Information in Group Decision Making: Biased Information Sampling During Discussion' (1985) 48(6) *J Pers Soc Psych* 1467; Sunstein (n 9) 67–69, 86–88; Devine (n 6) 166–167, 185; Li Liu, Connie Yuan and Poppy Lauretta McLeod, 'Twenty-Five Years of Hidden Profiles in Group Decision Making: A Meta-Analysis' (2012) 16(1) *Pers Soc Psych Rev* 54.

14 On different conceptions of accountability, see Richard Mulgan, 'Accountability: An Ever-Expanding Concept?' (2000) 78(3) *Pub Adm* 555.

15 Thus, following Mulgan's typology, I'm not referring to *accountability* as "responsiveness." Mulgan (n 14) 556.

16 On how the idea of deliberation has evolved, see André Bächtinger, *John Dryzek, Jane Mansbridge and Mark Warren*, 'Deliberative Democracy: An Introduction' in André Bächtinger, John S Dryzek, Jane Mansbridge and Mark E. Warren (eds), *The Oxford Handbook of Deliberative Democracy* (Oxford University Press 2018).

17 Impartial reasons are reasons that don't just appeal to the speaker's self-interest. Jon Elster, *Securities Against Misrule: Juries, Assemblies, Elections* (Cambridge University Press 2013) 45.

do so with the aim of changing their peers' judgements, along with being open to having their judgements changed by their peers' claims. Thus, in principle, deliberation implies seeking unanimous agreements on decisions,[18] but only insofar as these agreements stem from rational argument – not from misrepresenting one's judgements to manipulate one's peers,[19] nor from making credible promises or threats to them.[20] This doesn't mean that unanimity is *necessary* for decision processes to be deliberative,[21] but according to the deliberative ideal – and insofar as agreements stem from a rational argument – all else equal, the more judges agree with each other when deciding, the better.

Judicial deliberation is seen as cognitively sound since, at best, deliberation boosts judges' accuracy[22] – that is, their capacity as a group for correctly resolving constitutional cases – while at worst, deliberation clarifies judges' grounds for disagreement. In turn, judicial deliberation is seen as boosting judges' accuracy since (1) deliberation enlarges the pool of arguments available to judges; (2) deliberation screens out good arguments from bad arguments; and (3) deliberation may lead to agreements, based on impartial reasons, on the constitutionality of legislation.[23]

At face value, the assumption that constitutional adjudication needs judicial deliberation seems rather evident. Indeed, salient legal scholars and philosophers have underscored the relations between deliberation and constitutional adjudication. For Ely[24] and Habermas,[25] constitutional adjudication guards the conditions that enable deliberation at the societal level. And for Dworkin,[26] Rawls,[27] and Ferejohn and Pasquino,[28] among others,[29] constitutional courts

18 Deliberative democracy theorists disagree on how stringent this condition should be, but in general, they tend to prefer more rational agreement to less rational agreement. Bächtinger and others (n 16) 7–8.

19 Elster (n 17) 72–84. Following Steiner, I assume that 'mis-representing one's judgment' includes not sharing data that goes against such judgement. Jürg Steiner, 'Concept Stretching: The Case of Deliberation' (2008) 7 *Eur Pol Sci* 186.

20 Elster (n 17) 30–36.

21 So, in principle, deliberation is compatible with judges issuing separate opinions.

22 There are other benefits attributed to deliberation, but I won't tackle them here. For an overview, see Conrado Hübner Mendes, *Constitutional Courts and Deliberative Democracy* (Oxford University Press 2013) 22–36.

23 Kornhauser and Sager (n 11) 101; Hélène Landemore, *Democratic Reason: Politics, Collective Intelligence, and the Rule of the Many* (PUP 2013) 97–103.

24 John Hart Ely, *Democracy and Distrust: A Theory of Judicial Review* (Harvard University Press 1980) ch 4.

25 Jürgen Habermas, *Between Facts and Norms: Contributions to a Discourse Theory of Law and Democracy* (MIT Press 1996) ch 5, 7. See also Mattias Kumm, *Institutionalising Socratic Contestation: The Rationalist Human Rights Paradigm, Legitimate Authority, and the Point of Judicial Review* (2007) 1 *Eur JLS* 153.

26 Dworkin (n 2) ch 2.

27 Rawls (n 2) 215–216, 231–240.

28 Ferejohn and Pasquino (n 2) 1692–700.

29 E.g., see Christopher L. Eisgruber, *Constitutional Self-Government* (Harvard University Press 2007) ch 1–3; Robert Alexy, 'Balancing, Constitutional Review and Representation' (2005) 3(4) *ICON* 572, 579.

are archetypal examples of institutions whose authority rests on the quality of the reasons that judges can formulate. Further, law is a deliberative practice since one of its key tenets is the need to exchange arguments for solving cases. If there's an idea that most legal theories share, that idea arguably is that law is a sort of rational discourse, and thus an activity that needs deliberation. Certainly, legal scholars may strongly disagree on the kinds of claims that should be considered 'legal' arguments.[30] But the premise that law requires formulating and expressing reason-based arguments is shared by most of them.

Yet, law's deliberative character does not exactly imply that judges must discuss cases with each other. After all, one may think of constitutional adjudication systems in which, after the judges receive the case's data – and without communicating among themselves – each judge issues their decision along with the reasons behind it, and then these decisions are just added. It has been argued that this happened in the UK House of Lords,[31] and that it's happening in the High Court of Australia[32] and the supreme courts of Brazil,[33] Mexico,[34] and the United States.[35] In these cases, the respective court's decision could be considered deliberative insofar as it's based on impartial (and perhaps, even highly thought through) reasons, though it wouldn't be deliberative insofar as it wouldn't stem from previous discussions or debates between judges. Thus, even if law is a kind of rational discourse, this doesn't seem to suffice for arguing that judges must deliberate among themselves: one needs more reasons to argue so.

Still, a missing factor that, all else equal, tips the balance in favour of judicial deliberation is the need to boost legal certainty – the need to boost the likelihood that constitutional provisions are expounded in relatively uniform ways, so that their application is impartial and predictable. After all, if rather than mostly being group products, constitutional courts' decisions predominantly become just the sum of their judges' opinions, it becomes increasingly difficult

30 For an overview of these debates, see Hübner Mendes (n 22) 54–61.

31 Alan Paterson, *Final Judgment: The Last Law Lords and the Supreme Court* (Hart Publishing 2013) 84–91.

32 In Australia, this debate was sparked by a speech given by former High Court Justice Dyson Heydon. See Dyson Heydon, 'Threats to Judicial Independence: The Enemy Within' (2013) 129 *LQR* 205. For responses, see Peter Heerey, 'The Judicial Herd: Seduced by Suave Glittering Phrases?' (2013) 87 *ALJ* 460; Anthony Mason, 'Reflections on the High Court: Its Judges and Judgments' (2013) 37 *Aust Bar Rev* 102. I'm thankful to Gabrielle Appleby for sharing this data with me.

33 Virgilio Afonso da Silva, 'Deciding Without Deliberating' (2013) 11(3) *ICON* 557; André Rufino do Vale, *La deliberación en los tribunales constitucionales* (Centro de Estudios Políticos y Constitucionales 2017) 173–195.

34 Francisca Pou Giménez, 'Changing the Channel: Broadcasting Deliberations in the Mexican Supreme Court' in Richard David and David Taras (eds), *Justices and Journalists: The Global Perspective* (Cambridge University Press 2017).

35 Lee Epstein, Jeffrey A. Segal and Harold J. Spaeth, 'The Norm of Consensus in the US Supreme Court' (2001) 45 *AJPS* 362; Pamela Corley, Amy Steigerwalt and Artemus Ward, *The Puzzle of Unanimity: Consensus on the United States Supreme Court* (Stanford Law Books 2013) ch 1; Lawrence Baum, *The Supreme Court* (13th edn, CQ Press 2019) 116–119.

for citizens to expound the content of these decisions, thus hindering citizens' capacity to plan their lives in ways compliant with the law. In this sense, judicial deliberation is worthy since, by increasing the odds that judges reach common decisions supported by shared reasons – by increasing the odds that, following Cohen, judges agree on 'concessions and accommodations required for [their court] to speak with a more unified voice'[36] – deliberation boosts legal certainty.

Now that we've reviewed why judges must deliberate with each other, let's build the hypotheses for testing whether they really do so.

The hypotheses

Early voting makes judges stubborn

Analytically speaking, when groups decide, it's worth distinguishing between at least two ways in which their decisions may be made: namely, 'non-opposition'[37] (also called 'decision by interpretation'[38] or 'consensus')[39] and 'voting'.[40] In practice, many groups mix non-opposition and voting when deciding. Yet, these decision procedures have key differences that are useful to consider when analysing their effects, thus justifying a separate examination.

In non-opposition, decision making resembles the phrase generally used in Christian wedding ceremonies: 'speak now, or forever hold your peace'. When groups decide by non-opposition, group members talk among themselves until they seem to reach a unanimous agreement on what should be done. In non-opposition, after discussing possible decisions, a group member (usually the member directing the discussion) suggests a decision that isn't resisted by other group members (herein the name 'non-opposition'). Thus, due to the lack of resistance against the last decision proposal made inside the group, this decision proposal becomes the group's decision.

For example, suppose that Jean, Jeanne, and Juana must choose whether to go to a BTS concert or watch the latest *One Piece* anime movie. And suppose that Juana suggests that, since BTS won't be in town for long, they should go to the BTS concert first and watch the *One Piece* anime movie the following day. In this case, if nobody opposes Juana's plan and everyone follows it (even if nobody openly said that they agreed with that plan), that's deciding by non-opposition.

36 Mathilde Cohen, 'Ex-Ante versus Ex-Post Deliberations: Two Models of Judicial Deliberations in Courts of Last Resort' (2014) 62 *Am J Comp L* 951, 1006.

37 Phillipe Urfalino, 'The Rule of Non-Opposition: Opening Decision-Making by Consensus' (2014) 22(3) *J Pol Phil* 320.

38 Jürg Steiner and Robert H Dorff, 'Decision by Interpretation: A New Concept for an Often Overlooked Decision Mode' (1980) 10(1) *BJ Pol S* 1.

39 Sherif El-Hakim, 'The Structure and Dynamics of Consensus Decision-Making' (1978) 13(1) *Man, New Series* 55.

40 Elster (n 17) 30–36.

Conversely, unlike non-opposition, voting is about adding, aggregating, or counting individual preferences or judgements to collectively decide. Unlike non-opposition – in which a decision is understood as made just because nobody resisted the last decision proposal made inside the group – in voting, each group member's preferences or judgements must always be ***added*** to decide. So, in my previous example, if instead of deciding by non-opposition, Jean, Jeanne, and Juana decide by voting, each one of them must openly say which option they prefer, and the option that gets most individual support – the option that gets most 'votes' – wins.

Psychological studies[41] suggest that, if done early in a decision process, voting halts deliberation by anchoring group members to the judgements expressed in their votes.[42] Conversely – when compared against early voting – by not forcing group members to issue judgements until different possible decisions have been thoroughly analysed, non-opposition boosts agreements among group members since it allows them to change their minds more easily.

These studies suggest that, when people publicly voice a judgement (as judges do when voting), they somehow commit to that judgement, hence becoming less open to changing it than they would be if they hadn't expressed it,[43] along with supporting it more extremely.[44] The results of these studies may be linked to the cognitive bias called 'choice-supportive misremembering'.[45] Due to this bias, when one decides something, one automatically attributes positive traits to such a decision, while simultaneously attributing negative traits to its alternatives. Further, these results overlap with Carson's[46] and Carson and Schecter's[47] experience in organising deliberative mini publics. For these authors, voting early during a mini public discussion hampers deliberation by making people resistant to changing their minds.

41 For overviews, see Stuart Oskamp and P. Wesley Schultz, *Attitudes and Opinions* (3rd edn, Psychology Press 2005); Robert J. MacCoun, 'Psychological Constraints on Transparency in Legal and Government Decision Making' (2006) 12(3) *Swiss Pol Sci Rev* 112, 116–117.

42 Lewin was the first to suggest this hypothesis. Kurt Lewin, 'Group Decision and Social Change' in Eleanor E. Maccoby, Theodore M. Newcomb and Eugene L. Hartley (eds), *Readings in Social Psychology* (3rd edn, Holt, Reinhart and Winston 1958) 203–204.

43 Milton E. Rosenbaum and Isabel Madry Zimmerman, 'The Effect of External Commitment on Response to an Attempt to Change Opinions' (1959) 23(2) *Pub Op Q* 247; Michael S. Pallak, David A. Cook and John J. Sullivan, 'Commitment and Energy Conservation' (1980) 1 *App Soc Psych Ann* 235; Robert M. Bohm, 'Death Penalty Opinions: A Classroom Experience and Public Commitment' (1990) 60 *Soc Inquiry* 285.

44 Jerald M. Jellison and Judson Mills, 'Effect of Public Commitment upon Opinions' (1969) 5 *J Exp Soc Psych* 340; Charles A. Kiesler and Paul A. Munson, 'Attitudes and Opinions' (1975) 26 *Ann Rev Psych* 415, 423–424, 437–438.

45 Martina Lind, Mimì Visentini, Timo Mäntylä and Fabio Del Missier, 'Choice-Supportive Misremembering: A New Taxonomy and Review' (2017) 8(2062) *Front Psych* 1, 1–3.

46 Lyn Carson, 'Deliberation' (Research and Development Note, newDemocracy Foundation 22 March 2017).

47 Lyn Carson and David Schecter, 'The Role of Voting in Citizens' Juries' (Research and Development Note, newDemocracy Foundation 8 March 2017).

Similarly, studies on US criminal juries show that the earlier jurors vote, the likelier it is that jurors that made up an initial majority of the jury stick to their initial judgements.[48] According to these studies, in general, US criminal juries may be divided into 'evidence-driven' juries and 'verdict-driven' juries.[49] In evidence-driven juries, jurors usually try to build shared stories to which they later attempt to link unanimously agreed on decisions. In these juries, '[voting] is infrequent and tends to occur later in the deliberation'.[50] And since in these juries, jurors try to build shared understandings of the evidence, in these juries it is likelier that jurors widely agree on their decision. Contrariwise, in verdict-driven juries, jurors vote before debating the case, along with taking several votes during the debate before taking a final vote.[51] In verdict-driven juries, opinion-changes are infrequent since jurors tend to act as advocates for particular verdicts,[52] trying to 'align themselves with those who are on the same side and talk about the evidence that supports their faction.'[53]

Evidence-driven juries tend to decide in ways akin to deciding by non-opposition. Specifically, by postponing voting as much as possible, and by emphasising the search for common understandings of the case, evidence-driven juries' decision procedures closely resemble non-opposition in how they avoid unnecessary divisions among jurors, thus boosting intra-group agreements. Thus – as it happens with non-opposition – since evidence-driven juries' decision procedures boost agreements among jurors, it has been argued that such procedures 'appear to be more in keeping with the legal ideal associated with deliberation and would seem to be the preferred style for juries to employ.'[54]

Among constitutional courts, one may see a split akin to that between verdict-driven and evidence-driven juries. According to Baum,[55] Songer and others,[56] Cohen,[57] Kelemen,[58] Kirby,[59] and Paterson,[60] some constitutional courts – particularly those of the common law tradition, such as those of Australia, Canada, the United Kingdom, and the United States – decide by voting procedures that, broadly speaking, resemble those of verdict-driven juries. In these

48 Harry Kalven Jr and Hans Zeisel, *The American Jury* (special edn, The Legal Classics Library 1993) 486–491; Saks (n 6) 37, 39–41; Vidmar and Hans (n 6) 142–144; Devine (n 6) 156–157, 158-161, 185–186.

49 Vidmar and Hans (n 6) 142–144; Devine (n 6) 156–157, 171–172.

50 Vidmar and Hans (n 6) 143.

51 Vidmar and Hans (n 6) 142–144; Devine (n 6) 156–157, 171–172.

52 Devine (n 6) 156.

53 Vidmar and Hans (n 6) 143.

54 Devine (n 6) 172.

55 Baum (n 35) 116–120.

56 Donald R. Songer, Susan W. Johnson, Cynthia Lynne Ostberg and Matthew Edward Wetstein, *Law, Ideology, and Collegiality* (MQUP 2012) 87–93.

57 Cohen (n 36) 980–992.

58 Kelemen (n 12) ch 3.

59 M. D. Kirby, 'Judicial Dissent – Common Law and Civil Law Traditions' (2007) 123 *LQR* 379.

60 Paterson (n 31) 84–91.

courts, after the parties orally present their claims, the judges immediately meet face-to-face to debate the case and vote on a decision, which is then put into writing by a drafting judge. As in verdict-driven juries, in these courts, judges vote early in the process. Obviously, while the decision is being drafted, the judges may change their vote. But these judges still hold a vote *before* such drafting.

Conversely, as in evidence-driven juries, many European constitutional courts (such as those of France, Germany, Italy, and Spain) tend to decide by non-opposition, thus postponing voting as much as possible and using it only if unanimous agreements aren't reached.[61] Unlike courts deciding in ways akin to verdict-driven juries, in European constitutional courts, after the parties present their claims, one of the judges – called the 'reporter judge' or 'reporting judge' (*rapporteur* in French, *Berichterstatter* in German, or *ponente* in Spanish) – drafts a decision proposal to be later debated by all the respective judges in face-to-face meetings.

A key aspect that makes these courts' decision procedures non-oppositional is that – to gain as much support as possible – reporter judges actively seek out their peers' opinions and try to accommodate them in their drafts *before* the judges meet face-to-face.[62] (Actually, to save time, in France, reporter judges may write two opposing decision drafts in case one of them isn't supported by most of their colleagues.)[63] So, reporter judges generally try to boost the odds that the decision drafts they present get unanimous approval by previously discussing them with their peers.[64] And as Cohen claims, to do this, reporter judges' 'agenda setting power is perhaps [their] most significant prerogative. It gives [them] the opportunity to present [their] analysis in the best light so as to win over [their] colleagues'.[65] As it happens with verdict-driven juries vis-à-vis evidence-driven juries, when the US Supreme Court is compared with European constitutional courts (particularly the German court),[66] it's been noticed that the number of separate opinions tends to be higher in the former court than in the latter courts.[67]

61 Ferejohn and Pasquino (n 2) 1692–1696; Cohen (n 36) 963–980; Rufino do Vale (n 33) ch 1; Kelemen (n 12) ch 2. See also Alec Stone Sweet and Giacinto della Cananea, 'A Conversation with Dieter Grimm' (2021) 22 *Germ LJ* 1541, 1545–1547; Alec Stone Sweet and Giacinto della Cananea, 'A Conversation with Sabino Cassese' (2021) 22 *Germ LJ* 1526, 1529–1532.

62 Cohen (n 36) 963–975; Rufino do Vale (n 33) 48–61; Kelemen (n 12) 39–45.

63 Cohen (n 36) 965.

64 Ferejohn and Pasquino (n 2); Cohen (n 36) 973–975, 979–980; Kelemen (n 12) 39–44.

65 Cohen (n 36) 966.

66 For detailed quantitative data on the US Supreme Court, see Lee Epstein, Jeffrey A. Segal, Harold Joseph Spaeth and Thomas G. Walker, *The Supreme Court Compendium: Two Centuries of Data, Decisions, and Developments* (7th edn, CQ Press 2021) ch 3. For detailed quantitative data on the German Federal Constitutional Court, see Federal Constitutional Court – Bundesverfassungsgericht, 'Annual Statistics' <www.bundesverfassungsgericht.de/EN/Verfahren/Jahresstatistiken/jahresstatistiken_node.html> accessed 31 March 2023.

67 Ferejohn and Pasquino (n 2) 1672–1674, 1677–1679, 1692–1700; Kelemen (n 12) 83–95.

Considering this difference, this chapter's first hypothesis is that – all else equal – in constitutional courts, early voting produces a resistance to changing one's judgements akin to that of verdict-driven juries. Due to this resistance, if judges vote early, they are more reticent at changing their minds than they would otherwise be. In sum, this chapter's first hypothesis is that early voting makes judges stubborn. Thus, if one wants to promote deliberation (in the sense of boosting agreements among judges), constitutional courts' decision procedures should be more like those of European constitutional courts than those of the US Supreme Court. Therefore, after receiving the parties' claims, judges should try to agree on decision drafts by non-opposition, and only use voting if unanimous agreements aren't reached.

Unanimity coerces dissenting judges

Along with the timing of voting, another aspect of this decision procedure which matters for deliberation are voting thresholds. Meaning, the thresholds that indicate the number of votes needed to decide.

Based on thresholds, one may distinguish between at least four kinds of voting rules.[68] First, there is 'plurality rule' (also called 'relative majority' rule). Under this rule, decisions are made if most members present[69] support them, even if such support is less than half of the group members present. Second, there is 'majority rule' (also called 'absolute majority rule'). Under this rule, decisions are made if half of the group members present plus a group member present support them. Third, there are supermajority rules. Under these rules – and depending on the specific supermajority – decisions are made if they are supported by a threshold ranging between more than half of the group members present plus one group member present, but less than unanimity rule. So, supermajority rules are a range of voting rules. Finally, there is 'unanimity rule'. Under this rule, decisions are made if all group members support them.

In most constitutional courts, the voting rule for declaring statutes unconstitutional is majority rule. Still, in polities[70] such as Chile,[71] the Czech Republic,[72]

68 On voting rules generally, see Eerik Lagerspetz, *Social Choice and Democratic Values* (Springer 2006).

69 I use the word *present* due to possible quorum requirements.

70 I use the word *polities* rather than *countries* due to Taiwan's contested international situation.

71 In Chile, a four-fifths rule is used to void statutes, but the Chilean Constitutional Court can also dis-apply statutes by majority rule. Art. 93 inc. 1° N° 7 Constitución Política de la República [Constitution].

72 § 13 odst Zákon č 182/1993 Sb, o Ústavním soudu, ve znění pozdějších předpisů [Constitutional Court Act].

Mongolia,[73] Mexico,[74] Peru,[75] and South Korea[76] (along with the US states of Nebraska[77] and North Dakota),[78] constitutional courts declare statutes unconstitutional by supermajority rules.

There aren't many empirical studies on voting rules' effects on intra-group deliberation. Deliberative democracy theorists often see unanimous agreements as desirable – which suggests that they may support unanimity rule – while seeing plurality rule and majority rule as a sort of second-best decision procedure if unanimity isn't reached.[79] But there's not much evidence for holding that this mix between voting rules helps intra-group deliberation.

In turn, when comparing voting rules, social choice theorists often see a trade-off between speed and reflection. For them, the lower voting thresholds are, the quicker groups decide,[80] though such decisions are likely not as reflected on as they would be under higher voting thresholds. Conversely, the higher voting thresholds are, the more reflexive decisions are, though such decisions are likely not as quick as they would be under lower voting thresholds.[81] Some partial exceptions to this logic may be found in the works of Condorcet[82] and Laplace,[83] which suggest that – rather than enhancing deliberation – unanimity rule coerces dissenters (particularly lone dissenters) by promoting peer pressure and social influences. But empirical research to ground these claims still seems insufficient.

Yet, studies on mini publics in deeply divided societies, and on parliamentary debates, seem to confirm some of deliberative theorists' intuitions. Studies

73 In principle, the Mongolian Constitutional Court decides by majority rule. But to produce legal effects, the Court's decisions need the legislature's approval. If the legislature refuses its approval, the decision goes back to the Court for re-consideration. The Court can only trump the legislature's refusal by two-thirds. Tom Ginsburg, *Judicial Review in New Democracies: Constitutional Courts in Asian Cases* (Cambridge University Press 2003) 165–173; Constitution of Mongolia, art. 66(2); Law of Mongolia on the Constitutional Court (Tsets), art. 8(2).

74 Constitución [Constitution], art. 94 inc 2°; Ley Orgánica del Poder Judicial de la Federación [Organic Law of the Judicial Branch of the Federation], art. 7°.

75 Art. 5° inc. 1° Ley No 28.301 Ley Orgánica del Tribunal Constitucional [Organic Law on the Constitutional Court].

76 Hyonbop [Constitution] Art. 113(1) (RO Korea).

77 Neb Const. art. V-2.

78 ND Const. art. VI, §§ 4–5.

79 Bächtinger and others (n 16) 7–8.

80 Kenneth O May, 'A Set of Independent Necessary and Sufficient Conditions for Simple Majority Decision' (1952) 20(4) *Econometrica* 680, 681–682; Lagerspetz (n 68) 36–38.

81 Marie Jean Antoine Nicolas de Caritat, marquis de Condorcet, *Plan de Constitution présenté a la Convention Nationale* (first published 1793, Imprimerie Nationale 1793); Melissa Schwartzberg, *Counting the Many: The Origins and Limits of Supermajority Rule* (Cambridge University Press 2013) 93–94.

82 Marie Jean Antoine Nicolas de Caritat, marquis de Condorcet, *Essai sur l'application de l'analyse à la probabilité des décisions rendues à la pluralité des voix* (first published 1785, Cambridge University Press 2014) cxxxix–cxlii.

83 Pierre-Simon Laplace, *Essai philosophique sur les probabilités* (first published 1825, Cambridge University Press 2009) 171–174.

on Belgian mini publics undertaken by Caluwaerts[84] and by Caluwaerts and Deschower[85] suggest that, insofar as group members don't vote before debating (among other conditions), supermajority rules and unanimity rule boost deliberation among group members more than majority rule.[86] Similar results may be seen in research by Steiner and others on the Belgian legislature, in which they concluded that 'the highest level of deliberation occurred when unanimity was required, the lowest with majority rule, with the two-thirds rule in between'.[87] In these studies, deliberation was assessed by an indicator called 'the Discourse Quality Index' (DQI).[88]

Still, research on US verdict-driven criminal juries showing jurors' resistance to changing their judgements has been interpreted by Schwartzberg[89] as confirming Condorcet's and Laplace's intuitions that unanimity rule may coerce dissenters, hence hampering rather than aiding deliberation among group members. True, considering the secrecy of jury debates, peer pressure and social influences can't be directly seen. Yet the fact that these juries must usually decide unanimously – along with the fact that, when jurors vote early, juries' decisions tend to mirror the judgement of most jurors in the initial vote – gives us strong clues that minority jurors may have somehow been coerced into adopting their peers' judgement.

Considering that constitutional courts resemble juries since they both adjudicate cases, this chapter's second hypothesis is that, when declaring statutes unconstitutional, unanimity rule hinders deliberation, in the sense that it coerces dissenting judges into adopting their peers' opinion. After all, it's not clear why the results of studies involving unanimity rule are different in mini publics (or legislatures) when compared with US verdict-driven criminal juries. It may be that, in juries, the initial vote plays a major role in triggering unanimity rule's potentially coercive effects. But there may be other factors at play. So, unanimity rule's potentially coercive effects in constitutional adjudication require further testing.

After presenting this chapter's first two hypotheses – which focus on voting – let's turn to the third hypothesis, which tackles the effects of publicising judicial debates.

84 Didier Caluwaerts, *Confrontation and Deliberation: Deliberative Democracy in Divided Belgium* (Peter Lang 2012).
85 Didier Caluwaerts and Kris Deschouwer, 'Building Bridges Across Political Divides: Experiments on Deliberative Democracy in Deeply Divided Belgium' (2014) 6(3) *Eur Pol Sci Rev* 427, 433–434, 442–447.
86 Steiner (n 8) 211; Ian O'Flynn and Didier Caluwaerts, 'Deliberation in Deeply Divided Societies' in André Bächtinger, John S. Dryzek, Jane Mansbridge and Mark E. Warren (eds), *The Oxford Handbook of Deliberative Democracy* (OUP 2018) 747–748.
87 Steiner (n 8) 211.
88 There's been several versions of this index. On its development, see Steiner and others (n 7) 52–73, 170. For a newer version, see Steiner (n 8) 268–271.
89 Schwartzberg (n 81) 79, 87–88.

Publicity makes judges divas

Theoretically speaking, a most debated issue in deliberative theory is whether deliberation must happen secretly or publicly. For Habermas[90] and Landwehr,[91] publicity is a necessary trait of deliberative processes. Conversely, Shapiro,[92] Chambers,[93] Ferejohn and Pasquino,[94] Goodin,[95] and Elster[96] question this view. For these scholars, there's a trade-off between publicity and deliberation among group members. When groups must decide on behalf of others, disclosing their debates can make their members accountable to third parties affected by their decisions, along with allowing these parties to know – and thus to contest – the reasons behind such decisions. So, insofar as it helps disclosing groups' reasons for deciding to people outside the group, publicity may be considered positive for deliberation.

Yet, when promoting deliberation among group members, publicity may be detrimental. If debates are public, group members may feel more anxious about how they appear to potential audiences than about engaging with their peers' ideas. Thus, publicising debates may hinder group members' capacity to convince others, and their openness to change their judgements. Public debates may intimidate group members, making them less willing to say what they really think out of fear of social punishment. And as suggested by psychological research showing people's resistance to change their judgements once they have openly voiced them,[97] public debates may encourage group members to stick to their minds out of fear of appearing weak or indecisive before potential audiences, particularly if group members represent such audiences.

A key study on the effects of publicising debates is Elster's[98] comparison of the US Constitutional Convention with the 1789 French Constituent Assembly. For Elster, when compared with the French Assembly, the main factor explaining why the US Convention could mitigate 'passion, interest, bias, or prejudice'[99] in its debates is that such debates were secret, while in the French Assembly, debates were public.

90 Jürgen Habermas, 'Political Communication in Media Society: Does Democracy Still Enjoy an Epistemic Dimension? The Impact of Normative Theory on Empirical Research' (2006) 16 *Comm Theory* 411, 413.
91 Claudia Landwehr, 'Discourse and Coordination: Modes of Interaction and their Roles in Political Decision-Making' (2010) 18(1) *J Pol Phil* 101, 105–107.
92 Ian Shapiro, 'Optimal Deliberation' (2002) *J Pol Phil* 196.
93 Simone Chambers, 'Behind Closed Doors: Publicity, Secrecy, and the Quality of Deliberation' (2004) 12(4) *J Pol Phil* 389.
94 Ferejohn and Pasquino (n 2) 1692–1700.
95 Robert Goodin, 'Sequencing Deliberative Moments' (2005) 40 *Acta Politica* 182, 193–194.
96 Elster (n 17) 7–11, ch 2, 228–232.
97 Oskamp and Schultz (n 41) 250; MacCoun (n 41) 116–117.
98 Elster (n 17) 201–202, 228–232.
99 Elster (n 17) 201–202.

Further, research by Steiner and others[100] on parliamentary debates from the late 1980s through the 1990s in Germany and Switzerland[101] shows that, though some aspects of deliberation are strengthened by publicising debates, others are weakened by such publicity.[102] Using the DQI, Steiner and others compared the public debates of the studied legislatures' plenary sessions with the secret debates of their committee sessions.[103] These researchers found that, though in plenary sessions there were 'high levels of logical justification'[104] and 'frequent references to the common good',[105] there was also 'little respect for the arguments of others'.[106] Conversely, Steiner and others found that committee sessions were exactly the opposite: in these sessions, group members had high levels of inter-personal respect,[107] but 'low levels of logical justification'[108] and 'infrequent references to the common good'.[109] Thus, when promoting agreements among group members, this research suggests that the anxiety that publicity may hinder deliberation has some merit.

Moreover, a study by Meade and Stasavage[110] reveals that publicising debates may hamper dissent due to some degree of self-censorship by group members. Meade and Stasavage examined the minutes of the US Federal Reserve's Open Market Committee before and after a decision made by the US Congress in 1993 to publish them. Before 1993, the Open Market Committee's members didn't know that the minutes of their meetings would eventually be disclosed, but after 1993, they knew this would happen.[111] Analysing these minutes, Meade and Stasavage found that, after 1993, dissent among Committee members sharply decreased.[112] According to them, before 1993, Federal Reserve governors (who are part of the Open Markets Committee) had 'a 10% likelihood of verbally dissenting'[113] to an interest-rate policy proposal made by the Federal Reserve chairman, while after 1993, they only had 'a 3% likelihood'[114] of voicing such dissent.

100 Steiner and others (n 7) ch 4–6.
101 Steiner and others (n 7) 100–107.
102 Steiner and others (n 7) 128–131.
103 Though the debates of the German and Swiss legislatures' committee sessions were secret, once these debates ended, transcripts of them were published. Steiner and others analysed these transcripts. Steiner and others (n 7) 54.
104 Steiner and others (n 8) 128.
105 Steiner and others (n 8) 128.
106 Steiner and others (n 8) 128.
107 Steiner and others (n 8) 128.
108 Steiner and others (n 8) 128.
109 Steiner and others (n 8) 128.
110 Ellen E. Meade and David Stasavage, 'Two Effects of Transparency on the Quality of Deliberation' (2006) 12(3) *Swiss Pol Sci Rev* 123.
111 Meade and Stasavage (n 110) 123, 126–127.
112 Meade and Stasavage (n 110) 127–131.
113 Meade and Stasavage (n 110) 130.
114 Meade and Stasavage (n 110) 130.

Similar results may be seen in psychological studies[115] and in Naurin's research on business lobbyists in Sweden and the European Union.[116]

In most constitutional courts, judicial debates are secret. Still, there are at least two salient constitutional courts in which judicial debates are broadcast live on television, namely, the Federal Supreme Court of Brazil[117] and the Supreme Court of Mexico.[118]

In the Brazilian court, after the oral hearings, face-to-face meetings among the justices are broadcast. According to da Silva[119] and de Mendoça Lopes,[120] this broadcast hinders judicial deliberation. For these authors, broadcasting judicial debates has discouraged judges from engaging with their peers' ideas, while encouraging them to constantly develop, guard, and promote a public persona towards Brazilian citizens; even if that means not reaching possible (and even desirable) agreements with their peers.

In this respect, a study undertaken by André Rufino do Vale[121] comparing the Brazilian and Spanish constitutional courts is quite illustrative. This study includes interviews of active judges in both courts. Though do Vale's study doesn't use statistics, this study suggests that Spanish judges tend to agree with each other more than Brazilian judges. For do Vale, while in the Spanish court, there are actual exchanges of opinions among judges in their face-to-face meetings,[122] in Brazil, these meetings tend to be monologues in which each justice just states their decisions (and their underlying reasons) without really considering their peers' claims.[123] Do Vale's conclusions are partially confirmed by de Mendoça Lopes'[124] statistical analysis of the Brazilian court's decisions, which shows that, after publicising judicial debates, the length of justices' opinions increased, along with their odds of dissenting. Similar results can be seen in a recent study made by da Silva, which also includes interviews of former and active Brazilian justices.[125]

In the Mexican supreme court, broadcasting judicial debates seems to produce similar effects as in the Brazilian court. According to Pou Giménez,[126] when justifying their decisions (particularly in politically salient cases), Mexican justices

115 Robert J. MacCoun, 'Psychological Constraints on Transparency in Legal and Government Decision Making' (2006) *Swiss Pol Sci Rev* 12(3) 116–117.

116 Daniel Naurin, *Deliberation Behind Closed Doors: Transparency and Lobbying in the European Union* (ECPR Press 2007).

117 da Silva (n 33) 580–583.

118 Pou Giménez (n 34) 209.

119 da Silva (n 33) 580–583.

120 Felipe de Mendoça Lopes, 'Television and Judicial Behavior: Lessons from the Brazilian Supreme Court' (2018) 9(1) *Econ Anal L Rev* 41, 43, 59–62.

121 do Vale (n 33) 48–80, 146–185.

122 do Vale (n 33) 63–81.

123 do Vale (n 33) 173–185.

124 de Mendoça Lopes (n 120) 43, 59–62.

125 Virgilio Afonso da Silva, 'Big Brother Is Watching the Court: Effects of TV Broadcasting on Judicial Deliberation' (2018) 51 *VRÜ* 437, 443–449, 454–455.

126 Pou Giménez (n 34) 213–218.

show extreme divisions. For her, these divisions are linked to broadcasting judicial debates, since doing so incentivises justices to 'deliver . . . eloquent speech[es] and never go back',[127] rather than 'com[ing] to terms with one another to the extent necessary to reach . . . identifiable collective institutional outcome[s]'.[128]

Pou Giménez's insights are partially backed by Gustavo Marín Hernández's[129] statistical analysis of the change in the number of separate opinions in the Mexican court before and after 2007, the year when judicial debates started to be broadcast. According to this study, after 2007, having television cameras where Mexican justices debate boosts the odds that they'll dissent, particularly if such dissents are issued by single justices. (Though under the same conditions, the odds that justices concur diminishes.)[130] This leads Marín Hernández to conclude that, if in a collective institution, one mainly seeks coherency and unity, one should opt for secrecy – or lower publicity levels – when shaping its decision procedures.[131]

Considering this research on the Brazilian and Mexican courts – along with the research on the effects of publicising debates on other groups – this chapter's third hypothesis is that publicising debates hinders judicial deliberation, in the sense that it stimulates judges to agree with each other less than they would if judicial debates were secret. Indeed, publicity's effects on judicial deliberation may be gradual: the more public judicial debates are, the less judges are willing to agree with each other, and vice versa. In short, this chapter's third hypothesis is that publicising judicial debates makes judges divas.

Possible research

Let's briefly restate this chapter's hypotheses before examining how they may be studied. The first hypothesis is that, compared with non-opposition, early voting deters judicial agreements. The second hypothesis is that, in constitutional adjudication, unanimity rule coerces dissenting judges into adopting their peers' view. The third hypothesis is that publicising judicial debates discourages judicial agreements.

A key challenge for testing the first and third hypotheses – as I argue further, it doesn't seem possible to test the second hypothesis through comparative studies – is that there doesn't seem to be much comparative research focused on constitutional courts' voting rules, or their debates' publicity levels. And studies suggesting that European judges tend to agree with each other more than other judges often compare European constitutional courts with the US Supreme Court. This lack of comparative research doesn't allow us to screen

127 Pou Giménez (n 34) 223.

128 Pou Giménez (n 34) 223.

129 Gustavo Marín Hernández, '¿Protagonismo ante las Cámaras de TV? Deliberación Pública y Disenso Judicial en la Corte Suprema Mexicana, 1998–2012' (Master's thesis, Centro de Investigación y Docencia Económicas 2018).

130 Marín Hernández (n 129) 21–28.

131 Marín Hernández (n 129) 27.

out for factors unrelated to constitutional courts' decision procedures (or just applicable to the US) that may influence judicial deliberation.

Indeed, one of the few salient studies focused on decision procedures that compares a European constitutional court with a court other than the US supreme court is do Vale's.[132] As mentioned earlier, this study suggests that publicising judicial debates hinders judicial agreements. Yet, this study mainly focuses on judicial debates' publicity, saying little on non-opposition's and voting rules' effects on deliberation. Further, a limit of do Vale's study is that the Brazilian and Spanish constitutional courts not only differ on publicity levels – they also differ on aspects such as whether they decide in plenary sessions (the Brazilian court)[133] or divided into panels (the Spanish court);[134] whether they allow oral hearings (the Brazilian court does,[135] while the Spanish court generally doesn't);[136] or whether they allow amici curiae (the Brazilian court does,[137] while the Spanish court doesn't).[138] So, though Rufino do Vale's study is a necessary, deep, and insightful contribution, by itself, this study isn't enough for isolating publicity's effects on Brazilian justices from other procedures' effects.

Thus, considering do Vale's methods, a good way of studying the effects of non-opposition, voting rules, and publicity on judicial deliberation might be to do more studies like his. If focused on the effects of non-opposition and voting rules, publicity would have to be controlled for. So, these studies should only consider courts in which judicial debates are secret. These studies may start comparing European courts with constitutional courts other than the US Supreme Court on which we already have in-depth analyses – or even just basic data on their decision procedures.[139] In turn, if focused on publicity's effects on judicial deliberation, the Brazilian or Mexican courts may be compared with courts that may be more like them in aspects other than publicity levels. For example, the Brazilian court may be compared with other constitutional courts in the Americas. And considering that, in the Brazilian court, judges issue their opinions *seriatim*,[140] the Brazilian court may be compared

132 Rufino do Vale (n 33).
133 do Vale (n 33) 126.
134 do Vale (n 33) 47.
135 do Vale (n 33) 170–173.
136 Ferejohn and Pasquino (n 2) 1677, 1692.
137 do Vale (n 33) 170–173.
138 do Vale (n 33) 44–46.
139 E.g., along with the literature I've already cited on the Brazilian and Mexican courts, for Latin America, we may consider data in Ferrer Mac-Gregor (n 12); Manuel José Cepeda Espinosa and David Landau, *Colombian Constitutional Law: Leading Cases* (OUP 2017). For Asia, we may consider data in Ginsburg (n 73); Albert H. Y. Chen and Andrew Harding (eds), *Constitutional Courts in Asia: A Comparative Perspective* (CUP 2018). For Africa, we may consider data in Charles M. Fombad (ed.), *Constitutional Adjudication in Africa* (Oxford University Press 2017).
140 da Silva (n 33) 570–572.

with other courts following this decision procedure, such as the Australian High Court[141] or the UK Supreme Court.[142]

Still, for testing the first and third hypotheses, it's worth complementing comparative studies with statistical analyses akin to de Mendoça Lopes'[143] and Marín Hernández's;[144] and particularly with controlled trials involving judges or former judges. After all, though controlled trials' effects aren't fully applicable in real-world cases, controlled trials are still the most reliable tool we have for assessing variables in isolation. And considering the relevant differences among legal systems – differences that affect how their constitutional courts are shaped – in comparative research, it's very hard (if not impossible) to find two courts that are equal in everything except the decision procedures one wants to study.

Moreover, on examining publicity's effects on judicial deliberation, the speeches of Mexican and Brazilian judges could be analysed through Steiner and others' Discourse Quality Index.[145] As in Steiner and others' study,[146] if after this analysis, it is found that – though having logical justifications, and often referring to ideas of group well-being – these speeches show little respect for other judges' claims, this would partially show that, in constitutional courts, publicity likely produces Steiner and others' observed trade-offs between different aspects of deliberation. (Naturally, in controlled trials focused on assessing publicity's effects on deliberation, the speeches of participants involved in these trials may also be analysed through Steiner and others' method.)

However, we may face a contradiction here between accountability and judicial deliberation. Up to now, I've assumed that accountability and judicial deliberation are compatible, that judges should be accountable for whether they deliberate among themselves, and that to generate such accountability, we need research to get more data on how they really decide cases. Yet, if studies on publicity's effects on judicial deliberation show that this deliberation is hindered by publicity, accountability and judicial deliberation wouldn't be as compatible any longer. As with many publicity measures, in Brazil[147] and Mexico,[148] publicising judicial debates was introduced to bolster citizens' chances of checking judicial behaviour. But if publicising judicial debates lessens the odds that judges deliberate, then, to foster such deliberation, one may have to forgo the accountability given by publicity.

If accountability and judicial deliberation are partially incompatible, studies on publicity's effects on judicial deliberation are still worthy since they would confirm that – when shaping a constitutional court – trade-offs must be made between

141 Kirby (n 59).
142 Paterson (n 31) 11.
143 de Mendoça Lopes (n 120).
144 Marín Hernández (n 129).
145 Steiner and others (n 7) ch 3.
146 Steiner and others (n 7) 100–107, 128–131.
147 da Silva (n 33) 580–581.
148 Pou Giménez (n 34) 209–210.

these two aims. If one can't simultaneously have a maximally accountable and a maximally deliberative constitutional court, it's still quite useful to have information on the areas in which accountability and judicial deliberation can be boosted, or the areas in which one can only boost one of these aims by decreasing the other. Trade-offs may be certain, but it's better knowing so than acting blindly.

Lastly, on the second hypothesis – that is, that in constitutional adjudication, unanimity rule coerces dissenting judges into adopting their peers' view – this hypothesis would mainly have to be assessed via controlled trials: it doesn't seem possible to assess them by comparing constitutional courts since, to the best of my knowledge, no constitutional court uses unanimity rule to declare statutes unconstitutional.

Conclusion

In a recent article, Donald Bello Hutt criticised the idealisation of constitutional courts as the fora in which deliberation is best realised.[149] Further, he showed scepticism in our ability to study judicial deliberation for two reasons: first, since judicial debates are secret, we can't see judges' interactions;[150] and second, the DQI is a questionable index since, among other things,[151] it is only based on a sketchy version of Habermas' ideas[152] and it can't assess speakers' sincerity.[153]

I share Bello Hutt's critique of court idealisations, but I don't fully share his scepticism on empirically studying judicial deliberation. Indeed, in most polities, judicial debates are secret. Thus, Bello Hutt is right in holding that 'we are in no position to know whether judges are deliberative during the parts of the procedure in which they gather to decide'.[154] But this also happens in US criminal juries, and researchers have still been able to draw valuable empirically backed insights on how debates among jurors unfold. Granted, these studies may not allow us to build optimally deliberative decision procedures, but comparatively speaking, they at least give us enough information on the kinds of procedures in which it's likelier that group members deliberate with each other (e.g. in the jury context, the procedures of evidence-driven juries when compared against those of verdict-driven juries). This information may not be much. But in a context of limited data due to the secrecy of debates – and indeed, a context in which such data may have to be limited for deliberation to happen – this information seems better than nothing.

In turn, on the DQI, it's worth noting that Bello Hutt hasn't questioned the parts of this index that assess whether speakers' claims are logically justified, whether these claims refer to group well-being, or whether speakers show

149 Donald Bello Hutt, 'Measuring Popular and Judicial Deliberation: A Critical Comparison' (2018) 16(4) *ICON* 1121, 1136–1140.
150 Hutt (n 149) 1139, 1145–1146.
151 Hutt (n 149) 1131–1132, 1135–1136.
152 Hutt (n 149) 1132–1134.
153 Hutt (n 149) 1134–1135.
154 Hutt (n 149) 1139.

respect for their peers' claims. This matters since these parts of the DQI allow us to examine the trade-offs involved in publicising debates. So, despite the DQI's flaws, if these parts of the DQI are strong, this index may still be useful for studying whether these trade-offs also occur in constitutional courts.

Therefore, following a more optimistic path than Bello Hutt's, in this chapter, after reviewing key literature, I have presented three hypotheses for empirically studying judicial deliberation that assume that some decision procedures hinder this aspect of constitutional adjudication. Any study made to test these hypotheses may generate information that would enable citizens to check whether judges really deliberate with each other when deciding. I started by hypothesising that – when compared against non-opposition – in constitutional courts, early voting hinders deliberation by making judges less likely to change their minds. Later, I hypothesised that, if used to declare statutes unconstitutional, unanimity rule coerces dissenting judges into accepting their peers' opinion. Finally, I hypothesised that publicising judicial debates discouraged judges from agreeing with each other.

On a final note, some constitutional courts publish annual reports or annual statistics that include the number of yearly decisions issued by the respective court.[155] To aid data collection, it would be quite helpful if these reports or statistics included (1) the number of yearly unanimous decisions; (2) the number of yearly decisions with dissenting opinions, including separate data on different numbers of dissenting opinions; and (3) the number of yearly decisions with concurrences, including separate data on different numbers of concurrences. For example, on (2) and (3), these statistics or reports may show 'number of decisions with one dissent (or concurrence),' 'number of decisions with two dissents (or concurrences),' and so forth.[156]

After all, it's likely that much of the research needed to test these chapter's hypotheses are highly resource-intensive and time-consuming, especially when gathering data on majority opinions and separate opinions in large sets of judicial decisions; something which is needed to quantitatively study judicial deliberation. Thus, presenting this data wouldn't only ease the researcher's task; it would also show a strong commitment to public scrutiny – and to help improving decision procedures – that, in the long run, would likely benefit the respective court reputationally among researchers, legal practitioners, and citizens as a whole.[157]

155 E.g., the German and Spanish courts present this data, along with data on the yearly number of separate opinions. Yet, it isn't clear how many of these opinions are dissents or concurrences. On the German court, see Federal Constitutional Court (n 66). On the Spanish court, see Tribunal Constitucional de España, 'Memorias del Tribunal Constitucional' *Tribunal Constitucional de España* (26 July 2021) <www.tribunalconstitucional.es/es/memorias/Paginas/default.aspx> accessed 10 April 2023.

156 A useful format for presenting this data may be that of the US *Supreme Court Compendium*. Epstein and others (n 66) ch 3.

157 Of course, this means I'm against the French criminal ban on studying judicial behaviour. Malcolm Langford and Mikael Rask Madsen, 'France Criminalises Research on Judges' *Verfassungsblog* (22 June 2019) <https://verfassungsblog.de/france-criminalises-research-on-judges/> accessed 10 April 2023.

8 How to hold constitution's defenders accountable? Reflections on the specificity of the constitutional judges' accountability

Radosław Puchta

Introduction

Although the idea that constitutional actors should be accountable for their actions is quite old, it was only recently that a theoretical concept of their accountability gained – not without some resistance – a fixed place among other concepts being at the centre of attention of the contemporary legal doctrine, including constitutional law scholars.[1] Moreover, due to the high complexity of the issue in question, the doctrine still seems to be far from reaching a consensus on the very meaning of accountability, its nature and limits, as well as adequate measures of its enforcement. While some scholars employ a broad and sometimes vague definition of the accountability, comprising not only an obligation to submit information, but also the need for sanctions of both political and legal nature, others insist on adopting a narrow meaning so as to distinguish the concept of accountability from other constitutional concepts, such as political responsibility or legal liability.[2] As Nicholas Bamforth and Peter Leyland summarize it:

> Discussion of accountability begs the question concerning what it means to be 'accountable', which parties an accountability relationship might

1 See Nicholas Bamforth and Peter Leyland, 'Introduction: Accountability in the Contemporary Constitution' in Nicholas Bamforth and Peter Leyland (eds), *Accountability in the Contemporary Constitution* (Oxford University Press 2013) 1–24; note esp. their assertion, at 1, that '"Accountability" is one of the more frequently used terms in today's constitutional vocabulary, whether in the United Kingdom, the European Union more broadly, the United States, or other liberal democracies'.

2 From the latter point of view, accountability as a separate category is oriented 'only to obtain a report on the authority exercised and not to apply specific sanctions. . . . [I]t is a set of institutions consisting of obtaining knowledge about the undertaken actions with the possibility of their further use (also in order to implement other form of account), and not of the assessment (approval or rejection) of the subject's power'. Anna Młynarska-Sobaczewska and Jacek Zaleśny, 'Accountability as a Category of Constitutional Law – Terminological Considerations' (2020) 26 *Comp L Rev* 199.

DOI: 10.4324/9781003557852-11

> or must exist between and in relation to which issues, and the sanctions which should be attached to an actor's failure to behave in an appropriate fashion, however this is defined.[3]

Regardless of the various controversies that surround the issue of accountability, which this chapter does not intend to resolve, it seems to be commonly accepted that the judicial branch of government is not exempt from being accountable. In modern democracies, it is uncontroversial that '[j]udges wield public power, and they ought to be accountable to the people to the extent that they exercise discretion'.[4] Since the very beginning of constitutionalism, the way in which judges exercise their official powers has been subject to multiple requirements regarding their compliance with the constitution, the laws and the oath of office, the fairness of trials, as well as the clarity and reliability of the motives of court decisions. Judges are expected to exercise their office independently and cannot be deposed except for cases of misconduct. Today, however,

> the growing demand for efficiency, economic rationality, responsiveness and accountability in the public sector, along with the growing autonomy of the judiciary as a self-governing branch in the latter half of the twentieth century, have had implications for these traditional notions of judicial accountability.[5]

The constitutional requirement of accountability is no longer limited to the mere obligation to act on the basis and withing the limits of the law. It is accurate to say that nowadays the aim of judicial accountability is to ensure that judicial personnel and institutions discharge their duties not only in compliance with the law, but also efficiently, effectively and transparently.[6]

While analysing the concept that this book focuses on, scholars are asking themselves questions about the legal basis of the judicial accountability, the appropriate procedures and the possible sanctions, as well as the necessary limitations capable of ensuring the proper scope of judicial independence.[7] As the other

3 Bamforth and Leyland (n 1) 3.

4 Mark Tushnet, 'Judicial Accountability in Comparative Perspective' in Nicholas Bamforth and Peter Leyland (eds), *Accountability in the Contemporary Constitution* (Oxford University Press 2013) 57.

5 Shivaraj S. Huchhanavar, 'Conceptualising Judicial Independence and Accountability from a Regulatory Perspective' (2022) 9 *Oslo L Rev* 129.

6 See Huchhanavar (n 5) 111.

7 As Mark Tushnet stressed: 'in examining judicial accountability we must ask: accountability to whom, and how much? One answer is that judges in modern democracies are to be accountable to the people roughly contemporaneously, just as other wielders of public power are. Judges wield public power, and they ought to be accountable to the people to the extent that they exercise discretion. Call this political accountability. Yet, "too much" political accountability is troublesome, because it conflicts with the independence we seek in judges. . . . Yet, "too much" judicial independence can also be troublesome, if the mechanisms of indirect accountability are so weak that judges are in practice politically unaccountable except in some quite loose, even

chapters clearly show, the legal academia considers various aspects and dimensions of judicial accountability. One can note, however, that doctrinal discussions tend to focus on common courts' duties in this area. Meanwhile, one of the inherent elements of modern democratic constitutional systems (at least those within the continental legal tradition) is an institution known as 'constitutional court' or 'constitutional tribunal'. The organization of such institutions (hereinafter collectively referred to as 'constitutional courts'), their competences and mode of action may vary from one country to another, but their basic function is the same everywhere. Their task is to ensure the compliance of activities of all other government authorities with constitutional norms and, therefore, their role is crucial in liberal democratic societies. At the same time, constitutional courts are one of the state authorities and, as such, they act on the grounds of the law and within its limits. Thus, the following question arises: how can it be ensured that a constitutional court itself performs its tasks in compliance with the constitution? Indeed, as examples from same central European countries show, there is a real risk of malfeasance when a particular constitutional court ceases to act as a guardian of a democratic constitution and becomes its gravedigger.

This chapter is, therefore, devoted to the issue of constitutional courts' accountability. It is assumed that the principle of independence of these institutions should not be interpreted in a manner that would entirely rule out the need for their accountability as collective bodies and for the accountability of their individual members. Thus, both collective and individual accountability of constitutional judges will be considered. Since decisions, whether of judicial[8] or administrative[9] nature, are usually taken by constitutional judges

metaphorical sense: "Too much" independence, and judges wield power in service of their own aims, mediated only by their own understanding of what "the law" requires from them, which may not be much'. Tushnet (n 4) 57.

8 One shall bear in mind the fact that, while adjudicating, the possibility for an individual judge to notify and publicly present his or her dissenting opinion does not at all seem commonly accepted due to the need to preserve the independence and integrity of a court as a whole. To date, dissenting opinions cannot be presented neither by members of the Italian Constitutional Court nor by their peers sitting on the French Constitutional Council. The German Constitutional Court's members began issuing dissenting opinions in 1971, after two decades of operation of this institution. On the other hand, the right to present their dissenting opinion is guaranteed by law for judges of the Spanish Constitutional Court and those of the Polish Constitutional Tribunal.

9 As far as administrative management is concerned, although day-to-day affairs are run by a constitutional court's president, matters of a fundamental importance for the functioning of a constitutional court, and particularly budgetary matters, are to be settled by all judges acting as a general assembly. For example, as far as the German Federal Constitutional Court is concerned, the Plenum deliberates and decides, most importantly, on the budget of the Court, on all questions directly concerning the members of the Court, their status as well as their working conditions, and, as required, on general principles relating to the administration of the Court. The President of the Court, apart from exercising the powers conferred upon him or her by law or by decisions of the Plenum, oversees the administration of the Court; nevertheless, he or she should consult matters of fundamental importance with the Plenum. Each member of the Court must be kept informed of any important matter that affects the Court. See Rules of Procedure of the Federal Constitutional Court of 19 November 2014, §§ 1 and 7 (2015) 1 Federal Law Gazette 286.

collectively, the question relating to their collective accountability is the first one to emerge. The principle of collectiveness, however, may not exempt them from individual accountability. Constitutional judges enjoy relatively extensive powers in comparison with other public officials and are authorized to use them as long as they do it 'during good behaviour'. This chapter examines the feasible measures and procedures aimed at holding these 'guardians' of constitutionality accountable for their actions to the public and its representatives. The framework of the analysis has been narrowed down to selected European constitutional courts. The main aim of this chapter is to outline the characteristic features of constitutional judges' accountability.

Collective accountability of constitutional judges

There is no doubt that the primary function of constitutional courts is to resolve legal disputes that fall within their respective spheres of competence. In some constitutional systems, these institutions are considered explicitly a part of the judiciary,[10] whereas in other systems they are regarded as a specific constitutional guarantee located outside the classical structure based on the concept of the three branches of government.[11] In general, however, at least within the legal framework of the Council of Europe, constitutional courts fulfil their adjudicatory functions with respect to the standards inherent in the due process of law. These standards have been established on the basis of Article 6 of the European Convention on Human Rights, which protects the right to a fair and public hearing within a reasonable time by an independent and impartial tribunal established by law.[12]

10 This is the case, among others, in Germany and Poland. See Article 92 of the Basic Law for the Federal Republic of Germany of 8 May 1949: 'The judicial power shall be vested in the judges; it shall be exercised by the Federal Constitutional Court, by the federal courts provided for in this Basic Law and by the courts of the *Länder*'. As far as the organization of Poland's state authorities is concerned, according to Article 10(2) of the Constitution of the Republic of Poland of 2 April 1997, the judicial power is vested in courts and tribunals. Article 173 of that Constitution specifies that courts and tribunals (namely the Constitutional Tribunal and the Tribunal of State) constitute a separate branch of government and are independent of other branches.

11 See, for example, the Constitution of the Italian Republic of 22 December 1947, in which the provisions concerning the Constitutional Court are collected in Title VI of Part II, entitled 'Constitutional Guarantees' (*Garanzie costituzionali*), which also contains provisions regulating the procedure for amending the Constitution.

12 According to the case-law of the European Court of Human Rights, proceedings fit within the scope of Article 6(1) of the Convention even if they take place before a constitutional court. It matters little whether a constitutional court considers a case following a question referred for a preliminary ruling, or following a constitutional appeal lodged against judicial decisions. The same is true where a constitutional court examines a legal action lodged directly against a law, if the domestic legislation provides for such a remedy. The relevant test aimed to determine whether proceedings fit within the scope of Article 6(1) of the Convention, even if they are conducted before a constitutional court, is whether their outcome is decisive for the determination of the applicant's civil rights and obligations or of any criminal charge against him or her. *Xero Flor v. Poland* App no 4907/18 (ECHR, 7 May 2021), §§ 188–191.

In the context of the accountability of constitutional judges, the requirements relating to the public nature of constitutional proceedings are essential. What is more, such requirements should not be seen only as a mere guarantee protecting possible interests of the parties to these proceedings, but – taking into account the nature of the legal disputes adjudicated by constitutional courts – essentially as an instrument for the public and mass media to acquire information on the activity of these institutions, as well as on the persons performing mandates of their members. Therefore, a public hearing, ensuring the right of the public and mass media to enter the courtroom, should be the rule. This is the case with most European constitutional courts.[13] It used to be the case with the Polish Constitutional Tribunal, too.[14] However, as a result of the statutory changes aimed at undermining its autonomy and ability to act, adopted successively in 2015 and 2016, an *in camera* session became, in fact, the rule.[15] Moreover, in 2017 the President of the Tribunal implemented a new policy regarding the Tribunal's cooperation with the media, which in effect has further restricted the work of journalists reporting on the Tribunal's activities.[16] At the same time, the access of journalists or nongovernmental

13 See, for example, § 17a of Federal Constitutional Court Act in the version of 11 August 1993 (Federal Law Gazette I 1473), last amended by Act of 20 November 2019 (Federal Law Gazette I 1724).

14 The statutory provisions in force between 1997 and 2015 specified that the Constitutional Tribunal must examine each case at a public hearing. Only a constitutional complaint brought by an individual was allowed to be examined during a closed session, provided that written statements of the participants in the proceedings clearly proved a violation of the constitutional rights or freedoms of the plaintiff. See Article 59 of Act on Constitutional Tribunal of 1 August 1997 (Journal of Laws of the Republic of Poland 102 643, as amended). A hearing before the German Federal Constitutional Court, including pronouncements of decisions, must be public. Audio and television or radio recordings, as well as audio and video recordings intended for public presentation or for publication of their content are allowed during oral hearings, until the Court has established that the parties are present, and during public pronouncements of decisions. Audio transmissions to a workspace for persons reporting for the press, radio, television or other media may be authorised by the presiding judge. Making or transmitting recordings may by prohibited, entirely or in part, by the presiding judge in order to protect the legitimate interests of the parties or of third parties, and to ensure the proper course of the proceedings.

15 According to Article 91 of the Act of 30 November 2016 on the Organisation of the Constitutional Tribunal and Mode of Proceedings Before the Constitutional Tribunal (Journal of Laws of the Republic of Poland 2072; hereafter referred to as Constitutional Tribunal (Organisation and Mode of Proceedings) Act 2016), the Constitutional Tribunal must consider an application, a question concerning law submitted by a common court or a constitutional complaint filed by an individual at a public hearing or at an *in camera* session. If written statements of all participants in proceedings as well as other evidence constitute a sufficient basis for issuing a ruling or if the case concerns a legal matter that has already been sufficiently explained in case law, then – in light of Article 92(1) of this Act – a case may be examined at an *in camera* session, which, in practice, is most often the case.

16 According to these new rules, journalists are allowed to be present during a public hearing, but recording or taking photos are prohibited without a prior individual permission. The public opinion may observe the hearing via a live streaming available on the Tribunal's website.

organizations to public information concerning the cases pending before the Tribunal,[17] and the official activities of its members has also been restricted to such an extent that in 2021 Poland was finally convicted by the European Court of Human Rights of violating Article 10 of the ECHR.[18] The less transparent the actions of a court and its officials, the weaker the principle of accountability, which may be a symptom of a systemic deterioration of the rule of law. This problem becomes particularly serious when it begins to affect the 'guardian' of the constitutionality itself.

To ensure transparency, constitutional courts are obliged to prepare and present, usually to the parliament, an annual report containing not only statistical data, but also general remarks regarding systemic problems of constitutional importance that arose from the recent case law. In Italy, at the beginning of the calendar year, the President of the Constitutional Court gives an annual address to the public and presents a report on the work of the Court during the previous year, giving an account of the most important decisions and statistics on the Court's activity. The report is then printed and made available to the public, as are the Court's decisions, which are published every Wednesday in a special issue of the 'Official Gazette of the Italian Republic'.[19] In Poland, the relevant statutory provisions require the President of the Constitutional Tribunal to submit to the Sejm and the Senate (the two houses of the Polish parliament) an annual report on significant problems arising from the

Access to the Tribunal's official recordings is also allowed, at least theoretically, through the procedure for access to public information.

17 Particularly controversial was the refusal to make publicly available information about the orders issued by the Tribunal's President for the purpose of appointing and changing the composition of adjudicating panels. Not only nongovernmental organisations (NGOs), but also the constitutional judges themselves reported irregularities in this respect. See 'Functioning of the Constitutional Tribunal 2014–2017. Report of the Stefan Batory Foundation Legal Expert Group. Introduction' <www.batory.org.pl/upload/files/Programy%20operacyjne/Forum%20Idei/Functioning%20of%20the%20Constitutional%20Tribunal%202014.pdf> accessed 1 April 2024.

18 See *Sieć Obywatelska Watchdog Polska v. Poland* App no 10103/20 (ECHR, 21 March 2024). The applicant was a Polish NGO, which in 2017 lodged numerous requests for access to various types of information regarding the official activities of the President and Vice-President of the Polish Constitutional Tribunal, including their meetings diaries. These requests were aimed, most importantly, at confirming, whether there were, or were not, any meetings between these Tribunal's officials and the members of the Council of Ministers, especially the Minister Coordinator of Special Services, during the period when the Tribunal was about to examine some cases sensitive to the new government formed by the conservative Law and Justice Party. The requests were rejected. The European Court of Human Rights found out that such a denial of information amounted to interference with the applicant NGO's right to receive and impart information (§ 65), and no convincing argument was presented by the Polish authorities to prove that this denial had pursued any legitimate aim or had been 'necessary in a democratic society' (§ 76).

19 See 'The Italian Constitutional Court' (Rome 2019) 19 <www.cortecostituzionale.it/documenti/download/pdf/The_Italian_Constitutional_Court.pdf> accessed 1 April 2024.

Tribunal's activities and case law.[20] This report is also sent to other constitutional state authorities.[21] The statutory provisions do not determine, however, any specific content of that document, which depends only on the discretion of the Tribunal itself. It is within the competences of the General Assembly of the Judges to approve the final version of annual report.[22] Once a year, the Tribunal's President is obliged to convene a public session of the General Assembly during which the annual report is presented and the most significant issues arising from the case law are publicly discussed in the presence of representatives of the top state authorities and other guests.[23] Regrettably, recent experience shows a rather lamentable practice of presenting a report for a previous year at the end of a current one, which is another example of the deterioration of the transparency of the Constitutional Tribunal's activities.

However, the key problem related to the concept of constitutional judges' collective accountability concerns not only the way in which they perform their judicial duties, but also, and most importantly, the content of the decisions they make, and thus, in essence, the values that guide their rulings. It is well known that the centralized model of constitutional review, formed according to Hans Kelsen's ideas, was originally based on the assumption of a hierarchical structure of the legal system. Within such a system, each norm of a lower order should be directly and explicitly rooted in a higher-order norm, as the latter should authorize a competent authority to establish a lower-order norm with a predefined normative content. In that view, any assessment of compliance would be solely procedural and thus the role of a constitutional court would be limited to verifying whether the lawmaker acted in compliance with the authorization resulting from the higher-order norm. It might appear to be a purely technical, almost mathematical operation, excluding any sort of evaluation so as to the values underlying a lawmaker's decisions. However, this has never been the case, since constitutions adopted in continental Europe contain provisions defining the values on which the political and social order is founded, as well as citizens' fundamental freedoms and rights, the protection of which shall be granted by all public authorities, especially the legislature. As a consequence, the control exercised nowadays by constitutional courts is not limited to a merely technical verification of whether the legislator acted in

20 The Constitutional Tribunal's annual report may not, however, be subject to any vote in the Sejm and the Senate. See Article 13 of the Constitutional Tribunal (Organisation and Mode of Proceedings) Act 2016.

21 Those are, primarily, the President of the Republic of Poland, the Prime Minister, the First President of the Supreme Court, the President of the Supreme Administrative Court, the Chairman of the National Judicial Council, the Prosecutor General-Minister of Justice, as well as the Commissioner for Human Rights, the Commissioner for Children's Rights and President of the Supreme Audit Office.

22 See Article 6(2) of the Constitutional Tribunal (Organisation and Mode of Proceedings) Act 2016.

23 See Article 9 of the Constitutional Tribunal (Organisation and Mode of Proceedings) Act 2016.

line with its competency and procedural limitations; it also includes a substantive evaluation of the normative content of any legislative measure, which, in turn, implies the need for a constitutional court to 'balance' the conflicting constitutional principles and to assess the proportionality of the legislature's interference with the freedoms and rights of citizens. For this reason, European constitutional courts, instead of being just passive, 'negative' reviewers of legislatures' choices, have become true active decision makers[24] on matters of crucial political and social importance.[25]

As for the merits of constitutional courts' rulings, the accountability principle encounters a far-reaching constraint related to the required independence of such courts and impartiality of their members. Therefore, the common rule is that judicial decisions issued by constitutional courts are final and legally binding *erga omnes*.[26] They may not be challenged before any other public authority.[27] In particular, constitutional courts' rulings are not subject to any parliamentary approval.[28] Judges serving in these institutions are certainly not

24 See Monika Florczak-Wątor (ed.), *Judicial Law Making in European Constitutional Courts* (Routledge 2020).

25 Referring again to the Polish experience, this is well illustrated by the recent abortion case. In 2019, a group of conservative deputies of the Law and Justice party, which then held the majority in the parliament, instead of proposing a bill to amend statutory provisions regulating the access to abortion, decided to lodge an application, demanding the Constitutional Tribunal to declare these provisions inconsistent with the Constitution. This manoeuvre achieved the intended effect. In its judgment of 22 October 2020, no K 1/20, the Constitutional Tribunal ruled that access to the pregnancy termination procedure – where, on the basis of prenatal tests and/or on other medical grounds, there is a high probability of a severe and irreversible impairment or a life-threatening incurable illness of the foetus – is not sufficiently justified in light of constitutional values and, as such, constitutes the unproportionate interference with the right to life of an unborn child. See Aleksandra Gliszczyńska-Grabias and Wojciech Sadurski, 'The Judgement that Wasn't (But Which Nearly Brought Poland to a Standstill) – "Judgement" of the Polish Constitutional Tribunal of 22 October 2020, K 1/20' (2021) 17(1) *Eur Const L Rev* 130; Tadeusz Tomasz Koncewicz, 'When Legal Fundamentalism Meets Political Justice: The Case of Poland' (2022) 53(3) *Isr L Rev* 302.

26 See, among others, Article 62(3) of the French Constitution ('No appeal shall lie from the decisions of the Constitutional Council. They shall be binding on the state powers, as well as on all administrative authorities and all courts'), and Article 190(1) of the Polish Constitution ('Judgments of the Constitutional Tribunal shall be of universally binding application and shall be final').

27 Article 137(3) of the Italian Constitution clearly states that 'no appeals are allowed against the decision of the Constitutional Court'. Similarly, according to Article 164(1) of the Spanish Constitution, the judgments of the Spanish Constitutional Court 'have validity of *res iudicata* from the day following their publication, and no appeal may be brought against them. Those which declare the unconstitutionality of a law or of a rule with the force of law, and all those which are not limited to the subjective acknowledgment of a right, shall be fully binding on all persons'.

28 In this context, it may seem strange that the Polish constitution-maker established a mechanism that enabled the Sejm (i.e. the lower house of the Polish parliament) to reject a judgment of the Constitutional Tribunal by a two-third majority vote in the presence of at least half of the statutory number of Sejm's members, if such a judgement concerned statutory provisions

politically accountable to any political body, either the parliament or the head of state. However, their decisions have grave political implications. The margin of the legitimate reaction of the parliament – as the representative body of the people – is limited. In fact, the only constitutionally possible way to overrule potential legal and social consequences resulting from a constitutional court's ruling involves amending the constitution itself,[29] but that measure usually requires the consensus of a qualified majority of members of parliament, as well as the overcoming of some other procedural barriers. A problem may arise when a democratically elected parliamentary majority is not of sufficient size to amend the constitution on its own and does not gain the support of the opposition to do so. In such a situation, the ruling group may be tempted to adopt a constitutionally questionable strategy.

This, in fact, is the root cause of the constitutional crisis that Poland has been facing since 2015. It started in the autumn of 2015, when the right-wing Law and Justice party, immediately after winning the parliamentary elections, undertook a series of legal and political measures designed at inhibiting the Constitutional Tribunal and depriving it of its legitimacy. First, the freshly made appointments of five members of the Constitutional Tribunal were revoked and new nominees were elected by the Sejm,[30] which constituted a classic example

adopted before the Constitution came into force. That mechanism, however, was conceived as one of the instruments of the constitutional transition and is no longer used since 17 October 1999. See Article 239(2) of the Polish Constitution.

29 Actually, it seems to be a somehow 'normal' way to moderate legal effects of judicial decisions issued by a constitutional court, which – as a 'guardian of the constitution', and not its creator – must feel subordinated to the choices made by the constitution-maker. The French Constitution has been amended several times to allow the ratification of international agreements that had been previously found by the Constitutional Council incompatible with the previous version of this act. The Polish Constitution also had to be amended following the judgement of the Constitutional Tribunal of 27 April 2005, no P 1/05 (OTK ZU 4/A/2005, 42), declaring the incompatibility of the statutory provisions implementing the European EAW mechanism with the constitutional prohibition of extradition of a Polish citizen, which was absolute at that time.

30 In the autumn of 2015, the terms of office of 5 of the 15 judges serving at the Polish Constitutional Tribunal were going to expire. Three of these judges were about to leave the office in November, and the next two of them in December. On 8 October 2015, just before the parliamentary elections, the Sejm of the 7th term – back then dominated by the centrist Civic Platform party – elected five candidates to fill all five positions that were to become vacant shortly. However, the President of the Republic of Poland, closely associated with the Law and Justice party, did not take the oath of office from the newly elected judges. On 25 November 2015, the newly composed Sejm of the 8th term, already having a conservative majority, passed resolutions declaring the resolutions of 8 October invalid and of no legal effect. Following that, on 2 December 2015, five new judges were appointed, and four of them were immediately sworn in by the President of the Republic of Poland during the night of 2 December. On the following day, 3 December 2015, the Constitutional Tribunal ruled in its judgment no K 34/15 (OTK ZU 11/A/2015, 185) that the appointments made on October 8 ware consistent with the Constitution insofar as they concerned the judges whose terms of office would end in November, and affected the competences of the new Sejm only

of 'court-packing'.[31] Second, the governing majority formed by the Law and Justice party rapidly pushed through a law intended, most importantly, to enforce the inclusion of all five newly elected judges in the Tribunal's works and to give them at least the right to block decisions that could be made by the 'old' judges.[32] The publicly declared justification of such measures was that the Constitutional Tribunal – openly defined by the chief of the Law and Justice party as an 'organ' of the Civic Platform party – was deemed to be likely to block the social reforms that constituted the core of the Law and Justice party's electoral program. The leaders of that party assumed that, because their election program received the support of the majority of Polish citizens, they may, acting directly on the basis of the mandate allegedly granted by the Polish Sovereign itself, cut off the 'old' constitutional judges from the decision-making process. That turned out to be the first step towards dismantling the rule of law standards in Poland during the rule of the Law and Justice party.[33]

Nevertheless, at the present time, the former Polish democratic opposition is undergoing a kind of constitutional maturity test, too. After winning the parliamentary elections of 15 October 2023, the 'October 15 Coalition' is expected to fulfil its election promises, which include the declared 'reset' of the Constitutional Tribunal inherited from the predecessors (i.e. a body that is regarded as unlawfully composed, dysfunctional and socially discredited, and the legitimacy of which is denied by both international[34]

insofar as they concerned the judges whose terms of office would end in December. Nevertheless, that ruling of the Constitutional Tribunal has never been implemented by either the President of the Republic of Poland or the Government, and even the Prime Minister refused its immediate publication in the Journal of Laws.

31 See Anna Śledzińska-Simon, *'Poland's Constitutional Tribunal under Siege' VerfBlog* (4 December 2015) <https://verfassungsblog.de/polands-constitutional-tribunal-under-siege/>, DOI: 10.17176/20170529-160952; Tomasz Tadeusz Koncewicz, '"Court-Packing" in Warsaw: The Plot Thickens' *VerfBlog* (18 December 2015) <https://verfassungsblog.de/court-packing-in-warsaw-the-plot-thickens/>; Tomasz Tadeusz Koncewicz, 'Of Institutions, Democracy, Constitutional Self-Defence and the Rule of Law: The Judgments of the Polish Constitutional Tribunal in Cases K 34/15, K 35/15 and Beyond' (2016) 53(6) *CMLR* 1753–1792.

32 These new statutory provisions established, most importantly, the mandatory participation of at least 13, instead of 9, of the 15 judges during the session of the full bench; the requirement of a two-thirds majority for issuing a ruling (despite the fact that Article 190(5) of the Constitution requires only a simple majority) and the obligation for the Tribunal to examine cases according to the date of their receipt. These new procedural restrictions were found inconsistent with the Constitution by the Constitutional Tribunal itself in its judgement of 9 March 2016, no K 47/15 (OTK ZU A/2018, 31). But this time again the ruling was neither respected nor implemented by the Government, so that the sentence of this ruling was not published by the Prime Minister until 5 June 2018, when the publication was finally made with an annotation of its mare 'historical' significance.

33 Wojciech Sadurski, *Poland's Constitutional Breakdown* (Oxford University Press 2019).

34 In 2021, the ECtHR found that 'the actions of the legislature and the executive amounted to unlawful external influence on the Constitutional [Tribunal]. It found that the breaches in the procedure for electing three judges . . . to the Constitutional [Tribunal] on 2 December 2015

and domestic institutions),[35] and a restoration of a 'true guardian' of constitutionality. However, the new governing formation also does not have a qualified majority required for amending the Polish Constitution. Despite that, the Ministry of Justice has announced a constitutional amendment bill providing for the Tribunal's reset.[36] At the same time, an ordinary bill on the Constitutional Tribunal has been submitted to the Sejm.[37] Some of the transitional provisions of the bill may raise serious constitutional objections; an example is the provision stating that any Tribunal's ruling issued by a panel on which 'a person who was not authorised to adjudicate' sat is invalid and has no legal effect, and all procedural steps in such cases must be repeated.[38]

---

were of such gravity as to impair the legitimacy of the election process and undermine the very essence of the right to a "tribunal established by law" [in the meaning of Article 6 of the ECHR]' (*Xero Flor v. Poland*, cited above, § 287). That conclusion is not without consequences for the further assessments of the Court concerning the lawfulness of any interference with the rights protected under the ECHR. Assessing the abusive effects of the Polish Constitutional Tribunal's ruling concerning access to abortion (no K 1/20, cited above), the ECtHR stated that 'the interference with the applicant's rights cannot be regarded as lawful in terms of Article 8 of the Convention because it was not issued by a body compatible with the rule of law requirements'. It was so because, 'given that the irregularities in the election procedure of the above-mentioned judges compromised the legitimacy of the Constitutional [Tribunal]'s bench which introduced the impugned restriction as a "tribunal established by law", its ruling fell short of what the rule of law required'. *M.L. v. Poland* judgment no 40119/21 (ECHR, 14 December 2023) §§ 174–175.

35 In the opinion of the Polish Supreme Administrative Court, 'the presence of the irregularly appointed judges among the members [of the Constitutional Tribunal] means that the entire Polish constitutional court has been somehow "infected" with illegality, and therefore has lost, in a material sense, the ability to adjudicate in accordance with the law, because there is a high degree of probability that an adjudicating panel would include at least one of the so-called "doubles" [i.e. the persons appointed for those three judicial posts that had been legally filled]' (judgement of 16 November 2022, III OSK 2528/21 <https://orzeczenia.nsa.gov.pl/doc/19E3B22F74>). One of the Polish Supreme Court's panels composed of 'old' judges stated that 'a body composed of persons appointed to the seats previously filled is not the body described in the Constitution as the Constitutional Tribunal, and therefore decisions issued by such a body do not have the legal effects provided for in Article 190(1) of the Constitution'. Ruling of 13 December 2023, I KZP 5/23 <www.sn.pl/sites/orzecznictwo/OrzeczeniaHTML/i%20kzp%205-23.docx.html>.

36 According to the announcement of the Ministry of Justice, the term of office of all incumbent constitutional judges would expire on the date of entry into force of this constitutional amendment and the Sejm would be convened to elect a new full composition of the Tribunal within 14 days by a three-fifths majority. In the absence of such a majority, judges would be elected in a second step by an absolute majority. See 'Pakiet rozwiązań uzdrawiających Trybunał Konstytucyjny' [Package of Solutions to Restore the Constitutional Tribunal] <www.gov.pl/web/sprawiedliwosc/pakiet-rozwiazan-uzdrawiajacych-trybunal-konstytucyjny> accessed 1 April 2024.

37 See Daniel Tilles, 'Polish Government Unveils Planned Overhaul of "Defective" Constitutional Court' *Notes from Poland* (4 March 2024) <https://notesfrompoland.com/2024/03/04/polish-government-unveils-planned-overhaul-of-defective-constitutional-court/> accessed 1 April 2024.

38 The legislative reform related to the Constitutional Tribunal has been finally adopted by the Polish parliament on 13 September 2024. However, on 7 October 2024 the President of the Republic decided to refer new legislative measures, before signing them, to the Constitutional

These legislative measures have, however, little chance of entering into force, at least until a new President of the Republic is elected in 2025. For this reason, on 6 March 2024 the ruling Coalition pushed through the resolution of the Sejm stating that three of the incumbent members of the Tribunal are not judges in the meaning of the Constitution, and therefore any Tribunal's decision issued with their participation must not be taken into account by any public authority without violating the very principle of the rule of law.[39] In fact, the resolution of 6 March 2024, which formally has no direct legal effect as it is not of a universally binding character, puts onto the common courts the burden of remedying the defectiveness of the Polish 'guardian' of constitutionality, showing the lack of capability of the parliament to enforce on its own the accountability of the constitutional judges.

Individual accountability of constitutional judges

According to the well-established constitutional tradition, judges, once appointed, hold office for life or until they reach a mandatory retirement age – provided, however, that they perform judicial duties 'during good behaviour'.[40] This condition, known as the 'good behaviour clause', has for centuries been seen as one of the cornerstones of judicial independence.[41] Generally speaking, judges may not be dismissed at will. They are not politically accountable to either the head of state or the houses of the parliament, especially when it comes to the substance of their judicial decisions.[42] The relevant constitutional provisions in Italy stress explicitly that 'the judges of the Constitutional Court are not subject to any control, nor can they be persecuted for opinions expressed and votes given in the performance of their duties'.[43] Nevertheless, as wielders of public power, judges may not act arbitrarily or be

---

Tribunal for an adjudication upon their conformity to the Constitution. The case, registered under the number Kp 3/24, is still pending up to now. See P. Pacuła, 'President Andrzej Duda Refers Sejm's Constitutional Tribunal Bills for Preventive Review Instead of Singing Them', Rule of Law (7 October 2024) <https://ruleoflaw.pl/this-was-a-long-anticipated-decision-by-president-duda-as-expected-the-president-intends-to-block-the-proposed-reforms-to-the-constitutional-tribunal-which-had-been-politicized-by-the-law-and-justi/>.

39 That Resolution of 6 March 2024 was found unconstitutional by the Constitutional Tribunal in its judgment of 28 mai 2024, no U 5/24. However, up till now, the tenor of this judgement has not been published by the Government pursuant to Article 190(2) of the Constitution of the Republic of Poland.

40 See Act of Settlement 1701, 12 & 13 Will. 3, c. 2. See also Constitution of the United States, s III(1).

41 One must note, however, that the good behaviour clause does not grant judges immunity from criminal prosecutions.

42 One must agree with the opinion of Mark Tushnet that 'using some obviously political process to remove a judge from office because of her rulings is perhaps the strongest possible form of direct political accountability, and is, I believe, widely thought to be fundamentally incompatible with judicial independence and the rule of law'. Tushnet (n 4) 60.

43 See Constitutional Law no 1 of 11 March 1953, defining Some Supplementary Constitutional Rules Concerning the Constitutional Court (Gazzetta Ufficiale 14 March 1953, n 62), art. 5.

exempted from any responsibility. As the meaning of 'good behaviour' is still the subject of debate and controversy,[44] it is necessary to establish as clearly as possible a general rule for the performance of judicial duties. For these reasons, judicial codes of ethics have started to be adopted, often by judges themselves. Moreover, certain international standards have also been developed to reconcile the principle of independence of judges and that of their accountability.[45]

The process described above has, of course, influenced the legal arrangements concerning members of constitutional courts, regardless of the numerous differences in their constitutional roles and legal status when compared to that of members of common courts. It is well known that the constitutional courts do not administer justice in 'day-to-day' civil and criminal cases. As 'guardians of constitutionality'[46] and 'supreme interpreters' of constitutional provisions,[47] they intervene only when legal disputes involve issues of constitutional importance, such as *ultra vires* measures taken by a constitutional authority and/or violations of citizens' freedoms and rights. Therefore, cases subject to the competence of constitutional courts are, in general, of great importance to the social and political life of a nation. At the same time, due to the relatively small number of members serving in each constitutional court (by comparison, for instance, to the usual number of judges in supreme courts),[48] the influence that each judge individually exerts on the outcome of a case is significant. One may say that, given the nature and importance of cases, a group consisting of about a dozen 'sages' decides on matters that are essential for the life of a political community. For this reason, the individual accountability of these 'sages' is also of crucial constitutional importance. Yet, they enjoy strong constitutional protection, sometimes even stronger than that granted to their colleagues from common courts.

44 See, as an example, Saikrishna Prakash and Steven D. Smith, 'How to Remove a Federal Judge' (2006) 116 *YLJ* 72, and Martin H. Redish, 'Response: Good Behavior, Judicial Independence, and the Foundations of American Constitutionalism' (2006) 116 *YLJ* 139.

45 See, for examples, UN 'Basic Principles on the Independence of the Judiciary' (endorsed by General Assembly resolutions 40/32 of 29 November 1985 and 40/146 of 13 December 1985), as well as 'Judges: Independence, Efficiency and Responsibilities' (recommendation CM/Rec(2010)12 adopted by the Committee of Ministers of the Council of Europe on 17 November 2010).

46 See, for example, Article 83 of the Czech Constitution, which refers to the Czech Constitutional Court as 'soudní orgán ochrany ústavnosti' (judicial body for the protection of constitutionality).

47 The Spanish Constitutional Tribunal Organic Law 1978, art. 1, expressly refers to the Constitutional Tribunal as 'intérprete supremo de la Constitución' (supreme interpreter of the constitution).

48 In France, there are nine elective members of the Constitutional Council, while approximately 200 judges sit (*magistrats du siège*) on the Court of Cassation. The Federal Constitutional Court of Germany consists of 16 judges divided into two separate Senates, while the number of Federal Supreme Court justices exceeds 150.

Firstly, in terms of their role as 'negative legislators', the position of constitutional judges may be strengthened vis-à-vis the parliament. This manifests itself not only in the fact that decisions of a constitutional court are legally binding for the legislature, but also in the fact that the legislature's decisions may not, at least under certain circumstances, be binding for a constitutional court. The Polish Constitution expresses such a peculiarity in a specific way. According to the explicit wording of the Constitution, while Polish judges serving in common courts are subject to the Constitution and statutes, the members of the Constitutional Tribunal are subject 'only' to the Constitution.[49] As the constitutional case law shows, the Constitutional Tribunal may, as a result, refuse to apply statutory provisions regulating its organization and the mode of proceedings whenever such provisions are challenged before the Tribunal itself as violating its independence and preventing it from carrying out its constitutional functions. In such a case, the Tribunal may rule directly on the basis of the Constitution, supplementarily applying only those statutory provisions that are not contested. As the Polish Constitutional Tribunal has explained it,

> the subordination of a judge of the Constitutional Tribunal to the Constitution alone is primarily derived from the judicial tasks of that constitutional court, which include the review of statutes in force. However, this subordination is not limited to the basis of the final decision concerning the compatibility of contested statutory provisions, which crowns the proceedings. It also includes all acts of application of the law by the Tribunal, and thus any procedural actions that are a necessary element of the entire complex process of review of the constitutionality of a statute and issuing a ruling on the merits.[50]

Secondly, unlike judges of common courts, who in general are appointed for an undefined period of time, members of constitutional courts are usually appointed for a fixed term of office,[51] which normally lasts from 9 to 12 years.[52] As a rule, they cannot be re-elected or reappointed for a second term.[53] This

49 Cf. Articles 178(1) and 195(1) of the Polish Constitution.

50 See Constitutional Tribunal, 9 March 2016, K 47/17, OTK ZU A/2018, 31.

51 Although introducing lifelong tenure for constitutional court judges is not a common idea, in Austria judges of the Constitutional Court are appointed for an undefined period of time and they hold office till they reach the retirement age of 70 (see Article 147(6) in fine of the Austrian Basic Law 1920).

52 A nine-year term of office is provided for constitutional judges in France, Italy, Poland, Portugal and Spain. In the Czech Republic, constitutional judges hold office for ten years (see Czech Constitution, art. 84(1)). A 12-year term of office is provided for constitutional judges in Germany and Hungary. However, German judges leave the office when they reach the retirement age of 68.

53 In Italy, the Constitution, in its Article 135, initially only ruled out an immediate re-election (*una rielezione immediata*). However, since the constitutional reform adopted in 1967, the

particularity of the constitutional judges' legal status is not irrelevant to the question of their accountability. Since the 'sages' do not hold office for life, the risk of a jurisprudential stagnation and lack of awareness of modern social needs seems lower. However, the average term of office of a constitutional judge is still longer than the mandate of state authorities whose democratic legitimacy derives from universal and direct elections, such as the legislature. In many situations, the latter may not want to wait until the expiry of the term of office of the judges appointed by its predecessor in order to adopt laws it has promised to adopt. The fixed term of office constitutes a form of individual guarantee for a constitutional court's judge that he or she will not be dismissed before its end, except in cases precisely described in law.[54] The possible grounds for early termination of their mandate only relate to rather objective circumstances, such as death, reaching the mandatory retirement age, inability to hold the office due to the state of health, resignation from the office, and a final criminal conviction for a crime. However, these conditions do not allow any way of enforcing the individual accountability of constitutional judges for the way in which they perform their judicial duties by the parliament or any other state authority.

In order to establish some rules regarding 'good behaviour', the legislature sometimes decides to adopt statutory provisions specifying certain duties incumbent on constitutional judges. Nonetheless, the scope of such provisions is usually narrow because it is limited to defining the incompatibility clauses[55] and expressing the general obligation of reserve.[56] The statutory measures are then expanded and elaborated either in sub-statutory provisions issued at the request of a constitutional court,[57] or in purely internal regulations

---

Italian constitutional judges may not be re-elected at all. See Antonio Ruggeri and Antonino Spadaro, *Lineamenti di giustizia costituzionale* (7th edn, Giappichelli 2022) 53. In Germany, neither immediate nor subsequent re-election of a member of the Federal Constitutional Court is permissible according to the explicit wording of Article 4(2) of the Federal Constitutional Act 1951. Also in Poland, Article 194(1) of the Polish Constitution precludes any candidate from being elected for more than one term of office.

54 According to usual constitutional provisions, judges of a constitutional court shall be independent and irremovable during the term of office. See, as an example, Article 159(5) of the Spanish Constitution.

55 As a rule, constitutional judges are not allowed not only to exercise any parliamentary or governmental mandate, but also to hold other public offices. They can be members neither of political parties nor of trade unions or other similar organizations. In general, the office of a constitutional judge is incompatible with any private or public professional activity, possibly except from that of an academic lecturer or researcher.

56 See, for example, French Constitutional Council Organic Law 1958, introduced by Ordonnance no 58–1067 of 7 November 1958, which, in Article 7, prohibits members of the Constitutional Council, during their term of office, from taking any public position on issues that have been or may be subject of decisions by the Council, or consulting on such issues.

57 For example, in France, duties incumbent on the members of the Constitutional Council are defined by a presidential decree issued at the request of the Constitutional Council itself (see Decree no 59-1292 of 13 November 1959).

autonomously adopted by constitutional judges.[58] In this context, the Polish constitutional practice has brought an exception, since in 2016 the parliament passed a separate law entirely dedicated to the rights and duties of the members of the Polish Constitutional Tribunal.[59] Some of the provisions contained in that law may seem strangely detailed, such as those minutely prescribing the rules under which judges are obliged to submit to the Tribunal's President their financial statements. The failure to fulfil the obligation to submit a proper annual financial statement is to be considered tantamount to resignation from the office.[60] One must bear in mind, however, that such extraordinarily detailed statutory regulation of judges' rights and duties may result from a rather populist idea of judges being all members of an untrustworthy caste whose privileges should be curbed by the legislature. It was, at least, the case within the Polish political context of that time. In practice, such financial statements were not always disclosed to the public or mass media.

As far as possible procedural arrangements aimed at enforcing the individual accountability of constitutional judges are concerned, their catalogue seems quite limited. The constitutional principles protecting the independence of the constitutional court's members and the stability of their mandates rule out any form of political responsibility of the 'guardians' of constitutionality to the Sovereign (the people) or its representatives. Since constitutional judges are not elected by universal suffrage, they are also not subject to procedures such as a recall referendum. Therefore, citizens cannot in any way respond on their own to actions and decisions that harm, in their opinion, the fundamental rights and freedoms or any best interest of the nation.[61] Citizens' representatives, acting in the capacity of members of the parliament or the head of state, cannot remove a judge from office, either.[62] In Poland, the Sejm, which has

58 See, as an example, 'Code of Conduct for the Justices of the Federal Constitutional Court' (Germany) <www.bundesverfassungsgericht.de/EN/Richter/Verhaltensleitlinie/Verhaltens leitlinie.html> accessed 31 March 2024.

59 Hereinafter cited as Constitutional Tribunal (Status of the Judges) Act 2016.

60 See Article 18 of the Constitutional Tribunal (Status of the Judges) Act 2016.

61 However, citizens may always express their disapproval of what a constitutional court has decided by means of assemblies, protests and, eventually, ballot cards. One can keep in mind that the Polish Constitutional Tribunal's judgement restricting the access to abortion, issued in 2020 (no K 1/20, cited above), sparked a widespread, long-lasting, and sometimes violent protest movement which forced some leaders of the Law and Justice party to distance themselves from the initiative of their own camp's members to bring the case to the Tribunal. Social and political consequences of this judgement have contributed to the Law and Justice party's defeat in the 2023 parliamentary elections. See Dominika Tronina and Kaja Kaźmierska, 'Abortion Rights and Election Campaigns: The Case of Poland' *LSE Blog* (11 October 2023) <https://blogs.lse.ac.uk/gender/2023/10/11/abortion-rights-and-election-campaigns-the-case-of-poland/> accessed 1 April 2024.

62 Lithuania is, however, an exception. According to Article 108 of the Lithuanian Constitution, the powers of a judge of the Constitutional Court cease when the Seimas (the Lithuanian unicameral parliament) removes him or her from office in accordance with the procedure for impeachment proceedings. Article 74 of this act specifies that the President and judges of the

the competence of appointing all 15 judges of the Constitutional Tribunal,[63] has no power to dismiss, for any reason, a judge once he or she is appointed. The situation is the same in France, where the three supreme state authorities competent to nominate members of the Constitutional Council (i.e. the President of the Republic as well as Presidents of the National Assembly and the Senate)[64] may not remove them from office before the end of their nine-year term. In addition, constitutional judges are not subject to any form of evaluation at the end of their term of office because of the commonly accepted principle that they may not be re-elected or reappointed for a second term. At most, citizens or their democratically chosen representatives may try to influence judges indirectly through measures such as street protests, individual or collective petitions, as well as desiderata adopted by the parliament.[65] Still, the 'sages' are not legally bound by any external instructions and cannot be brought to the political responsibility in any way.

As a result, the legal liability of constitutional judges may appear to be the only way for holding them individually accountable. Yet, the judicial legal liability encounters far-reaching limitations resulting from the fact that constitutional provisions are meant to protect the independence and autonomy of these institutions and their members from the interference of any authorities other than the constitution-maker. Within some legal systems, constitutional judges are protected by immunities which cover even those situations where the alleged actions are not linked to the performance of their judicial duties. In such cases, judges can be neither held criminally liable nor deprived of liberty without a prior consent granted by the court on which they sit.[66] There are very few constitutional systems where the protection resulting from such immunities may be suspended by a political authority, such as a house of the parliament.[67] In most countries of continental Europe having a constitutional court, disciplinary proceedings are seen as the principal, and usually the sole, mechanism for enforcing

---

Constitutional Court who have grossly violated the Constitution or breached their oath, or have been found to have committed a crime may be removed from office by a 3/5ths majority of all the members of the Seimas. This is done according to the procedure for impeachment proceedings, which is established by the Statute of the Seimas.

63 See Article 194(1) of the Polish Constitution.

64 See Article 56(1) of the French Constitution.

65 See, as an example, the Resolution of the Polish Sejm of 6 March 2024 (cited above).

66 See Article 196 of the Polish Constitution. According to Article 23(1) of the Constitutional Tribunal (Status of the Judges) Act 2016, such consent can be granted at the request of the Prosecutor-General in a resolution adopted by an absolute majority of the votes cast by the judges of the Constitutional Tribunal participating in the session of the General Assembly of Judges (the incriminated judge being excluded from participation).

67 In the Czech Republic, a judge of the Constitutional Court may be criminally prosecuted only with the consent of the Senate. However, if the Senate withholds its consent, such criminal prosecution is foreclosed for the duration of the mandate of the judge of the Constitutional Court. See Article 86(1) of the Czech Constitution.

the individual legal accountability of a constitutional judge and, if this is the case, removing him or her from office for severe disciplinary misconduct. However, in this regard, the idea of judicial accountability seems to unduly give way to the principle of the independence and autonomy of constitutional courts.

It is in the name of the constitutional court's independence and autonomy, though, that, as a rule, the court itself has the exclusive jurisdiction over disciplinary cases involving its members. In Poland, disciplinary proceedings concerning constitutional judges are administrated by the Constitutional Tribunal acting as a disciplinary court. A disciplinary case is heard in the first instance by a three-member panel, and in the second instance by a panel of five members. The adjudicating panels are composed solely of incumbent judges of the Tribunal, selected by a draw carried out by the Tribunal President.[68] Statutory provisions explicitly preclude any further challenge to the ruling issued in the second instance, including any cassation appeal to the Supreme Court.[69] As a result, Polish constitutional judges are accountable solely to the Constitutional Tribunal, which means that they are accountable solely to themselves. What is more, only they can initiate proceedings against their colleagues. To protect the Tribunal from any possible 'chilling effect' from the outside, the power to launch a disciplinary procedure is usually restricted for subjects external to this institution. Thus, the power to demand the appointment of a 'disciplinary officer' in order to examine a case has been vested in each member of the Constitutional Tribunal acting alone, as well as to the President of Poland who, however, may act only upon request of the Prosecutor General and after consultation with the First President of the Supreme Court.[70] No one else may make accusations against a judge. Furthermore, the initiation of proceedings ultimately depends on the decision issued by a 'disciplinary officer', that is, by one of the incumbent members of the Constitutional Tribunal who is appointed to this role in each case by a draw carried out by the Tribunal's President. The role of such a disciplinary officer is to take all preliminary steps to investigate all circumstances that may be relevant for the determination of the nature of the alleged misconduct. If there are grounds for launching disciplinary proceedings, he or she provides the accused judge with a written account of the allegations and, after having heard the explanations of the latter, if any, files an application for the case to be examined in the first instance by the disciplinary court.[71] Whether it is determined that there was a misconduct

68 See Article 25 of the Constitutional Tribunal (Status of the Judges) Act 2016. A draw to select judges for the disciplinary court of second instance does not include those judges of the Tribunal who have adjudicated in the first-instance proceedings.

69 See Article 28 of the Constitutional Tribunal (Status of the Judges) Act 2016.

70 See Article 26 of the Constitutional Tribunal (Status of the Judges) Act 2016.

71 If, on the other hand, the disciplinary officer finds no grounds for presenting any disciplinary allegations, he or she issues a decision on refusal to institute disciplinary proceedings, and then the one who has 'reported' that the judge had committed a misconduct, may file an appeal to

or not is entirely at the discretion of the colleagues of the accused judge. For this reason, the October 15 Coalitions, ruling in Poland since autumn 2023, has proposed, a new mechanism for enforcing the disciplinary liability of the constitutional judges. According to the relevant provisions contained in the new Law on Constitutional Tribunal adopted on 13 September 2024, members of the panels appointed for adjudicating disciplinary cases would be composed of not only the incumbent judges of the Tribunal, but also of retired ones, selected by a draw carried out by the Tribunal President. Notifications concerning a misconduct of a constitutional judge could be submitted by another judge (either incumbent or retired).[72]

Conclusion

The recent experience of some European countries, especially those located in Central Europe, shows that the ancient question of 'who shall guard the guardians?' is not just a rhetorical device when it comes to the role played by constitutional courts in modern systems of government. In this context, the problem of constitutional judges' accountability requires particular attention and further in-depth study. The establishment of constitutional courts in Europe was usually associated with a specific historical moment when the most urgent issue for the constitution-maker was to consolidate the rule of law and respect for fundamental freedoms and rights of citizens after an infamous period of rule of an undemocratic regime (e.g. in Italy and Germany after the Second World War, or in Poland at the end of the communist period in the late 1980s). For that reason, constitutional courts have been granted far-reaching guarantees of independence and autonomy. Nowadays, when the rudiments of constitutionalism are deemed to be well established, it seems reasonable to rethink the relations between the 'guardians' of constitutionality

---

the disciplinary court of the first instance. See Article 27(1–5) of the Constitutional Tribunal (Status of the Judges) Act 2016.

72 The inclusion of retired constitutional judges in the mechanism for enforcing dyscyplinary liability was in general positively assessed by the Venice Commission, which stated that 'retired judges are still very much tied to the Constitutional Tribunal, which could justify providing them with a role in disciplinary proceedings. While the Venice Commission has some reservations about the workability of this (also in that it may lead to a great variety in disciplinary jurisprudence), it appreciates the creativity of this somewhat unusual scheme, in that it ensures that the competency to adjudicate in disciplinary proceedings remains with the Tribunal, while guaranteeing that there are an adequate number of judges to provide for a solid appeal procedure (which is all the more important to avoid any misuse of disciplinary proceedings – or perception thereof – to change the composition of the Tribunal) and ensuring at the same time that the fact that all the current judges of the Constitutional Tribunal have been appointed by the same political majority does not constitute an obstacle to holding constitutional judges to account' (Opinion on the draft constitutional amendments concerning the Constitutional Tribunal and two laws on the Constitutional Tribunal, adopted by the Venice Commission at its 141st Plenary Session (Venice, 6–7 December 2024), § 63).

and the people and other constitutional state authorities, especially the parliament. There is no question that judicial decisions made by constitutional courts in individual cases – no matter how controversial or even questionable they may be – remain final and cannot be overturned by anyone except the constitution maker itself. Nevertheless, the full transparency of constitutional court's actions needs to be ensured. Moreover, the principle of independence and autonomy of the court may not give its members immunity from disciplinary or criminal liability for their misconduct. Each mechanism aimed at enforcing the disciplinary liability must be effective, which means that the initiation of proceedings, as well as the investigation and adjudication of a disciplinary case must not be left entirely in the hands of the accused judge's colleagues, but instead should be entrusted to an impartial authority. Taking into account not only the legal, but also the socio-political consequences of constitutional courts' rulings, it is worth discussing at least some kind of quasi-political responsibility of constitutional judges to the parliament. This would allow representatives of citizens to dismiss, by a qualified majority, the president or an individual judge of a constitutional court for breaching the oath they took.

Part IV

Samples of accountability mechanisms

9 Autonomy and boundedness as internal values in the practice of the Court of Justice of the European Union

Alexander Lazović

Introduction

The ongoing rule of law crisis has once again drawn attention to the conflict between autonomy and boundedness of legal decision-making with much of it revolving around the Polish judicial Disciplinary Chamber (C-791/19; weitere Quellen).[1] However, the tension between judicial accountability and judicial independence exists in any legal system based on the rule of law. Any institution that may hold judges to account is automatically put in a position by which it may unduly influence their decision-making. And yet, both are fundamental values of the rule of law. In this chapter I will discuss how Judges at the Court of Justice (hereinafter also "the Court")[2] hold each other to account. Inspired by Bourdieu's theory of practice, I will argue that the institutional structure of the Court enforces a specific form of legal discourse that discourages biased or illicit arguments. This gives the Judges the means not only to punish inappropriate behaviour by their colleagues in a subtle way but even, to some degree, prevent their occurrence in the first place. This form of inner-judicial accountability is both necessary due to the strong protection of the Judges' independence at the Union level, and presents a viable alternative to outside control. However, it may pose a different threat to judicial independence from within and serves the independence of the judiciary more than the independence of the individual judge.

The argument will be structured the following way. I will first discuss both independence and accountability as fundamental elements for a judiciary under the rule of law and how the European Union judicial system puts a stronger emphasis on independence than (external) accountability. I will then briefly discuss Bourdieu's theory of practice and how I apply it to the judicial practice

1 See, e.g., Court of Justice, judgement of 15 July 2021, C-791/19, *Disciplinary regime for judges* [ECLI:EU:C:2021:596] (subsequently, *Disciplinary regime for judges*); Wojciech Sadurski, 'The Disciplinary Chamber May Go – but the Rotten System' 11 August 2021 https://verfassungsblog.de/the-disciplinary-chamber-may-go-but-the-rotten-system-will-stay/.

2 For clarification, due to the unfortunate nomenclature of the Union judicial system, I will only be referring to the Court, not the larger institution of the Court of Justice of the European Union, unless otherwise stated.

DOI: 10.4324/9781003557852-13

at the Court before discussing the elements that shape the Judges' practice in such a way as to create inner-judicial accountability and how it developed over the years. In the conclusion, I will discuss how this form of inner-judicial accountability today may threaten the individual independence of Judges.

Accountability and independence

The Court of Justice highlights the strong connection between judicial independence and the rule of law, emphasising that in a democratic society, trust in the judiciary's operation and autonomy is essential to upholding the rule of law itself.[3] And while judicial independence is not always regarded as a central design element of the rule of law,[4] this connexion is all but far-fetched.[5] This becomes apparent when one follows Martin Krygier in taking a teleological view of the rule of law. According to Krygier, the point of the rule of law is to prevent the arbitrary exercise of power and temper its use.[6] In any political system where courts are used as an institution to further this goal by ensuring the equal, impartial and disinterested application of law, judicial independence automatically becomes a requirement for the rule of law to persist. If judges are not independent from those in power, then they cannot fulfil their function in enforcing laws against them. Who "those in power" are changes depending on the context. On the national level, judicial independence is generally concerned with independence from the government.[7] On the international level, the focus is commonly on those who would nominate them.[8] However, the point of judicial independence is not to curtail the risk of arbitrary exercise of power by one actor by granting it to another. Judges are supposed to be subject to the law themselves[9] and, thus, there must be accountability mechanisms to prevent autonomy from turning into autocracy.[10] Independence and accountability can therefore be seen as roughly antagonistic.[11]

3 Court of Justice, *Disciplinary regime for judges*, para. 83.
4 It is, for example, missing in Fuller's famous account in *The Morality of Law* (rev edn, 15 print, Yale University Press 1978).
5 Jeffrey L. Dunoff and Mark A. Pollack, 'The Judicial Trilemma' (2017) 111 *Am J Int L* 255, 273; Jeremy Waldron, 'The Concept and the Rule of Law' (2008) 43 *GaL Rev* 1, 55.
6 Martin Krygier, 'The Rule of Law: Legality, Teleology, Sociology' in Gianluigi Palombella and Neil Walker (eds), *Relocating the Rule of Law* (Hart 2009) 57–60.
7 Frank B. Cross, 'Thoughts on Goldilocks and Judicial Independence' (2003) 64 *Ohio State L J* 195, 196–197.
8 Dunoff and Pollack (n 5) 226.
9 Although this is not an unproblematic task in itself, see in varying degrees of gravity, Joxerramon Bengoetxea, *The Legal Reasoning of the European Court of Justice: Towards a European Jurisprudence* (Clarendon Press; Oxford University Press 1993) 123–133; Dieter Simon, *Die Unabhängigkeit Des Richters* (Wissenschaftliche Buchgesellschaft 1975) ch 4.
10 Martin Krygier, 'What's the Point of the Rule of Law?' (2019) 67 *Buff L Rev* 743, 784.
11 Cross (n 7) 196–199.

At the Court of Justice, the institutional set-up places a great emphasis on independence. The Judges must be "chosen from persons whose independence is beyond doubt".[12] Their oath of office requires them to perform their functions impartially and conscientiously,[13] and the Court's Code of Conduct tasks them to perform their duties with complete independence and integrity, neither seeking nor following any instructions from the institutions, bodies, offices or agencies of the Union, the governments of the Member States or any private or public entities.[14]

Accountability, on the other hand, figures less prominently in the various legal bases for the Court's working. There is a conspicuous absence of norms requiring the Judges to rule only in accordance with the law, although the Court's task is described as ruling "in accordance with the treaties."[15] Judges are immune from all legal proceedings and continue to be so after the end of their terms regarding any acts performed in an official capacity while in office. This immunity can only be waived by the Court itself sitting as a full Court.[16]

Accountability could, in theory, be established via the reappointment procedures. The six-year terms of office and the possibility for re-election[17] would make them beholden to their Member States.[18] This is exacerbated by the fact that until the establishment of the so-called 255-panel by the Treaty of Lisbon,[19] there existed an unspoken agreement among the Member States that each would nominate one Judge that the others would not veto.[20]

In fact, however, the structural setup of the Court is such that, at least individually, the Judges are effectively shielded from outside accountability. The Court issues *per curiam* decisions without the possibility of dissent, making it difficult to identify the Judges individually responsible for an undesired decision

12 Consolidated Version of the Treaty on the European Union (2012) OJ C 326/13, art. 19 para. 2 subpara. 3 cl 1 (hereinafter TEU), Consolidated Version of the Treaty on the Functioning of the European Union (2012) OJ C 326/47, art. 253 para. 1 (hereinafter TFEU).

13 Consolidated Version of Protocol No 3 on the Statute of the Court of Justice of the European Union, annexed to the Treaties (2016) OJ C 202/210, art. 2 (hereinafter Statute).

14 Code of conduct for Members and former Members of the Court of Justice of the European Union (2021) OJ C 397/1, art. 2 para. 2.

15 TEU, art. 19 para. 3.

16 Statute, art. 3.

17 TEU, art. 19 para. 2 subpara. 3 cls 2 and 3, TFEU, art. 253 paras. 1 and 4.

18 R. Daniel Kelemen, 'The Political Foundations of Judicial Independence in the European Union' (2012) 19 *J Eur Public Policy* 43, 55.

19 A seven-person panel that gives an opinion on a candidates' suitability to perform the task of Judge (or Advocate-General) at the Court, TFEU, art. 255.

20 Sally J. Kenney, 'The Members of the Court of Justice of the European Communities' (1998) 5 *Colum J Eur L* 101, 101–102; Henri de Waele, 'Not Quite the Bed that Procrustes Built: Dissecting the System for Selecting Judges at the Court of Justice of the European Union' in Michal Bobek (ed.), *Selecting Europe's Judges: A Critical Review of the Appointment Procedures to the European Courts* (Oxford University Press 2015) 26.

(even though, of course, the members of the deciding panel are known).[21] The Judges are sworn to protect the secrecy of the deliberations,[22] – a term that the Court interprets broadly: even for those case files made accessible in the Court's Archives, any drafts or notes that precede the deliberations and may give an indication of the judge's preferred position is removed.[23] This strong emphasis on secrecy was apparently a conscious decision by the drafters of the Treaty.[24] More than that, the Court apparently cultivates a collegial approach to decision-making. By having outvoted members continue to participate in the writing of a decision, the Judges try to bring as many of their colleagues on board with a decision as possible.[25] Thus, a Judge-Rapporteur outvoted on the outcome of a case may continue to be influential in how the reasoning is presented. This makes it difficult to pinpoint who exactly is responsible for a decision. Even if this does not prevent accountability for the Court as a whole, by legislative override or noncompliance,[26] it effectively protects Judges from any potential retaliation by nominating Member States.[27] This focus on securing independence against the nominating Member States has culminated in a strongly worded note in the most recent Activity Report

21 David Edward, 'How the Court of Justice Works' (1995) 20 *Eur L Rev* 539, 557; Kenney (n 20) 103; Michal Bobek, 'Of Feasibility and Silent Elephants: The Legitimacy of the Court of Justice Through the Eyes of National Courts' in Maurice Adams, Henri de Waele and Johan Meeusen (eds), *Judging Europe's Judges: The Legitimacy of the Case Law of the European Court of Justice* (Bloomsbury Publishing 2013) 204–205; whether such shielding is still necessary is today called into question, see, e.g., Joseph H. H. Weiler, 'Epilogue: Judging the Judges – Apology and Critique' in Maurice Adams, Henri de Waele, Johan Meeusen and Gert Straetmans (eds), *Judging Europe's Judges: The Legitimacy of the Case Law of the European Court of Justice* (Hart Publishing Limited 2013) 252.

22 Statute, art. 2. and 35.

23 With the famous exception of the preparatory material by Trabucchi for the *Van Gend* decision, see Morten Rasmussen, 'Law Meets History: Interpreting the *Van Gend En Loos* Judgment' in Fernanda Nicola and Bill Davies (eds), *EU Law Stories* (Cambridge University Press 2017) 115.

24 Dunoff and Pollack (n 5) 244.

25 Edward (n 21) 556; Ulrich Everling, 'The Court of Justice as a Decisionmaking Authority' in Eric Stein and Michigan Law Review Association (eds), *The Art of Governance: Festschrift zu Ehren von Eric Stein* (2., unveränd. Aufl, Nomos-VerlGes 1987) 157; Koen Lenaerts, 'The Court's Outer and Inner Selves. Exploring the External and Internal Legitimacy of the European Court of Justice' in *Judging Europe's Judges: The Legitimacy of the Case Law of the European Court of Justice* (Bloomsbury Publishing 2013) 45; Gil Carlos Rodríguez Iglesias and Fernando Castillo de la Torre, 'The Procedure Before the Court of Justice of the European Communities' in Carlos Jiménez Piernas (ed.), *The Legal Practice in International Law and European Community Law: A Spanish Perspective* (Martinus Nijhoff Publishers 2006) 365.

26 This is heavily contested; see in this regard to discussion between Clifford J. Carrubba, Matthew Gabel and Charles Hankla, 'Judicial Behavior Under Political Constraints: Evidence from the European Court of Justice' (2008) 102 *Am Polit Sci Rev* 435; and Alec Stone Sweet and Thomas L. Brunell, 'How the European Union's Legal System Works and Does Not Work: Response to Carrubba, Gabel, and Hankla' (2010) *SSRN Elec J.*

27 Christoph Krenn, 'Self-Government at the Court of Justice of the European Union: A Bedrock for Institutional Success' (2018) 19 *Ger L J* 2007, 2024–2025; Edward (n 21) 557; Kenney (n 20) 103.

by the 255-panel, addressing the issue of a Member State intending not to renew the term of a Judge who, replacing another Member mid-term, had only sat for five months. Although nothing in the Treaties grants a right to term renewal and, according to the report, the Member State had a tradition of non-renewal, the 255-panel pointed out that this may call into question the independence of Judges nominated by this Member State. The conflict was resolved when the new appointee withdrew their application.[28]

The Court, thus, seems to be geared very strongly towards judicial independence and individual judges shielded from outside accountability, and reluctant to use the overt mechanisms for internal accountability. This aligns with the narrative of an unrestrained court which, to use the term coined by the former President of Germany and the Constitutional Court, Roman Herzog, must be stopped.[29] And yet, this is clearly not the full picture. Accountability can come in many forms, not just in the forms of non-reappointment or disciplinary committees. Judges can be held to account by their fellow judges in their everyday experience by constantly reminding each other of the "rules of the game" in which they are interlocked, by "keeping each other honest." This is not supposed to indicate some active discourse in which Judges are praised or reprimanded for the way they conduct themselves, but a much more subtle effect of their working environment. This "inner judicial accountability" arises simply from the fact that "not playing by the rules" will cause a judge to become sidelined, ineffective and shunned. The following section will flesh out this notion based on Bourdieu's concept of habitus and *illusio*.

The illusion of accountability

Bourdieu describes habitus as the structures of our perception of the world,[30] or "schemata of perception."[31] Habitus is both objective, arising from objective structures such as family, education, professional experience, etc., and subjective, as each agent's trajectory is distinct.[32] Because habitus is subjective, it allows for agency – but because it is also objective, this agency is not unbound and must be exercised within the structures of the practice that gives rise to it.[33] Practice is the key word here. In order to participate successfully in an

28 Panel provided for by Article 255 of the Treaty on the Functioning of the European Union, *Seventh Activity Report* (Publications Office 2019) 15.

29 Roman Herzog and Lüder Gerken, 'Stop the European Court of Justice' *EUobserver* (10 September 2008) <https://euobserver.com/opinion/26714>.

30 Pierre Bourdieu, *The Logic of Practice* (trans. Richard Nice, Polity Press 1992) 53; Pierre Bourdieu, *Outline of a Theory of Practice* (trans. Richard Nice, Cambridge University Press 1977) 86.

31 Pierre Bourdieu, 'Social Space and Symbolic Space' in Brian McHale (ed.), Gisele Sapiro (trans.), *Practical Reason* (Polity Press 1998) 9.

32 Bourdieu, *Outline of a Theory of Practice* (n 30) 80–81, 85–87.

33 Gerd Nollmann, 'Luhmann, Bourdieu Und Die Soziologie Des Sinnverstehens. Zur Theorie Und Empirie Sozial Geregelten Verstehens' in Armin Nassehi and Gerd Nollmann (eds), Bourdieu und Luhmann. Ein Theorievergleich (Suhrkamp 2004), 118, 142–143.

interaction – whether it consists of everyday social interactions or specific professional discourse – an agent has to internalise the rules of that practice.[34] They have to adopt them as their own and follow the logic of that practice.[35] For law, for example, jurists must accept outwardly – and thus also inwardly – the rules of legal discourse. They must be "pious sinners," as Bourdieu puts it.[36] This deeply inculcated belief in the self-presentation of law, the value ascribed to legal practice, the *illusio*,[37] involves a dedication to the practice that goes beyond mere lip service. Commonly perceived values of legal practice must be upheld not only outwardly but also inwardly. Actions that undermine the belief in the *illusio* must be marked as unacceptable. Thus, the structures of legal decision-making require judges to converge around commonly shared perceptions or values of this practice.

For inner-judicial accountability this means two things. First of all, Judges remain strategic actors in that they partake in a struggle to impose their understanding of the law and sanctify their preferred outcome of a case.[38] Secondly, however, any judge must present any decision or even argument to their colleagues as genuinely legal. They simply cannot expect to be heard with outwardly political or private arguments. To do so, they must believe in the existence and effectiveness of legal discourse to begin with, so that they can distinguish genuine from non-genuine arguments.[39]

Additionally, Judges must dismiss and sanction any attempts by colleagues to break the rules. Not only because it would strategically disadvantage them to consider themselves bound but others free of these rules. The self-understanding and presentation of legal decision-making as a disinterested practice is also the source of law's symbolic power, its presentation as a legitimate mechanism to resolve social conflicts.[40] By sanctioning deviances and overtly political or private acts by their colleagues, judges reaffirm the rules of practice to which they adhere. In short: judges must take law seriously and ensure that other judges do so as well. They must hold themselves and other judges to account.

34 Bourdieu, *The Logic of Practice* (n 30) 68.

35 Pierre Bourdieu, 'The Force of Law: Toward a Sociology of the Judicial Field' (1987) 38 *Hastings L J* 814, 816, 844–846.

36 Pierre Bourdieu, 'Die Juristen. Torhüter der kollektiven Heuchelei' in Andrea Kretschmann (ed.), Sergej Seitz and Anna Wieder (trans.), *Das Rechtsdenken Pierre Bourdieus* (Velbrück Wissenschaft 2019) 142–143.

37 Anja Böning, 'Rechtswissenschaft, juristische Ausbildung und soziologische Praxistheorie – Eine Theorieübung mit Bourdieu' (2014) 1 *Zeitschrift für Didaktik der Rechtswissenschaft* 195, 199; Simon Susen, 'Hermeneutic Bourdieu' in Lisa Adkins, Caragh Brosnan and Steven Threadgold (eds), *Bourdieusian Prospects* (Routledge; Taylor & Francis Group 2017) 3–4.

38 Bourdieu, *Outline of a Theory of Practice* (n 30) 88; Bourdieu (n 35) 835, 848.

39 Bourdieu (n 36) 30–31; Pierre Bourdieu, 'Is a Disinterested Act Possible?' in Randal Johnson (trans.), *Practical Reason* (Polity Press 1998) 76–77.

40 Bourdieu (n 35) 818, 844.

Since these standards arise from (judicial) practice, they are impacted by the structure in which this practice takes place.[41] For Judges, this typically includes their legal education, their training, and their professional experience. Here, the court system plays a pivotal role,[42] and the structure provided by the Court is even more central to unifying the perception of its Members. Independence and accountability may be shared values among the Member States; however, their centrality for judicial work is likely much more deeply engrained in the habitus of a former judge than in that of a former bureaucrat who was subject to instructions in a formal hierarchical system or even a former politician who had to take political accountability. Additionally, the selection process for Judges at the Court of Justice is particularly prone to political appointments. Effectively, one Judge is nominated per Member State with no specific rules for the procedure on the national level, and accepted by all others (lest they risk their appointments being blocked).[43] With the Treaty of Lisbon, some more oversight has been introduced with the 255-panel which has already rejected multiple nominations even for the Court of Justice.[44] But within the formal requirements set by the panel, such as a base understanding of the specific problems of EU law, much leeway remains for the Member States. For inner-judicial accountability to function, the practice at the Court must inculcate in all of them a habitus that causes them to consider themselves bound by law and expect the same from their colleagues.

This inculcation process functions essentially in the same way as any socialisation process on the national level as well. As they are emerging from practice, structures are not immutable. As practice changes, they, too, will change. But since they structure practice, this change is not arbitrary.[45] Different aspects of Court practice may make it more or less likely that new Judges converge around established values and practices. The stronger this convergent pull, the more Judges will share one outlook, and the more inert the structures will become. In a national system, the prospect of promotion within the national system may present a strong incentive for Judges to adopt the judicial habitus;[46] but, they cannot be mirrored at the European level.

The next section will provide insight to how the practice at the Court is structured.

41 Bourdieu (n 35) 816; for the approach of analysing organisations rather than fields, see Mustafa Emirbayer and Victoria Johnson, 'Bourdieu and Organizational Analysis' (2008) 37 *Theory Soc* 1, 5–9.

42 Kenney (n 20) 101; de Waele (n 20) 24–25.

43 Kenney (n 20) 101–102; de Waele (n 20) 26.

44 Panel provided for by Article 255 of the Treaty on the Functioning of the European Union, *Seventh Activity Report*, 9.

45 Bourdieu, *Outline of a Theory of Practice* (n 30) 169–171; Bourdieu, 'The Force of Law' (n 35) 837–839, 847–848.

46 Simon (n 9) 22–30; Raymund Werle, *Justizorganisation und Selbstverständnis der Richter. Eine empirische Untersuchung* (Kronberg/Ts.: Athenäum Verlag 1977) 97.

Structuring accountability

Looking at the structure of the Court requires a holistic approach that not only takes into account the formal rules of conduct,[47] but also the way in which Judges deliberate, the way panels are composed and chambers are chosen, and the roles played by different Judges.

Socialising judges

Cases at the Court are decided either by a chamber of three (small chambers) or five judges (large chambers), by the Grand Chamber, or – rarely anymore – by the full plenary. The five small chambers each consist of three to four Judges who rotate on the positions.[48] They are presided over by a President elected for a term of one year.[49] Additionally, this position rotates, although re-elections were common in the past.[50] Large chambers today consist of five Judges. They are presided over by Presidents elected for three-year terms.[51] Large Chamber Presidents may be re-elected once,[52] and they usually are. Since the overhaul of the chamber system in 2003, which introduced the three-year terms and re-election rule, almost all Large Chamber Presidents were re-elected for a consecutive term, if they continued to remain with the Court. The exception was Judge Bonichot, who was not re-elected after his first term in 2012 but became the Court's Grover Cleveland when he was elected again in 2018.[53] Chamber compositions are suggested by the President but confirmed by the Court as a whole.

The Grand Chamber always includes the President and the Vice-President of the Court, but elsewise has not a stable formation. Instead, it includes three of the five Presidents of the five judge chambers, rotating.[54] Until 2012, all Presidents of large chambers were permanent members of the Grand

47 Although apparently, the Court scarcely uses these mechanisms, Christoph Krenn, *The Procedural and Organisational Law of the European Court of Justice: An Incomplete Transformation* (Cambridge University Press 2022) 54.

48 Consolidated version of the Rules of Procedure of the Court of Justice of 25 September 2012, art. 28 para. 1 <https://curia.europa.eu/jcms/upload/docs/application/pdf/2012-10/rp_en.pdf> (hereinafter RoP), for the current composition see <https://curia.europa.eu/jcms/jcms/Jo2_7029/en/>.

49 RoP, art. 12 para. 1.

50 Edward (n 21) 543; Alexander Lazović, *Structuring Perception: How Structures of Practice Influence Decision-Making at the Court of Justice of the European Union* (European University Institute 2023) 61 <https://data.europa.eu/doi/10.2870/896180> accessed 18 April 2024.

51 Statute, art. 16 para. 1 cl 3.

52 Statute, art. 16 para. 1 cl 4.

53 Lazović (n 50) 268–269, which also contains an overview of the Chamber Presidents in Annex B.

54 RoP, art. 27 para. 1.

Chamber.[55] The remaining ten positions are filled with the "regular" Judges, rotating on the basis of alternating seniority.[56]

For all cases, the chamber includes the Judge-Rapporteur[57] who is designated by the President,[58] and who prepares the case and writes the preliminary report which not only suggests the chamber formation, but also measures such as the dispensation of oral proceedings and the Advocate-General opinion, on which the Court votes as a whole.[59] They also commonly write the first draft of the decision.[60]

This chamber system effectively establishes a certain measure of indirect control on new Judges that at the same time respects their independence. None of the mechanisms directly impacts how a Judge may vote or position themselves. At the same time, however, it structurally places more senior Judges in central positions in the decision-making process and allows oversight over new Judges to monitor their behaviour.

First of all, it places the President of the Court in a nexus position. The President appoints the Judge-Rapporteurs and can suggest chamber formations. Both mechanisms can be used strategically. For the Judge-Rapporteur appointment, this is fairly obvious. As the Judge-Rapporteur is the one who prepares the case and drafts the decision, they are situated in a way that can give them a greater impact on the case outcome: their greater knowledge of the details of the case serves as a form of cultural capital in the deliberations,[61] while their selection by the President can function as symbolic capital.[62] Research suggests that this greater impact is indeed measurable,[63] although this should not be overstated. The other Judges partaking in the decision are also experienced jurists who can critically scrutinise the Judge-Rapporteur's report.[64] According to reports by former Members, all Judges usually actively partake in the deliberations (and thus the shaping of the decision), even if they have been

55 Codified version of the Rules of Procedure, (2003) OJ C 193/1, art. 11b para. 1 cl 1.

56 RoP, art. 27 paras. 1, 2 and 3, art. 7.

57 RoP, art. 27 para. 1 cl 1, art. 28 para. 1 cl 1.

58 RoP, art. 15 para. 1.

59 RoP, art. 59.

60 Don C. Smith, Interview with David Edward, 'Interviews, the Judge David Edward Oral History Project. Session IV – Years on the Court: Part 1–1989–2004, How the Court Operated' (21 November 2005) 8 <www.law.du.edu/documents/judge-david-edward-oral-history/transcript-2006-05-17-session-4.pdf> accessed 2 January 2020.

61 Christoph Krenn, 'A Sense of Common Purpose: On the Role of Case Assignment and the Judge-Rapporteur at the European Court of Justice' in Mikael Rask Madsen, Fernanda Nicola and Antoine Vauchez (eds), *Researching the European Court of Justice* (Cambridge University Press 2022) 191–192; Lazović (n 50) 65–66.

62 Lazović (n 50) 66.

63 Jens Frankenreiter, 'Judges, Politics, and the Law: Empirical Studies on Judge Behavior, with a Focus on the European Court of Justice' (Doctoral Thesis, ETH Zürich 2016) 121–122, DOI: 10.3929/ethz-a-010675121, accessed 2 January 2020.

64 Krenn (n 47) 110–111.

outvoted.[65] Still, it is likely that the more routine a case is, the more influence the Judge-Rapporteur will have, since the overworked Judges are likely to pay less attention to such cases. By picking the Judge-Rapporteur, the President can thus help to advance a certain direction of the Court's jurisprudence (although, of course, other aspects may also influence who the President picks, such as workload and experience).[66] With regard to the composition of chambers, research suggests that chamber composition is used to create politically moderate chambers where the decisive vote is less likely to fall to Judges close to the fringes of the political spectrum.[67] Both mechanisms work to incentivise new Judges to align themselves with the Court majority perception (adopt its habitus): being assigned Judge-Rapporteur for interesting and important cases not only increases their impact within the Court; it is also one of the few ways in which Judges can signal to the outside world that their work at the Court is appreciated and valued – and thus improve their position for a post-Court career.[68] However, this requires them to prove to be reliable Members, and not to stick out. Judges who exhibit a tendency towards overt political reasoning may find themselves on the fringes and be "neutralised" by strategic placement in a chamber that may outvote them. Krenn found that newer Judges are commonly assigned to cases that end up being deliberated by three- or five-judge chambers.[69] Such cases can be understood as being labelled "routine cases".[70] Cases marked as routine are less likely to invite debate since the underlying issues are considered "solved" by the participants.[71] As mentioned, it is likely that the Judge-Rapporteur has a greater impact in such cases. However, it is also less prudent for the Judge-Rapporteur to attempt to push for a change in case-law or advance any form of a personal agenda, since it would immediately be noticeable. Effectively, in such cases new Judges can learn to inculcate the Court's positions and show that they follow in line – learning the rules, thus adopting them as their own. If they prove themselves, they are slowly rising in the Court's unofficial hierarchy, being picked for more important cases.

Similarly to Judge-Rapporteurs, Chamber Presidents are likely to also have a greater impact on the outcome of the case due to the symbolic capital associated with their position. This is particularly true for Presidents of the five-judge chambers, who are elected for three years and – due to their more

65 Edward (n 21) 157; Everling (n 25) 157.

66 Juliane Kokott and Christoph Sobotta, 'Der EuGH – Blick in eine Werkstatt der Integration' (2013) 40 *Europäische Grundrechtezeitschrift* 465, 469; Krenn (n 27) 2016–2017.

67 Frankenreiter (n 63) 157–158.

68 Silje Synnøve Lyder Hermansen and Daniel Naurin, 'Will Do? Selecting Judges on the Basis of Policy Preferences or Performance Indicators' (2019) 11–15; Krenn (n 61).

69 Krenn (n 61) 197–198.

70 Sacha Prechal, 'The Many Formations of the Court of Justice: 15 Years After Nice' (2016) 39 *Fordham Int L J* 1273, 1281.

71 Martin Morlok, Ralf Kölbel and Agnes Launhardt, 'Recht als Soziale Praxis: Eine soziologische Perspektive in der Methodenlehre' (2000) 31 *Rechtstheorie* 15, 34–35.

regular presence in the Grand Chamber – have a closer relationship to the President of the Court and a greater impact on the Court jurisprudence than other Judges. As Chamber Presidents are elected by the whole Court, the position favours both Judges who represent a majority position and who are well connected within the Court (hold social capital). Both are more likely for more senior members, of whom the other Judges know how they tend to position themselves in deliberations and who would have had more time to connect to other Judges. Like the position as Judge-Rapporteur, the position as Chamber President is a way for Judges to signal to the outside world that their work at the Court is considered successful.[72]

Both positions – Judge-Rapporteur (for important decisions) and Chamber President – are thus desirable. And both require Judges to "fall in line," to fully submerge themselves in the Court's habitus and show that they take the rules of conduct seriously. At the same time, the system reduces the potential impact of dissenters – impious sinners, if you will. It is set up in a way that will minimise their chances to be the decisive vote, especially in important cases, and allows the President to lower their influence by excluding them from cases in which they would likely display disregard for judicial modes of reasoning by, on the one hand, not appointing them Judge-Rapporteur for such cases and, on the other hand, appointing as Judge-Rapporteurs Judges who are part of a different chamber. This picture is completed by the composition of the Grand Chamber: while not forming a majority within it, the more regular appearance of the Chamber Presidents of the five-judge chambers together with the President and Vice-President of the Court places as a relatively stable core at the centre of the Grand Chamber a group of regularly more senior Judges. The alternating seniority mode of picking the remaining members means that junior Judges will always sit together with more senior Judges in cases considered of particular importance. This strong emphasis on seniority favours stability: more senior Judges will have had more time to adopt the habitus of the Court, the likelihood to increase seniority (by being reappointed by their Member State) rises when they adopt the habitus (as they are more likely to be appointed Judge-Rapporteur for important decisions, or even elected President of a large chamber), and they are well positioned in the Grand Chamber and as Chamber Presidents to pass this habitus on to more junior Judges.

Judicial accountability

However, the mere installation of an (indirect and unofficial) hierarchy to further socialisation of new members is insufficient to hold Judges accountable to the law. To speak of judicial accountability, the socialisation needs to be such that it installs in the Judges a sense of shared judicial values and forms of argumentation – a legal perception specific to the Court that the

72 Hermansen and Naurin (n 68) 13.

other Judges recognise (or recognise when someone deviates from it). As the primary mode to control Judges in this way is judicial deliberation,[73] installation of judicial values concerns primarily the mode in which these deliberations function – such as the arguments deemed eligible or the approach to case-law taken by the Court. This makes stable case-law an important factor in inner-judicial accountability. The more stable the jurisprudence of the Court is, the easier it is to recognise an argument as acceptable or pinpoint deviations from established case-law. If such deviations are identified, the reasons for the deviation may be questioned more severely – and Judges who deviate must be able to defend their position with a legally acceptable argument, the canon of which has been established by the previous practice. This is, however, where practice at the Court shows greater problems.

It has been noted regularly, that the decisions of the Court can often be terse or even opaque.[74] This alone would not necessarily be a problem. The claim is more common for Common law lawyers than Continental lawyers, as the latter are more used to this style of reasoning – the Court's decisions are, for example, more deliberative than the French style.[75] And – as Bobek points out – the argument is also made more often by academics than by practitioners for whom more concise decisions are much more feasible to work with.[76] After all, various legal systems in Continental Europe manage to establish a stable and intelligible jurisprudence despite the more concise decisions compared to common law systems.

The problem with the Court's style thus lies less in the terseness itself and more in the arguments that are being used. The Court prefers teleological (or, more precisely teleo-systemic) arguments.[77] Again, this is not in itself a problem and likely related to the peculiarities of a multilingual legal system.[78] However, oftentimes the *teloi* and values to which the Court refers are themselves, although legal in nature, so abstract that they remain open to debate even after a decision has been issued. Broad European legal values like integration, equality or proportionality often remain vague and lawyers can reasonably disagree as to their correct meaning.[79] The reason for this is, apparently, that the

73 Krenn found that the disciplinary procedures are rarely used, (n 47) 54. However, the conduct of the Judges is heavily regulated including a requirement that external activities are authorised in advance and are closely related to the performance of their duties, Code of Conduct, art. 8 para. 3.

74 Bengoetxea (n 9) 211; Mitchel de SO -l'E Lasser, *Judicial Deliberations: A Comparative Analysis of Judicial Transparency and Legitimacy* (Oxford University Press 2004) 107.

75 Lasser (n 74) ch 8; Christoph Schönberger, '"Mi attendu, mi dissertation." Le style des décisions de la Cour de justice de l'Union européenne' (2015) 91 *Droit et Société* 505, 514–516.

76 Bobek (n 21) 204–205.

77 Bengoetxea (n 9) 250–251; Lasser (n 74) 210.

78 Bengoetxea (n 9) 231; Jan Komárek, 'Legal Reasoning in EU Law' in Damian Chalmers and Anthony Arnull (eds), *The Oxford Handbook of European Union Law* (Oxford University Press 2015) 45–46.

79 Bengoetxea (n 9) 252; Lasser (n 74) 135–140.

Judges at the Court attempt to bring as many of their colleagues on board as possible. This can be achieved by using values on which most Judges can agree on principle, without going into detail concerning their content.[80] Such values used as arguments open the door to non-judicial considerations being scarcely disguised as judicial arguments.[81] Due to the single-voice decisions issued by the Judges, this allows even outvoted members to find themselves represented by the decision. The downside is that, at times, arguments are either dismissed or it is unclear which argument was supposed to be decisive, because no agreement could be reached among the deciding panel.[82] As a result, such decisions become much less apt at creating convergence among the Judges for future decisions.

Similarly, the Court's approach to its own case-law has proven to be a major destabilising factor. In keeping with its continental tradition, the Court uses a *jurisprudence contante* rather than an in-depth analysis of ratio decidendi.[83] The Court acknowledges its own case-law, but seldom discusses it in detail.[84] And while it is now not uncommon that the Court explicitly distances itself from earlier decisions, implicit reversal is still abundant.[85] Additionally, the lack of discussion of previous decisions makes it easy to reinterpret them or cite them selectively.[86] In such cases, Judges use earlier decisions as a source for arguments, rather than strings of reasoning. This allows them to pick and choose which sentences fit their narrative of the Court's case-law and may disregard other elements of a decision that could cast doubt on their interpretation. As with the terse style, this may allow Judges to diverge from established case-law less noticeably and thus reinterpret decisions in light of their own preferences. Overall, this makes case-law a less stabilising factor than it may otherwise could have been.

Therefore, the Court's legal approach is not necessarily as apt in creating accountability as the structure of the working process would allow it to be. However, there are additional elements that may rectify such shortcomings.

80 Michal Bobek, 'The Court of Justice of the European Union' in Anthony Arnull and Damian Chalmers (eds), *The Handbook of European Union Law* (Oxford University Press 2015) 171; Lorna Woods, 'Consistency in the Chambers of the ECJ: A Case Study on the Free Movement of Goods' (2012) 31 *Civil Justice Quarterly* 339, 350.

81 Frankenreiter (n 63) 41–42; Jan Komárek, 'Precedent and Judicial Lawmaking in Supreme Courts: The Court of Justice Compared to the US Supreme Court and the French Cour de Cassation' (2008) 11 *Camb Yearb Eur Leg Stud* 399, 418.

82 Schönberger (n 75) 518; Edward (n 21) 556–557.

83 Bobek (n 80) 157; Lasser (n 74) 116; Jan Komárek, 'Reasoning with Previous Decisions: Beyond the Doctrine of Precedent' (2013) 61 *Am J Comp L* 149, 157.

84 Komárek (n 83) 431; Urška Šadl, 'Case – Case-Law – Law. Ruiz Zambrano as an Illustration of How the Court of Justice of the European Union Constructs its Legal Arguments' (2013) 9 *Eur Const L Rev* 205, 212.

85 Giuseppe Federico Mancini and David T. Keeling, 'Language, Culture and Politics in the Life of the European Court of Justice' (1995) 1 *Colum J Eur L* 397, 402.

86 Komárek (n 83) 159; Lazović (n 50) 292–293; Šadl (n 84) 220–240.

Of course, it is not uncommon for supreme courts in particular to be more inventive than lower-level courts when it comes to legal arguments and to their own case-law. Binding such courts too strictly would make jurisprudence inert and unapt to deal with the changing nature of social reality.[87] And as the Union's highest court, the Court of Justice falls within this category. However, the inner structure of the Court is such that cases of importance should be deliberated in the Grand Chamber (or, in rare occasions, by the full plenary). These would be the cases where "innovation" would more likely be expected. In such cases, the mere fact that the case is assigned to the Grand Chamber indicates to all participating Judges the relevance of the case. The greater number of Judges partaking in the deliberations means that "outliers" are less likely to be decisive. Arguments made by individual members will always be more thoroughly dissected by a larger number of colleagues. And the "core" of the Court is better placed to call out and prevent suspicious forms of reasoning. In short, innovation should happen in a space of scrutiny.

This is different in the smaller chambers: here a canon of acceptable forms of argumentation and a stable case-law are more relevant to detect unwarranted and suspicious deviations. Research on the Court's case-law on childcare-related leave has shown that case-law becomes more stable where the Judges opt for concrete values and goals anchored in directives or secondary sources instead of broader values.[88] Such goals also appear to make it more difficult to deviate from previous decisions as they are picked up more regularly by subsequent decisions. A key aspect in creating such stability has been increased routinisation in the work of the smaller chambers. Routinisation can happen in various ways. Sending a case to a smaller chamber already indicates that it is considered to be a routine matter that should not require extensive debate of legal issues.[89] In such cases, it would be expected that Judges work with case-law citations rather than deep legal argumentation.[90] Additionally, the President's power to appoint Judge-Rapporteurs can further routinisation in two ways: by the reappointment of a Judge-Rapporteur who had worked on similar cases before (or the appointment of Judges who sat on such cases) and by ensuring that the chamber that will deliberate the case has had prior experience with such cases (thus making deviations more obvious to the remaining panel members).[91] The ability to use such routinisation methods has increased in the past 20 years by increasing the number of five-judge chambers which allows for less rotation within the panels (there are no "oversized" panels any more with seven or even eight Judges).[92] The Court also

87 Niklas Luhmann, *Das Recht Der Gesellschaft* (6th edn, Suhrkamp 2013) 380–381.

88 Lazović (n 50) 286.

89 Lazović (n 50) 75.

90 Lazović (n 50) 92.

91 Lazović (n 50) 284–286.

92 Alan Dashwood, Angus Johnston and European Commission (eds), 'The Report by the Working Party on the Future of the European Communities' Court System ("The Wise

introduced or made use of other mechanisms to mark cases as routine, such as dispensing with the Advocate-General opinion or the hearing.[93] The introduction of such mechanisms and the increased use since the mid-2000s broadly coincides with the expansion of the European Union and the accompanied influx of new Judges.[94] One can thus assume that the Court was prepared to increase inner-judicial accountability for the new members out of concern (well-founded or not) that they required additional supervision.[95]

Two final factors that should be mentioned briefly in establishing a set of accepted forms of argumentations and highlight deviations from them are the *référendaires* and the Court's language service. *Référendaires* are the Court's law clerks, of which each Judge has three.[96] While the Judges are completely free in choosing their *référendaires* and follow vastly different ways in doing so,[97] it appears to be common practice for new Judges to pick at least some *référendaires* with experience working at the Court.[98] And while Judges are also free in how to use their *référendaires*,[99] and, as experienced lawyers, possess the capabilities to critically examine their work,[100] *référendaires* are usually heavily involved in the drafting of the decisions,[101] often using self-made glossaries composed of previous decisions.[102] This system is commonly seen as giving the Court a slightly conservative structure – the *référendaires* acting as the human embodiment of the decisions past.[103]

Similarly, the Court's multilingual system – decisions are translated into all official languages of the Court – means that decisions have to be easily translatable.[104] As thus, Judges are encouraged not to use new formulations where

---

Persons" Report or "The Due Report")' in *The Future of the Judicial System of the European Union* (Bloomsbury Publishing 2001) 196–199; Mitchel de SO-L'E Lasser, *Judicial Dis-Appointments: Judicial Appointments Reform and the Rise of European Judicial Independence* (1st edn, Oxford University Press 2020) 44–49; Lazović (n 50) 77–78.

93 Lazović (n 50) 285.

94 Lazović (n 50) 71–72.

95 On these fears by some of the old Member States, Krenn (n 27) 2017 fn 65.

96 Gillian Cahill, 'The Référendaire as Unseen Actor: A Comparative Look at the Court of Justice of the EU, the US Supreme Court and International Arbitral Tribunals' in Freya Baetens (ed.), *Legitimacy of Unseen Actors in International Adjudication* (Cambridge University Press 2019) 497–498; Sally J. Kenney, 'Beyond Principals and Agents: Seeing Courts as Organizations by Comparing Référendaires at the European Court of Justice and Law Clerks at the U.S. Supreme Court' (2000) 33 *Comp Polit Stud* 593, 609–611.

97 Cahill (n 96) 498–499; Smith (n 60) 21.

98 Kenney (n 96) 612.

99 Cahill (n 96) 503–504; Kenney (n 96) 611.

100 Kenney (n 96) 617–618.

101 Cahill (n 96) 503–504; Kenney (n 96) 611.

102 Karen McAuliffe, 'Hybrid Texts and Uniform Law? The Multilingual Case Law of the Court of Justice of the European Union' (2011) 24 *Int J Semiot L – Revue internationale de Sémiotique juridique* 97, 110.

103 Kenney (n 96) 596.

104 Bobek (n 80) 912.

there are existing ones.[105] This leads to a situation where arguments are commonly reproduced and innovation (or deviation) stands out.

Conclusion: inner and outer independence?

Overall, the Court is structurally geared towards inculcating a distinct "Court of Justice habitus" in its new judges. It does so by creating a system in which they can be easily held to account for deviating from existing case-law. The chance to be appointed to relevant Grand Chamber decisions or even be elected Chamber President for one of the five-judge chambers present strong incentives to converge around the accepted values and modes of reasoning in the Court. Decisions must be translatable and are commonly drafted largely by the *référendaires* who recycle previously used terminology so that divergences stick out. Routinisation makes it easy to spot deviations within the chamber system, and innovation is regulated to the Grand Chamber where more experienced Judges hold a more central position. While the case-law system and the use of broader and vaguer *teloi* and values make it easier to use existing arguments or case citations formally, while filling them with new meaning, the Court's increased use of routinisation and goals anchored in secondary legislation curtail these possibilities to some degree.

Thus, there is a high degree of inner-judicial accountability at the Court of Justice. However, it is questionable whether this form of accountability is purely judicial in nature. It is possible that its rigidity can cause accountability to the Court, rather than to the law, particularly if the Court's practice does not present a strong tradition of legal reasoning but rather brisk and often imprecise references to established case-law. More optimistically, this system may be used to enshrine a certain interpretation of the law and disincentivise rivalling (but acceptable) interpretations. Given the social structure of the Court, in which now academics appear to hold the most social capital,[106] this may favour academic interpretations of law over more judicial or bureaucratic approaches. Judges who diverge from the Court's majority opinion, but do so with valid legal reasoning, may still find themselves sidelined.[107] New Judges may be disincentivised from engaging in deeper legal argumentation and rather attempt to simply reproduce their colleagues' positions.

The justification given for the Court's structure is commonly that it protects judicial independence.[108] Outside accountability is replaced by inner-judicial accountability and thus Judges are shielded from retaliation by their Member States. However, inner-judicial accountability may just as well encroach

105 McAuliffe (n 102) 105.

106 Lasser (n 92) 379–380.

107 See, e.g., the concerns by Hjalte Rasmussen, 'Present and Future European Judicial Problems After the Enlargement and the Post-2005 Ideological Revolt' (2007) 44 *CMLR* 1661, 1674.

108 Edward (n 21) 557; Kenney (n 20) 10; Weiler (n 21) 252.

on judicial independence where it allows for a system where Judges can be sidelined for defending legally feasible positions that diverge from majority positions (that may also be legally defensible; this is not to suggest that the majority opinion presents any form of politicised jurisprudence). By protecting the independence of the Court, the independence of the Judges may be encroached.

This would be less problematic if a stable case-law could be equated with judicial "correct" decisions. After all, it would create foreseeable decisions and thus fulfil an important judicial function. However, adaptability is an equally important judicial function, particularly in an international court. The Court must be able to react to changing social realities in different Member States so that their case-law does not become irrelevant.[109] The Court has shown in the past that its case-law continues to be adaptable. But the increasing rigidity of the inner-judicial accountability may create the danger that the Court – involuntarily – becomes inflexible as Judges merely look inward rather than outward.

This is a dilemma not easily solved. It is unlikely that merely addressing one factor would prevent this effect. For example, abolishing the single-voice approach, as is often suggested,[110] may make it easier for minority positions to be heard and allow for outside critique of the majority opinion. But it is questionable whether this would really increase the quality of the decision or be effective in preventing partisan argumentation, as a look to the US Supreme Court easily shows. Additionally, the interconnectedness of the factors addressed means that any changes to the Court's working structure may have knock-on effects on the system overall. Random case allocation, for example, would decrease the risk of sidelining minority judges. However, it would also reduce the likelihood of panel consistency (the same panel deciding similar cases) and negatively affect routinisation and thus the stability of the case-law. Any reduction of inner-judicial accountability would have to be carefully balanced so as not to open the door for partisan argumentation.

109 Alexander Lazović, 'Converging on Structures – the Influence of Court-Structure on Convergence and Divergence Among Judges' in Maja Sahadžić, Marjan Kos, Jaka Kukavica, Jakob Gašperin Wischhoff and Julian Scholtes (eds), *Accommodating Diversity in Multilevel Constitutional Orders: Legal Mechanisms of Divergence and Convergence* (Routledge 2023) 194–195.

110 Weiler (n 21) 252.

10 Vetting as a judicial integrity enhancement tool

Arnisa Tepelija and Teodora Miljojković

Introduction

This chapter addresses the complex challenge within the rule of law framework concerning the management of incumbent judges amidst circumstances where the judiciary's legitimacy is compromised due to systemic transformations, corruption, or a confluence of both factors. Specifically, it explores vetting as a distinct approach to addressing the status of incumbent judges in such contexts. It follows the transformation of the underlying concerns around incumbent judges due to system failures through the lenses of two countries that have aimed at cleansing the system through the vetting process. In several countries, the foundational rationale for implementing vetting processes is intricately linked with the demands of the European Union (EU) accession procedure, mainly to bolster judicial systems to meet the requirements stipulated in relevant chapters of the EU Accession Procedure and the Copenhagen criteria.[1] Beyond procedural compliance, these initiatives are deeply embedded within the broader framework of transitional justice concerns, aiming to address past injustices and ensure a more equitable legal system. This chapter seeks to dissect the synergies between the principles of transitional justice and the EU's judicial reform objectives, primarily through the lens of vetting processes designed to enhance judicial integrity and accountability. It will scrutinise the implications of these intertwined paradigms when applied within the complex socio-political landscapes of specific nations. To this end, Albania and Moldova are selected as focal points, given their status as contemporary exemplars of the dynamics at play. They offer insight into the practical challenges and outcomes of navigating the intersection of transitional justice and EU accession-driven judicial reforms.

This chapter is structured as follows. Initially, it explores the overarching concept of vetting within the context of its origins in transitional justice, providing a foundation for understanding its role and purpose. Subsequently, the

1 See in general Christopher Hillion, 'The Copenhagen Criteria and Their Progeny' in Christopher Hillion (ed.), *EU Enlargement: A Legal Approach* (Hart Publishing 2004).

DOI: 10.4324/9781003557852-14

discussion shifts to the nuanced transformation in the rationale behind vetting procedures in post-transitional contexts, where vetting evolves from a tool of transitional justice to a mechanism for enhancing the rule of law (RoL), particularly in alignment with international standards and the criteria for European Union (EU) Accession. The final section presents detailed case studies of Albania and Moldova, selected for their relevance as contemporary manifestations of the phenomena under review. Through these case studies, the chapter aims to elucidate critical insights relevant to the theoretical discourse on judicial vetting and, more broadly, to the principles of judicial accountability.

Judicial vetting as the transitional justice tool to enhance accountability

As it is already well recognised in the literature, judicial independence is limited by judicial accountability as its "other side of the coin."[2] Judicial accountability is yet another multifaceted concept, which, as well as judicial independence, needs to be conceived to other state and non-state actors.[3] Mauro Cappelletti proposed a typology that delineates four distinct categories of judicial accountability (JA): (1) political accountability, subdivided into interbranch and constitutional accountability; (2) public accountability, oriented towards the general public; (3) legal accountability of the state; and (4) personal legal accountability of individual judges.[4] This theoretical framework is significant as it illuminates the facets of judicial status particularly vulnerable to politicisation and potential encroachments by other government branches.

When governments refer to accountability as the reason behind judicial reform, they usually consider the first two types – political and public accountability of the judiciary as a whole. According to Charles Gardner Geyh, political-institutional judicial accountability responds to three objectives underpinning this concept – promotion of the rule of law, public confidence, and institutional responsibility.[5] In transitional contexts characterised by sensitive political realities, these principles acquire heightened significance due to the potential for divergent understandings of the RoL in regular times and post-transition.[6]

2 Stephen B. Burbank, 'What Do We Mean by Judicial Independence?' (2003) 64 *Ohio State L J* 323.

3 As Burbank posed – independence and accountability from whom or what? See Stephen B. Burbank, 'Judicial Independence, Judicial Accountability, and Interbranch Relations' (2007) 95 *Geo L J*. 909.

4 Mauro Cappelletti, 'Who Watches the Watchmen – a Comparative Study on Judicial Responsibility' (1983) 31 *Am J Comp L* 1.

5 Charles Gardner Geyh, 'Rescuing Judicial Accountability from the Realm of Political Rhetoric' (2006) *Case West Reserve L Rev* 911, 912.

6 "Adherence to the rule of law during periods of political upheaval creates a tension between rule of law as backward-looking and forward-looking, as settled versus dynamic. In this dilemma, the rule of law is ultimately contingent; rather than grounding legal order, it serves

A notable challenge occurs when the imperatives of judicial accountability clash with the foundational principle of judicial independence, notably its element of judicial irremovability. This phenomenon is acutely observed within the context of nations in the throes of political and legal transitional phases. Haldemann and Unger highlight the dilemma of judicial irremovability in transitional regimes, where the principle complicates the dismissal of judges in contrast to other public sector employees, potentially jeopardising the new regime's commitment to judicial independence and the rule of law.[7] Additionally, a retrospective rule of law tension exists, as David Dyzenhaus points out, regarding the legitimacy of prosecuting acts deemed legal under the former regime, raising similar questions about dismissing judges appointed legally by previous authorities.[8] Preserving the tenure of judges from an erstwhile regime necessitates careful consideration of their potential impact on the new government's functionality and moral evaluation of their role in supporting past injustices, with the risk that their continued presence may undermine the rule of law principles in the nascent democracy.

In the realm of transitional justice, vetting emerged as a pivotal strategy aimed at reconstituting state capacity during crisis resolution or regime transition phases.[9] This procedure is delineated as "a means of assessing integrity to ascertain suitability for public employment," thereby excluding individuals with significant integrity deficits from public service to foster civic trust and re-legitimise public institutions.[10] Throughout the 1990s, vetting served to restructure public sector entities, including the judiciary, in the post-communist countries of the CEE region, aiming to depart from their communist past.[11] It was also present in the post-conflict context in several countries, such as Bosnia and Herzegovina and Libya, with its implementation closely monitored by international organisations.[12]

---

to mediate the normative shift in justice that characterizes these extraordinary periods." Ruti Teitel, 'Transitional Jurisprudence: The Role of Law in Political Transformation' (2019) 106 *Yale L J* 2009, 2016.

7 Thomas Haldemann and Thomas Unger (eds), *The United Nations Principles to Combat Impunity: A Commentary* (Oxford University Press 2018) 325.

8 David Dyzenhaus, 'Judicial Independence, Transitional Justice and the Rule of Law' (2003) 4 *Otago L Rev* 345, 346.

9 Alexander Mayer-Rieckh, 'Vetting to Prevent Future Abuses: Reforming the Police, Courts, and Prosecutor's Offices in Bosnia and Herzegovina' in Alexander Mayer-Rieckh and Pablo de Greiff (eds), *Justice as Prevention: Vetting Public Employees in Transitional Societies* (Social Science Research Council 2007).

10 United Nations Development Program, *Vetting Public Employees in Post-Conflict Settings: Operational Guidelines* (Bureau for Crisis Prevention and Recovery 2006) 4.

11 Cynthia M. Horne, 'Transitional Justice: Vetting and Lustration' in Cheryl Lawther, Luke Moffett and Dov Jacobs (eds), *Research Handbook on Transitional Justice* (Elgar Publishing 2017).

12 For the BiH context, see Per Bergling, 'Adaptation, Compensation and Imposition: Paradigms for Purging the Bosnian Judiciary' (2008) 15 *Int Peacekeep* 362. For Libya's context

From a procedural standpoint, vetting embodies a hybrid mechanism, integrating aspects of various judicial status procedures, notably resembling conventional evaluation processes, while also possessing the capacity to lead to a judge's dismissal. This particular nature of vetting underscores the imperative for embedding due process principles akin to those applied in evaluations and dismissals within the vetting framework. Distinctively, vetting diverges from standard procedures concerning judicial status in its pronounced impact, meticulousness, and the criteria employed. Within the ambit of transitional justice, vetting primarily focused on assessing judges' political and moral suitability for roles within emergent democratic frameworks (assessing, e.g., if the judges were in any capacity involved in establishing and upholding the previous regime). Conversely, contemporary vetting practices, oriented towards enhancing the rule of law, align more closely with routine judicial assessments, emphasising efficiency and competence.

Within scholarly discourse, the concept of vetting frequently becomes entangled with that of lustration and purging. Nonetheless, distinctions between these concepts, although nuanced, can be identified. While lustration represents a measure of dealing with the past, vetting is considered a forward-looking measure aiming to bolster public trust in institutions and strengthen new democracies.[13] Unlike purging, which historically lacked due process and was primarily retaliatory, the rationale behind the vetting design is to support democratic transition and the building of citizens' trust in state institutions.[14]

In transitional justice processes within post-conflict societies, international actors have predominantly concentrated on reconciliation efforts and reparative measures for human rights violations, while there has been a tendency to overlook the crucial areas of administrative and judicial reforms.[15]

In the contemporary landscape, vetting practices have been developed against the backdrop of democracies characterised by systemic deficiencies in the rule of law, requiring enhancements in their judiciary systems to align with the requirements for EU membership.[16] The EU, alongside the Council of Europe, has expressed robust support for these significant measures within

---

see Betsy Popken, 'Vetting the Public Sector' in Paul R. Williams and Milena Sterio (eds), *Research Handbook on Post-Conflict State Building* (Elgar Publishing 2020).

13 Adam Czarnota, 'Lustration, Decommunisation and the Rule of Law' (2009) 1 *HJRL* 307, 311.

14 L. Stan and N. Nedelsky (eds), *The Encyclopedia of Transitional Justice* (Cambridge University Press 2013).

15 Richard Sannerholm, 'Legal, Judicial and Administrative Reforms in Post-Conflict Situations: Beyond the Rule of Law Template' (2007) 12 *JJC & SL* 65, 83.

16 For the definition of a systemic deficiency in the EU context, see Armin Von Bogdandy, 'Principles of a Systemic Deficiencies Doctrine: How to Protect Checks and Balances in the Member States' (2020) 57 *CMLR* 718; Robin Gadbled and Cecilia Rizcallah, 'Unpacking the Multifaced Nature of the Systemic and the Particular in European Law: An Introduction' (2023) 24 *Ger L J* 941.

several candidate countries yet to close Chapters 23 and 24 of the accession negotiation process. This support indicates a commitment within the European context to narrow the disparity in the adherence to the rule of law among the Member States, particularly in the context of the core-periphery divide.[17] The recent decline in rule of law standards within some EU Member States has led to an expansion of the EU's rule of law toolkit. This includes introducing new tools such as the annual rule of law report and the rule of law conditionality regulation, in addition to the RoL framework, consisting of the Commission's recommendations to the Member States.[18] This enhanced scrutiny is expected to spill over to the accession process, modifying the EU's scrutiny under the Copenhagen criteria for aspiring member states. Consequently, vetting the judiciary to improve the rule of law compliance serves as a preemptive measure to avoid potential violations under Articles 2 and 19 (1) of TEU after full membership is achieved.

The efficacy of vetting to attain the necessary rule of law standards for European Union (EU) membership continues to be contested, especially given the current absence of long-term results in nations such as Albania and Moldova. Simultaneously, the post-accession implementation of the Cooperation and Verification Mechanism in Romania and Bulgaria, aimed at similar objectives, has been demonstrated to lack efficiency over time.[19]

Transitioning from a broad discussion of judicial vetting within transitional justice contexts, we now focus on specific instances that illustrate the dynamic evolution of these processes in the pursuit of European Union integration. Albania and Moldova represent critical case studies in this exploration, shedding light on the nuanced challenges and achievements of aligning domestic judicial reforms with the stringent criteria set by the European Union. These examples are particularly informative as they reveal the intricate relationship between national reform initiatives and international standards, providing a deeper understanding of how vetting procedures are tailored and executed to fulfil local imperatives and EU accession requirements. As this analysis delves into the experiences of these two nations, it highlights the critical role of vetting in enhancing the rule of law standards while also considering the long-term effectiveness and sustainability of reforms driven mainly by international influence.

17 See Ziya Öniş and Mustafa Kutlay, 'Reverse Transformation? Global Shifts, the Core-Periphery Divide and the Future of the EU' (2020) 28 *JCES* 197.

18 Petra Bard, Nóra Chronowski, Zoltán Fleck, Ágnes Kovács, Zsolt Körtvélyesi and Gábor Mészáros, 'Is the EU Toothless? An Assessment of the EU Rule of Law Enforcement Toolkit' (2022) MTA Law Working Papers 08/2022.

19 Radosveta Vassileva, 'Threats to the Rule of Law: The Pitfalls of the Cooperation and Verification Mechanism' (2020) 26 *Eur Pub L* 741.

Albania and Moldova: navigating the crossroads of transition and European Union aspirations

The EU as a normative power[20] has produced significant results in the frame of conditionality, famously coined as the *logic of consequences* as opposed to the *constructivist logic of appropriateness*.[21] This paradigm is projected into vertical interrelations (top-down imposture of norms) instead of horizontal interrelations (based not on a legal obligation but on a voluntary transfer of concepts by interpretation, influence, dialogue, transnational networks, etc.). Under the revisited external incentive model, the logic of persuasion is another horizontal interrelation typical for intra-court exchanges and can transform legal reasoning and legal culture. While there are generally accepted paradigms in the conception and diffusion of judicial independence standards and norms between actors engaged with the judicial reforms in transforming countries, there is also an agreement that the EU has had differentiated results in different countries. Research also broadly suggests that more focus should be given to the idiosyncrasies of a particular environment where the paradigms are exported.[22] The Europeanisation process in the diffusion of rule of law paradigms has been criticised extensively because of the rigidity of the patterns deployed[23] and because of the method of evaluation of progress, which has, at its most criticised, been considered failed[24] or pathologic.[25]

The institution-building process within the judiciary without transforming mentalities that do not move at the same pace with structural reforms has also been depicted as highly problematic.[26] This argument also relates to the issue of the alignment of judges'

> beliefs, values, attitudes, and understanding of the law, which overall constitutes the cultural traits of a judiciary, which, from the experience of past judicial reforms, does not go on the same pace with the institutional adjustments and constitutes the mental transition of the judge.[27]

20 Ian Manners, 'Normative Power Europe: A Contradiction in Terms?' (2002J, 20 CMS: *Journal of Common Market Studies*), 235–258.

21 Frank Schimmelfennig and Urlich Sedelmeier, 'The Europeanization of Eastern Europe: The External Incentives Model Revisited' (2020) 27 *J Eur Public Policy* 814.

22 Tanja A. Börzel and Thomas Risse, 'When Europeanisation Meets Diffusion: Exploring New Territory' (2012) 35 *West Eur Politics* 192.

23 Anja Seibert-Fohr, 'European Standards for the Rule of Law and Independent Courts' (2012) 20 *Journal für Rechtspolitik* 161.

24 Dimitry Kochenov, *EU Enlargement and the Failure of Conditionality: Pre-Accession Conditionality in the Fields of Democracy and the Rule of Law* (Kluwer 2007).

25 Martin Mendelski, 'Europeanization and the Rule of Law: Towards a Pathological Turn' (2016) 40 *SEE* 346.

26 Lisa Louwerse and Eva Kassoti, 'Revisiting the European Commission's Approach Towards the Rule of Law in Enlargement' (2019) 11(1) *HJRL* 223–250.

27 Michal Bobek 'The Fortress of Judicial Independence and the Mental Transitions of the Central European Judiciaries' (2008) *Eur Pub L* 99–123.

Albanian judicial reforms through dealing with old judges

Albania has been chosen as a case study because it represents an exceptional case, even in the Western Balkan region. Firstly, it has unravelled the full potential of the latest trend tool of radical integrity international vetting with regards to its impact: Albania lost around 40% of its judges, prosecutors and assistant-judges in this process, which considerably more than initially expected. Secondly, it is a clear-cut case of the differentiation between lustration and vetting, which is not always the case in CEE and SEE countries. In countries such as Albania, which have entered the fourth decade after the fall of communist regimes and do not have statehood problems, there has been a departure from vetting as a tool checking whether judges serving in the communist regime are fit for purpose in a liberal democracy, replacing it with an instrument to tackle the lack of accountability and endemic corruption. The intensification of the EU accession perspective has mediated this change. The full transformational power of the EU as a normative power and authority is unleashed in the case of the re-design and re-shuffling of all the judicial governance apparatus, starting at the constitutional design level and projected into every aspect of the judiciary. The intervention is believed to have reshaped the notion of Europeanisation of the judiciary through enlargement again, as this is considered inspirational for other countries that are reforming under the label of potential EU candidates.

The legacies of past transformations: reformation in distrust

In the three decades following the overturn of the most hardcore communist dictatorship in Europe, Albania has adopted the paradigms of democracy, human rights, and the rule of law with modest success. Building a strong, independent, and accountable judiciary as the cornerstone of the rule of law has been and still is an ongoing process that has produced various results. The attempts to bring the judiciary in Albania closer to European standards have often forced the international and national legal community alike to reconsider their approach towards judicial reform in terms of institutional configurations and individual judges.

The first endeavours towards judicial reform started in 1991 with the law on the Main Constitutional Provisions,[28] which established the first provisional liberal constitutional basis that would be used to build democratic institutions and transitional justice mechanisms up until the adoption of the Constitution of Albania by referendum in 1998. This legal framework was insufficient to drive transitional justice processes with due procedural guarantees, as the political scene at the time was quite volatile, the actors did not have the maturity to drive this process forward, and the institutions were weak. All the lustration attempts that followed in 1991–1998 were ineffective, erratic, targeted at political or

28 Law No. 7491 of 21/05/1991, "On the Main Constitutional Provisions."

other opponents, and led without the guarantees of due process. The Verification Law passed in 1995 and expired in 2001, provided a frame to clean the system from officials, politicians, and judges who had served in the previous system.[29] The law established a Verification Commission that could not guarantee its integrity and impartiality, as it was politically composed. This law was mainly used to target political opposition and politicians stemming from the dictatorial system, while there is no record of the persons who underwent lustration in the judiciary. In fact, due to the lack of transparency, systemic approach, and procedural means, the number and details of the process are unknown.[30]

The inability to enable proper transitional processes and the need for this new liberal system to be equipped with more judges for the new courts led to the decision to train existing and new magistrates with the infamous "six months" training.[31] So, instead of removing the "old judges," new ones were added to the system quickly. The turbulent years that followed in Albania did not contribute to strengthening the judiciary regarding independence, accountability, or quality, which also accounts for the individual level. The institutions mandated to preserve judicial independence, such as the High Council of Justice did not properly perceive the principle of separation of powers. By 1998, due to the adoption of the new constitution and the renewal of its composition, the High Council of Justice was mandated to reevaluate the judges and prosecutors based on the legislation in force.[32]

The evaluation consisted of an exam that tested their knowledge, and the judges who failed turned to the Constitutional Court, which reinstated them by concluding that

> the evaluation of the exam result only, regardless of the work results of the judge and his theoretical and practical contribution in the legal field, is an unconstitutional stance that goes beyond the content of the Constitution.[33]

29 Law No. 8043 of 30/11/1995 "On the verification of the moral character of officials and other persons connected with the defense of the democratic state."

30 "There is not an official number of the persons lustrated/vetted by Genocide Law and Verification Law. In the annual report of 2017, the Albanian Authority on Access to Information on the former State Security Service (Authority) confirm that all the documents created by Verification Commission are not elaborated or inventoried as the archives law demands, so there is not a list of persons controlled or verified by the Verification Commission. In addition, there is not a list of persons who have a clearness certificate. These entire documents are being processed from the Authority in respect to the Law No.45/2015." In Englantina Reka Lustration and Vetting in post-communist Albania inter-linked with civic trust in governmental institutions, in *Transitional Justice in Albania*, A Compilation of Papers by Young Albanian Researches (OSCE Presence in Albania and Konrad-Adenauer-Stiftung 2019) <www.osce.org/files/f/documents/e/4/445090.pdf>.

31 See Aurela Anastasi, 'The Albanian Justice Reform in the Framework of the European Integration Process' (2021) 2 *Euro-Balkan L Econ Rev* 1.

32 Anastasi (n 30) 1.

33 Decision of the Constitutional Court of Albania (CC) no. 59, 1999.

Even though transitional justice tools are meant to (re-)build trust in institutions through truth, transparency, and due process, this was not achieved during the democratic transition period of the country, and the processes carried no meaningful results from which to learn. Several authors argue that there is a causal link between the country's inability to instill the rule of law through further reforms and the lack of proper implementation of transitional justice in the early years.[34] Indeed, further changes to the legislation of institutions governing justice did not serve much of the purpose of attaining judicial independence, proper accountability, and overall integrity among individual judges.

In 2016, three decades later, the comprehensive and systemic vetting process of all judges and prosecutors was offered as the present solution for regaining the trust of the citizens in the judiciary. It was part of a comprehensive judicial reform, which changed one-third of the constitution with unanimity in the Parliament[35] and passed 27 organic laws to strengthen the structural independence of the judiciary and the status of magistrates and provide more guarantees against politicisation. Dsevoid of any intent to include transitional justice elements, it is instead an extraordinary accountability mechanism to address the systemic corruption and clientelist judiciary in Albania. Furthermore, it was incorporated amongst the political criteria as a precondition for Albania's opening of accession negotiations with the European Union.

> Judicial reforms are deemed an essential element for the accession of the Western Balkans to the EU as a process mainly driven by EU assistance.[36]

This process was just one of the pillars of the encompassing judicial reform, which was adopted with unanimity in 2016 by the General Assembly. Indeed, at the time, the judiciary was the power with the lowest trust amongst the citizens, based also on the measurement of perceptions and the interviews conducted by the Venice Commission with expert interlocutors.[37] Therefore, cleaning the judiciary using extraordinary accountability measures was meant to precede the organisation of the judiciary and the building of other mechanisms to preserve a balance between accountability and independence. The implications of the vetting were slightly more complex than the expectations.

34 Ines Stasa, 'Transitional Justice in Post-Communist Societies – the Case Study of Albania' in Anja Mihr (ed.), *Between Peace and Conflict in the East and the West* (Springer 2021).

35 Arta Mandro, 'Albanian parliament approved the new constitutional reform on justice system' July 27, 2016, *Constitutional Change*, <https://www.constitutional-change.com/albanian-parliament-approved-the-new-constitutional-reform-on-justice-system/>

36 European Commission for Democracy through Law (Venice Commission), 'Albania – Interim Opinion on the Draft Constitutional Amendments of the Judiciary' (CDL-AD(2015)045).

37 European Commission for Democracy through Law (Venice Commission), 'Albania – Interim Opinion on the Draft Constitutional Amendments of the Judiciary' (CDL-AD(2015)045).

Only a one-time thing: extraordinary vetting proceedings and their implications

In 2014, international and national legal experts conducted a comprehensive analysis of the justice system, which evidenced the system's vulnerabilities. Politicisation, corporatism, and endemic corruption suggested that a rather radical intervention toward accountability should be made before reforming the judiciary structurally. For years to come, this would turn the balances of the judiciary weighing on accountability. The "transitional reevaluation of judges and prosecutors"[38] is to make each judge, magistrate, prosecutor, and assistant judge responsible in three core areas: assets, professionalism, and integrity.

This reevaluation would be an extraordinary process, conceived "as a one-time action"[39] following sof the Venice Commission Opinion, which stressed the necessity to conduct it "by an assumption that the level of corruption in the Albanian judiciary is extremely high, and the situation requires urgent and radical measures."[40]

The Venice Commission clarified further what the process entails by differentiating between *pre-vetting* of judges and prosecutors[41] in cases of selection and appointment, *integrity checks regularly*[42] (such as yearly declaration of assets and performance evaluation), and fully-fledged *extraordinary vetting*, such as the one initiated in Albania in 2016.

The extraordinary vetting proceedings "should be regarded as wholly exceptional and subject to extremely stringent safeguards to protect those judges who are fit to occupy their positions."[43]

38 See Annex "Transitional Qualification Assessment" to the Constitution of Albania <www.venice.coe.int/webforms/documents/default.aspx?pdffile=CDL-REF(2016)064-e>.

39 *Xhoxhaj v. Albania*, App no 15227/19 (ECtHR 9 February 2021), para. 362.

40 European Commission for Democracy through Law (Venice Commission), 'Albania – Interim Opinion on the Draft Constitutional Amendments of the Judiciary' (CDL-AD(2015) 045).

41 See European Commission for Democracy through Law (Venice Commission), 'Republic of Moldova – Joint opinion of the Venice Commission and the Directorate General of Human Rights and Rule of Law (DGI) of the Council of Europe on some measures related to the selection of candidates for administrative positions in bodies of self-administration of judges and prosecutors and the amendment of some normative acts' (CDL AD (2021) 046).

42 See European Commission for Democracy through Law (Venice Commission), 'Ukraine – Urgent Joint Opinion of the Venice Commission and the Directorate General of Human Rights and Rule of Law (DGI) of the Council of Europe on the Legislative Situation regarding anti-corruption mechanisms, following Decision N° 13-R/2020 of the Constitutional Court of Ukraine' (CDL-AD(2020) 038).

43 European Commission for Democracy through Law (Venice Commission), 'Ukraine – Joint Opinion of the Venice Commission and the Directorate of Human Rights (DHR) of the Directorate General of Human Rights and Rule of Law (DGI) of the Council of Europe on the Law on the Judicial System and the Status of Judges and Amendments to the Law on the High Council of Justice of Ukraine' (CDL-AD(2015) 007).

The severity of the corrupt, clientelist, and politicised judiciary led to the recommendation for the vetting process to encompass all judges of all instances, including Constitutional Court judges, assistant judges, and prosecutors, which made the process a considerable undertaking. The case here presents a difference from other cases, such as in Kosovo,[44] where the vetting will only be applied to members of the judicial councils, court presidents, and chief prosecutors, or Moldova, which initially offered a pre-vetting process.

The transitional revaluation of judges and prosecutors (from now on, the vetting) was highly internationally driven, with working groups designing the reform being composed in equal parts by national and international scholars, legal experts, and judges,[45] which supported the work of an ad hoc parliamentary commission.[46] Driving lessons from previous reforms in similar contexts, which were made expeditiously, with a weak legal basis, without due process guarantees and therefore overturned quickly in higher instances, such as the reappointment case of Serbian dismissed judges in 2009, the designation of the vetting was made at the constitutional level.[47] Beyond the changes to the permanent constitutional provisions causing a whole re-organisation of the judiciary, a unique transitional annex was added to the constitution to regulate the vetting process. This Annex provided for the ad hoc bodies with judicial functions, namely the Independent Qualification Commission, which acted as a first instance court, and the Specialized Qualification Chamber (Appeal Chamber), which formed a two-tier administrative court. It was decided that these bodies, with the functions of courts, be locally composed, amongst judges with integrity and professionalism, in contrast with Ukraine, for instance, in which the vetting bodies were ad hoc courts composed of international judges, and the process was quoted as an international integrity vetting.[48]

The international community has been very present, de jure and de facto, in the planning, designing, and active monitoring phase. While the ad hoc courts were locally composed, their activity has been constantly scrutinised and sometimes oriented by a monitoring body made of international judges named the International Monitoring Operation (IMO). This is a constitutional body, as the Annex to the Constitution of Albania that frames the whole vetting process establishes this body for the whole vetting period, with oversight and counseling functions. IMO has had a crucial role in (1) monitoring the selection of the

44 See CDL-AD(2022)011-e Kosovo - Opinion on the Concept Paper on the Vetting of Judges and Prosecutors and draft amendments to the Constitution, adopted by the Venice Commission at its 131st Plenary Session (Venice, 17–18 June 2022).

45 The High-Level Experts of the Albanian Judicial Reform <www.reformanedrejtesi.al/ekspertet>.

46 Established with the Decision 96/2014, 27 November 2014.

47 Teodora Miljojkovic, 'Vetting as a Tool for Strengthening Judicial Integrity in the OSCE Region' in Anja Mihr and Chiara Pierobon (eds), *Polarization, Shifting Borders and Liquid Governance* (Springer 2024).

48 UNCAC Guest Blog with Tilman Hoppe, *International Integrity Vetting of Public Officials* (2023) <https://uncaccoalition.org/international-integrity-vetting/> accessed 13 July 2024.

reevaluation bodies; (2) providing recommendations to the Assembly regarding the qualification of the members of the reevaluation bodies and Public Commissioners; and (3) filing findings and opinions with the Commission and the Appeal Chamber and in particular may contribute to the background assessment.[49]

The vetting process was initiated in 2016 and is still ongoing, even though it was initially projected to be concluded within five years.[50] It is an extraordinary administrative exercise of accountability that entails reviewing the lifetime activity of judges and prosecutors in three main areas: asset assessment (wealth), background control (ethics), and proficiency assessment (professionalism). This disciplinary process leads to three possible results: an end of the judge's tenure, a return to the School of Magistrates for a year, or confirmation in duty. The exceptional specificity in this process is that, as distinct from other administrative proceedings, it is the reverse of the burden of proof: there were, in fact, the judges themselves who provided all the proofs necessary to be able to justify their assets and integrity.

Whether the process succumbs to political intents, there is a need to understand that the process is substantially political. It requires negotiations, legitimacy, international approval, and, mainly, good governance of the judiciary. While the process has been inclusive and has had public and international support, it fell short of foreseeing and managing the impacts of this sort of intervention. The shockwaves are very visible and long-term, and it would be naïve to say that the vetting process can be seen as easily differentiated or compartmentalised from the rest of the judicial mechanism of independence and accountability, as it is the process that has deeply scarred every aspect of it.

The first immediate consequence of this reformation phase was that the judiciary remained empty. In 2022, an estimated "45% of the 408 judges are out of the system, due to the vetting process, resignations or other reasons."[51] The Constitutional Court and High Court were not operational for two years and could not form minimal quorums for decision-making. Two High Court Judges had to undergo criminal proceedings for failure to declare previous convictions in other jurisdictions. Access to justice for citizens and piling the backlog of cases from the bottom up became a threatening and systemic problem not yet solved, amounting to 36,000 cases in 2020, by a non-functioning High Court, only exacerbating the breaching of the European standards on the length of proceedings.[52] Furthermore, the vetting has delayed the establishment and the consolidation of the new bodies of governance, such as the

49 See Article B to the Annex of the Constitution of Albania.

50 See Law No. 16/2022 of 10/02/2022 which changed the mandate of the vetting bodies from five years to eight years <https://qbz.gov.al/eli/ligj/2022/02/10/16/66ca1099-24a8-48bb-b8bb-b34fcb014eed;q=r.%2016%2F2022,%20dat%C3%AB%20 10.2.2022>.

51 <https://europeanwesternbalkans.com/2022/06/16/despite-its-weaknesses-the-vetting-process-remains-the-reform-of-paramount-importance-in-albania/> accessed 12 September 2024.

52 See *Bara and Kola v. Albania* App no 43391/18 and 17766/19 (ECtHR 12 October 2021).

High Judicial Council, the High Prosecutorial Council, and the High Inspector of Justice, which had the mission to ensure the normal flow of work of the judiciary and set up guarantees for independence and permanent mechanisms for maintaining accountability of the judiciary.

This created a blackout and suspension of the judiciary's work and the balances of power relying on judicial review, coined by the academic community as the "rule of law paradox."[53]

Due process considerations and international monitoring

In 2021, the first pivotal case in the Albanian vetting saga, *Xhoxhaj v. Albania*,[54] was decided by ECtHR, which led to a series of other cases following the ECtHR's interpretation of the civil limb of Article 6/1 ECHR also pertaining to individual complaints of judges in the frame of their subjective right to judicial independence[55] and Article 8/2 ECHR as the right to private life.[56] The ECtHR considered the extraordinary process of reevaluation of judges and prosecutors as a necessary intervention in the private life of judges and prosecutors (Article 8 ECHR), as well as considered the ad hoc two-tier vetting bodies (the General Commission of Qualification and the Appeals College), to be courts within the meaning of Article 6/1 ECHR. This line of reasoning legitimised the vetting as a whole, including the unusual reverse to the burden of proof in administrative proceedings from state bodies to applicants. The Court followed the Venice Commission's rationale[57] in justifying the radical intervention with the extraordinary circumstances the judiciary in Albania found itself in. The ECtHR became the missing Constitutional Court for dismissed judges, handling a comprehensive and ever-growing number of applications stating alleged breaches to the right to a fair trial, privacy, and access to justice for judges dismissed by the system.

Even though the vetting was considered a legitimate process, due process considerations produced different results in different individual complaints. In *Cani v. Albania*[58] there was a breach of the right to a tribunal established by law, as the composition of the vetting court, in this case, was deemed unlawful, while in *Thanza v. Albania*[59] the applicant's claim that he was never able to encounter

53 Darinka Piqani, 'The Rule of Law Paradox in the 2016 Constitutional Amendments in Albania', in Uladzislau Belavusau, and Aleksandra Gliszczynska-Grabias (eds), Constitutionalism under Stress (Oxford, 2020; online edn, Oxford Academic, 22 Oct. 2020), <https://doi.org/10.1093/oso/9780198864738.003.0007>, accessed 12 Feb. 2025.

54 See *Xhoxhaj v. Albania* App no 15227/19 (ECtHR 31 May 2021).

55 See *Baka v. Hungary* App no 20261/12 (ECtHR 23 June 2016).

56 *Oleksandr Volkov v. Ukraine* App no 21722/11 (ECtHR 9 January 2013) and *Denisov v. Ukraine* App no 76639/11 (ECtHR 25 September 2018).

57 European Commission for Democracy through Law, 'Albania Amicus Curiae Brief for the Constitutional Court on the Law on the Transitional Re-Evaluation of Judges and Prosecutors (The Vetting Law)' (CDL-AD(2016)036-e).

58 *Cani v. Albania* App no 37474/20 (ECtHR 4 January 2024).

59 *Thanza v. Albania* App no 41047/19 (ECtHR 4 October 2023).

the claims of the vetting bodies because they were not made known to the applicant during vetting, led the Court to consider it a breach of Article 6/1. In *Sevdari v. Albania*,[60] the Court ruled that there were disproportionate measures from the vetting bodies concerning the right to privacy and family enshrined in Article 8 ECtHR, so as in *Nikehasani v. Albania*[61] and *Gashi and Gina v. Albania*.[62] There are several other cases of dismissed judges waiting for the ECtHR verdict, and since the process is ongoing, there is no possibility to draw definite conclusions in terms of whether, overall, the vetting has been conducted with integrity and following the European standards of the right to a fair trial.

The post-interventionist period

The mandate of the reevaluation bodies was six and nine years, respectively, for the Qualification Commission and the Specialized Qualification Chamber (Appeal Chamber) when the vetting was supposed to finish. In 2022, eight years later, due to the rhythm of the process and COVID-19, only one-third of the judges and prosecutors were vetted. Therefore, the provisional constitutional amendments were voted on in the Parliament to extend the mandate of the reevaluation bodies by 36 months. When this chapter is written, the structures of the vetting (ad hoc tribunals, public commissioners, the International Monitoring Operation) co-exist with the permanent structures of ordinary accountability of the judiciary.[63] The latter are new structures, with new procedures, situated ideally in the supposedly 'clean' judiciary. After the harsh accountability intervention, four whole new judicial self-governing bodies (The High Judicial Council, the High Prosecutorial Council, the High Inspector of Justice, and the Judicial Appointment Council) should provide for a total self-governance of the judiciary and take on the permanent constitutional duties involving the initial vetting of the new magistrates (pre-vetting), and the integrity checks conducted regularly. The fear has arisen that the judicial councils, together with the anti-corruption body in charge of checking the assets of high officials and judges before and while on duty (High Inspectorate for Declaration of Assets and Conflict of Interest [HIDAACI]), who are now responsible for the "normal" and perpetual mechanisms of accountability, are not upholding the same standards attained by the vetting bodies and the vetting process.[64]

According to investigative sources, at the initial vetting performed on new magistrates, HIDAACI and the judicial councils found no problems on the

60 *Sevdari v. Albania* App no 40662/19 (ECtHR 13 March 2023).

61 *Nikehasani v. Albania* App no 58997/18 (ECtHR 22 May 2023).

62 *Gashi and Gina v. Albania* App no 29943/18 (ECtHR 4 July 2023).

63 See European Commission for Democracy through Law (Venice Commission), 'Albania – Opinion on the Extension of the Term of Office of the Transitional Bodies in charge of the re-evaluation of Judges and Prosecutors' (CDL-AD(2021)053).

64 See the Investigative Network Albania, Family members of dismissed judges and prosecutors take their place in the justice system; those who resigned during the vetting, teachers of new magistrates <https://ina.media/?p=7729>.

asset declarations of the expelled judges' wives, sons, and daughters who are accessing the system as new magistrates. Expelled judges are also not banned from teaching in the School of Magistrates, where the new magistrates are trained and socialized into the judiciary. While the system should bear no prejudice on individuals and their right not to bear the responsibilities of other people's actions and decisions, the risk of falling back into the path-dependency of the clientelist structure is higher when international scrutiny is not present.

This brings us to two main problems of initial pre-conceptions of the vetting, to which this chapter wants to bring attention:

1 In most cases, the overreliance on international intervention is not sustainable enough to recreate the same practices to ensure integrity and provide due process in the immediate aftermath of the intervention. Other socialisation processes need to be in place, and a legitimisation of the vetting process as a standard upholding the rule of law needs to happen within the community of judges, prosecutors, and legal practitioners to replicate practices of integrity building. The process per se' does not offer the guarantees or the legacy of permanent integrity building within the judiciary.
2 The overreliance on vetting to secure integrity "once and for all" needs to be reckoned with permanent mechanisms in place. The conception of integrity as a once-and-for-all, pre-packaged product solved with vetting is followed by empowerment that would create a lack of accountability as a path-dependent practice.

The Albanian experience with vetting process, being more established, provides a substantive body of evidence, whereas Moldova has only recently embarked on its vetting journey after acquiring EU candidacy status. The eventual outcomes of Moldova's vetting initiatives remain to be seen. Although the execution of vetting procedures exhibits differences between Moldova and Albania, the underlying rationale and narrative surrounding judicial vetting in both cases purport a similar objective – asserting the need for substantial reforms to combat corruption and inefficiency in the judiciary, ostensibly to comply with the international norms set by the Council of Europe and the EU acquis.

Moldova

On 23 June 2022, Moldova was granted Candidate Status to the European Union and Ukraine in the context of Russia's war aggression. In its opinion on Moldova's application, the European Commission recognised that the 2020 presidential and 2021 parliamentary elections in Moldova suggested "a clear alignment of the presidential, executive, and legislative powers on a pro-reform, anti-corruption European path for the first time since independence."[65] For

65 European Commission, 'Commission Opinion on the Republic of Moldova's application for membership of the European Union of June 17th' (COM 2022) 1.

the country to comply with the Copenhagen criteria and hard acquis of the EU negotiation chapters, a sturdy judicial reform was announced by the current government, which would be conducted with the assistance of international expert bodies such as the OSCE Office for Democratic Institutions and Human Rights (ODIHR) and European Commission for Democracy through Law (Venice Commission).

The international community has widely recognised and thoroughly analysed the endemic corruption and lack of independence within Moldova's judiciary.[66] According to the National Survey of 2017, even after extensive reforms in 2011–2017 under JSRS (Justice Sector Reform Strategy), more than 81% of the general population did not trust the judiciary.[67] The corruption scandals involving judges, such as the Russian Laundromat in 2016[68] and local corruption schemes in 2018, further eroded the public opinion on the independence of the judiciary.[69]

Recent legal developments

Ever since 2019's change of government, one of the proposed solutions for the problem of corruption in the judicial sector has been external evaluation in the form of vetting, as it became apparent that the internal self-cleansing of the judiciary would not take place.[70]

In March 2022, the Law on Some Measures related to the Selection of Candidates for Members' Positions in the Self-Administration Bodies of Judges

66 ODIHR, Election Observation Mission Final Report (22 May 2019) 4; Parliamentary Assembly of the Council of Europe (PACE), Resolution 2357 (2021); European Commission, 'Association Implementation Report on Moldova' (12 September 2019); Council of Europe, Directorate of Human Rights (DHR) of the Directorate of Human Rights and the Rule of Law (DGI) (CoE DHR-DGI), 'Justice Sector Reform Strategy of the Republic of Moldova – Review of Implementation – Assessment and Recommendations'(5 December 2017); International Commission of Jurists, 'Only an Empty Shell" – The Undelivered Promise of an Independent Judiciary in Moldova" (13 March 2019).

67 Survey conducted for the Superior Council of Magistracy by Open Justice, USAID funded program, and ATRECO, 'Increased Efficiency, Accountability and Transparency of Courts in Moldova' (2018) <http://crjm.org/wp-content/uploads/2018/02/Brosura_finala.compressed.pdf>.

68 Press conference of the head of the Anticorruption Prosecution Office and the head of the criminal investigation of the National Anticorruption Center of 21 September 2016 <www.realitatea.md/live–viorel-morari-si-bogdan-zumbreanu–conferinta-de-presa-privind-bilantuloperatiunii-de-retinere-a-celor-15-magistrati-si-3-executori-judecatoresti-pentru-fapte-de-coruptie_45501.html>.

69 International Commission of Jurists, " 'Only an Empty Shell" – the Undelivered Promise of an Independent Judiciary in Moldova' (13 March 2019) 7.

70 Vitalie Călugăreanu, 'Ultimatum for CSM' (25 June 2019) <www.dw.com/ro/ultimatum-pentru-csm-s%C4%83-cure%C8%9Be-ograda-magistra%C8%9Bilor-de-corup%C8%9Bi-compromi%C8%99i-%C8%99i-slujitori-ai-lui-plahotniuc/a-49348590>.

and Prosecutors was adopted without the support of the political opposition.[71] The law has envisioned an ad hoc Evaluation Committee vested with the mandate to check the integrity of the candidates for administrative positions in the Superior Council of Magistracy (SCM), the Superior Council of Prosecutors (SCP), and their specialised bodies.[72] The composition of the envisioned ad hoc Evaluation Committee would entail three members appointed by the Ministry of Justice at the proposal of the parliamentary factions based on the proportionality principle, as well as one alternate member in the same order, and three members and two alternates proposed by the development partners and approved with the vote of three-fifths by the deputies of the Parliament.[73] The developing partners stand for the international community active in Moldova's judicial development. As mandated by Moldovan law, the formation and functioning of the Evaluation Commission have revealed some procedural and structural flaws that impact its legitimacy and effectiveness.

Despite their roles, there was no provision for background checks or integrity evaluations of the ad hoc Evaluation Committee members themselves before the appointment, which is incongruent with the Commission's critical mandate of judicial evaluation.[74]

Furthermore, the procedures for appointing national and international members could have benefited from greater transparency and inclusivity, including broader consultation with civil society and more transparent communication about the selection criteria. The approval process in the Parliament did not thoroughly evaluate the qualifications or the suitability of candidates, particularly for international members who were confirmed without the opportunity to undergo a hearing before the legislators.[75]

The lack of accountability checks for the international members of the ad hoc committee reflects a broader challenge in the contemporary rule of law vetting of judges, as already seen in the Albanian case. In both contexts, the vetting process granted ample authority to the international community,

71 National Assembly of the Republic of Moldova, Law no. 26 of 10/03/2022 Regarding Some Measures Related to the Selection of Candidates for the Position of Members in the Self-administration Bodies of Judges and Prosecutors, Official Gazette no. 32, Art. 103.

72 On 22 April 2022 the Evaluation Commission established by the mentioned law adopted the Rules of Procedure of the Independent Evaluation Commission for assessing the integrity of candidates for the position of member in the self-administration bodies of judges and prosecutors ("Rules of Procedure"), which were followed by the adoption of Evaluation Rules in May 2022. Both acts represent the law's implementation and further regulate the evaluation criteria, stages of the evaluation, and procedural safeguards.

73 Article 5 of the Law no. 26 of 10/03/2022.

74 Office for Democratic Institutions and Human Rights (ODIHR), 'Report on the Evaluation (Pre-Vetting) of Candidates for Members of the Superior Council of Magistracy in Moldova' (1 June 2022–1 August 2023), para. 39.

75 Office for Democratic Institutions and Human Rights (ODIHR), 'Report on the Evaluation (Pre-Vetting) of Candidates for Members of the Superior Council of Magistracy in Moldova' (1 June 2022–1 August 2023), para. 43.

lacking sufficient oversight and accountability mechanisms. This aspect raises significant concerns about the long-term effectiveness of judicial vetting once international involvement ceases. In the long run, Moldova's judiciary should function independently within its national framework. This issue underscores the need for a balanced approach that ensures effective oversight and sustained institutional integrity post-international intervention, considering the radical nature of the vetting process itself.

The Evaluation Commission faced significant challenges with adhering to established deadlines, which raised concerns about its efficiency and effectiveness. Initially, the government had optimistic expectations for a swift evaluation process, but numerous delays undermined these timelines. Changes to legislation shortly after the establishment of the Commission extended various deadlines, contributing to the sluggish pace of proceedings. These delays slowed the momentum of judicial evaluations, highlighting a disconnect between the Commission's objectives and operational capabilities.[76]

Substance-wise, the law's introduction announced the commencement of the first phase of Moldova's judicial reforms, and, assessed through the comparative prism, it represented a novel solution in judicial vetting to strengthen the rule of law.[77] By opting first to assess the integrity of the bodies that will be in charge of the appointment, dismissal, and disciplinary procedures of the judges in the future, Moldova's mentioned law introduced a "filtering process" instead of the vetting process, which, according to the Venice Commission, had the potential to introduce "a balance between the benefits of the measure, in terms of contributing to the confidence of the judiciary, and its possible negative effects."[78] If the vetting process were confined solely to candidates for judicial self-administrative bodies, the procedure would effectively serve as a "filtering" mechanism. Following this rationale, these judicial and administrative bodies would subsequently filter the broader judiciary, thereby maintaining the judicial system's integrity while distancing the process from the extremities inherent in more comprehensive vetting approaches. However, subsequent legislation expanded the vetting bodies' mandate, encompassing the vetting of the broader judiciary and prosecutors. Consequently, what was initially a filtering procedure has evolved into a standard vetting process.

76 Office for Democratic Institutions and Human Rights (ODIHR), 'Report on the Evaluation (Pre-Vetting) of Candidates for Members of the Superior Council of Magistracy in Moldova' (1 June 2022–1 August 2023), para. 43.

77 The law has been so far analyzed by expert bodies such as the ODIHR, Venice Commission, and the Directorate General of Human Rights and Rule of Law (DGI) of the Council of Europe. See Joint opinion of the Venice Commission and the Directorate General of Human Rights and Rule of Law (DGI) of the Council of Europe on some measures related to the selection of candidates for administrative positions in bodies of self-administration of judges and prosecutors and the amendment of some normative acts' (L-AD(2021)046); OSCE Office for Democratic Institutions and Human Rights, Opinion-Nr.: JUD-MDA/439/2022 of September 28, 2022.

78 Venice Commission, CDL-AD(2021) 046, para. 43.

In March 2023, two laws were passed that regulated the institutional outlook of the Supreme Court and a vetting regime for its justices.[79] Finally, the Law on External Evaluation of Judges and Prosecutors and the Modification of Some Normative Acts was passed as the third step in the legislative process on judicial vetting of Moldova.[80] While the former stipulates that the Evaluation Commission conduct the vetting of Supreme Court justices, the latter establishes separate assessment commissions for judges and prosecutors from other judicial instances.[81] All vetting bodies maintain functional independence, and critical principles govern the vetting procedure, including (1) the independence of evaluation commissions, ensuring unbiased assessments; (2) fairness in the assessment process; (3) transparency through the public disclosure of evaluation documents; and (4) the distinct and extraordinary nature of the evaluation process.[82] Although the final decision on a particular judge or a prosecutor is on the Superior Council of Magistracy or the Superior Council of Prosecutors, which were pre-vetted, the assessment commissions' reports still carry significant weight. The decision of the SCM or SCP can be appealed before the Supreme Court of Justice only in the case of serious procedural errors or new facts which could have changed the outcome of the decision.[83] The legislative framework governing the vetting process includes allowing judges to resign before evaluation, effectively incorporating a self-cleansing element into the procedure.[84]

While the Moldovan government collaborated with international organisations to align the vetting procedures with global standards, certain aspects remained problematic. Notably, the provision that disqualifies individuals from serving on vetting bodies if they have held judicial or prosecutorial positions in Moldova within the last three years has elicited significant criticism from both the domestic judicial sector and international standard-setting organisations. Although it appears prudent to ensure that members vetting the new judiciary are independent of current structures, concerns arise regarding the legitimacy of vetting body members who lack prior involvement with Moldova's judicial sector. This adds to concerns about international members' legitimacy in the vetting process.

While the vetting process continues, Moldova is concurrently addressing judicial corruption by deliberating on establishing a specialised anti-corruption

79 Republic of Moldova, Law No. 64 of 30/03/2023 on the Supreme Court of Justice, Official Gazette, No. 117–118 art. 190; Republic of Moldova, Law No. 65 of 30/03/2023 on the external evaluation of judges and candidates for the position of judge of the Supreme Court of Justice, Official Gazette No. 117–118 art. 192.

80 Law No. 252 of 08/17/2023 on the External Evaluation of Judges and Prosecutors and the Modification of Some Normative Acts, Official Gazette No. 325–327 art. 581.

81 Law No. 64 of 30/03/2023, Article 4; Law No. 252 of 08/17/2023, Article 7.

82 Law No. 252 of 08/17/2023, Article 2 (2).

83 Law No. 252 of 08/17/2023, Article 19 (6).

84 Law No. 252 of 08/17/2023, Article 3 (c), Law No. 65 of 30/03/2023, Article 3 (b).

court system, again with significant involvement from the international community.[85]

Conclusion

It remains to be seen whether the extraordinary vetting procedure will leave a long-lasting trace in the modus operandi of the judicial governance institutions and their ability to strike a balance between institutional independence and the individual right of independence for judges in ensuring due process. Extending it further, it remains to be seen whether the vetting will leave a trace of better-managing integrity in the appointments and activities of judges and prosecutors. At the same time, securing enduring legitimacy and contextual expression in practice is essential for determining whether path-dependent practices prevail over extraordinary cleansing interventions. This argument becomes even more relevant when placing it in the overall social legitimisation of such internationally driven actions in their contexts and not just as mere transactional instruments of EU integration processes. The reorientation of vetting procedures towards facilitating EU accession and adherence to international standards marks a significant shift in their purpose and implementation. Initially envisioned as tools for transitional justice, these procedures are increasingly geared towards meeting the stringent requirements of EU integration and establishing a judiciary that aligns with global norms of independence and accountability. This strategic pivot reflects an evolving understanding of vetting as a corrective measure and a foundational step toward international compliance. However, this approach raises questions about such reforms' sustainability and long-term effectiveness.

Predominantly driven by the international community, these vetting processes often lack substantial and nationwide impetus, which is critical for ensuring their acceptance and integration into the domestic legal culture. The heavy reliance on external guidance and oversight may lead to reforms perceived as imposed rather than organically adopted, potentially undermining their legitimacy and efficacy in the eyes of the local population. Moreover, the focus on aligning with international standards through vetting can overshadow the need to cultivate a robust and independent judicial culture domestically. While vetting can temporarily enforce standards and remove unsuitable individuals from positions of power, it cannot instill a deep-seated culture of judicial independence and ethical governance. The risk then emerges that once the external pressure subsides or the international community's involvement diminishes, the judiciary may revert to previous practices or fail to advance the principles of transparency and accountability.

85 International Monetary Fund, 'Republic of Moldova: Technical Assistance Report – Analysis of the Draft Law on the Anti-Corruption Judicial System and on Amending Some Normative Acts' (22 March 2024).

The sustainability of vetting outcomes thus hinges on developing internal mechanisms and a judicial ethos that values independence as a fundamental principle rather than a conditional requirement of EU accession. Without this internalisation of judicial independence, the effectiveness of vetting remains contingent on external validation and support, which is neither viable nor desirable in the long term. This dependence on external drivers for judicial reform through vetting also poses a significant challenge: can such a process genuinely replace a lacking or weak culture of judicial independence? The answer seems complex. While vetting can set the groundwork by removing corrupt or compromised individuals, it cannot alone create the systemic and cultural change necessary for a judiciary to operate independently and impartially. True reform requires a multifaceted approach that combines vetting with comprehensive education, ongoing monitoring, and cultural shifts within the judiciary and broader society. Therefore, while vetting is essential to aligning with EU standards and improving judicial systems, it must be part of a broader strategy that fosters genuine judicial independence from the ground up. Ensuring reforms are implemented and embraced nationally is crucial for their success and sustainability. As such, the challenge moving forward will be to balance the influence of international norms with the cultivation of a domestic legal culture that supports and sustains the ideals of an independent judiciary. Only through such balanced approaches can vetting genuinely contribute to the long-term stability and effectiveness of judicial institutions in transitioning countries.

11 The conundrum of judicial accountability and independence in military courts from a comparative perspective*

Arianna Vedaschi and Micol Ferrario

Introduction

Military justice can be defined as the system put in place to deal with both disciplinary and criminal offences committed by military personnel[1] and, in some cases, by civilians closely associated with them.[2] Originally, the development of military justice was meant to maintain discipline and order within the armed forces. For this reason, its administration initially remained in the hands of military commanders, who served it via a set of specific rules and procedures different from those used in the civilian system.[3] However, this commander-centred arrangement presented several downsides, especially regarding the alleged arbitrariness and summariness of proceedings.[4]

Against this background, starting in the seventeenth century, a trend towards the "civilianisation" of military justice took hold, namely the progressive incorporation of civilian principles (such as the respect of human rights, including procedural fairness) within the military legal system.[5] After World War II, this process went as far as abolishing, in some states, military justice in peacetime and delegating its handling to civilian courts. In other states, the change has been less dramatic, resulting in the establishment of standing special courts.

* Arianna Vedaschi authored the paragraph "Italian military jurisdiction: a hybrid leading model?" and the Conclusion.

Micol Ferrario authored the Introduction and the paragraph "A taxonomy of military justice". The authors are grateful for funding from MIUR – PRIN Bando 2020 – prot. 2020M47T9C "Decision-Making in the Age of Emergencies: New Paradigms in Recognition and Protection of Rights". The authors would especially like to thank Pierpaolo Rivello, along with David Brunelli and Maria Michela Teresa Mazzilli, for their useful suggestions.

1 Matthew Nathan Groves and Alison Duxbury, 'The Reform of Military Justice' in Groves and Duxbury (eds), *Military Justice in the Modern Age* (Cambridge University Press 2016) 2.

2 Mindia Vashakmadze, 'Understanding Military Justice: A Practice Note' (2018) *DCAF* 1, 2.

3 Gwenaël Guyon, Jean Paul Laborde and Stéphane Baudens, 'Introduction' in Guyon, Laborde and Baudens (eds) 93 *Revue Internationale de Droit Pénal: Military Justice. Contemporary Challenges, History and Comparison* (2022) 1, 10.

4 Claire Simmons, *Military Investigations in Armed Conflict: Independence and Impartiality Under International Law* (Routledge 2024) 17.

5 Eugene R. Fidell, *Military Justice: A Very Short Introduction* (Oxford University Press 2016) 22ff.

DOI: 10.4324/9781003557852-15

Nevertheless, military justice, as an act of administration of justice, must follow the same precepts of the rule of law that traditionally apply to the judiciary.[6] There have been major concerns regarding the independence, impartiality, and accountability of military judges. As for judicial accountability, it has been widely posited that states should implement a set of mechanisms to make military judges accountable for their decisions or behaviours. With reference to independence and impartiality, it has been stressed that military courts should be detached from both the legislative and executive branches of government, as well as from the military hierarchy. Such concerns do not normally arise in countries where military justice falls under the jurisdiction of civilian courts. On the contrary, when the handling of military justice belongs to special military courts, it is necessary to take steps to ensure the same principles governing the administration of civilian justice. In this vein, in the early 2000s, the United Nations drafted the principles governing the administration of justice through military tribunals, which were formally articulated and presented before the United Nations Human Rights Council in 2006 and then updated in 2018 (the so-called Yale Draft of the Decaux Principles).[7] Among other things, this document stresses that military judges "should have a status guaranteeing their independence and impartiality, in particular vis-à-vis the military hierarchy" (principle n. 4) and be accountable (principle n. 20). Regarding the former, it has been pointed out that a proper course of military justice would be achieved if all the undue influences from politics and military command were expunged. Indeed, since military courts normally consist of one or more servicepersons appointed by the armed forces or by the defence ministry, significant apprehensions arise regarding the separation of powers and the potential lack of independence and/or impartiality.[8] In this respect, even the European Court of Human Rights (ECtHR) has repeatedly expressed its concerns.[9] Regarding accountability, efforts should be made to build a military justice system that is accountable before both the law and the public. This means that, on the one hand, a way to hold military judges liable for their performances should be established; on the other hand, it would be necessary to make their decisions available to the public.

6 Rachel E. VanLandingham, Grazvydas Jasutis and Kristina Cernejute, 'Military Justice' (2023) *DCAF* 1, 11.

7 Principles Governing the Administration of Justice Through Military Tribunals (the Yale Draft) <www.court-martial-ucmj.com/files/2018/06/The-Yale-Draft.pdf>.

8 Martin Baumgartner, 'Military Tribunals' in Christina Binder, Manfred Nowak, Jane A. Hofbauer and Philipp Janig (eds), *Elgar Encyclopedia of Human Rights* (1st edn, Edward Elgar 2022) Vol. 1, 475.

9 See, among others: ECtHR, *Findlay v. the United Kingdom*, application n. 22107/93, 25 February 1997; ECtHR, *Incal v. Turkey*, application n. 22678/93, 9 June 1998; ECtHR, *Moore v. the United Kingdom*, application n. 37481/97, 30 May 2000; ECtHR, *İbrahim Gürkan v. Turkey*, application n. 10987/10, 3 July 2012; ECtHR, *Mustafa v. Bulgaria*, application n. 1230/17, 28 February 2020.

The current geopolitical landscape has led to increasingly questioning the role and the proper functioning of military justice. Indeed, after the outbreak of the Russia-Ukraine conflict and the possible involvement of some European states in military interventions, these concerns are growing in importance. It suffices here to consider French President Emmanuel Macron, who on 26 February 2024 stated his refusal to rule out putting ground troops in Ukraine,[10] or the Swiss military justice, which already opened several proceedings against Swiss nationals accused of joining the Ukrainian war.[11]

In view of this, the first part of the chapter puts forward a typology of military jurisdictions showing how divergent systems are vulnerable to different criticisms with respect to judicial independence, impartiality, and accountability. Here, the main Western advanced democracies will be considered and sorted on the grounds that they belong to a common law-based (courts-martial) or a civil law-based (standing courts) tradition. Within the latter group, a further distinction is drawn between the legal systems in which military justice falls within the competence of civilian courts and those in which the jurisdiction over military justice pertains to special military courts. The chapter later takes Italy as a case study, considering it an illustrative example in terms of military judicial independence, impartiality, and accountability. The reason for such a choice is twofold: first, Italian military tribunals feature a mixed composition, namely civilian judges sit alongside military personnel; and second, the Italian military jurisdiction has its own self-governing body. A brief insight into its origins and a focus on its structure and jurisdiction are given. A deepening discussion on the composition and the functioning of its self-governing body (the Council of Military Judiciary) follows. In this passage, particular attention is paid to a recent reform affecting its composition. The chapter ends with an assessment of whether a system of military justice such as the Italian one may be a leading model in terms of judicial independence, impartiality, and accountability.

A taxonomy of military jurisdictions

Over the years, the idea that "where there is an army, there is military justice"[12] took hold. Consequently, it has been broadly argued that military courts began to exist as soon as the military apparatus came into existence. This assumption has nevertheless been widely challenged, given that several countries with armies do not have military courts tasked with punishing the military's wrongdoing but rather civilian courts or disciplinary bodies are in charge of doing so.

10 In such a scenario, the jurisdiction would be regulated by the Code de Justice Militaire.

11 Indeed, pursuant to art. 94 of the Swiss Military Criminal Code, foreign service is subject to a term of imprisonment up to three years or to a fine.

12 John Gilissen, *Évolution actuelle de la justice militaire* (Recueils de la société internationale de droit pénal militaire et de droit de la guerre 1981) 38.

Against this background, several issues with the taxonomic classification of military jurisdictions have been raised. Over time, several attempts have been put forward and relied on different factors, such the systems of law they belong to,[13] the composition of military courts,[14] the power they hold or, again, the body tasked with adjudicating military offences.[15] Although there are now common trends in military justice, several differences still exist from country to country. A major one subsists between the common law-based and civil law-based systems of military justice.

Military justice in the common law tradition

The common law (Anglo-Saxon) tradition has historically been acquainted with ad hoc military tribunals convened on a case-by-case basis.[16]

Among others, the United Kingdom features a service justice system with exclusive jurisdiction over offences against service law. Following the enactment of the Armed Forces Act (AFA) 2006, the Court Martial (a standing, permanent court) was established. Pursuant to section 50, (1), AFA "has jurisdiction to try any service offence" (as punctually listed in section 50, (2), AFA). It is chaired by the judge advocate (a civilian judge), and the jury consists of three to six lay members. Its judgments may be appealed before the Court Martial Appeal Court (section 272 AFA), which is composed of senior judges serving in civilian courts. Even in cases of summary trials (for non-criminal conduct military offences, such as misconduct through alcohol or drugs), there are two tiers of jurisdiction: the first level falls under the competence of the commanding officer of the accused, while the second falls under the summary appeal court. Furthermore, in the United Kingdom, there is a body responsible for minor offences committed by civilians working for the armed forces, namely the Service Civilian Court.

Similar to other former British colonies, the United States initially borrowed its system of military justice from the United Kingdom.[17] However, over the years, the US system has evolved significantly, especially in times of

13 Gilissen (n 12) 46ff. Gilissen classified them on the basis of the systems of law they belonged to (civil law systems, Roman law system, and socialist law system).

14 Gilissen (n 12) 48.

15 Mindia Vashakmadze, *Understanding Military Justice* (Geneva Centre for the Democratic Control of Armed Forces 2011). According to this author, four models of military justice can be observed: the purely civilian model, in which the jurisdiction over military offences is held by civilian courts; the purely military model, in which military courts have an exclusive jurisdiction over military offences; the jurisdictionally hybrid model, in which military and civilian courts have overlapping jurisdictions over military offences; and the structurally hybrid model, in which civilian court also deals with issues of military judicial nature.

16 David Denton QC, 'The Australian Military Justice System: History, Organization and Disciplinary Structure' (2016) 6 *VULJ* 27, 28.

17 Brett J. Kyle and Andrew G. Reiter, *Military Courts, Civil-Military Relations, and the Legal Battle for Democracy: The Politics of Military Justice* (Routledge 2021) 197.

severe security threats.[18] Currently, the substantive and procedural rules governing the US military justice system are settled down in the Uniform Code of Military Justice (UCMJ) 1951, which applies to all branches of military service. Under the UCMJ, courts-martial have the power to judge military personnel. Depending on the military offence, a different type of court-martial may be set up. The general court-martial (section 816, art. 16, lett. b, UCMJ) adjudicates the most serious crimes (e.g. felonies) and consists of a military judge and a panel of not less than five members of the service. This is the only court-martial that can impose the death penalty. The special court-martial (section 816, art. 16, lett. c, UCMJ) is a misdemeanour court and consists of a military judge and a panel of at least three members of the service. Finally, there is the summary court-martial (section 816, art. 16, lett. d, UCMJ), which has jurisdiction over less serious offences and consists of one commissioned officer. Military convictions can be appealed before the courts of criminal appeals (section 866, art. 66, UCMJ). There are four courts of criminal appeal (one for each branch of the military service), and they are composed of one or more panels, counting a minimum of three military judges. In some cases, a complaint against their decisions may be filed before the Court of Appeals for the Armed Forces (section 867, art. 67, UCMJ), which is made up of three civilian judges. A final appeal may be filed before the US Supreme Court by writ of certiorari (section 867a, art. 67a, UCMJ).

In the common law tradition, military judicial independence, impartiality, and accountability have been a key issue. This is mainly because military justice was traditionally served by courts existing intermittently, which were exclusively made up of military representatives.[19] Nevertheless, as the two previous experiences show, in the last few decades, several efforts have been put forward to boost these fundamental principles. It is worth noting that, as the UK case plainly reveals, common law military tribunals are now increasingly shifting towards a system of military standing courts.[20] Moreover, as clearly displayed by both the United Kingdom and the United States, there has been an important increase in the number of civilian judges serving in courts-martial.[21] Therefore, several efforts have been put forward to foster the independence, impartiality, and accountability of military tribunals in the common law tradition.

Military justice in the civil law tradition

In the civil law tradition, jurisdiction over military offences belongs to standing courts, which are either civilian or special. An attempt at classification may

18 After 9/11, military commissions were largely resumed to try terrorists labelled as unlawful enemy combatants detained in Guantánamo: Brian J. Foley, 'Guantanamo and Beyond: Dangers of Rigging the Rules' (2007) 97 *JCLC* 1009, 1036ff.

19 Fidell (n 5) 68.

20 Ovidiu-Horia Maican, 'New Evolutions of Military Justice' (2022) 11 *Perspectives L Public Adm* 463, 464.

21 Fidell (n 5) 70.

therefore be made on the basis of the position occupied by military courts within the national judiciary system. Accordingly, two macro-models of military justice can be identified: the first gathers all the civil law countries where military courts are incorporated into civilian jurisdiction, and the second captures countries where military courts are separated from civilian ones and constitute a parallel special branch of jurisdiction.

Military justice in civilian courts

Especially after World War II, several Western states ran into huge popular dissatisfaction with their wartime military justice.[22] Following this war-generated criticism, countries such as Austria and Germany abolished their military court systems.

The decision to abolish military jurisdiction in Austria was made shortly after the end of World War I. Indeed, over the course of several official investigations, all the shortcomings of wartime military justice emerged.[23] Consequently, the Code of Criminal Procedure of 1920 stipulated that in peacetime, the members of the army must be subjected to the jurisdiction of civilian courts.[24] This decision was reproduced in the Austrian Constitution of 1929 (Osterreich Bundesverfassung), which in art. 8, provides that "[m] ilitary jurisdiction – except in time of war – is repealed". Nevertheless, in late 1933, martial law was reintroduced at the hands of the authoritarian Chancellor Engelbert Dollfuß. Following the Austrian annexation to Germany (the so-called Anschluss) in 1938, German military law began to be applied.[25] It was not until after World War II that all these Nazi residues were abolished, and the Austrian system was finally re-established. Thus, Austrian law currently provides that in peacetime military jurisdiction belongs to civilian courts and that, in wartime exclusively, special military courts may be established. The military offences are listed in the Militärstrafgesetz, § 1 of which provides that it applies to soldiers exclusively (with certain few exceptions).

Similar to Austria, Germany lacks a separate branch of military justice. In the country, in peacetime, the jurisdiction over military offences lies with civilian courts.[26] Only during the so-called state of defence[27] or when the members

22 Edward F. Sherman, 'Military Justice Without Military Control' (1973) 82 *Yale L J* 1398, 1398.

23 Steven R. Welch, 'Military Justice' in *International Encyclopedia of the First World War* (1st edn, 2014) 2: <https://encyclopedia.1914-1918-online.net/>.

24 Federico Andreu-Guzmán, *Military Jurisdiction and International Law: Military Courts and Gross Human Rights Violation* (International Commission of Jurists 2004) 180.

25 Martin Moll, 'Militärgerichtsbarkeit in Österreich (circa 1850–1945)' (2016) 6 *Beiträge zur Rechtsgeschichte Österreichs* 324, 324–344.

26 Only in cases of disciplinary offences soldiers are tried before the German army disciplinary and complaints court. Eventually, its rulings may be appealed before the federal administrative court and before its two military affairs divisions.

27 Arianna Vedaschi, *À la guerre comme à la guerre? La disciplina della guerra nel diritto costituzionale comparato* (G. Giappichelli Editore 2007) 310ff.

of the armed forces are serving abroad or are stationed on warship (art. 96, § 2, Basic Law)[28] may the federation establish a special military criminal court. Due to the experience of World War II, the jurisdiction of special military criminal courts is restricted to offences committed by members of the armed forces.[29] These are punctually listed in the Military Criminal Code (Wehrstrafgesetz, hereinafter WStG). In general, all the offences pertaining to military service or running counter to military duties can be defined as such (e.g. desertion, disobedience, and mutiny).[30] In peacetime, the scope of the WStG is broader, since it addresses both soldiers and civilians. More precisely, under § 1 WStG, it applies to soldiers actively serving in the German armed forces; former soldiers who violate provisions on secrecy; civilians acting as military superiors if they commit an offence against the duties of a superior; and civilians who commit a military offence.

With specific reference to judicial independence and impartiality, it has been widely argued that having civilian courts dealing with military offences may be an advantage. Indeed, in contrast to army judges, civilian judges are not serving members of the armed forces; thus, it is less likely that in a trial they show deference towards the army and its arguments. Although this macro-model of military justice ensures these fundamental principles, it has several potential downsides. One negative aspect may be related to the alleged lack of the necessary expertise to deal with military affairs. Unlike army judges, civilian judges normally neither have specialistic knowledge of military affairs nor share the militaries' professional standards and values, and they are not accustomed to practicing military criminal law. Another potential drawback concerns efficiency, particularly the recurrent delays in civilian trials.

It is worth underlining that to overcome these difficulties, some civil law countries have opted to establish a specialised division within their civilian courts. This is the case in France, where pursuant to art. 112–1 Code of Military Justice (Code de justice militaire, hereinafter CJM),[31] military courts can be set up only in wartime. Consequently, in peacetime, no special military courts exist, and military justice administration is performed by civilian judges in specialised divisions in military matters. Their jurisdiction varies *ratione*

28 "The Federation may establish federal military criminal courts for the Armed Forces. These courts may exercise criminal jurisdiction only during a state of defence or over members of the Armed Forces serving abroad or on board warships. Details shall be regulated by a federal law. These courts shall be under the aegis of the Federal Minister of Justice. The judges officiating there as their primary occupation shall be persons qualified to hold judicial office".

29 Monika Jachmann-Michel, 'GG Art. 96' in Günter Dürig, Roman Herzog and Rupert Scholz (eds), *Grundgesetz kommentar* (Verlag C.H. Beck 2023) §§ 25–26.

30 Georg Nolte and Heike Krieger, 'Military Law in Germany' in Nolte (ed), *European Military Law Systems* (De Gruyter Recht 2003) 415.

31 "Un décret en Conseil d'État fixe le siège des tribunaux et leur ressort ainsi que le nombre de chambres qui les constituent. Il détermine les autorités militaires qui exercent les pouvoirs judiciaires sous l'autorité du ministre de la défense".

loci.[32] If the act has been committed within the French national borders, the jurisdiction lies with the specialised chamber of the civilian courts, particularly the civilian tribunals in the case of an offence (*délit*) and the assize court in the case of a crime (*crime*) (art. 111-1, § 1, CJM and art. 697 Code de procédure pénale, hereinafter CPP). On the contrary, if the offence has been committed beyond French national borders, the jurisdiction lies with the specialised chambers of the civilian courts located in Paris (art. 111-1, § 2, CJM and art. 697-4 CPP).[33] As in the previous cases, military offences are enumerated in the CJM. Under this code, four main typologies of military offences exist: offences tending to exempt their perpetrator from their military obligations (arts. 321-1 to 321-24); offences against honour or duties (arts. 322-1 to 322-18); offences against discipline (arts. 323-1 to 323-23); and offences against orders (arts. 324-1 to 324-11).

Military justice in special military courts

In contrast to the previous examples, in several civil law countries, military courts represent a special branch of jurisdiction that is separated and, therefore, independent from the civilian branch. First, within this second macro-group, a further distinction may be traced on the basis of the courts' composition. By taking a comparative perspective, we immediately observe special military courts consisting exclusively of military judges and others with a mixed composition, namely, civilian judges sitting alongside military personnel.

Among others, to the first cluster belongs Switzerland, which features a highly structured military justice system[34] where all the judges are recruited from troops. At the head of the Swiss military justice system, there is the armed forces attorney general, who must hold the rank of brigadier and is the chief prosecutor in matters of military criminal law. The jurisdiction over military offences lies, in the first instance, with the military tribunals (three, one per each linguistic region) and, in the second one, with the military courts of appeal (three, one per each linguistic region). Each military tribunal is made up of a presiding judge (who must be a colonel or a lieutenant colonel) and four judges (two officers and two non-commissioned officers).[35] A similar composition[36] can be found in the military courts of appeal, the only difference being that they must have had legal training. The third tier of jurisdiction is provided by the Military Supreme Court. Similar to the previous ones,

32 Alessandro Arlotto, 'La giustizia penale militare in Francia' (2022) *Rivista di informazione giuridica* 1, 1–14.

33 Prior to 2012, it was the Paris army court (Tribunal aux armées de Paris) that had peacetime jurisdiction over the offences committed outside the French territory.

34 For an in-depth analysis, see Thierry Godel, 'La justice militaire suisse *de lege lata*' (2021) 139 *Revue Pénale Suisse* 279, 279–311.

35 Swiss Code of Criminal Military Procedure of 23 March 1979 (RS 322.1), art. 8.

36 Swiss Code of Criminal Military Procedure of 23 March 1979 (RS 322.1), art. 12.

it is made up of a presiding judge (who must have the rank of colonel) and four other judges (two officers and two non-commissioned officers).[37] All of them must hold a law degree or must have passed the Swiss bar examination. All military judges stay in office for four years. All the military offences over which the Swiss military tribunals have jurisdiction are punctually listed in the Military Criminal Code of 1927[38] that, pursuant to art. 7, § 1, may also apply to civilians.

Similarly, Spain features military courts composed of representatives of military personnel, with the sole exception of the Fifth Chamber of the Supreme Court. Spanish military courts are established under art. 117, § 5, of the Spanish Constitution, which stipulates that their jurisdiction "is limited to a strictly military scope in respect of the actions defined as military offences by the Military Criminal Code and to cases of state of siege".[39] Its bodies are listed in Ley Orgánica 4/1987.[40] The Fifth Chamber of the Supreme Court (Sala de lo Militar del Tribunal Supremo) is at the pinnacle of the military justice system and is composed of eight judges, four of which are from the civilian magistracy and four of which are from the troops (art. 24, Ley Orgánica 4/1987). The Central Military Tribunal (Tribunal Militar Central) has nationwide jurisdiction and is a centralised court for dealing with all the issues attributed to it (art. 34, Ley Orgánica 4/1987). As previously mentioned, it is composed of military representatives exclusively and, more precisely, by one president, four *vocales togados* (having the rank of generals), and a variable number of *vocales militares* (having the rank of brigadier generals or rear admirals) (art. 36, Ley Orgánica 4/1987). There are also the territorial military tribunals (*tribunales militares territoriales*) that are responsible for the criminal proceedings in their area of jurisdiction and consist of one president, four *vocales togados* (two auditor lieutenant colonels and two auditor commanders), and a variable number of *vocales militares* (having the rank of commanders or corvette captains) (art. 46, Ley Orgánica 4/1987). In peacetime, their jurisdiction is confined to the offences listed in the Military Criminal Code,[41] with the exception of troops displaced outside the national territory over whom they have exclusive jurisdiction. In wartime, instead, it is provided that their jurisdiction may be broadened (arts. 157ff., Ley Orgánica 4/1987).

The status of the judges composing a court is not irrelevant to judicial independence and, consequently, impartiality. Indeed, as we previously hinted, judges who are serving members of the armed forces may suffer from the command undue influences. In this respect, it has been claimed that if a special military court features a mixed composition, judicial independence and

37 Swiss Code of Criminal Military Procedure of 23 March 1979 (RS 322.1), art. 15.
38 Swiss Code of Criminal Military Law of 13 June 1927 (RS 321.0).
39 Ley Orgánica 6/1985 of 1 July, art. 3.
40 Ley Orgánica 4/1987 of 15 July.
41 Ley Orgánica 14/2015 of 14 October.

impartiality should be better granted.[42] Moreover, in such cases, concerns related to the lack of a specialistic understanding are also reduced.

This arrangement is obvious in Italy, which is a *unicum* in the comparative panorama, since besides featuring special military courts where military judges sit with the representatives of the military personnel, it also disposes of a self-governing body for the military judiciary (the Council of Military Judiciary).

Italian military jurisdiction: a hybrid leading model?

A historical background

Most legal scholars believe that the origins of the Italian military jurisdiction can be traced back to the years before the unification of Italy, specifically to the enactment of the Sardinian Military Criminal Code in 1859.[43] This code was thought to be applied exclusively to the Sardinian army, and it was at the forefront (for that time), both with respect to the prescribed penalties and the procedural guarantees.[44] Regarding this last point, the code established a system of military justice separate from civilian justice. Under its art. 274, during peacetime, there were several bodies in charge of the military jurisdiction, namely the commission of enquiry, the territorial military tribunals, the military tribunals on board ship, and the supreme war tribunal.[45] During wartime (art. 545), it was possible to establish extraordinary military tribunals, and the commission of enquiry did not operate.[46]

Following the unification of Italy in 1861, this structure was almost equally taken up in the Military Criminal Code of the Italian Kingdom (1869).[47] From that time until the outbreak of World War I, military jurisdiction fell under 12 military tribunals, four maritime tribunals, and one supreme tribunal in charge of the military jurisdiction. Throughout the conflict (to which Italy took part starting in 1915), the military jurisdiction was significantly extensive. First, it was competent over some charges brought against people not belonging to the army; this happened, for instance, in cases of treason, espionage, or

42 Benjamin Heng, Rain Liivoja, Daniel Ng and Bruce O. Oswald, 'Military Justice in a Comparative and International Perspective' (2016) 20 *J Int Peacekeep* 133, 135.

43 Antonio Intelisano, 'La Giurisdizione Penale Militare in Italia: Sguardo Retrospettivo e Attuali Tendenze Evolutive' (1980) 19 *MLLWR* 422, 423.

44 Marco Rovinello, 'Una giustizia senza storia? I codici penali militari nell'Italia liberale' (2012) *Le Carte e la Storia* 59, 60.

45 Giovanni Dallera, 'Premessa storica concernente l'ordinamento giudiziario militare' in Pierpaolo Rivello (ed), *Manuale del diritto e della procedura penale militare. Ordinamento giudiziario militare* (G. Giappichelli 2023) 500.

46 Dallera (n 45) 501.

47 Arturo Bruchi, *I tribunali militari e la scienza del diritto criminale* (Lazzeri 1890) 146 (esp. footnote 1).

subornation causing significant damage to the military administration.[48] Second, several extraordinary military tribunals were established, often on the orders of the commander of a military unit.[49] Finally, summary justice was extensively employed. Consequently, several arbitrary executions of soldiers and, for collective crimes, their decimations took place.[50] With the signing of the Armistice of Villa Giusti on 3 November 1918, military justice returned to being as it was prior to the conflict.

Under the fascist regime of Benito Mussolini, peacetime and wartime military criminal codes were adopted.[51] The system of military justice established at that time was made up of territorial military tribunals, military tribunals onboard ships, and the military supreme court.[52] The military tribunals decided in a composition including a president (holding the rank of brigadier-general), three military judges (two of whom were required to be superior officers), and a judge rapporteur (holding the rank of colonel and being the only one with a legal background). The military supreme court was competent over the appeal against the judgment of the military tribunals. This court included a president and six judges (three of whom were magistrates). In such a system, which encompassed only two tiers of jurisdiction, the process took place in conditions of severe disparity between the accused and the judges. Military justice was therefore conceived of as a system of jurisdiction that was separate and different from the civilian one.

When the Constitution of the Italian Republic entered into force, the issue of military justice was addressed. Art. 103, § 3, of the Constitution establishes that in peacetime, military courts have jurisdiction only over military personnel who commit a military offence. Moreover, pursuant to arts. 102 and 108 of the Constitution, read jointly, the jurisdictional function should be exercised by civilian magistrates in an independent way. These guarantees also apply to military jurisdiction. Although the Italian Constitution entered into force in 1948, the previous system of military jurisdiction remained in force until 1981.[53] Indeed, it was not until Law n. 180 of 7 May 1981 that the

48 Carlotta Latini, 'Una giustizia "d'eccezione". Specialità della giurisdizione militare e sua estensione durante la Prima guerra mondiale' (2006) *Deportati, Esuli, Profughe* 67, 75.

49 Dallera (n 45) 503.

50 Irene Guerrini and Marco Pluviano, 'Extrajudicial Executions in the Italian Army During World War I' in Jean Marc Berlière, Jonas Campion, Luigi Lacchè and Xavier Rousseaux (eds), *Justice militaire et guerres mondiales: Europe (1914–1950)* (Presses universitaires de Louvain 2013) 32. See also, Guido Crainz, Stefano Santoro and Andrea Zannini, *L'ingiustizia militare nella Grande Guerra: Le fuciliazioni 'per l'esempio' in Friuli e nella Venezia Giulia* (Forum 2023).

51 Royal decrees nos. 303 and 1022 of 1941. Despite with several amendments, these codes are still in force.

52 Andreu-Guzmán (n 24) 287.

53 This is extensively defined by Venditti as a jurisdictional system "impermeable to the constitutional principles and which is also derogated to the principles of criminal law" (our translation): Rodolfo Venditti, 'Il percorso evolutivo della giustizia militare nell'ultimo cinquantennio' in

system of military jurisdiction during peacetime was revised, and both the military tribunals onboard ship and the military supreme court were abolished.[54] By that time, the government was contrary to the abolition of military courts, since it aimed at maintaining their existence in accordance with the Italian Constitution 1948.[55] As a result, Law n. 180/1981 established new judicial bodies and endowed them with guarantees of independence. More precisely, this system foresees three tiers of jurisdiction: military tribunals as courts of first instance (art. 2, Law n. 180/1981); the courts of military appeal (art. 3, Law n. 180/1981); and the Court of Cassation as the supreme court (art. 6, Law n. 180/1981).

This reform acknowledged military judges and prosecutors as having the same status and financial benefits as their civilian counterparts (arts. 12 and 14, Law n. 180/1981). Moreover, with Law n. 561 of 30 December 1988, the Council of Military Judiciary (the self-governing body of military judiciary, see *infra* § 4) was established. Both Law n. 180/1981 and Law n. 561/1988 have been merged into the Military Code approved in 2010 (Decree Law n. 66/2010, of 15 March 2010).

Italian military jurisdiction nowadays: the structure

Art. 103, § 3, of the Constitution states that "[m]ilitary tribunals in times of war have the jurisdiction established by law. In times of peace they have jurisdiction only for military offences committed by members of the armed forces". Pursuant to this provision, the Italian military jurisdiction features two distinct systems, one for wartime and one for peacetime. In wartime, the 1941 Wartime Military Criminal Code still applies.[56]

In peacetime, the Italian military jurisdiction encompasses military tribunals, the military court of appeal, and the Court of Cassation. As previously hinted, the first two have a mixed composition, namely they consist of military judges and military personnel. To become a military judge, there is a "biphasic" mechanism.[57] In the first phase, recruitment is done among civilian judges through a competition based on their qualifications. After the first phase, if

Nicola Labanca and Pierpaolo Rivello (eds), *Fonti e problemi per la storia della giustizia militare* (G. Giappichelli Editore 2004) 253.

54 Vito Maggi, 'Non è mai troppo tardi: la riforma della giustizia militare' (1981) 104 *Il Foro Italiano* 167, 167–184.

55 It is worth an underlying notion that the maintenance of special military courts was also debated in the Constituent Assembly. One group (to which belonged Calamandrei) favored the suppression of military courts. Another one (including Leone) spoke in favor of establishing special sections within the civilian courts. In the end, the opinion that prevailed is that special military courts had to be maintained: Giuseppe de Vergottini, 'Attualità della giustizia militare e Costituzione' (2021) *Federalismi* 1, 2.

56 Albeit with several amendments among which, for instance, the abolition of the death penalty (Law n. 589/94).

57 Rodolfo Venditti, *Il processo penale militare* (Giuffrè Editore 1997) 31.

there are still vacant seats to be filled, a new recruitment competition based on examinations is organised. In terms of judicial impartiality and independence, it is noteworthy that the number of military representatives (i.e. military personnel) is always lower than the number of military judges.[58] Following the 2010 reform, the number of military tribunals (and the respective military prosecutions) was reduced[59] from nine to three (one in Naples, one in Rome, and one in Verona). The tribunals decide in a composition that includes a presiding judge, one military judge, and one military representative "from the Italian Army, the Navy, the Air Force, the Carabinieri, or the Financial Guard" who must have "a rank equal to that of the defendant and in any case no lower than that of an officer" (art. 54, § 2, lett. c, Military Code). Currently, there is only one military court of appeal headquartered in Rome. The deciding composition includes one presiding judge, two military judges, and two military representatives "from the Italian Army, the Navy, the Air Force, the Carabinieri, or the Financial Guard" who must have "a rank equal to that of the defendant and in any case no lower than that of colonel" (art. 57, § 4, lett. c, Military Code). The decisions issued by the military court of appeal can be challenged before the Court of Cassation.

Italian military justice nowadays: the jurisdiction

As laid down in art. 103, § 3, of the Constitution, in peacetime military judges have jurisdiction "only for military crimes", if and only if they are "committed by members of the armed forces".

The notion of "military crimes" represents the "objective constitutional limit to the jurisdiction of military tribunals".[60] Its definition is nonetheless not provided by the Constitution but deferred to the law. The main legislative provision regarding the notion of military crimes is art. 37 of the Peacetime Military Criminal Code (hereinafter, PMCC), which stipulates that "[a]ny violation of the military criminal law constitutes a crime". Nevertheless, this is a purely formal definition[61] that does not clarify what concretely falls under this category. So far, only a few military offences have been qualified as such by the military criminal codes and in the military special laws. As a result, many criminal offences that can occur in the military context have yet to be typified as military crimes.[62] Prior to being repealed in 1956, art. 264 PMCC foresaw that military courts also had jurisdiction over the so called "militarised

58 Rivello (n 45) 533.

59 This is also the consequence of abolishing the military compulsory service in 2005.

60 David Brunelli and Giuseppe Mazzi, *Diritto penale militare* (4th edn, Giuffrè 2007) 43 (our translation).

61 Venditti (n 57) 97; Rivello (n 45) 28.

62 That is why Block speaks of a "randomised" or "patchy" jurisdiction: Maurizio Block, 'L'art. 103 della Costituzione, comma 3' (2022) *La magistratura*, § 2.1.

crimes",[63] namely common offences that infringed upon military interests. Against this background, the configuration of a "military crime" is still highly randomised, and, consequently, the competence over them is often attributed to civilian courts. In an attempt to find a common criterion to define what a military crime is and to outline the borders of the military jurisdiction, most scholars[64] currently agree that a military crime is any offence that jeopardises or harms the military interests. In general, within the category of "military crimes", it is possible to identify two different categories: "exclusively military crimes" and "objectively military crimes".[65] The former consists of "a fact that, in its core elements, is not, in whole or in part, foreseen as a crime under criminal law".[66] The latter includes instead "all those military crimes that, in their core element, are, in whole or in part, foreseen as crimes under criminal law".[67]

By providing that military courts have jurisdiction only if the military crime is "committed by members of the armed forces", art. 103, § 3, of the Constitution also sets a subjective limit. According to scholars, those serving in the army, navy, air force, Carabinieri, and Guardia di Finanza belong to this category.[68] For many years now, the idea that military courts have jurisdiction over them as long as they maintain a relationship with the army has been consolidated. In other words, they are under the military jurisdiction until they are *sub signis*. This approach has been embraced even by the Italian Constitutional Court with judgment n. 429/1992. In this ruling, the Court declared art. 263 of the PMCC unconstitutional to the extent that it did not provide that military courts have jurisdiction only over military personnel (or considered as such) at the time when the criminal offence was committed.

In a nutshell, in times of peace, military courts have jurisdiction only over military crimes committed by the members of the armed forces, excluding both the ordinary crimes committed by the members of the armed forces and the military crimes committed by civilians.[69] Accordingly, pursuant to art. 103, § 3, of the Constitution, military courts do not have exclusive jurisdiction over military crimes. As the Constitutional Court stated in judgment n. 29/1958, the word "only" in art. 103, § 3, of the Constitution, shall not be interpreted in the sense that military courts exercise an exclusive jurisdiction over military

63 This wording has been coined by the Italian scholarship. See, among the others, Domenico Notaro, *Lineamenti di diritto penale militare italiano* (G. Giappichelli Editore 2020) 49; Gaetano Sucato, *Istituzioni di diritto penale militare, vol. I, parte generale* (Stamperia reale 1941) 125.

64 Rivello (n 45) 29. See also Constitutional Court, judgment n. 298/1995.

65 This distinction was first introduced by Di Vico: Pietro Di Vico, 'Il reato esclusivamente militare' (1935) *Rivista di diritto e procedura penale militare* 1, 5. It has been then endorsed by the Constitutional Court with judgment n. 213/1984.

66 Art. 37, § 2, PMCC.

67 Venditti (n 57) 103.

68 Block (n 62) § 3.

69 Piermaria Corso, 'Art. 103' in Giuseppe Branca and Alessandro Pizzorusso (eds), *Commentario della Costituzione* (Zanichelli 1975) 127.

crimes; rather, it means that the military jurisdiction must never cross over into the civilian one. In this respect, it has been argued that art. 103, § 3, of the Constitution has a merely limitative function[70] and aims at precluding military courts from adjudicating the crimes that fall under the competence of the civilian ones.[71] On the contrary, the civilian courts may have a say in criminal military law.[72]

Over the years, the field of action of civilian courts in criminal military law has been widened and, consequently, the competence of military courts has been extremely reduced. A clear example is Law n. 230/1998, which provides that the ordinary judge (and not the military judge) has jurisdiction over refusals to serve in the armed forces. The Italian Constitutional Court passed some judgments in this regard too: among the others, in judgment n. 78/1989, the Court stated that art. 263 PMCC was unconstitutional to the extent that it prevented civilian juvenile courts from trying minors enrolled in the armed forces who committed military crimes. Against this background, some scholars have even argued that the military jurisdiction should be considered an "exceptional jurisdiction, in peacetime, even with respect to military crimes".[73]

With reference to the jurisdiction of military courts in wartime, art. 103, § 3, of the Constitution states that "[m]ilitary tribunals in times of war shall have the jurisdiction established by the law". The wording "times of war" refers to the "state of war" declared by the President of the Republic (art. 87 of the Constitution) upon deliberation of the Houses of Parliament (art. 78 of the Constitution).[74] Hence, military jurisdiction is undoubtedly wider in wartime than in peacetime, insofar as, in case a state of war is declared, there are neither objective nor subjective limits to it.

The role of the Council of Military Judiciary

In an attempt to secure a proper balance between judicial independence and judicial accountability, several states around the world have (especially in the

70 Rivello (n 45) 554.

71 Francesco Caprioli, 'Giurisdizione penale ordinaria e giurisdizione militare: una tormentata coesistenza' (2023) *Archivio Penale* 1, 2–3.

72 See, among others, Constitutional Court, judgment nos. 196/1976, 207/1987, and 429/1992.

73 Giuseppe Mazzi, 'La giurisdizione militare come giurisdizione eccezionale e i suoi limiti costituzionali' (1993) *Cassazione penale* 1627, 1627.

74 Corso (n 69) 127. Nevertheless, it is worth noting that some Italian scholars argue that the "times of war" may exist prior to the declaration of the "state of war". See, among others: Maurizio Block, 'Introduzione. Il ruolo della giustizia penale nazionale ed internazionale nella prospettiva del *peacebuilding*. Riparto di giurisdizione e ipotesi di conflitto' in Ida Caracciolo and Umberto Montuoro (eds), *Ricostruzione della pace, giustizia e tutela dei diritti umani* (G. Giappichelli Editore 2021) XI. Nevertheless, art. 78 of the Constitution has so far never been invoked: Arianna Vedaschi, 'Costituzionalismo, declinazione del principio pacifista e conflitti armati' (2024) *DPCE Online* 1, 14.

aftermath of World War II) introduced new forms of judicial governance.[75] To this end, the control over judicial careers, the appointment of judges, and the court administration have been progressively ascribed to judges with the establishment of judicial councils. For this purpose, pursuant to art. 104 of the Constitution, in 1948, Italy introduced the High Council of the Judiciary as "the cornerstone of the independence of the judiciary".[76]

In Italy, the military forms a special jurisdiction endowed with the same guarantees of independence and autonomy; thus, a separated self-governing body was set up, namely the Council of Military Judiciary. As the High Council of the Judiciary, it decides over recruitment, promotions, transfers, and disciplinary sanctions against military judges and prosecutors (art. 62, § 1, Military Code). It also has additional functions, such as issuing opinions and making proposals to the Ministry of the Defense or giving opinions on drafts related to military issues (art. 62, § 3, Military Code).

The way towards its establishment has been troublesome. To give accomplishment to art. 108, § 2, of the Constitution, which stipulates that the law "ensures the independence of judges of special courts", Law n. 180/1981 applied a transitional regime. Under art. 15 of this Law, in absence of an ad hoc self-governing body, all the measures concerning military judges shall have been taken by the President of the Republic on the proposal of the Ministry of the Defense, and after having consulted a committee composed of several institutional bodies.[77] Initially, this regime was supposed to remain in force for only one year. Nevertheless, this deadline expired without a reform. In front of the legislative inertia, the Constitutional Court was called into question. With a first judgment (n. 67/1984), the Court addressed a "warning" to the Legislature (*sentenza di monito*), suggesting the adoption of a new law to settle a specific body. However, no new legislation was enacted; thus, four years later, a new question of constitutional legitimacy was raised before the Constitutional Court. This time, with judgment n. 266/1988, the Court declared art. 15, Law n. 180/1981 partially unconstitutional to the extent that it allowed that the measures over military judges could still be taken through a procedure that was supposed to last only for one year.

Against this background, the Legislature passed Law n. 561/88 and definitively established the Council of Military Judiciary. In outlining its structure, the model of the High Council of the Judiciary was followed.[78] Until recently,

75 Katarína Šipulova, Samuel Spáč, David Kosař, Tereza Papouškova and Viktor Derka, 'Judicial Self-Governance Index: Towards Better Understanding of the Role of Judges in Governing the Judiciary' (2023) *Regul Gov* 22.

76 Simone Benvenuti and Davide Paris, 'Judicial Self-Government in Italy: Merits, Limits and the Reality of an Export Model' (2018) 19 *GLJ* 1641, 1643.

77 Namely the military general prosecutor at the Court of Cassation, the president, and the military general prosecutor of the military court of appeal, and the presidents of the two detached sections of the military court of appeal.

78 Maria Michela Teresa Mazzilli, 'Il principio di indipendenza e l'autogoverno della magistratura militare' (2023) *PasSaggi costituzionali* 207, 211.

the Council of Military Judiciary counted five members, two sitting as of right – that is, the president of the Court of Cassation (who chairs it) and the military general prosecutor at the Court of Cassation – one elected by the presidents of the Houses of Parliament (lay member), and two military magistrates elected by their colleagues ("gowned" members) (art. 60, § 1, Military Code). They all stay in office for four years (art. 61, § 3, Military Code). Following the entry into force of the Legislative Decree n. 8 of 29 January 2024, the composition of the Council of Military Judiciary has been amended by increasing the number of gowned members from two to four, who have been finally granted the majority over the others (four out of seven). In this respect, it has been argued that the utmost independence and autonomy of the military judiciary from the legislative and executive powers has been definitively granted. Indeed, as suggested by the Committee of Ministers of the Council of Europe in 2010,[79] to achieve a fully-fledged independence, "not less than half the members of such councils should be judges chosen by their peers".[80] Moreover, in this way, the arrangement of the Council of Military Judiciary has been definitively adapted to that of the High Council of the Judiciary, in which pursuant to art. 104, § 3, of the Constitution, "[t]he two thirds of the members are elected". The reform has also provided that while sitting at the Council of Military Judiciary, the gowned members stay in office, and, in case they are out of position at the time of their election, they go back in office (art. 60, § 2, Military Code). This decision has been justified in view of the fact that the total number of military judges is narrow (maximum 60), and the outplacement of four of them may jeopardise the functioning of the military jurisdiction.[81] Interestingly, some of the current members of the Council of Military Judiciary have disputed this decision under several profiles.[82] First, they claimed that this would generate a discrepancy with the High Council of the Judiciary, whose model should be followed. Indeed, all its gowned members are placed out of office during their mandate at the council. Second, this would lead to an increasing concentration of powers in the hands of the same few people, which would at once undermine its correct functioning. Third and most importantly, they have stressed that this would concretely prejudice the autonomy and independence of the Council of Military Judiciary, since the magistrate would no longer be sheltered from possible conditionings posed by their staying in office. In this respect, it has been emphasised that it seems

79 Committee of Ministers of the Council of Europe, Recommendation CM/Rec(2010)12 and explanatory memorandum, of 17 November 2007.

80 Committee of Ministers of the Council of Europe, Recommendation CM/Rec(2010)12 and explanatory memorandum, of 17 November 2007, Chapter IV, § 27.

81 Study Service of the Senate of the Republic, Disposizioni sul funzionamento del Consiglio della magistratura militare e sull'ordinamento giudiziario militare. Atto del Governo n. 91, 21 November 2023, p. 14.

82 Study Service of the Senate of the Republic, Disposizioni sul funzionamento del Consiglio della magistratura militare e sull'ordinamento giudiziario militare. Atto del Governo n. 91, 21 November 2023, p. 15.

contradictory to raise the number of the gowned members to ensure a higher degree of autonomy and independence and, at the same time, providing that they must stay in office during the term.[83]

The decisions of the Council of Military Judiciary are validly adopted with the simple majority, provided that the necessary quorum of four members (of which two elected members) is met (art. 61, § 2, Military Code). Concerning disciplinary sanctions, the procedure that applies is the same as that for civilian judges (art. 67, § 1, Military Code). Here, it is interesting to note that the failure to establish a "special" section[84] to decide over the disciplinary sanctions of military judges and prosecutors has sparked considerable controversy. The Court of Cassation raised a question of constitutionality before the Constitutional Court, claiming that, since the Council of Military Judiciary acts as a judicial body in disciplinary matters, there is an infringement of art. 102, § 2, of the Constitution (which prohibits the establishment of extraordinary or special judges). With judgment n. 71/1995,[85] the Constitutional Court declared the question to be manifestly unfounded, as "[t]he Council of Military Judiciary is not to be conceived as a new special judge in the meaning given by art. 102 of the Constitution".[86] This positioning has been then repeatedly reaffirmed by the Constitutional Court, which, in several judgments, has confirmed that the Council of Military Judiciary does not represent a special judge.[87]

Conclusion

Independence, impartiality, and accountability have always been the cornerstones of the civilian jurisdiction. As we have seen, the same does not apply to the military. Depending on the tradition considered, this is determined by a plethora of factors. In the common law tradition, these principles are mainly threatened by the fact that military courts have traditionally been composed of representatives of military personnel who are usually convened on a case-by-case basis. In the civil systems featuring special military courts where all the judges are recruited from troops, the same concerns arise.

Against this background, the Italian military justice system represents a unicum. Its independence, impartiality, and accountability seemed better secured

83 Maurizio Block, Opinion, Military Council of the Magistracy, Dossier 290/2023/RR. See also David Brunelli, Opinion, Military Council of the Magistracy, Dossier 290/2023/RR.

84 As exists for the High Council of the Judiciary.

85 For a comment, see Anna Maria Poggi, 'La sentenza che salva il Consiglio della magistratura militare: un passo indietro nell'attuazione del principio di unicità della giurisdizione?' (1995) *Giurisprudenza italiana* 561, 561–572.

86 Judgment n. 71/1995, § 5.

87 Saulle Panizza, 'Materiali per uno studio della responsabilità disciplinare dei magistrati militari attraverso l'esame dei provvedimenti adottati dal Consiglio della magistratura militare (anni 1990–2008)' in Giuseppe Campanelli (ed), *Indipendenza, imparzialità e responsabilità dei giudici speciali* (Pisa University Press 2013) 218ff.

by a double set of factors: first, the mixed composition of its military courts and, second, the presence of a self-governing body. As for the former, we have stressed that having military judges sitting side by side with the members of the Italian army boosts its autonomy from the command while diminishing the lack of a specialistic understanding. Regarding the latter, we have pointed out that the presence of the Council of Military Judiciary deciding over recruitment, promotions, transfers, and disciplinary sanctions against military magistrates best guarantees their independence, impartiality, and accountability.

Nevertheless, following the very recent adoption of Legislative Decree n. 8/2024, this aspect has been questioned. Indeed, besides augmenting the number of the gowned members, this reform has established that once they sit at the Council of Military Judiciary, they must remain in office; that is, they must continue to serve as military judges. In the opinion of several of its components, such a choice may undermine the possibility of not being freed from conditioning.

In the last decades, the complex interplay between the general distrust towards military courts, the ongoing process of civilianisation, and the developments in human rights in Europe[88] has resulted in the reduction of military courts. In Italy, especially after the compulsory military service was abolished, proposals to remove or radically reorganise the system of military justice mushroomed. The rationale behind these drafts was that this apparatus was in an extended decrescendo and therefore appeared to be uneconomic.[89] On the contrary, the current return of heavy warfare in Europe suggests that in the near future, military justice may be resorted to more often. Thus, in contrast to the past, the usefulness of military courts may be rediscovered. In such a case, Italy could provide insightful suggestions, at least concerning the safeguarding of the independence, impartiality, and autonomy of military justice.

88 Frederik Rosén, 'The End of Military Justice in Europe: An Agenda for Juridical Civil – Military Relations' (2013) 21 *SWI* 335, 335–348.

89 Giuseppe de Vergottini, 'Giurisdizione militare: la crisi della specialità' (2007) *Quaderni costituzionali* 364, 364.

12 Judicial financial autonomy

How performance-based budgeting can impact on independence and accountability of judges

Grzegorz Kuca and Elżbieta Gudowska-Natanek

Introduction

The level of remuneration received by judges, making sure the amount received corresponds to the importance and significance of the tasks they perform, is a material guarantee of judicial independence.[1] Each year, this number is determined based on objectified economic indicators, here taking into account the multiplier of the remuneration factor and base rate. The statutory regulation of judges' compensation mechanisms aims to prevent any influence on their judicial activity by a superior, on whose decision the amount of such compensation could be determined.[2] On the one hand, the increasing number of court cases and their level of complexity and, thus, the longer time taken to process them, has prompted the search for various forms of accountability for judges; this can be understood not as disciplinary responsibility but accountability, which should ultimately lead to an increase in remuneration of judges. On the other hand, because of the need to mitigate the effects of crises (financial, pandemic, military) that significantly affect the level of public debt, the remuneration of judges is subject to a freeze in a given year or even a reduction below the level set in previous years.[3] The subject of this chapter is the functioning of horizontal and vertical accountability mechanisms, here in the sense that Guillermo A. O'Donnell gives it. The purpose of this chapter is to attempt to reconstruct the constitutional standard for the remuneration of

1 See Frank Cross, 'Judicial Independence' in Gregory A. Caldeira, R. Daniel Kelemen and Keith E. Whittington (eds), *The Oxford Handbook of Law and Politics* (Oxford University Press 2008) 557–575; Mike McConville and Luke Marsh, *The Myth of Judicial Independence* (Oxford University Press 2020); Martin H. Redish, *Judicial Independence and the American Constitution. A Democratic Paradox* (Stanford University Press 2017) 54–60; Peter H. Russell, 'Towards a General Theory of Judicial Independence' in Peter H. Russell and David M. O'Brien (eds), *Judicial Independence in the Age of Democracy Critical Perspectives from Around the World* (The University of Virginia Press 2001) 1–24.

2 Katarzyna Gonera, '*Status pracowniczy sędziego. Czy sędzia jest pracownikiem?*' in Ryszard Piotrowski (ed.), *Pozycja ustrojowa sędziego* (Wolters Kluwer Business 2015) 54.

3 See Guillermo A. O'Donnell, 'Horizontal Accountability in New Democracies' (1998) 3 *J Democr* 112–126.

DOI: 10.4324/9781003557852-16

judges and conditions (rationale) that justify freezing in a given year or reducing salaries below the level set in previous years.

Choosing this subject was dictated by the lack of studies on the issue of judicial remuneration, the different constitutional regulations of this issue in the EU countries, and, moreover, the preliminary questions to the ECJ,[4] which provided an opportunity to re-examine and develop the existing case law in the context of the principles of judicial independence and effective judicial protection. In judgement C 64/16,[5] the Court of Justice of the European Union (CJEU) took the position that the level of remuneration received by members of the judiciary, here corresponding to the importance of the tasks they perform, constitutes a guarantee of judicial independence. For this requirement to be fulfilled, the court must perform its tasks completely autonomously, without subordination within the official hierarchy, without subordination to anyone, and in a manner free from orders or directives from any source, thus remaining protected from outside interference and pressures that may jeopardise the independence of its members' judgement and that may influence their decisions.[6] The CJEU considered this requirement as important as the immutability of judges, thus linking security of tenure to material security.[7]

Exploring the aim of this chapter should be preceded by several preliminary assumptions. First, judges have a special status resulting from the principle of judicial independence and its guarantees, and among these is the level of their remuneration appropriate to the importance and importance of the tasks performed. Second, with the replacement of the traditional budget with a task-based budget, there has been no change in the mechanism of remuneration of judges depending on their work (the number of cases on the court, the number of completed cases, the number of justifications or the stability of jurisprudence). Third, with the introduction of performance-based budgeting (PBB), there has been no introduction of responsibility or accountability of judges when it comes to the effects of performing judicial activity, and possible changes in this regard cause a lot of controversy. Fourth, in connection with the need to mitigate the effects of crises, the salaries of judges in the system are subject to freezing in a given year or even reduced below the level set in previous years. Fifth, national laws, as well as EU law, establish impassable limits on the budget deficit and limits on public debt, which can provide important interpretative guidance in deciding whether to 'freeze' or reduce

4 Request for a preliminary ruling from the Vilniaus apygardos administracinis teismas (Lithuania) – (Case C-374/23) and Request for a preliminary ruling from the Sąd Rejonowy w Białymstoku (Poland) – (Case C146/23).

5 Judgment of the Court (Grand Chamber) of 27 February 2018 *Associação Sindical dos Juízes Portugueses v. Tribunal de Contas*, case: C-64/16.

6 The Court of Justice made similar statements in its judgments of September 19, 2006, Wilson, C-506/04, EU:C:2006:587, paragraph 51; and February 16, 2017, Margarit Panicello, C-503/15, EU:C:2017:126, paragraph 37 and the case law cited therein.

7 Case: C-64/16.

the remuneration of judges. And finally, at the constitutional level, provisions are introduced to regulate the remuneration of judges, protecting them from unjustified freezes or reductions in their remuneration, hence constituting a significant restriction on the legislative or executive power from interfering in the sphere of the functioning of the judiciary.

Judicial financial autonomy

A significant qualitative transformation in the approach to the formation and execution of the judicial budget emerged with the shift from traditional budgeting to PBB. The performance-based method is related to developing new ways of managing the state and improving, among other things, the management of public finances, here along the lines of techniques previously used only in the private sector.[8] The main advantages of PBB models include transparency and accountability by making explicit the link between resources and results; efficiency by measuring and stimulating improvement; and evidence-based policymaking by basing decisions on performance data[9]. Nevertheless, on the one hand, too much emphasis being placed on these otherwise legitimate values guiding the PBB may adversely affect the independence of the courts and independence of judges, here to the detriment of the quality of personnel and jurisprudence; on the other hand, 'excessive financial independence of the judiciary could be used by some judiciary to shield themselves against legitimate reform efforts and reasonable expectation regarding performance'.[10] In a traditional budget, only politicians are accountable to the public for the tasks performed by the administration. In contrast, the officials who directly perform them are held accountable by their superiors but remain anonymous to citizens. The situation is different in PBB because, by introducing accountability mechanisms, the accountability for the quality of the implementation of public tasks is also borne by their direct executors, including task coordinators.[11]

In EU countries, by far the largest portion of the judicial budget is allocated to remuneration, the share of which varies widely, ranging from 40% to 90%. Of the judiciary's budget, the most (about 90%) is spent on remuneration

8 Federica Viapiana, 'A Performance-Based Budget in the Judiciary: Allocation of Resources and Performance Variability in First Instance Courts. An Analysis of Three Case Studies' (2019) 9 *JPBAFM* 23.

9 Ronnie Downes, Delphine Moretti and Scherie Nicol, 'Organisation for Economic Co-Operation and Development (OECD) (2017), Budgeting and Performance in the European Union. A Review in the Context of EU Budget Focused on Results' (2017) 1 *OECD J Budge* 1–38.

10 Klaus Decker, Christian Mohlen and David F. Varela, *The World Bank. 2011. Improving the Performance of Justice Institutions* (The World Bank 2011) 15.

11 Urszula Zawadzka-Pąk, 'Racjonalizacja procesu wdrażania budżetu zadaniowego w Polsce na podstawie wybranych rozwiązań zagranicznych' in Renata Przygodzka (ed.), *Instrumenty i metody racjonalizacji finansów publicznych* (Wydawnictwo Uniwersytetu w Białymstoku 2012) 102.

in four EU countries (Croatia, Portugal, Lithuania, Greece) and the least in Ireland (about 46%). The share of the remuneration fund ranges from 70% to 80% of the judiciary's expenses, and sometimes falls to 65% (Poland, Denmark, Bulgaria).[12] The courts are of particular importance in this regard because they sometimes exercise financial autonomy. Symptomatically, the constitutional legislators of EU countries are quite cautious about the constitutionalisation of this issue. In only five EU countries (Belgium, Bulgaria, Denmark, Luxembourg, Spain) can one find constitutional provisions on the financial autonomy of specific entities; these concern the competence of the legislature (Bulgaria, Belgium, Spain), the head of state (Belgium, Denmark, Luxembourg, Spain) or the judiciary (Bulgaria) to set or dispose of their own budget.

Obviously, comparative analysis will look different if one analyses financial autonomy through the prism of the relevant statutory. After considering their results, financial autonomy is characteristic of EU countries. It most often applies to the parliament (Belgium, Bulgaria, Estonia, Finland, France, Germany, Greece, Hungary, Ireland, Italy, Latvia,[13] Luxembourg, Poland, Portugal, Romania, Spain, Sweden, United Kingdom), the head of state (Belgium, Denmark, Luxembourg, Poland, Spain), the courts (Bulgaria,[14] Germany, Hungary, Ireland, Latvia,[15] Poland), the supreme audit bodies (Denmark, Estonia, Finland, Germany, Hungary, Italy, Lithuania, Luxembourg, Poland, Romania,[16] Slovakia, Sweden, United Kingdom) and often many other bodies and institutions.[17]

In some cases, entities exercising financial autonomy are excluded from management by results. This is the case in France,[18] where the President of the Republic, the Senate, the National Assembly, the Constitutional Council and the Court of Justice are financed by grants (*dotations*), the awarding of

12 Andrzej Siemaszko, Beata Gruszczyńska, Marek Marczewski, Paweł Ostaszewski and Anna Więcek-Durańska, *Sądownictwo. Polska na tle pozostałych krajów Unii Europejskiej* (Wydawnictwo Instytutu Wymiaru Sprawiedliwości 2016) 26.

13 See Article 6 Latvian statutory of 24.03.1994 on the state budget and financial management.

14 In addition, in Bulgaria, the draft budget of the judiciary is adopted by the Supreme Judicial Council (Article 130(6)(4) Constitution of the Republic of Bulgaria).

15 See Article 8 of the Latvian statutory of 24.03.1994 on the state budget and financial management.

16 See Article 5 Romanian statutory no. 94 of 8.09.1992 on the organization and functioning of the Court of Accounts.

17 The statement was prepared based on the following: 'International Budget Practices and Procedures Database, Question 37 on How the State Budget Is Planned' <http://qdd.oecd.org/subject.aspx?Subject=7F309CE7-61D3-4423-A9E3-3F39424B8BCA#> accessed 11 August 2024 and information on Bulgaria, Croatia, Cyprus, Lithuania, Latvia, Malta collected from other sources, See Ian Hawkesworth, Richard Emery, Joachim Wehner and Kristin Saegert, 'Budgeting in Bulgaria' (2009) 3 *OECD J Budget* 146–146; Ian Hawkesworth, Richard Emery, Joachim Wehner and Jannick Saegert, 'Budgeting in Lithuania' (2010) 3 *OECD J Budget* 2010, 32; Michael Ruffner, Joachim Wehner and Matthias Witt, 'Budgeting in Romania' (2005) 4 *OECD J Budget* 39.

18 Jolanta Adamiec, 'Budżet zadaniowy w krajach Unii Europejskiej' (2010) 10 *Analizy BAS* 2.

which does not require the submission of an 'annual performance plan' and, thus, are not subject to evaluation in an 'annual performance report' (*rapport annuel de performance*).[19] The exclusion of this group of bodies from the obligation to submit an annual performance plan and the inclusion of their funding by grants has won the approval of the French Constitutional Council,[20] which states that this allows these institutions to maintain their financial autonomy, which is a direct consequence of the principle of separation of powers.[21] Nevertheless, there is nothing to prevent entities exercising budget autonomy from being subject to PBB. For example, in Poland, the Constitutional Court, the Supreme Court, the Supreme Administrative Court along with the provincial administrative courts, the National Council of the Judiciary and the general judiciary enjoy budgetary autonomy, but at the same time, they prepare PBBs.[22] The primary role of budget autonomy is to protect the body's self-reliance from potential threats from the entity responsible for determining the amount of finances allocated.[23]

In addition, judicial financial autonomy does not always result in an automatic exclusion of the Minister of Finance from interfering with the courts' draft budget. For example, in Sweden, the draft budget of the parliament submitted by the parliamentary administration can be amended by the government, but in practice, the government does not exercise this power. In Slovenia, in the process of drafting the budget of so-called direct users, an agreement is sought with the Minister of Finance, who suggests the necessary adjustments. If this agreement is not reached, then the government incorporates its proposals into the draft budget, and the attached explanatory notes include the proposals made by the budget administrators. In Slovakia, on the other hand, the draft budget submitted by budget self-users is subject to negotiation with the Minister of Finance.[24]

The constitutional standard for the remuneration of judges

A comparative analysis of regulations in EU countries shows that the rules for the remuneration of judges are relatively rarely elevated to constitutional status. Of the 27 EU countries, 10 (Belgium, Cyprus, Denmark, Greece,

19 See Caroline Expert-Foulquier, 'The Financial Independence of the Judiciary in France' (2020) 1 *IJCA* 3.

20 Décision n° 2001–448 DC du 25 juillet 2001 <www.conseil-constitutionnel.fr/conseil-constitutionnel/francais/les-decisions/acces-par-date/decisions-depuis-1959/2001/2001-448-dc/decision-n-2001-448-dc-du-25-juillet-2001.504.html>

21 Nevertheless, there is nothing to prevent entities exercising budget autonomy from being subject to performance budgeting (e.g. in the Czech Republic).

22 See Article 139 (2) of the Public Finance Law.

23 Wojciech Brzozowski, *Niezależność konstytucyjnego organu państwa i jej ochrona* (Sejm Publishing House 2013) 276.

24 Zofia Szpringer, 'Procedura budżetowa w Polsce na tle innych państw' (2010) 3 *Studia BAS* 43–44.

Hungary, Ireland, Lithuania, Luxembourg, Malta, Poland) have regulated the rules for the remuneration of judges, while the remaining 17 have not. This means that the rules for the remuneration of judges are rare in the constitutions of EU countries. The second comparative finding indicates that the EU countries that have constitutionalised the rules for remuneration of judges can find three basic approaches to this issue. The constitutional legislators most often decide to refer to the regulation of this issue by law (Belgium, Cyprus, Greece, Hungary, Ireland, Luxembourg),[25] less often formulate a ban on changing the amount of remuneration to the detriment of a judge (Cyprus, Ireland)[26] and in only one country to provide judges with conditions of remuneration corresponding to the dignity of their office and the scope of their duties (Poland).[27] In the case of an order to regulate the issue of the remuneration of judges by statute, the material status of judges is protected from too far-reaching interference from the executive branch, here in the case of a prohibition on changing the amount of remuneration to the detriment of a judge – the possibility of reducing the level of remuneration is limited and in the case of linking the amount of remuneration to the dignity of the office and the scope of duties – there is a comprehensive regulation of this issue.

EU law does not impose on its member states a specific constitutional model governing the relations and interactions between different state organs, especially regarding the definition and division of their powers. In choosing constitutional models, member states are obliged to respect, among other provisions of EU law so as not to undermine judicial independence or interfere with the activities of the judiciary.[28] Because of the diversity of structures and political and constitutional traditions of EU countries, the roles played by the actors involved in the process of determining the level and components of judges' remuneration can significantly differ. The principle of separation of powers and the need to safeguard the judiciary from unauthorised external influence exerted by the legislature or the executive branch, among others, do not deprive the latter two of the ability to decide on many aspects of the organisation of the state's judicial branch.[29]

25 Article 154 Constitution of Belgium, Article 153 Constitution of the Republic of Cyprus, Article 88(2)(2) Constitution of the Republic of Greece, Article 36 Constitution of Ireland, Article 92 Constitution of Luxembourg, Article 25(7) Constitution of Hungary.

26 Article 153(12) and Article 158(3) Constitution of the Republic of Cyprus; Article 35(5) Constitution of Ireland.

27 Art. 178(2) Constitution of the Republic of Poland.

28 Judgment of the Court (Grand Chamber) of 22 February 2022 proceedings brought by RS Request for a preliminary ruling from the Curtea de Apel Craiova – Romania), case: C-430/21.

29 See Christoph Möllers, *The Tree Branches. A Comparative Model of Separation of Powers* (Oxford University Press 2013) 89–96; Tom Campbell, *Separation of Powers in Practice* (Stanford University Press 2004).

To maintain the independence of the judicial system in the long and short term, it will be necessary to provide the judiciary with adequate financial resources to enable courts and judges to meet the standards of the right to a court as set forth in Article 6 of the European Convention on Human Rights and in national constitutions and perform their duties with the integrity and efficiency that are essential to the fostering of public confidence in justice and the rule of law. It is the duty of every EU state to provide adequate funding for the judiciary. Even in times of economic downturn or crisis, the proper functioning and independence of the judiciary must not be jeopardised, and the courts should not be funded based on the discretionary decisions of official bodies but in a stable manner based on objective and transparent criteria.

Increase in the remuneration of judges

The standard of EU countries is the statutory formation of the remuneration of judges. Legislators generally prejudge the determination of remuneration of judges based on objectified economic indicators, here taking into account the multiplication factor of the remuneration coefficient and the base rate, equality of remuneration rates for judges of equivalent courts, and differentiation of remuneration amounts only according to seniority and additional functions (e.g. function or long service allowances). At the same time, legislators rule out differentiating the amount of remuneration according to time consumption (the number of cases on the court docket, the number of completed cases) or the complexity of the tasks assigned to judges (the number of justifications written and stability of jurisprudence). This may seem unfair from a common-sense view and incompatible with labour laws, which generally require that remuneration correspond to the type of work performed and take into account the quantity and quality of work performed. It may also be socially unacceptable, especially in the situation of protracted proceedings or the variation in the time taken to handle a given category of cases in peer courts.[30]

Guaranteeing equal (equal) remuneration of judges of different courts should be done by the appropriate distribution of full-time judges, hence equalising the burden between judges of the same court and providing support staff (number of full-time clerks, assistants, registrars) or other measures that fall under the concept of the administration of justice. However, even these measures may not have the desired effect, especially when a comparison is made between the number and complexity of cases of equivalent courts in different local courts. For this reason, it would be advisable to consider additional elements that would allow judges to be held accountable for their judicial work, which would allow their salaries to rise above those determined based on objectified economic indicators. This could significantly affect the realisation of the right to a court, including what is stipulated in Article 6 of

30 Gonera (n 2) 54.

the European Convention for the Protection of Human Rights and Fundamental Freedoms, which, *expressis verbis*, stipulates 'within a reasonable time' the consideration of a case as well as the realisation of the goals of the performance budget, along with reducing compensation proceedings from the Treasury for protracted proceedings. One of the more interesting proposals that would allow a change here would be Federica Viapiana's proposed concepts of equality in the distribution of resources and equality of access and performance, which could justify the introduction of an accountability mechanism for judges that would allow for a fuller realisation of the right to a court, here in terms of the consideration of a case 'within a reasonable time'.[31]

Decrease (or freeze) in remuneration of judges

Public debt and budget deficits are the most important elements of state financial management, and their excessive growth can have significant economic and social consequences. Unfortunately, with the state of public finances further deteriorating, the prerequisites have been given for initiating the EU's excessive deficit procedure against a few European countries: France, Hungary, Italy, Poland and Romania. Not only that, but a breach of the permissible deficit level has occurred, which is of a permanent nature and is projected to increase.[32] In these circumstances, EU countries may be forced to take measures to increase revenues or reduce expenditures, and the latter may prompt them to 'freeze' or reduce the remuneration of public officials, including judges. For this reason, it is worthwhile to analyse the settlements here, and as the Venice Commission points out, the example of Poland, which in the Constitution of 1997 guarantees judges remuneration adequate to the dignity of their office and the scope of their duties, is commendable.[33]

It is crucial to refer to the constitutional conditions for the remuneration of judges and to answer the question of whether, in practice, the legislator, together with the executive power, have not made an unauthorised interference

31 Viapiana (n 8) 10.

32 The purpose of the excessive deficit procedure (EDP) is for European Union countries to correct excessive deficits or debt levels. The European Commission can apply the EDP to a EU country that does not respect the Stability and Growth Pact (SGP), which is a set of rules to coordinate the fiscal policies of EU countries. In particular, the EDP can be launched if an EU country (1) has breached or is at risk of breaching the deficit threshold of 3% of GDP or (2) has violated the debt rule by having a government debt level above 60% of GDP that is not diminishing at a satisfactory pace, meaning that the gap between a country's debt level and the 60% reference needs to be reduced by 1/20th annually (on average over three years). The SGP aims to safeguard sound public finances and has two arms: (1) a preventive arm, which ensures EU countries' fiscal policy is conducted in a sustainable manner, and (2) a corrective arm, which lays down how countries should take action in the event their public debt or budget deficit is considered excessive.

33 'Report on the Independence of the Judicial System Part I: The Independence of Judges, 10' <https://rm.coe.int/1680700a63>

in the constitutionally protected principle of judicial independence affecting the right to a court by explaining this as a threat to the state finances, including state budget balance. The legislature and the executive are not authorised to arbitrarily and unjustifiably modify the amount of judges' remuneration, in the process of doing so disregarding the guaranteed principles and rules set out in Art. 178 section 1 of the Constitution and Art. 91 § 1c of the Act on the Organization of Common Courts (hereinafter referred to as p.u.s.p.). The incidental nonadjustment of the remuneration of judges and prosecutors, although not having a constitutional guarantee of a specific remuneration, would be constitutionally permissible in a normative way in the event of exceeding the constitutional debt limit resulting from Art. 216 section 5 of the Constitution.

In Art. 178 section 2 of the Constitution of the Republic of Poland, the constitution-maker decided to include the issue of the judge's remuneration corresponding to the dignity of the office held and the scope of duties as part of the guarantee of judicial independence. The essence of this approach is also emphasised by the fact that the issues of remuneration included in the Constitution concern only one professional group – judges – which is related to the systemic position of judges exercising the administration of justice, where the appropriate level of judges' remuneration affects the functioning of the judicial power, especially because judges have limited opportunities for additional earnings. Appropriate remuneration allows one to hold office without worrying about the financial resources needed to live but also without the temptation to give in to others when adjudicating in exchange for material benefits. Therefore, the proper functioning of the justice system is possible if the appropriate status of specific entities is guaranteed.

The European Charter of Statutory Rules for Judges highlights the following:

> The exercise of the profession of a judge entitles him to receive remuneration, the amount of which is determined in a way that protects the judge from the pressure exerted on him to influence the content of the decisions he issues, and more generally – on his attitude in the adjudication process, by negatively affecting his independence and impartiality.

Hence, appropriate remuneration is an element of the guarantee of judicial independence and, as such, constitutes a European standard. In the judgement of 4 October 2000, P 8/00, the Constitutional Tribunal stated that 'the justice system will function properly when the working conditions of judges and their remuneration are adequate to the dignity of the judge's office and the scope of his duties'. The lack of adequate remuneration becomes a threat to judicial independence and, as a result, may affect the right to court. Therefore, it is important to take care of the unique status of judges and provide them with remuneration commensurate with the dignity of the office and scope of their duties.

The very concept of the dignity of the office as an undefined concept does not allow us to determine what constitutes remuneration worthy of the office of a judge. Undoubtedly, however, the requirement to provide judges with remuneration commensurate with the dignity of the office can lead to a prohibition on a discretionary remuneration determination. Specified in Art. 178 section 2 of the Constitution, the norm regarding the dignity and scope of duties must be taken into account by the legislator responsible for shaping the level of judges' remuneration and implemented by state authorities. Certainly, Art. 178 section 2 of the Constitution limits the legislator's freedom to shape the remuneration of judges.

According to a consensus, in Art. 91 p.u.s.p., the legislator decided to adopt the principle that, first, the amount of remuneration of judges holding equivalent judicial positions varies depending on the length of service or functions performed, and second – most importantly for the present study – the basis for determining the basic remuneration of a judge in a given year is the average remuneration in the second quarter of the previous year, as published in the Official Journal of the Republic of Poland, *Monitor Polski*, by the President of the Central Statistical Office pursuant to Art. 20 point 2 of the Act of 17 December 1998 on pensions and annuities from the Social Insurance Fund;[34] this comes with the note that, if the average remuneration referred to in § 1c, is lower than the average remuneration announced for the second quarter of the preceding year, the basis for determining the judge's basic remuneration in the current amount is adopted. The basic remuneration of a judge is determined in rates, the amount of which is determined using multipliers of the basis for determining the basic remuneration referred to in § 1c. The rates of basic remuneration for individual judicial positions and multipliers used to determine the amount of basic remuneration of judges in individual rates are set out in the annex to the Act.

The above systemic regulations were created as a result of a consensus based on the interpretation of Art. 178 section 2 of the Constitution.[35] This consensus concerned making the issue of the principles of shaping judges' remuneration more objective so that the method of determining the remuneration would not depend on an arbitrary decision of the executive or the legislature. The adopted solution results in an automatic increase in wages when the average wage increases, regardless of the country's financial situation.[36] Art. 91 § 1c p.u.s.p. adopted a solution that is a kind of security for the remuneration

34 Journal of Laws of the Republic of Poland 2023, items 1251, 1429 and 1672.

35 M. Celej, 'System kształtowania wynagrodzeń sędziowskich w działalności Krajowej Rady Sądownictwa w latach 1990–2008' (2009) 1 *Bulletin of the NCJ* 58–69.

36 The remuneration system for judges was separated from the remuneration system for public sector employees. The amount of a judge's remuneration depends on objective criteria that do not have discretionary aspects, i.e., the position held, length of service and function performed.

of judges and protection against the country's economic and financial problems. Strictly speaking, the state's financial problems should not be relevant to the guarantees for determining wages included in the above-mentioned regulations. Established in this way, the regulation sets objective indicators of remuneration for judges. It appears to be independent of the interference of the executive and legislative authorities, although recent experience shows that the issue of freezing the remuneration of judges is an action tested within the framework of the adopted budget. At this point, the question must be asked of whether the government can be justified in blocking wage indexation.

Equally important is that the right to remuneration that can be determined based on the average remuneration in the second quarter of the year and that is acquired upon publication of a communique on this subject by the President of the Central Statistical Office (i.e. several months before the end of the year). In turn, the authority exercises the acquired right at the beginning of the following year. Therefore, judges, therefore, acquire the right to a specific amount of remuneration in the following year with a specific advance notice. This means that they acquire a right belonging to the legally protected category of maximum-formed expectancy. The adoption of the budget-related act takes place just before the right to remuneration – determined in accordance with the announcement of the President of the Central Statistical Office – is exercised. The principle of protection of rightfully acquired subjective rights cannot, in principle, be limited or abolished.

The constitutionality of laws related to the implementation of the Budget Act regarding the remuneration of judges after 2011 was examined by the Constitutional Tribunal twice: in 2012 and 2023.[37]

In 2011, the Act amending certain acts related to the implementation of the Budget Act provided that, in 2012, the basis for determining the remuneration of judges was the average remuneration in the second quarter of 2010, as announced by the President of the Central Statistical Office. This meant that judges would not receive remuneration in accordance with the regulations included in Art. 91 § 1c p.u.s.p. In fact, this case concerned not only the judges of common courts, but also the judges of the Supreme Court, administrative courts, the Supreme Administrative Court, and the Constitutional Tribunal. For the creators of the budget-related act, the reason for reducing remuneration in 2012 was the need to maintain a balanced budget, which is a constitutionally protected value. This decision resulted in a lack of salary indexation. Despite this, in the judgement of 12 December 2012, K 1/12, the Constitutional Tribunal found that the one-off, incidental suspension of the

37 The issue of judges' remuneration was the subject of the Constitutional Tribunal's decisions also earlier: decision of the Constitutional Tribunal of November 8, 2000, P 1/94; judgment of the Constitutional Tribunal of October 4, 2000, P 8/00; judgment of the Constitutional Tribunal of December 12, 2001, SK 26/01; judgment of the Constitutional Tribunal of February 18, 2004, K 12/03; judgment of the Constitutional Tribunal of December 17, 2009, P 73/08.

indexation of judges' remuneration in 2012 was consistent with the Constitution. 'Freezing' judges' salaries actually meant a decline in their value, resulting in a deterioration of the financial situation. The Constitutional Tribunal found the challenged regulation – consisting of a one-year 'freeze' of judges' remuneration – to be consistent with the Constitution. The Constitutional Tribunal emphasised that the recognition of the constitutionality of this solution results from its incidental nature and from taking into account the difficult financial situation of the state, which threatened a balanced budget, forming a constitutional value competitive with the values specified in Art. 178 of the Constitution. The Constitutional Court also indicated that the 'freezing' of judges' remuneration can only be tolerated exceptionally because of other constitutional values, in particular because of the state's budgetary difficulties. This practice, however, cannot, under any circumstances, become a systematic practice. Then, the 'freezing' of the remuneration of judges took place when Poland was in the excessive deficit procedure initiated by the European Commission, which is when the state public debt at the end of 2011 amounted to 56.4% of the country's GDP, so the second prudential threshold was exceeded in accordance with Article 86(1)(2) of the Finance Act public.

In this judgement, the Tribunal formulated unsurpassable 'boundary conditions' for remuneration commensurate with the dignity of the judge's office and the scope of their duties: First, 'judges' remuneration should be shaped in a way that excludes any discretion – both in relation to this entire professional group – on the part of the executive power, and in relation to individual judges, for whom it is unacceptable to make its amount dependent on an individual assessment of their work'. Second, 'the amount of remuneration of a judge, including a district court judge who is starting his career as a judge, should significantly exceed the average remuneration in the budgetary sphere'. Third, 'judges' remuneration should, over a long period of time, show an upward trend no less than the average remuneration in the public sector'. Fourth, 'in the difficult situation of the state budget, the remuneration of judges should be protected against excessively unfavourable changes to a greater extent than the remuneration of all other public officials and employees'. And finally, 'it is unacceptable to reduce the nominal amount of judges' remuneration by normative means, except for the situation provided for in Article 216(5) of the Constitution (exceeding the constitutional debt limit)'.[38]

Despite this, derogations from the general method of calculating the remuneration of judges were introduced not only in 2012 but also in 2021–2023.

38 A dissenting opinion to this judgment was expressed by Constitutional Tribunal judge Mirosław Granat, who emphasised that, in light of Art. 178 of the Constitution of the Republic of Poland, remuneration corresponding to the dignity of the office of a judge is not determined by the state budget but by the principle of independence. The Constitution links the dignity of the office with the independence of the judge, which means that this dignity cannot be made dependent on the state budget. As Mirosław Granat noted, 'even a modest state budget does not authorise the executive to "tinker" with a judge's salary'.

The Act of November 19, 2020, on special solutions for the implementation of the Budget Act for 2021[39] indicates that, in 2021, the basis for determining the basic remuneration of a judge is the average remuneration in the second quarter, not 2020, but 2019. The average salary in the second quarter of 2019 was PLN 4,839.24. The Act of December 17, 2021, on special solutions for the implementation of the Budget Act for 2022[40] provides that, in 2022, the basis for determining the basic remuneration of a judge is the average remuneration in the second quarter of 2020, which increased by PLN 26. The average salary in the second quarter of 2021 was PLN 5,504.52. In turn, in 2023, the Act of 1 December 2022 on special solutions for the implementation of the Budget Act for 2023[41] provides that the basis for determining the basic remuneration of judges is the amount of PLN 5,444.42. According to political regulations, this should have amounted to PLN 6,156.25. The basis for determining the basic remuneration of judges from 2021 to 2023 was lower than would result from the regulation adopted in the law on the system of common courts, the Act on the Supreme Court and the Act on the Constitutional Tribunal.

All this caused waves of anxiety among judges, resulting in numerous lawsuits. About a thousand lawsuits from judges were filed regarding the freezing of wages. The first judges were paid compensation.[42] Going to court resulted in additional costs related to, among others, interest and legal representation, thus additionally burdening the State Treasury.

The breakthrough came with the Constitutional Tribunal's judgement issued in November 2023.[43] The Constitutional Tribunal found that Art. 8 and Art. 9 of the Act of 1 December 2022 on special solutions for the implementation of the Budget Act for 2023[44] are inconsistent with Art. 178 section 2 of the Constitution of the Republic of Poland. The Constitutional Tribunal emphasised that the definition of the basis for the remuneration of judges in the budget-related act for 2023 violates the guarantees of judicial independence and the dignity of holding office by unilaterally and arbitrarily determining the basis for the remuneration of judges, making the judiciary dependent on other authorities. The judgement emphasised that the rules for remunerating judges formulated in the budget-related act for 2023 must meet all the boundary conditions specified in the Constitutional Tribunal's judgement of 2012.

Importantly, the 2023 budget does not indicate that the state debt level is below constitutional limits, that there are tragic economic indicators or that there is a collision of constitutional values resulting in the need to interfere

39 Journal of Laws, item 2400, as amended.
40 Journal of Laws, item 2445, as amended.
41 Journal of Laws, item 2666, as amended.
42 Judgment of the District Court in Nowa Sól of June 6, 2023, IV P 10/23.
43 Judgment of the Constitutional Tribunal of November 8, 2023, K 1/23.
44 Journal of Laws, item 2666, as amended.

with the acquired rights of judges. The actual situation did not justify such solutions. The Constitutional Tribunal emphasised that 'each of the modifications to the rules for remunerating judges under the budget-related act was, in fact, of a temporary nature because, as a rule, the basis for the basic remuneration of judges is established on the basis of the provisions of the Act on the Judiciary, the Act on the Supreme Court and the Act on the Constitutional Tribunal'. Meanwhile, for over three years, this rule has been 'temporarily' modified, each time in a different way. This calls into question the existence of norms regulating the basis of the basic remuneration of judges in the above-mentioned acts. This means that the use of one-year solutions means that the boundary condition mentioned in point 1 has been constructed in a completely discretionary manner, violating the constitutional protection of remuneration that is decent and consistent with the scope of a judge's duties. It was emphasised that the legislator shapes remuneration entirely at discretion, which violates the constitutional guarantee of a specific amount of remuneration, while a balanced budget is not in any way threatened. As a result, the government adopted an amendment to the Budget Act for 2024, resulting in judges receiving remuneration in accordance with the systemic regulations for the first time since 2021.

Conclusion

The establishment of court budgets in EU countries is a political decision and occurs within a system that is based on the principle of separation of powers, under which neither the executive nor the legislative branch can exert any pressure on the courts in determining their spending. Decisions on the allocation of funds to the courts must be made with the strictest respect for judicial independence, and the level of remuneration of judges must correspond to the importance and significance of the tasks they perform. The increasing number of court cases and their level of complexity in the era of PBB argues for introducing the accountability of judges, allowing for their remuneration to rise above the level set based on objectified economic indicators, which allows for the full realisation of the right to a court, and the possible decrease (freezing) of the remuneration of judges and the constitutional prohibitions applied in this regard are an important material guarantee of judicial independence. The constitutional provisions applied in EU countries supplement the catalogue of guarantees provided by other constitutional provisions, and statutory solutions regulating judges' salaries must be based on appropriate, objective and verifiable criteria. In practice, it is precluded to treat the obligation to remunerate judges as a source of their subjective rights, which would provide a basis for directing claims against the state.[45] However, it is not excluded to consider

45 Bogumił Naleziński, 'Komentarz do art. 178' in Piotr Tuleja (ed.), *Konstytucja Rzeczypospolitej. Komentarz* (Wolters Kluwer 2023) 582.

a specific provision of the law as a benchmark for controlling the constitutionality of the solutions adopted by the legislator, with the difference, however, being that the way of shaping the level of the remuneration of judges requires weighing between the two constitutional values of remuneration and budget balance and fiscal stability.[46]

46 Judgment of the Court (Grand Chamber) of 27 February 2018. *Associação Sindical dos Juízes Portugueses v. Tribunal de Contas* Request for a preliminary ruling from the Supremo Tribunal Administrativo, Case C-64/16.

Index

Note: Page numbers in **bold** indicate a table on the corresponding page.

FSC
www.fsc.org
MIX
Papier | Fördert gute Waldnutzung
FSC® C083411

Kolibri 360 GmbH
Ferdinand-Jühlke-Straße 7
99095 Erfurt, Deutschland
produktsicherheit@kolibri360.de